The Official America Online® for Macintosh™ Tour Guide

SECOND EDITION

The Official America Online®
for Macintosh™ Tour Guide
SECOND EDITION

Tom Lichty

VENTANA
PRESS

The Official America Online® for Macintosh™ Tour Guide
Copyright © 1994 by Tom Lichty

Library of Congress Cataloging-in-Publication Data
Lichty, Tom
    The official America Online for Macintosh membership kit & tour
  guide / Tom Lichty. -- 2nd ed.
       p. cm.
    Rev. ed. of: The official America Online membership kit & tour
  guide. c1992.
    Includes index.
    ISBN 1-56604-127-9
    1. America Online (Videotex system) 2. Macintosh (Computer)
  I. Lichty, Tom. Official America Online membership kit & tour guide.
  II. Title.
  QA76.57.A43L523 1994
    004.69--dc20   94-1492
                                  CIP

Book design: Marcia Webb
Cover design: IMAGE Communications; adaptation: John Nedwidek
Index service: Dianne Bertsch, Answers Plus
Technical review: Tim Barwick, David Peal, Kelly Richmond, Marshall Rens: America Online
Editorial staff: Angela Anderson, Laura Bader, Eric Edstam, Tracye Giles, Pam Richardson
Production staff: Patrick Berry, Cheri Collins, John Cotterman, Dan Koeller, Dawne Sherman,
  Marcia Webb, Mike Webster
Proofreaders: Eric Edstam, Sharla Green

Second Edition 9 8
Printed in the United States of America

Ventana Press, Inc.
P.O. Box 13964
Research Triangle Park, NC 27709-3964
919/544-9404
FAX 919/544-9472

Limits of Liability and Disclaimer of Warranty

Trademarks

Trademarked names appear throughout this book. Rather than list the names and entities that own the trademarks or insert a trademark symbol with each mention of the trademarked name, the publisher states that it is using the names only for editorial purposes and to the benefit of the trademark owner with no intention of infringing upon that trademark.

About the Author

Tom Lichty recently retired to devote full-time energies to research and writing. He is author of six computer books, including *Design Principles for Desktop Publishers* (voted Book of the Year by the Computer Press Association in 1988), *America Online's Internet for Windows* and *The Official America Online Membership Kit & Tour Guide* (Windows and Macintosh versions). Tom lives at the base of Oregon's Mount Hood, where he specializes in the design, desktop publishing and online communications fields of the computer industry. His Internet mailing address is majortom@aol.com.

Acknowledgments

Oh sure, I want to acknowledge people like Laura Bader, Tim Barwick, Mary Daffron, George Louie, Luis Montel, Bill Hartman, Marshall Rens, Pam Richardson, Kelly Richmond, Kathy Ryan, Matt Triplet, Matt Wagner and Elizabeth & Joe Woodman: they're the heart and soul of this book's production and editorial teams and without their assistance there would be no book.

Special thanks goes to Jennifer Watson, who coordinated the update of this book with expedience, professionalism and aplomb. Santa never had a better elf.

Most of all I want to acknowledge the thousands of readers (nearly 5000 at last count) who have written to me with comments and suggestions for improvements to the first edition. I read every message, and many of the suggestions are woven into this book's manuscript. Thus, this book is truly a community project. We all have reason to be proud of that.

—Tom Lichty

Contents

Chapter 15

Chapter 16

Foreword

I first got interested in online services in the early 1980s. I didn't know much about them then, but I knew enough to realize that they had a lot of potential. So when I bought my first personal computer in 1982, I decided to buy a modem and get online. This proved to be a very frustrating experience. It took me several months before I had all the equipment properly configured and was able to connect for the first time. Once I got connected, I found the services themselves hard to use and expensive. Nevertheless, despite all the hassles and shortcomings, I thought it was amazing that such a wealth of information and services were out there, waiting to be tapped into.

That was more than a decade ago. When we founded America Online, Inc., our objective was simple: to make online services more accessible, more affordable, more useful and more fun for people like you and me. America Online now serves more than a million customers and is the nation's fastest-growing online service.

Our success has been driven by a constant focus on making the power of online services accessible to everyone. In designing America Online, we worked hard to make it very easy to use. We didn't want people to have to read a book in order to get connected, so we made the software easy to install and easy to use. As a result, people are usually up and running with America Online in less than 15 minutes.

Although we've done a good job of making the process of connecting to America Online hassle-free, we still have a problem: once you're connected, what do you do? America Online has grown so quickly, and now contains so many different services, finding the services that best meet your specific needs can be a bit of a challenge.

That's where this book comes in. Think of it as your personal tour guide, helping you get the most out of America Online. It highlights a wide range of useful and fun services, so you can begin enjoying America Online immediately. After you're comfortable with the basics, it will take you to the next step by explaining some of the more advanced capabilities that are built into the service.

When Ventana Press first contacted us about publishing an America Online book, we thought it was a great idea. Our members had been asking for a book for some time, so we knew there was interest. And we felt that by working with an independent publisher, we'd end up with a better book than if we tried to write it ourselves.

Ventana's choice of Tom Lichty as the author was inspired. Tom had written a number of popular computer books, so he knew how to communicate information in an interesting and humorous manner. (A lot of computer books are deathly dull; Tom's are funny and engaging.) And since Tom was a novice user of online services, we felt his insightful observations as a novice would help others get the most out of America Online.

When the first edition of this Tour Guide was published in 1992, it got raves from readers, so this new, expanded version—highlighting our broader array of services (including Internet access), and introducing you to our new Main Menu and multimedia look—is certain to be even more popular.

As you'll soon discover, America Online is more than easy-to-use software and a collection of useful and fun services. It's a living, breathing "electronic community" that comes alive because thousands of people all across the country don't just passively read the information that scrolls by on their screens, they get involved and participate, exchanging ideas on hundreds of topics. We provide the basic framework; beyond, that, America Online is shaped by the collective imagination of its participants.

A new interactive communications medium is emerging, and it will change the way we inform, educate, work and play. America Online is at the forefront of this exciting revolution. Come join us, as we work together to shape this new medium.

Steve Case, President, America Online, Inc.
AOL E-Mail Address: SteveCase

CHAPTER 1

Starting the Tour

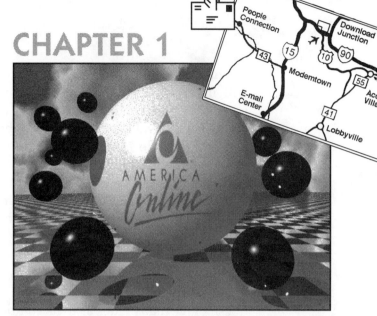

I'll never forget my first visit to the San Diego Zoo. I took the whole family. The cabby who drove us there told us to take the tour bus immediately upon arrival. After that, he reasoned, we would have an idea of how the zoo was organized and know what exhibits we would want to visit. We took his advice and hopped on the bus first thing.

The San Diego Zoo's buses are of the double-decker variety, and we sat on the top deck, baronially surveying the fauna below. The tour guide—wise San Diegan that he was—sat down below, out of the sun and away from the family of miscreants who shared the top deck with us, littering it with profanity, malcontent children and various artificially sweetened beverages. We never saw the tour guide, but we heard him. In anticipation of the Odious Family Robinson, the zoo had installed a megaphonelike loudspeaker on the top deck that immersed us in tsunamis of sound capable of drowning out not only the complaints of small children, but the bellows of elephants and screeches of orangutans alike. We left the tour at the first stop, wondering if our insurance covered auditory prosthetics.

With that preamble, allow me to welcome you to *The Official America Online Tour Guide*. I have good news: You won't encounter any orangutans, megaphones or tickets on this tour. You won't even see a bus. No signs will warn you to keep your hands and feet inside, and artificially sweetened beverages are permitted.

Frontispiece graphic: "Fantasy AOL Spheres," by Gwydian (Mike Wiseman). Use the keywords File Search and then the criterion AOLSPHER.GIF.

You can take this tour without ever leaving home or fraternizing with miscreants; and though I'm a tour guide, I'm here for your singular employ. I will endeavor to inform, entertain and enlighten—forever vigilant and always *sotto voce*. When the tour has concluded, you're welcome to explore on your own, secure in your familiarity with the territory and the attractions therein.

Best of all, the territory we're about to explore is every bit as diverse and wondrous as the San Diego Zoo. It's always at your fingertips, and about the most threatening creature you'll find here is a mouse.

What Is America Online?

This question isn't as easy as it seems. A term like "America Online" doesn't give many clues as to its composition. We can safely deduce its country of origin (it's in America, all right: Vienna, Virginia, to be exact—just outside Washington, DC; see Figure 1-1). But what's this "online" business? The word's not even in the dictionary.

Figure 1-1: America Online nestles snugly in this office building in the Virginia forests just outside Washington, DC.

You can define America Online in many ways. It is, after all, a great many things. It offers abundant resources: the latest news, weather reports, stock quotes, movie and book reviews, databases to research things as diverse as wine or hardware prices, online discussions of everything from politics to system software—even a service for reserving airline tickets, rental cars and hotel rooms.

America Online (AOL) is also an electronic mail (e-mail) service. You can use AOL to exchange e-mail with nearly anyone who uses e-mail, regardless of whether they are a fellow AOL member. If they don't use e-mail, you can use AOL to send them a fax. If they don't use fax, you can use AOL to send them printed mail via the US Postal Service.

America Online is an Internet gateway. The Internet is a vast superset of AOL itself, incorporating thousands of other communications systems from around the world similar to AOL. The extent of a thousand AOLs is almost incomprehensible, but that's what the Internet is, and AOL offers an elegant way of getting there.

America Online is also a community. In Chapter 9, "Entertainment," I compare AOL to the small Oregon town where I live. People are friendly here. They say hello when they pass you on the street, they invite you to their house for a chat, and they go out of their way to be of assistance. AOL does all these things: Instant Messages allow people who are online at the same time to say hello and hold "passing on the street" conversations; Chat Rooms are electronic "rooms"—public or private—where groups of members hold real-time conversations about subjects of their choosing; and Members Helping Members is a message board where members help one another with questions regarding AOL.

But how does all this communication take place? I can recall when I bought my first CD player. It offered more features than a 1973 Cadillac, and it sounded like the Boston Symphony on the bridge of my nose.

At first I was enamored with its technology. CDs were new to me. The player's booming bass and crisp treble commanded my respect; its aurora borealis of indicator lights illuminated my curiosity, and its scores of controls rivaled those of the Starship Enterprise. In the end, however, it's the music I enjoy. Mozart, Haydn, Vivaldi—these are my companions, and I treasure their company the most.

America Online is much the same. At first, ignoring the technology is difficult, but AOL is people—and in the end, you will treasure their company the most.

I am going to pursue the definition of AOL much as one might pursue any new technological acquisition. Over the next few pages, we'll allow its technology to dazzle us, but in the end it will be the community—the people who await us on AOL—who are the true reward.

It's a Telecommunications Service

Now there's a polysyllabic mouthful: "telecommunications." As the term is used here, telecommunications refers to two-way communications via telephone lines. A phone call, in other words, is a form of telecommunicating. Telephone lines are good for things other than phone calls. Fax machines use telephone lines to transfer documents; video phones use them to transmit pictures; and *modems* use them to transfer computer data (more about modems in the next chapter). I'm not talking about expensive, dedicated telephone lines here—I'm talking about the very same telephone lines that are already in our homes and offices.

Now we're getting somewhere. If you have a computer and I have a computer and we each have modems, we can use our existing telephone lines to connect our computers to one another. Once connected this way, our computers can exchange data: text, graphics, sounds, animation—even other computer programs.

Of course, you have to be at your computer and I have to be at mine—at the same time—and we have to know how to make our computers talk to one another, and we have to check for errors encountered in the transmission, and I'm just me and you're just you, and there's only so much computer data two people can exchange with one another before the whole thing gets to be pretty dull.

What we need is a *service* that will store our data so that we don't have to be at our computers at the same time. Instead of calling your computer, I have my computer call the service and store my data and messages there. When you're ready for that data, you can instruct your computer to call the service and retrieve the data at your convenience.

As long as we're imagining a service, we might imagine it to automate all the electronic technicalities as well. If we imagine it right, the service can mediate communications between the two computers, check for errors (and fix them when they're encountered) and even dial the telephone.

And who's to say that you and I should have the service all to ourselves? We can let everyone else with a computer in on it as well, regardless of the type of computer they own. Carried to its extreme, this scenario might result in hundreds of thousands—millions, actually—of people utilizing the service, exchanging and storing thousands of computer files. Most of this data can be public rather than private, so the exchange becomes multilateral.

Which is precisely what telecommunications services—and AOL—are: a vast network of "members," each of whom uses a computer, a modem and a telephone line to connect with a common destination—to "go online." Members can exchange public and private files; they can send and receive e-mail; and members who are online at the same time can "chat" in real time—they can even play online games with one another.

And what does this service cost? The economies of scale allow expenses to be distributed among the members. Moreover, even though AOL is near Washington, DC, few members pay for long-distance calls. America Online has local telephone numbers in more than 800 cities in the contiguous United States. Even if you live in the sticks, chances are you can find a local number you can call, or one that's a "short" long-distance call away.

It's One Big Thunder-Lizard Computer

Another way of defining AOL is by describing its hardware. Coordinating thousands of simultaneous phone calls and storing tens of thousands of files requires one Thunder Lizard of a computer complex. No little Stegosaurus will do. We're talking Brontosaurus here, a beastie who relocates continents whenever he gets the urge to sneeze. Forget prefixes like kilo and mega. Think giga and terra. When they turn on the power to this thing, lights dim all along the Eastern seaboard.

Open Architecture

I hate to disappoint you, but America Online isn't a single Brontosaurus-sized mainframe; it is, in fact, a number of refrigerator-sized computers, each having more in common with the adaptable Velociraptor than a leviathan as benign as the Brontosaurus.

Figure 1-2: A few of the many systems that comprise the heartbeat of America Online. A number of manufacturer's products are represented here, each selected on the basis of its suitability to a specific task. The homogenization factor is open architecture, which allows all of these diverse systems to work in concert.

By employing a technique called open architecture, AOL is able to utilize hardware, software and communications systems from a variety of manufacturers, each optimized for a specific task. America Online's open architecture permits it to use the most powerful hardware running the fastest software. The open communication architecture runs on the fastest local area and the most powerful wide area networks. The open architecture is AOL's key to the scalability it needs to keep up with its meteoric growth and the unpredictable mutations of the tele-communications industry.

Common Carriers

If you wanted to send a package to a friend across the country, you could probably hop in your car and drive it there yourself. Compared to the alternatives, driving across the country would be a perilous journey and would cost a fortune.

More likely, you'd hire a *common carrier*—a service such as United Parcel Service or Federal Express—to deliver the package for you. For a fraction of what it would cost you to do the job yourself, common carriers can do it more reliably, less expensively and much more conveniently.

For much the same reason, AOL hires common carriers to deliver goods to its members. And typical of AOL, it hires multiple common carriers to ensure reliability. SprintNet, a service of US Sprint, is the common carrier AOL most often uses in the United States. (Figure 1-3 shows SprintNet equipment at AOL.) Datapac, a subsidiary of Bell Canada, serves Canadian members. These common carriers offer *nodes*—local telephone numbers—in most cities in North America. They charge AOL for phone calls (placed or received) just as Federal Express would charge you to deliver a package.

Figure 1-3:
High-speed
telecommunications
equipment in use
at America Online
Headquarters.

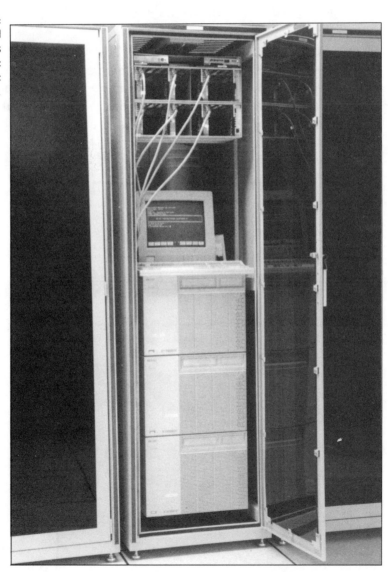

Again, the economies of scale operate to our advantage. Thousands of clients, of which AOL is only one, use these long-distance providers. Chances are when you're not using one of your local nodes, some corporate computer is phoning data to a parent mainframe in New Jersey or Chicago. The cost of this service is so insignificant that it's covered by your membership. No matter how many hours you're online per month, AOL never charges extra for the call. Indeed, the only connect charges are to those few members who have to make a long-distance call to reach a node.

It's Software Installed in Your Computer

Conceptualizing AOL as nodes and mainframe computers isn't very comforting. America Online is much more parochial than that. For many of us, AOL is software in our Macs—software that arrived on that little disk provided in *The Official America Online Membership Kit.* (Figure 1-4 shows the AOL logo.)

Figure 1-4: America Online's logo appears whenever you run the software installed on your Mac.

That's more like it. The software you use on your Mac to sign on to AOL more accurately represents the personality of the service than anything we've discussed so far. It makes noises, it's resplendent with windows and icons, and it automates those tasks and procedures that formerly were responsible for excluding most semi-normal people from using an online service.

Here's what I mean. Nearly every telecommunications program assumes you know how to set certain arcane but necessary attributes and protocols such as data bits, stop bits, parity or flow. Frankly, although I've used telecommunications software for years and though I have adjusted my data bits and parity, I have no idea what they are, and I have always been kind of nervous about shooting in the dark like that. America Online, on the other hand, uses its own custom software at both ends of the line. After you install the software on your Mac (a simple process I describe in the next chapter), all the technicalities are coordinated by the AOL host computer and your Mac. They simply talk things over and make adjustments as required. This is as it should be. People shouldn't be asked to do these things; that's why we have machines. America Online's software simply has no controls for setting data bits, stop bits, parity or flow (see Figure 1-5). It's all taken care of for you.

Figure 1-5:
America Online's
software never
asks you to set (or
even think about)
data bits, stop
bits, parity or flow.

Amazingly, the software is self-configuring. Whenever you sign on, a behind-the-scenes dialog transpires between your Mac and the AOL host computer. In effect, your Mac says, "Hey! Do you have any new features I should know about?" If new features are available, your Mac requests them from the host and adds them to its version of the local software (the copy of AOL that resides on your hard drive). This capability is significant: At any point, AOL can add features to the service and incorporate them immediately. No new software releases have to be sent out. No interminable decimal places have to be added to the version number. That convenience means the AOL staff can add features whenever they please. No disk duplication and mass mailings are required. Upgrade costs to you are nonexistent, and they hardly amount to anything at AOL either. America Online's staff operates in an environment that encourages, rather than stifles, improvement. Perhaps best of all, you don't have to lift a finger to take advantage of whatever changes or additions AOL makes to its service. Just sign on as usual, and you immediately have the most recent version available. (See Figure 1-6.)

Note: I'm discussing minor upgrades here. Major upgrades—from version 1 to version 2 for example—are handled with disk duplication and mass mailings. Minor upgrades are usually handled as described above; often members aren't even aware of them when they occur.

Figure 1-6: In July 1992, midway through the first edition of this book, America Online added a help icon to the Compose Mail window. The update took place automatically and online. No disks were sent out. No costs were incurred. America Online simply got better.

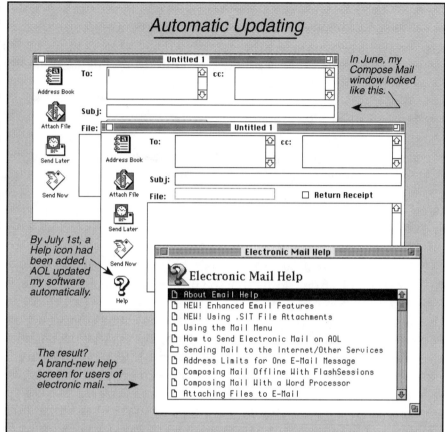

We're getting closer to the mark. The phrase "user-friendly" is properly used to describe this service. America Online's Mac software is real Mac software: familiar, predictable and comfortable. The File menu says Open, Save, Close and Quit. Its windows have title bars and close boxes. It even takes advantage of all those esoteric Mac commands you've come to know, such as Copy, Cut and Paste.

Another unique aspect of the AOL for Mac software is its interface and communication strategy. Though it's highly graphical, none of those graphical elements are transferred to your Mac online. Transferring graphics online takes time—much more than transferring text, for instance—which could make the service as sluggish as a hound in July. Instead, all of AOL's graphical components are stored on your hard disk. Only text is transferred. This capability makes AOL much faster than other graphically oriented services and saves you money in connect-time charges.

Here's the point: AOL is an advanced and aggressive telecommunications service that grows daily and contains the features necessary to accommodate that growth. The software features I described previously reflect a progressive attitude, and that attitude is a better way of defining AOL.

It's a Resource

News, sports, weather—sure you can get them on radio and television, but not necessarily when you need or want them. You can get them in a newspaper, too; but it's going to cost the environment a tree or two, the pictures are fuzzy, and about all you can do with a newspaper you've read is throw it away (consult the Environmental Club—clubs are described in Chapter 13, "Clubs & Interests"—for recycling information). America Online offers the news, sports and weather as well, available at your convenience and without sacrificing any trees. It's in electronic form, too; so you can file it, search it and include it in documents of your own.

This past winter, I kept tabs on China's nuclear testing in Today's News (discussed in Chapter 6), tracked the meager investments in my portfolio (discussed in Chapter 10, "Personal Finance") and monitored the progress of the Israeli/Palestinian peace accord while browsing the Newsstand (discussed in Chapter 7). I researched the purchase of a new hard disk for my computer in the Marketplace (discussed in Chapter 17) and actually bought that hard disk using Comp-U-Store. I booked both airplane and auto rentals for a trip to New Mexico using EAASY SABRE (discussed in Chapter 11, "Travel"). I constantly search the online video reviews before I rent a tape (the Entertainment Department is discussed in Chapter 9), and I check Wine & Dine Online (Chapter 13, "Clubs & Interests") for recommendations before I hazard the racks of wines at the shop down the street. Past issues of *MacWorld*, *National Geographic* and *Smithsonian*, and even *CNN*, are online for my review, as is *Comptons Encyclopedia* and the Gray Lady: the *New York Times*. I recently sold my old car after consulting AutoVantage (described in Chapter 17). As a professional member of the desktop publishing community, I constantly collect graphics (AOL has thousands of files online—described in Chapter 5, "Computing"; also see Figure 1-7), fonts (see Figure 1-8) and utilities, and the Desktop Publishing Forum is one of my favorite haunts.

Figure 1-7: Just a few of the thousands of graphics available in America Online's file libraries. ("Lise2," by David Palermo; "Dragonfly," from the Graphics Forum; and "High Tech Laurel & Hardy," by Lou Moccia.)

A Graphics Gold Mine

Figure 1-8: A quintet of fonts, all downloaded from the Desktop Publishing Forum. At top, *Eire* is by Paul Glomski; *Oregon Dry* is by Pat Snyder; Jim Pearson's *Oakwood ProFont* is particularly elegant; Brian Hendrix's *Windsor* is a traditional, Old World font; and Jonathan Macagba's *Smiley Face* is great for illuminating e-mail. Most are shareware and cost about $5 each.

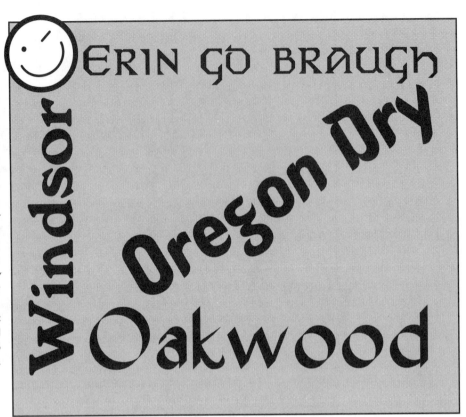

In other words, you could describe AOL as a resource of almost infinite potential. You don't have to drive anywhere to use it; it's continuously maintained and updated; and it's all electronic—available for any use you can imagine. Many members find the resource potential alone ample justification for signing on to AOL, but to limit your participation this way would be a disservice to AOL and to yourself. Above all, AOL is people: friends, associates, consultants—even lovers. It's a resource all right, but it's also a community, and therein lies its greatest value.

It's a Community

I've taken the easy way out. Yes, AOL is a telecommunications service. Yes, it's the host computer. Yes, it's software in your Mac; and yes, it's a resource. But that's like saying that Christmas is just another day of the year. There's much more to it than that. Christmas is reverence and good things; but for many of us, Christmas means people: family, friends and community. What really defines AOL is its people, as well. America Online is a *community*. My dictionary defines community as, "A social group sharing common characteristics or interests," and that is the best definition I can imagine for AOL.

As members, we have common interests, we all have computers, and we love to share. *That's* what AOL is all about. After a few weeks, the novelty of interconnection and graphical images wears off. After a few weeks, we stop wondering about the host computer and data bits. After a few weeks, we all discover the true soul of AOL, and that soul is its people.

Steve Case

I have never asked AOL President Steve Case where he lives. It would surprise and disappoint me to learn that he doesn't live in the suburbs: Steve Case is a character study of the suburban next-door neighbor. He's a clean-cut, casual guy. He wears rumpled chinos, cotton sportshirts and no tie. He looks as if he's about to mow the lawn. He took me to lunch at the Ringmaster's Pub in the Barnum and Bailey building next door. (America Online's building is next door to the world headquarters of the Ringling Brothers Circus.) We had iced tea and sandwiches. That's Steve's idea of a business lunch.

Steve's personality is reflected everywhere at AOL. I've never seen a necktie or a closed office door during my visits there. More important, the people in the AOL offices reflect the spirit of community. They never use titles. No one wears ID badges, not even guests. Everyone calls everyone else by his or her first name. Conferences happen in hallways.

Steve's eyes sparkle when the conversation turns to community. He sends e-mail to every new member and hopes for a reply. He's the president of the company, yet he spends as much time conversing with members as he does with his staff. Everyone calls him Steve.

With Steve Case steering the ship, AOL remains, foremost, a community. All corporate decisions are based on that concept; every change benefits the community. That's the way Steve wants it to be. If he could have his way, he'd have us all out to Virginia for a barbecue on the green. You'd know who he was the moment you got there: he'd be the one turning burgers on the grill. You couldn't ask for a better neighbor.

When I first signed on to write this book, community was the last thing on my mind. I have been a telecommunicator for years. I thought I'd seen it all. Now, however, I spend as much of my online time corresponding with friends—new friends in every part of the country—as I do conducting research. In Chapter 4, I admit to getting despondent if I don't hear the familiar mail notification when the In the Spotlight screen comes up. Throughout this book, I'll offer little tips on how to make friends online; follow these tips, and you'll become as much a part of this community as I am.

You really couldn't do much better.

How to Use This Book

The America Online Tour Guide serves two purposes: (1) It's the official documentation for the use of America Online; and (2) it's a guidebook for the explorer. As documentation, the book should be thoroughly indexed, strictly organized and pithy. As a guide, the book should offer entertainment, insight and advice. These goals are somewhat disparate, but not necessarily incompatible.

Fortunately, the people at AOL have an altruistic attitude toward the documentation for their service. *The America Online Membership Kit & Tour Guide* is a book, not a manual. I'm an independent author, not a staff technical writer. And AOL chose a traditional publisher—Ventana Press—to produce and distribute this book; it's not an AOL production. I therefore have the autonomy and elbow room to explore the subject with you independently, thoroughly and candidly. The people at AOL are to be commended for their courage in choosing this path. It could be perilous. Confidence in their product, however, emboldens them, and rightfully so.

How to Use This Book as Documentation

As you no doubt already know, documentation can be dull. Few people take a software manual to the hammock for a lazy afternoon of reading. The universe of technical documentation is far from the universe AOL inhabits. America Online is diverse, abstract and personable—hardly documentation material. Nonetheless, I've included a number of organizational and reference tools to serve the documentation need.

Finding Answers

I want you to be able to turn to *The America Online Tour Guide* whenever you have a question about AOL. I want you to be able to find the answer to your question with a minimum of effort, no matter how many different places the subject may appear in the book. Pursuant to that, a number of tools are at your disposal:

🔺 The *table of contents* lists titles, section heads and subheads for every chapter. When you need information on a specific subject, turn first to the table of contents. Nine times out of ten, it will be all you need.

🔺 A thorough *index* appears at the end of the book, with references to subjects, procedures and departments. If the subject you're after doesn't appear in the table of contents, turn to the index.

🔺 A listing of primary *keywords* is the first appendix item. Keywords are the interstate highway system at AOL. If you want to get somewhere in a hurry, use a keyword. As you discover places that appeal to you, grab your yellow pen and highlight the keyword corresponding to that location. Eventually, you'll commit a number of keywords to memory (or place them on your Go To menu, a process described in Chapter 13, "Clubs & Interests"), and the keyword appendix will have served its purpose.

🔺 A *listing of Command-key combinations* follows the keywords list. Few people memorize every Command-key combination for every program they use, but most people memorize some. If you're an occasional (or frequent) user of Command keys (or if you'd like to learn a few shortcuts that will cut down on mouse use), refer to Appendix B of the book.

🔺 A *glossary* of terms used in the book follows the appendices. The glossary is especially thorough in its inclusion of telecommunications terminology. I may never define "parity" in the text—with AOL, you never have to bother with it—but I want you to be able to find out what it means if you're curious.

Departmental Listings

Starting with Chapter 5, each chapter explores a department available online at AOL. If Entertainment is your game (forgive the pun), read Chapter 9. If you're interested in the Computing Department, read Chapter 5. America Online is infinitely too large and diverse to explore these departments thoroughly. Instead, I've attempted to capture the personality of each department with glimpses into a few areas of particular interest. Wherever possible, I offer insight into the department's features: where to find the really good stuff.

Subject Listings

Departments are also vehicles for exploring specific subject areas. In Chapter 13, I introduce the concept of the forum; in Chapter 5, we explore the subject of downloading. These subjects can be complex, and to document them without some relief could be as dry as white bread. Instead, I've made a sandwich of each technical subject, flavoring the presentation with the diversity of a department. This approach, I hope, will make for more effective documentation: If you're enjoying yourself, you'll learn more about the subject. Associating subjects with departments also provides a context that's practical rather than theoretical; learning by doing is always more effective than listening to a lecture.

A Documentation Strategy

My personal strategy for the use of software documentation is to first spend a half-hour browsing. With no specific need and in no particular order, I just thumb through the manual, trying to get a feeling for its contents and organization. I look for organizational signposts (chapter titles, icons, sidebars, heads and subheads); I peek at the index; I read a paragraph or two from sections that strike my fancy. This kind of random orientation buoys my confidence and orients my perspective.

If you're a new member and haven't yet installed the software or signed on, read Chapter 2, "Making the Connection," next. It's a "hand-holder," documenting every step of the installation and initial sign-on process. The chapter includes a suggested initial online session.

From then on—perhaps once a week—pick a department and tour it with me at your own pace. While we're there, we'll explore a procedural subject as well as the department itself. Each chapter should take about an hour. When we're finished, you will not only be familiar with the department, you'll learn about a feature that will make your online experience more productive and fun.

How to Use This Book as a Book

I would be flattered if you would read this book for the pleasure of it. As I spend time on AOL, I'm struck by its diversity. Last night I spent an hour contemplating the universe on the Online Home Companion (my favorite forum—forums are described in Chapter 13). This afternoon I visited the Lobby for some companionship. Tonight I plan to attend a Rotunda event (which we explore in Chapter 12, "People

Connection"). Online visits are often unstructured. Your rhythm is syncopated and your interests wander.

I have tried to organize this Tour Guide in much the same fashion. I have liberally splashed gobbets of material throughout the book, often with no other intention in mind than to relieve the page of textual tedium. I want your thoughts to wander; I want to pique your curiosity; I want to delight and provoke and intrigue you (see Figure 1-9). That's what AOL does: it discourages linearity and encourages randomness. It demands your regard and rewards your return.

I hope this book does the same.

Figure 1-9: A video review, the title screen for the Online Gaming Forum and a daily horoscope. These examples are just a tiny slice of the spectrum of opportunity that awaits you on America Online.

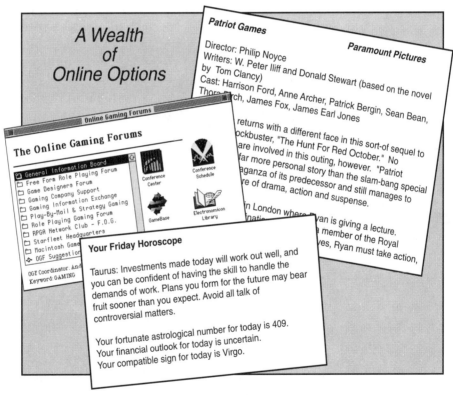

Moving On

Are you comfortable? Our journey is about to begin. Reach into that pocket in the seat in front of you and pull out the program. Here's where we're about to go:

- ♠ Chapter 2, "Making the Connection," walks you through the setup and initial sign-on process. Just as it relieves you from worrying about the complexities of most of the other technical aspects of telecommunications, AOL automates most of the process of getting started as well, so Chapter 2 isn't too technical. You'll be up and running in no time.

- ♠ Chapter 3, "Online Help & the Members," serves as an introduction to the AOL software—especially all of its offers of help. We'll pull down menus and peek at dialog boxes. We'll do most of this work off line, but you'll need your Mac (and a modem) handy. Eventually we'll sign on, visit the Lobby and get to know an online guide. Guides are usually there, waiting to help. We'll examine the members' directory and see if we can make a friend.

- ♠ Chapter 4 will teach you everything you need to know to master AOL's e-mail feature. We'll put some names into our Address Book, send (and receive) some mail, and attach a file to be uploaded to a friend.

- ♠ Chapter 5 goes for the heart: the Computing Department. We'll visit the Mac Operating System Forum, look over *MacWorld* magazine, catch up on the latest computing news and opinion, and solicit some assistance from a software vendor. Along the way, we'll explore the process of downloading files. We'll download a few for ourselves, decompress those that require it and perhaps upload a file in return.

- ♠ Chapter 6, "Today's News," reveals AOL's new news feature, including not only news, but business, entertainment, sports and weather. You can search them to find the stories of interest to you, and they're all updated on a continuing basis. We'll keep a log of our visit for review later, when we're off line and rested.

- Chapter 7 discusses the Newsstand. America Online features alliances with a number of contemporary magazines and newspapers, including *The Atlantic Monthly, Bicycling, Car & Driver, Consumer Reports, Chicago Tribune, San Jose Mercury News, The New York Times, Time, Road & Track, Popular Photography, WIRED* and dozens of others. The Newsstand is where you'll find them all. You can search these articles too (including back issues), talk with the editors, and in many cases download the graphics that accompany the stories.

- Chapter 8 is dedicated to sports fans. In addition to baseball, basketball, football, hockey, tennis and golf, there are even games you can play yourself.

- Chapter 9, "Entertainment," is simply for the fun of it. We'll read a few movie reviews, peek at a cartoon or two, have a (virtual) beer at LaPub and play a game or two.

- Chapter 10 explores AOL's extensive Personal Finance Department. There we'll start our portfolio of investments (cash optional), consult Morningstar and Hoover's financial profiles, and consult Real Estate Online.

- Chapter 11 offers a break from the workaday world, as we visit the Travel Department. We'll consult the experts (and fellow travelers) before we plan our dream vacation, then we'll book our reservations and set up correspondence with other members before we leave.

- Chapter 12 explores People Connection. We'll wipe the sweat from our palms, walk into the Lobby and say hello. We'll check out a few of AOL's Chat Rooms and see who we can find there. Perhaps we'll visit the Center Stage and participate in a game show.

- Chapter 13, "Clubs & Interests," explores AOL's clubs. Perhaps we'll try Wine & Dine Online, the Environmental and Star Trek Forums, and BikeNet. We'll learn about forums, read a few messages and post one of our own.

▲ Chapter 14 introduces the Internet and AOL's "Internet Connection." In the telecommunications industry, AOL is to Walla Walla what the Internet is to the universe. Over 30 million people visit the Internet every day, downloading files, exchanging mail, and acquiring data. America Online is your key to this universe, *if* you know enough to keep from getting stuck in orbit. This chapter is your official Internet primer.

▲ Chapter 15 reveals one of the newest departments: "Kids Only." Prominent among the offerings is KOOL (Kids Only OnLine), but Disney is here, and KIDSNET, and games, and TIME for Kids.

▲ Chapter 16 is devoted to education. *Comptons Encyclopedia* is here, of course, but so is the Online Campus. Perhaps we'll enroll in a class, or enroll in a correspondence course through the International Correspondence Schools. We'll make a special visit to the Library of Congress as well.

▲ Chapter 17 introduces The Marketplace, where you can buy or sell anything from computers to cars. And *Consumer Reports* magazine—past issues and present—ensures an informed decision.

▲ The Reference Desk is the subject of Chapter 18. The Career Center is here, along with Barron's Booknotes, the Bible and the CNN Newsroom.

▲ Chapter 19 explores FlashSessions and the Download Manager. This chapter covers the heavyweight stuff, but it's also some of the best telecommunications software ever offered. Even if you never use it, you've got to read this chapter just to appreciate two of the high-end features AOL offers.

▲ Chapter 20 offers my ten best ten-best lists—the ten best tips for using AOL, the ten most frequently asked questions of the AOL customer support team, the ten best files for downloading—that kind of thing. You'll be among the online illuminati after you've finished this chapter.

⚙ Five appendices conclude the book. A keyword listing offers warp-speed navigation through the AOL universe. The Command-key reference helps you Get It Done Fast; the "Modems, Localities & CCL Files" appendix is for the digitheads among us; an on-the-road reference serves those who take AOL to remote locations; and the "Preferences" appendix shows you how to configure AOL just the way you want. At the end of the book, an extensive glossary defines all those cryptic terms that have become requisite adjuncts to the telecommunications lexicon.

You'd better fasten your seat belt. Sometimes the ride gets a little bumpy, and when I get to talking, I forget to steer—hand gestures and all that, you know. Don't worry: I haven't lost a passenger yet. Have your camera ready, you have lots of stuff to see. And relax. Smile a bit. You're five years old again and Christmas morning is only a turn of the page away....

Making the Connection

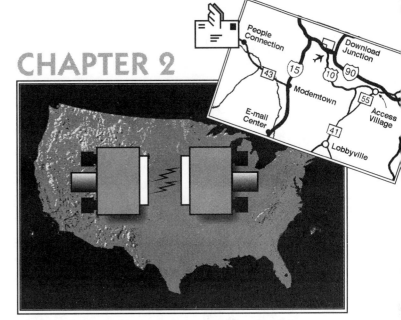

If you have never used America Online—if you have never even installed the software—this chapter's for you. It's written for the agnostic, the novice—those who hold disks in their sweaty palms and wonder if they are stalwart enough to connect their Macs to the outside world.

For most of us, computers are autonomous and independent. The only external device we've ever encountered is a printer. Our dialog with the computer has always been a singular one—isolated and solitary. We might personify our Macs. We might give them names and even voices, and we might think of their error messages and dialog boxes as communication, but we know better.

Computers don't think. Computers don't respond with imagination or indignation or intelligence. There are no threats to us here. Connecting to AOL will put human intelligence at the other end of the line. America Online isn't just a computer in Virginia; it's people, and people online expect a dialog. People respond, with innovation and humor. This is not the isolation we have come to expect of our computers.

So far, our ordered universe has been predictable and familiar. Why mess with it?

Frontispiece terrain map by Gail P. Thelin and Richard J. Pike, published by the US Geological Survey. Superimposed are the connector icons from the AOL sign-on screen. The terrain map (without the connectors) is available in the libraries of the Macintosh Graphics forum. Use the keywords File Search, and search using the criterion USGA. GIF files such as this (and how to view them) are discussed in Chapter 5, "Computing."

Because there's more to life, that's why. Think of your first car, your first love, your first child. Each was shrouded in anxiety, and each was resplendent with reward. We're talking about discovery here, and while the AOL opportunity might not rank with love and birth, it's an opportunity one should not deny.

Before you read any further, I want you to understand that this chapter describes the process of installing the AOL software and making the first connection with AOL itself. If you already have an established AOL account, then you probably won't need to read much of this chapter. Feel free to skim it or skip ahead to another part of the tour—I'll catch up with you soon enough.

Things You'll Need

Let's take inventory here. There are a few things you need before you can connect with America Online. No doubt you already have them, but let's be sure.

The Computer

You need a Mac, of course. Almost any Macintosh will do—a Mac Plus or better. That's one of the benefits of telecommunications: nearly any computer is adequate. I bought my first Macintosh in 1984. It's a bandaged relic, but I still use it to sign on to AOL and for that purpose it has power to spare.

You will need at least 1200k of available random-access memory (RAM) and a hard disk with at least 3mb of free space, but that's about it. If computers were cars, AOL would run on a Yugo.

The Telephone Line

You need access to a telephone line. Your standard residential phone line is fine. A multiline business telephone might be more of a challenge. What's really important is that your telephone plug into a modular telephone jack (called an *RJ-11 jack,* if you care about that sort of thing). It's the one with the square hole measuring about a quarter-inch on a side.

Whenever you're online, your telephone is out of commission for voice calls. It's as if someone is on the phone and you want to use an extension, except that you'll *never* want to eavesdrop on an AOL session. The screeching sound that modems make when communicating with each other is about as pleasant as fingernails on a blackboard—and about as intelligible.

Call Waiting

Call Waiting—a feature offered by most telephone companies today—allows you to receive notice of an incoming call while you're on the phone. This plays havoc with telecommunications signals. If you have Call Waiting, you'll need to disable it whenever you're online. It's discussed in Chapter 20, "Ten Best." Look in the index under "Call Waiting."

The Membership Kit

America Online membership kits come in a number of forms, but they all have some things in common: they include a disk, a temporary registration number and password. *The Official America Online Membership Kit & Tour Guide* includes a disk, account number and password in a little plastic pouch affixed to the inside back cover. Find all of this stuff, and set it by your Mac. Keep this book nearby as well.

It's a good idea to make a copy of the AOL disk right now. It's not copy-protected: standard Macintosh disk-copying routines work just fine. Your Macintosh manual contains the necessary instructions for copying a floppy, if you don't already know how. Put the original AOL disk away somewhere safe. You never know when you might need it again.

The Modem

A modem (short for *modulator/demodulator*) is a device that converts computer data into audible tones that the telephone system can transmit. Modems are required at both ends of the line: the AOL host computer has one too.

Modems are rated according to their data transmission speed. If you're shopping for a modem, get one rated at 9600 bps (bits per second—see the sidebar) or faster. Modem prices are quite reasonable nowadays—even 14.4-kbps modems are generally less than $150. Modems rated at 9600 bps are fast and capable of extracting every bit of performance AOL has to offer. Modems rated at 14.4 kbps are capable of extracting all of the performance AOL has promised for the foreseeable future. If you can afford it, get a 14.4-kbps modem. You'll regret it if you buy anything slower.

Baud Rates

The term *baud rate* refers to the signaling rate, or the number of times per second the signal changes. You might hear this term confused with *bits per second* (bps), which isn't entirely accurate. By using modern electronic wizardry, today's modems can transmit two, three or four bits with each change of signal, increasing the speed of data transfer considerably. Since it takes eight bits to make a byte, a rate of 9600 bps means that anywhere between 1200 and 4800 bytes per second can be transferred. A *byte* is the amount of data required to describe a single character of text. In other words, a baud rate of 9600 should transmit at least 1200 characters—about 15 lines of text—per second.

Alas, the world is an imperfect place—especially the world of phone lines. If static or interference of any kind occurs on the line, data transmission is garbled. And even one misplaced bit can destroy the integrity of an entire file. To address the problem, AOL validates the integrity of received data. In plain English, this means that the host computer sends a packet of information (a couple of seconds' worth) to your Mac, then waits for the Mac to say, "I got that!" before it sends the next packet. Validation like this means things run a little slower than they would without validation, but it's necessary. We're probably down to a minimum of 1000 characters per second once we factor in the time it takes to accommodate data validation.

Then there's noise. You've heard it: static on the line. If you think it interferes with voice communication, it's murder on data. Often your Mac says, "That packet was no good—send it again," and the host computer complies. The reliability of any particular telephone connection is capricious. Some are better than others. Noise, however, is a definite factor, and packets have to be re-sent once in a while. Now we're probably down to a minimum of 900 characters per second on a good telephone line on a good day—a little over 11 lines of text per second at 9600 bps.

In other words, a 9600-bps modem isn't four times faster than a 2400-bps model, and a 2400-bps modem isn't twice as fast as one rated at 1200 bps. On the other hand, a 2400-bps modem doesn't cost twice as much as a 1200-bps model, and a 9600-bps screamer doesn't cost four times as much as a 2400-bps pedestrian model. What I'm trying to say is that in terms of baud per buck, 9600 is your best buy.

I prefer modems with speakers and lights. A speaker lets you hear the phone being dialed and the modem at the other end answering—very reassuring stuff. At that point—when the connection is established—most modem speakers become silent so you don't have to listen to the screeching sound of two computers talking to each other.

As I said earlier, lights are nice. My modem has nine of them. I don't understand most of them, but they look important, and the one marked "RD" (receiving data) is worth watching when you are downloading a file (I discuss downloading in Chapter 5, "Computing"). It should stay on almost continuously. If, during a download, your "RD" light is off more often than it's on, you've got a noisy phone line or the system is extremely busy. Whatever the cause, it's best to halt the download (AOL always leaves a Cancel button on the screen for that purpose) and resume it another time. That's why I advise buying a modem with lights: if you don't have them, how can you tell what's going on?

A number of Macs now offer internal modems: modems inside the Mac itself. If you have an internal modem, you won't tie up the modem connection on the back of your Mac (leaving it available for some other purpose) but you won't have any lights to watch either. Life is full of compromises.

If your modem is the external variety, it will need power of some kind. Some external modems use batteries, but most use AC power and plug into the wall. Be sure a socket is available.

Most important, be sure you have the proper cables. For an external modem, you need two: one to connect the modem to the Mac and another to connect the modem to the phone jack. The modem-to-phone-jack cable bundled with many modems rarely exceeds six feet. If the distance between your modem and your phone jack exceeds that distance, you can buy an extension cable at a phone, electronics or hardware store. Extension cables are standard equipment and are inexpensive. Check your modem's manual to see if your modem requires a hardware-handshaking cable. If it does, it's essential that you use one, as it will provide for a more reliable connection at 9600 baud.

Few external modems include a Mac-to-modem cable. You will probably have to purchase one if you're buying an external modem.

You will also need the continued use of your phone, and will need to make some provision for that. It's less complicated if the modem has a jack for your phone. In that case, you can plug the modem into the phone jack, then plug the phone into the modem. The jacks on the back of the modem should be marked for this.

If your modem is internal, or if your external modem only has a single jack, and you want to continue using your phone as well as your modem, you might also want to invest in a modular splitter, which plugs into the phone jack on your wall, making two jacks out of one. You plug your phone into one of the splitter's jacks and your modem into the other. Plugging both devices into the same jack won't interfere with everyday telephone communications; incoming calls will continue to go to your phone, just as they did before. You should be able to find a splitter at a phone, electronics or hardware store for less than $3.

If all this sounds like a lot of wires to keep track of and you have trouble plugging in a toaster, don't worry. Most modems come with good instructions, and the components are such that you can't connect anything backward. Just follow the instructions and you'll be all right.

The Money

Before you sign on to AOL for the first time, there's something else you'll need: money. America Online wants to know how you plan to pay the balance on your account each month. Cash won't do. Instead, you can provide a credit card number: Visa, MasterCard, American Express or Discover Card are all acceptable. So are many bank debit cards. Or have your checkbook handy: AOL can directly access your checking account if you provide them with the necessary numbers.

The Screen Name

We're almost ready, but right now I want you to get all other thoughts out of your mind and decide what you want to call yourself. Every AOL member has a unique screen name. Screen names are how AOL tells us apart. You must have one and it has to be different from anybody else's.

A screen name must be three to ten characters in length—letters or numbers. Over a million people use AOL, and they all have screen names of ten or fewer characters. Ten isn't many characters; chances are the screen name you want most is taken. Have a number of alternates ready ahead of time, and prepare yourself for disappointment. Hardly anyone ever gets his or her first choice.

There's no going back, by the way. Once AOL accepts your initial screen name, it's yours as long as you remain a member. Though your account can have as many as five screen names (to accommodate other people in your family or your alter egos), your initial screen name is the one AOL uses to establish your identity. For this reason, your initial screen name can't be changed. Be prepared with a zinger (and a half-dozen alternates), or AOL will assign you something like TomLi5437, and you'll forever be known by that name. People have a hard time relating to a name like that.

MajorTom

I worked my way through college as a traffic reporter for an Oregon radio station. I was both reporter and pilot. It was a great job: perfect hours for a student, easy work and unlimited access to a flashy plane. It didn't pay much, but somehow that wasn't important—not in the halcyon days of bachelorhood.

I hate to date myself, but David Bowie was an ascending force on the music scene in those days. Impertinent, perhaps—a little too androgynous and scandalous for the conservative element of the Nixon era—but definitely a hit-maker. Our station played Bowie. On my first day, the morning-show disk jockey switched on his microphone and hailed "Ground Control to Major Tom"—a line from Bowie's *Space Oddity*—to get my attention. The name stuck. I was known as Major Tom from then on.

When the time came for me to pick my AOL screen name, it suggested TomLi5437 and I balked. How about just plain Tom? I asked. It's in use, said the host computer. I tried four others and AOL continued to remind me of my lack of imagination. In desperation I tried MajorTom, and the AOL accepted it. Once an initial screen name is accepted, there's no going back. I'm MajorTom on AOL now, and I will be forever more.

The Password

Oh yes, you need a password. Without a password, anyone knowing your screen name can log on using your name and have a field day on your nickel. Passwords must be from four to eight characters in length, and any combination of letters or numbers is acceptable. You're asked for your password every time you sign on, so choose something easy for you to remember—something that's not a finger-twister to type. It should be different from your screen name, phone number, social security number, address or real name—something no one else would ever guess, even if they know you well.

A Case for Elaborate Passwords

In his book *The Cuckoo's Egg*, Cliff Stoll describes computer hackers' methods for breaking passwords. Since most computers already have a dictionary on disk—all spelling checkers use dictionaries—the hackers simply program their computers to try every word in the dictionary as a password. It sounds laborious, but computers don't mind. (Cliff Stoll and *The Cuckoo's Egg* are mentioned again in Chapter 4, "Electronic Mail." Look in the bibliography for the specifics on his book.)

In other words, I'm making a case for elaborate passwords here. Don't make it personal, don't use your social security number, don't write it down, and select something that's not in a dictionary. That'll foil the rascals.

Installing the Software

Finally, we're ready to get our hands dirty. Installing the AOL software is a straightforward process: an installation program does all the work for you.

- Again, be sure you have at least 3mb of space available on your hard disk. Use the Finder to disclose your free disk space—your Mac manual will tell you how.

- Assuming you made a copy of the AOL disk, insert that copy into your floppy disk drive. (The original AOL disk works just as well, but making—and using—a copy is just standard paranoid procedure.) A window opens on your desktop and the installation program's icon is visible there.

- When you double-click the Install icon. A greeting screen appears, identifying the Installer program (see Figure 2-1).

- Installation options are disclosed via the Custom button pictured in Figure 2-1. Few installations require the use of these options.

Figure 2-1: The
Installer greeting
screen appears as
soon as the
program is
running.

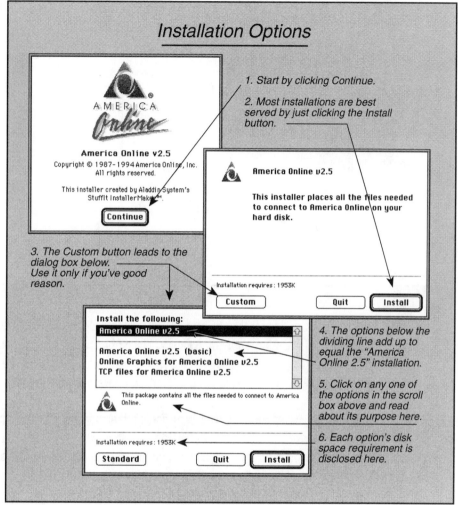

🔊 The Installer then produces the window pictured in Figure 2-2. It asks you where you want to place AOL's folder.

Select disk to install onto:

IBM

[Eject Disk]   [**Install**]

[Switch Disk] [Cancel]

IBM

Readers with eagle's eyes will note that the hard disk on my Macintosh is named "IBM." There's a good reason for this: my hard disk *is* an IBM. When I first received my Mac and popped open the case (not a recommended method for getting to know a Mac, but often educational), the striped-blue "IBM" logo was the first thing I saw. (It's hard to miss in that context.)

As it turns out, IBM makes hard disks and Apple doesn't. IBM is on Apple's list of suppliers and Apple buys hard disks from any supplier who offers the right price at the right time. Apparently, IBM's price was right when my Mac was constructed and it has been a mixed-breed computer ever since. It's kind of embarrassing, but it's mine and I'm not about to hide it.

The moral of the story: open the case only if you're prepared for the consequences.

🔊 Remember that you're about to install a folder, not a file. You needn't have a folder already prepared for AOL: it makes its own.

🔊 Once you click the Install button, the Installer does its work. This takes a couple of minutes. As it's working, a "thermometer" keeps you abreast of the Installer's progress (see the upper window in Figure 2-3). The Installer concludes with an announcement of its success (bottom window of Figure 2-3).

Figure 2-3: The
installation
process is
automatic: all
you have to do
is watch.

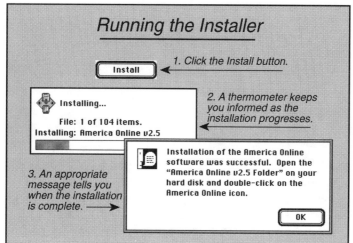

Running the Installer

1. *Click the Install button.*

Install

Installing...

File: 1 of 104 items.
Installing: America Online v2.5

2. *A thermometer keeps
you informed as the
installation progresses.*

3. *An appropriate
message tells you
when the installation
is complete.*

Installation of the America Online
software was successful. Open the
"America Online v2.5 Folder" on your
hard disk and double-click on the
America Online icon.

OK

After you click the OK button pictured in Figure 2-3, take a moment to explore your hard disk. The Installer has created a new folder where you told it to, containing the AOL application and four folders (see Figure 2-4). Note that the folder and its contents equal nearly 3mb, even though the floppy disk from which it came holds much less than that. The secret is file compression. Using a product called StuffIt (described in Chapter 5, "Computing"), the AOL folder's components were compressed (stuffed) before they were placed on the floppy disk; the compressed files were copied to your hard disk; then the Installer unstuffed them. It's all very logical, I suppose, but it's still magic to me.

Figure 2-4: The Installer places a folder on your hard disk containing the America Online software and all of the necessary folders.

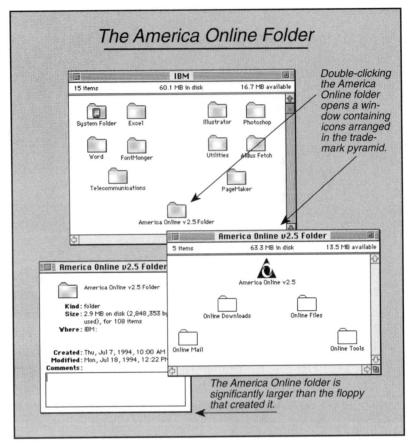

The America Online folder is significantly larger than the floppy that created it.

The Pyramid

Look again at the America Online v.2.5 window pictured in Figure 2-4. Note how the icons are arranged. Since the AOL logo is a pyramid, the programmers arranged the folder icons in a pyramid shape as well. Little details like this crop up everywhere at AOL; some are functional, some are fanciful like the pyramid. They're part of the fun, but they're also an indication of the care and vigilance that go into the product. In the end, we the members are the beneficiaries.

There, you've done it. You've installed the software and you're ready to sign on. Eject the floppy disk, put it in a safe place and let's get on with it.

The Initial Online Session

The initial online session takes about 15 minutes. Be sure you have the time and uninterrupted access to the phone before you begin. You needn't worry about money: though you'll be online for a while, the setup process is accomplished on AOL's dime, not yours. You needn't worry about indelibility either: plenty of Cancel buttons are offered during the initial session. If you get cold feet, you can always hang up and start over.

Configuring the Telephone Connection

Before it can successfully make the connection, AOL needs to know a number of things about your telephone. It needs to know whether you have Touch Tone or rotary dialing, whether it needs to dial a 9 (or something else) to reach an outside line and whether a 1 should be dialed before the 800 number. Canadian members will need to supply additional information. Your modem should be connected to the phone line and to your Mac by now, and everything should be turned on.

Don't let me scare you. Most of this stuff happens automatically. All you will have to do is watch.

🔺 You can resize and relocate the AOL window for a neater desktop if you wish—it's just like any other window. Double-click the AOL icon to launch the AOL software. A welcome screen greets you as soon as the software loads (see Figure 2-5).

Figure 2-5: This In the Spotlight screen greets you when you first run the America Online software.

Upgrading

If you're already an AOL member and you've been using an earlier version of AOL's software on your machine, you should now click the Upgrade button shown in Figure 2-5. The Installer will ask you for the location of your old AOL application and use information it finds there—access numbers, address books, preferences, screen names and mail files—to customize the new edition. The remainder of the installation process described here will be skipped.

> A second screen greets you when you click the Continue button shown in Figure 2-5. (This screen is shown in Figure 2-6.) Carefully read the list of assumptions presented here. If they describe your situation accurately, click the Continue button. If they don't, click the Change Options button. Change Options accommodates dial phones, modem connections to the Macintosh printer port, and members calling from Canadian exchanges.

Figure 2-6: If the assumptions aren't correct, click the Change Options button.

First, we will automatically dial a toll-free number to reach America Online. During this free call you will choose a number in your area that you will use regularly to sign on to America Online.

You probably...
- use a touch-tone phone
- have your modem connected to your Macintosh's modem port
- don't need to dial a '9' for an 'outside' call
- don't need to disable call waiting during calls to America Online
- are calling from the continental United States

If this is correct, click 'Continue.' If any one of the above does not apply, click 'Change Options.'

| Cancel | Change Options | Continue |

> When you click Figure 2-6's Continue button, the Installer checks your modem's speed and port, then asks you one more time if you're ready to sign on. Be sure no one is using your phone line, that you have your registration certificate (with its temporary registration number and password), and that your credit card or checking account number is nearby, then click Continue.

A Now the Installer dials an 800 number to temporarily connect to AOL and find a local access number for you. You will be able to monitor the call's progress by watching the window pictured in Figure 2-7. Once you see the message that says "Connected at XXXX baud" (the baud rate is determined by the speed of your modem) you can be sure that your Mac and modem are communicating properly. You can be sure that your modem and the telephone system are connected as well. If the AOL software finds anything amiss prior to this point, it notifies you and suggests solutions.

Figure 2-7: This window appears as America Online dials its toll-free number during the initial connection.

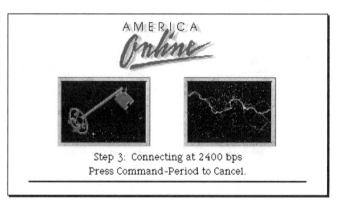

Isolating Connection Errors

Though they rarely do, things can go wrong during the connect process. The problem could be at your end (e.g., the modem or the phone lines), or it could be at AOL's end. You can be sure the problem is at your end if you don't hear a dial tone (assuming your modem has a speaker) before your modem begins dialing.

If your connection fails during the initial connect process, don't panic. The software will eventually hang up and display a message with a Change Configuration button. Click that button and select your modem's brand name and model from the Modem Type pop-up scroll box you'll see on your screen, then try the connection again.

The solution described in the previous paragraph solves about 90 percent of the connection problems. If yours persists, wait a few minutes and try again. If it fails a third time, call AOL Customer Service at 800-827-6364.

Selecting Your Local Access Numbers

Now you're connected to the AOL host computer and it's anxious to say hello. Its singular interest right now is to find some local access numbers for you. To do that, it needs to know where you are. It finds that out by requesting your local area code (see Figure 2-8).

Figure 2-8: Using your area code, America Online attempts to select two local numbers for access to the service.

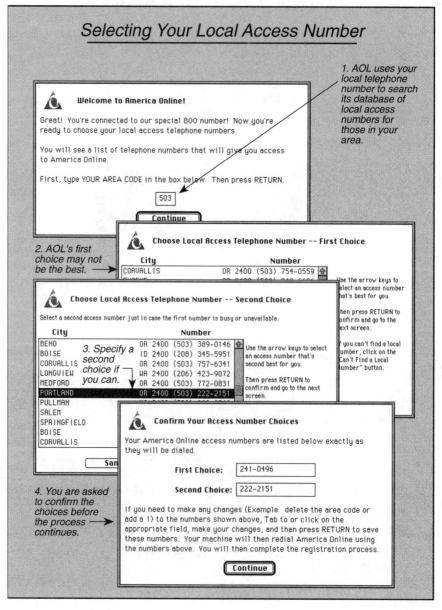

🔺 Using your area code, AOL consults its database of local access numbers and produces a list of those nearest you (see the second window in Figure 2-8). Look over the list carefully. The phone number at the top of the list isn't necessarily the one closest to you. Also, note the baud rates listed in the third column. Be sure the number you pick represents the baud rate you intend to use.

🔺 If there isn't a local number listed for your area, you might have to pay long-distance charges to your telephone company in order to connect to AOL. (You'll know this is true if you have to dial a 1 before your access number in order to complete the call.) If you believe that a local number is warranted for your area, complete the initial sign-on process described in this chapter, sign on, use the keyword: Access (I'll discuss keywords in Appendix A), and follow the online directions for petitioning for a local access number.

🔺 It's nice to have a secondary number as well. A secondary number (if available) is just that: a second number (the proper term is *node*—see the Glossary) for your modem to call if the first one is busy (which happens rarely) or bogged down with a lot of traffic (which happens more frequently). Interestingly, dozens of modems can use the same node at the same time by splitting the time available on that node into tiny packets. This is all very perplexing to those of us who think of phone numbers as being capable of handling one conversation at a time, but it's nonetheless true. There is a limit, however, and when it's reached, AOL tries the second number. The third window in Figure 2-8 illustrates the screen used to select this alternate.

Slow Down!
If your first-choice access number is rated at 9600 baud, make your second choice something slower. The number of high-speed incoming lines at AOL is limited, and when they're all in use, the AOL host computer will instruct your software to hang up and try the alternate number. If the alternate is also rated at 9600 baud you'll have the same problem. Select a 2400-baud alternate. At least you'll get online.

🔺 Finally, AOL presents the screen confirming your selections pictured at the bottom of Figure 2-8.

The Temporary Registration Number & Password

Assuming you've clicked on Figure 2-8's Continue button, your Mac will disconnect from the 800 number and dial your primary local access number. Once the connection is reestablished, AOL presents the screen shown in Figure 2-9. This is where you must enter the registration number and password printed on your certificate. These are the temporary equivalents of the permanent screen name and password you'll soon establish. Enter the words and numbers carefully; they're usually nonsensical and difficult to type without error.

Figure 2-9: Enter your temporary registration number and password here. Be sure to type them exactly as they appear on your certificate or label.

> **Welcome to America Online!**
>
> **New Members:**
>
> Please locate the Registration Certificate that was included in your software kit and, in the space below, type the certificate number and certificate password as they appear on the printed certificate.
>
> **Existing Members:**
>
> If you already have an America Online account and are simply installing a new version of the software, type your existing Screen Name in the first field and Password in the second. This will update your account information automatically.
>
> Note: Use the "tab" key to move from one field to another.
>
> Registration Number (or Screen Name): [   ]
>
> Registration Password (or Password): [   ]
>
> [Cancel]   [Continue]

Your Name & Address

When you click on the Continue button shown in Figure 2-9, AOL provides directions for using an online form like that shown in Figure 2-10. If you're not familiar with Mac conventions, you'll want to read the directions carefully. If you've used Mac software before—even a little bit—you already know this stuff. It's traditional Mac protocol. Hint: Use the Tab key to move from field to field.

Once you've read the form usage instructions, click on the Continue button and AOL will ask you for some personal information (see Figure 2-10).

Figure 2-10:
Provide your name,
phone number(s)
and address. Be
sure to use the
telephone number
format shown in
the illustration.

Please be sure to enter ALL of the following information

First Name: [ ]   Last Name: [ ]

Address: [ ]

City: [ ]

State: [ ]   Daytime Phone: [ ]

Zip Code: [ ]   Evening Phone: [ ]

Note: Please enter phone numbers area code first, for example,
703-555-1212, and enter state with no periods, for example, VA for
Virginia.

[Cancel]   [Continue]

America Online uses this information to communicate with you off-line. Though AOL never bills members directly (we'll discuss money in a moment), and though this information is not available online to other members (member profiles—which is what other members see—are discussed in the next chapter), AOL does, occasionally, need to contact you off-line, and they use this information to do so. They might want to send you a disk containing an upgrade to the software, or perhaps you've ordered something from them (this book, for example) that needs to be mailed. That's what this information is for.

Your Phone Number

Your phone number becomes an important part of your record at America Online, not because anyone at AOL intends to call you, but because AOL's Customer Service Department uses this number to identify you whenever you call. Should you ever find the need to call, the first question Customer Service will ask is, What's your phone number? It's unique, after all, so Customer Service uses it to look up your records. It's an efficient method, but only if you provide the number accurately during your initial sign-on.

Providing Your Billing Information

Let's be up front about it: America Online is a business run for profit. In other words, AOL needs to be paid for the service it provides. It offers a number of ways to accomplish this. Your VISA, MasterCard, Discover Card or American Express are the preferred methods of payment. If you don't have one of these (or if you prefer an alternate method), AOL accepts selected bank debit cards as well (verifying acceptability with the financial institution). AOL can also arrange to automatically debit your checking account. (There's a fee for this—more than a credit card costs you—so it should be your last choice.)

When you click on Figure 2-10's Continue button, another screen appears, identifying AOL's connect-time rates. Read it carefully (you need to know what you're buying and what it's costing you, after all), then move on (see Figure 2-11).

Figure 2-11: All major credit cards are welcome. Or, if you wish, AOL will debit your checking account directly.

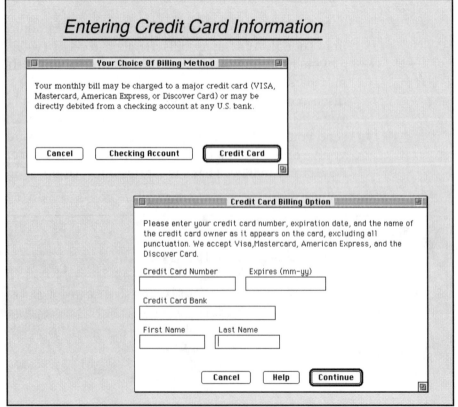

Figure 2-11 is an example of the billing information screen for MasterCard information, but the forms for VISA and Discover are about the same.

Choosing a Screen Name & Password

When you click the Continue button shown in Figure 2-11, AOL provides a series of screens discussing the significance of screen names, concluding with the screen name input form, pictured at the top of Figure 2-12. Do you see the screen name it picked for me? This is an incentive to have your own alternates at hand.

Figure 2-12: Conclude the registration process by entering your screen name and password.

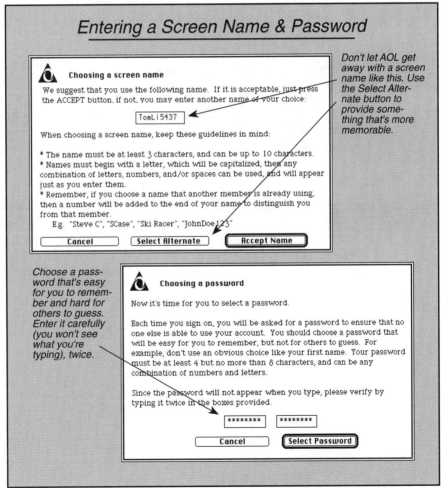

Note that your password doesn't appear on your screen as you type it. Substituting asterisks for the letters of your password is a standard security precaution. You never know who's looking over your shoulder. America Online asks you to enter your password twice, to be sure you didn't mistype it the first time.

A Letter From the President

Now that you've successfully finished setting up and signing on, you enter the AOL service itself. No doubt the first thing that will happen is you'll receive an announcement that you have mail. To read the letter, choose Read New Mail from the Mail menu, or press Command-R. The New Mail window appears, with mail from AOL President Steve Case. Click the Read button and read what he has to say.

Where to Go From Here

Once you're online, you have the entire AOL universe to explore. The thought is both enticing and overwhelming. Here's what I suggest: spend a half-hour wandering around right after you read Steve's letter. You have quite a bit of free connect time coming; don't worry about money. You'll find a button marked Discover AOL on the Main Menu screen shown in Figure 2-13. Click that button, then explore a few of the areas offered in the Discover America Online window. The America Online Highlights are always interesting; the Best of America Online may turn up some areas to which you'll return; and What's Hot This Month is always topical.

Figure 2-13: The
Discover America
Online feature is
an excellent way
to begin your
online journey.

Try the Discover AOL icon
for your first online journey.
Explore a couple of the
areas at right before you
sign off.

During this initial session, don't try to absorb the entire contents of
AOL. Rather, wander aimlessly, getting a feeling for the nature of the
AOL universe. Note how Mac-like it is. Everything is predictable and
familiar—at least to a Macintosh user.

After a half-hour or so, you might want to sign off by choosing Sign
Off from the Go To menu. Once the dust settles, turn to the chapter in
this book that describes an area of particular interest to you. Read that
chapter, then sign back on and explore that area. See if you can find the
things I described in the chapter. Spend another half-hour at this.

Now you're on your own. Explore another department if you wish,
or turn to Chapter 4, "Electronic Mail," and learn how to send mail to
somebody. You'll probably get a response in a few days. People at AOL
are very friendly. It really is a community.

Moving On

Speaking of the people online, that's one of the subjects covered in the next chapter, "Online Help & the Members." When you have the time (I know how enticing AOL can be—you might never return to this book now that you're online), read on. We have many more things to talk about.

Online Help & the Members

CHAPTER 3

Sounds like a
heavy-metal band: "Online Help & the Members." Dressed in black
leather, with chains draped around their waists, Online Help & the
Members take the stage accompanied by waves of cacophony and
pandemonium. As in a jailbreak, spotlights sweep the auditorium,
illuminating a mass of writhing supplicants below. The spotlights
converge on Online as he wrests the microphone from its stand. An
expectant hush fills the air. In a voice amplified by 2,000 transistors the
size of hubcaps, he speaks: "America Online Customer Relations! May I
help you?"

Getting Help

Much to my delight, software publishers have recently placed notable
emphasis on providing users with help. The version of Microsoft Word
I use, for instance, includes a help file measuring 1.8mb—larger than
Word itself. The help file is right on my hard disk. All I have to do is
tap on a couple of keys and there's the help I need: convenient, comprehensive and clear.

Frontispiece graphic by Chuck Carter/Cyan. The graphic was created in Infini-D
using Phong shading with shadows. Keywords: File Search; use the criterion: "Phong
shadows."

America Online is no different. Like all good software, AOL's help is always a simple keystroke away. America Online, however, has a unique advantage: since a good portion of AOL's help resides on the host computer, it can be updated any time. This means that AOL's help can be particularly responsive. If members are having trouble with a specific area, AOL can rewrite the help files to address the source of confusion. It's as if a Microsoft representative came to my home with a new help disk every time Word's help files needed to be changed.

There's a flaw in the plan, however. In order to access online help, I have to be online. While this isn't much of a restriction—online is the time I usually need help, after all—there are occasions when I would like to get help without signing on. What if I *can't* sign on? What if I'm traveling and need help finding an alternative number?

Getting Help: A Methodical Approach

If you have a question about AOL and require help, *don't write to me!* I'm just a writer, and everyone knows that writers don' know nuttin'.

Rather, I suggest you use the methods described below, in the order in which they appear. All of the topics mentioned are explained in detail later in this chapter.

1. Look up the topic in the index of this book to see if your question is answered here. I'd like to think that most of your questions will be answered this way.

2. Run the AOL software and choose Help from the Apple menu. In this chapter I refer to this kind of help as *off-line* help, since it's available when you're off-line (even though it's available online as well). Off-line help offers a searchable list of over 20 topics and will often answer your question, especially if it has to do with the most commonly asked AOL questions.

3. Go online, press Command-K (which is how you prepare AOL to accept a keyword— we'll discuss keywords later in this chapter) then type Help. Click the OK button and click the second OK button in response to the "Are you sure..." message. This will take you to AOL's Online Support Center, a particularly comprehensive (and free) resource.

4. Go online and use the keyword: MHM. This will take you to AOL's Members Helping Members bulletin boards. Post your question in the appropriate folder there. Within a day or so you will have a response to your question from another member. Peer help is often the best help you can find.

More

5. Go online and use the keyword: TechLive. This will take you to Tech Help Live, where you can consult AOL's Technical Support staff. This feature is free and open from 9 A.M. to 1 A.M. (Eastern time) weekdays, and from 12 P.M. to 1 A.M. weekends.

6. Ask a Guide. Sign on, choose Lobby from the Go To menu, and once you arrive, look around for someone with the word "Guide" in their name. Guides are a particularly friendly form of help, and they're on duty weekdays from 9 A.M. until 6 A.M. (Eastern time), 7 days a week, 365 days a year.

7. Send e-mail to Customer Relations. Sign on and use the keyword: Help. In the Help window, click the "Email the Staff" button. You'll hear back from them in a day or two.

8. Call Customer Relations at 800-827-6364. They're open from 9 A.M. to 2 A.M. (Eastern time) Monday through Friday , and 12 P.M. to 1 A.M. Saturday and Sunday. It's a toll-free call in the continental U.S., and there's never any charge for support from AOL.

Altruistically, AOL offers *both* online and off-line help. One set of help files resides on your hard disk available at any time regardless of whether you're online. The other set of help files resides on the host computer. This set is the one that's constantly being updated. It's not just comprehensive, it's downright monumental. It's available whenever you're online, and—incredibly—it's free. Whenever you access AOL's online help area, the clock stops and you aren't charged for your time there.

Off-line Help

Let's talk about off-line help first. America Online's off-line help is especially configured to answer the kind of questions you'll encounter when you're disconnected from the service. How do I connect when I'm away from my usual location? What's the Customer Relations telephone number and when are they on duty? How do I sign up my friends?

Choosing Help From the Apple Menu

There are two ways to access off-line help. Perhaps the most obvious one is to choose Help from the Apple menu. The list of topics that results is extensive (Figure 3-1).

Figure 3-1: Off-line help is always available: Just choose Help from the Apple menu.

As is always the case with items under the Apple menu, Help can be chosen at any time, whether you're online or off. These help topics are stored in a file on your hard disk, and as such don't require that you go online in order to access them; you just need to launch the AOL program and pull down the Apple menu.

Look carefully at the list of help topics in Figure 3-1. Some of them are specifically for first-time users. Others are primarily for members on the road: Changing Your Setup, Access Outside the Continental USA and so on. The other help topics are oriented toward AOL's menu bar: the File menu, the Help menu, the Go To menu and so on right across the menu at the top of AOL's screen.

Using Command-Slash

The reason so many of the topics pictured in Figure 3-1 relate to the menu bar is because AOL's off-line help is also intended to serve you as you explore the program off-line. To access AOL's off-line help, type Command-slash at any time (the Command key is the one with a cloverleaf or Apple symbol on it), especially when you're exploring the program off-line. Wondering about Preferences? Press Command-slash. From the Help screen's Topic menu, choose The Members Menu. Help with Preferences is available by selecting The Members Menu in the scroll box on the left, then scrolling down to that topic in the Description box at the right side of the window (Figure 3-2). (For a complete discussion of Members Preferences, see Appendix E.)

Figure 3-2: Help with the Preferences command is found under the topic The Members Menu.

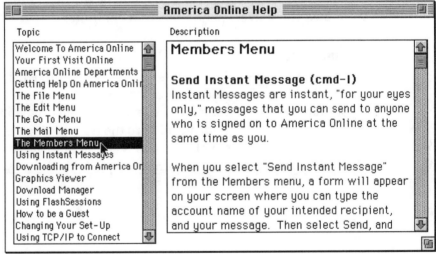

The slash—/—is used because its key is also the question-mark key, and the question mark just seems appropriate for help. This has become something of a universal Macintosh keystroke convention for software help.

My wife is a medical student. She learned a long time ago that it's an impossibility to memorize all of the things she has to know to become a successful practitioner. The sheer magnitude of the task was dragging her down until she realized that all she really had to know was *where to look for information*, not all of the information itself. She has a well-organized library and knows which books discuss which topics. When she needs assistance, she goes to her library and gets help.

You should do the same. Don't worry about memorizing all of the petty details—for any computer program. Instead, learn how to use help. It will take 20 minutes and it will be the most productive 20 minutes you'll ever spend with your computer.

Online Help

America Online's online help is especially comprehensive. Moreover, since the online help file is stored on the host computer (and not on your hard disk) only one file needs to be updated when the online help files require changing. In addition to the help you get using the online files, AOL staff and members stand ready to help you as well. This is world-class help and its breadth is unique to AOL.

Member Services

To access Member Services, choose Member Services from the Go To menu, use the keyword: Help or access it from the designated button on any department screen and the Main Menu. You must be signed on for this: Online help isn't stored on your hard disk, it's on AOL's host computer.

Just before you enter the Member Services area, AOL flashes the message pictured in the middle of Figure 3-3. Unprovoked dialog boxes like this often spell trouble, I know, but not this one. America Online is trying to say that you're about to pass through the "free curtain" (to use the AOL vernacular) and that you won't be charged for the time you're about to spend in Member Services. That's a comforting thought: Online help is free. You can spend all day perusing online help and AOL will never charge you a dime.

Random Acts of Help

The next time you sign on to AOL, click on Member Services from the Main Menu. This will take you to AOL's online help area.

Once you're there, relax (the clock's not running) and explore this area casually. Poke around as you would at a flea market. Don't try to memorize anything. Get the feel of the place. Get to know what's there and where it's found. Consider this an exploratory mission without any particular agenda. After 20 minutes or so, move on to something else.

You will be amazed at what this kind of unstructured behavior can do for you. You will acquire a familiarity with the layout of the place, and you will gain confidence in the use of online help. Most importantly, the next time you need help, you won't hesitate to use the keyword. And that, in the long run, is perhaps the most productive attitude you can adopt toward the use of AOL.

Figure 3-3: Online help is available whenever you're online, and it's absolutely free.

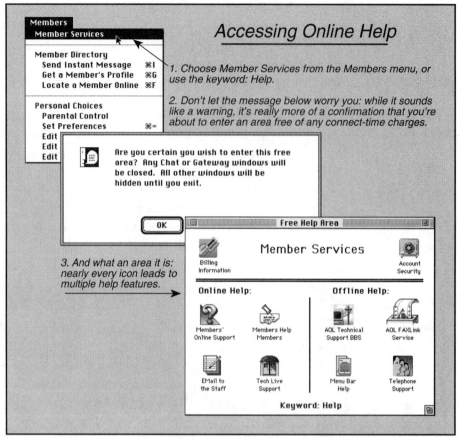

The subjects pictured in the list box on the left side of Figure 3-3's lower window offer immediate answers for nearly anything you encounter while online. Each of these help topics can be saved, printed or both. While the list of topics is extensive, the detail offered within each topic is bountiful (see Figure 3-4).

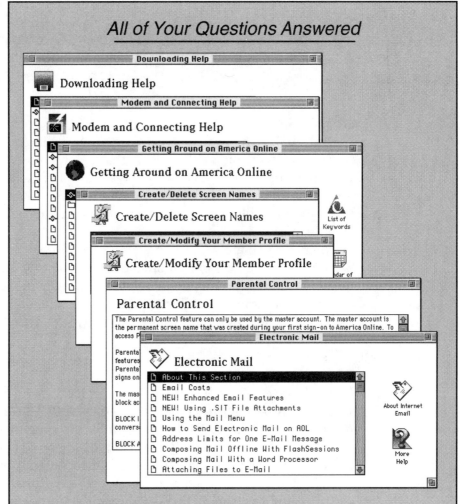

Figure 3-4: A few of the help topics available in the Member Services area.

Help Grab-bag

Nearly every online help feature discussed in this chapter is available via the keyword: Help. It's a free area, so get to know it well.

Saving Help

Though AOL's online help screens are primarily intended for you to read while you're online (there's no charge for the service, after all, so you can take your time), you might want to save a help topic or two on your disk. Doing so provides you with a text file that can be combined with other help files using a word processor, for instance, to create a comprehensive help manual.

To save a help topic that's on your screen, simply choose Save (or Save As—they're the same command in this context) from the File menu. America Online asks you what you want to name the file and where you want to save it. Provide the information it needs, and that help topic will be stored on your disk, ready for any purpose you might have in mind.

Printing Help

More likely, you'll want to print a help topic for ready reference. As you might expect, all you have to do is choose Print from the File menu. Printing from AOL works about like printing from any other Mac application. You'll receive the print dialog box associated with the printer you've selected via the Chooser (the Chooser is under the Apple menu). Configure this dialog as you please and print. By the way, you can print just about any text file you read online, not just the help files. If you run across a file description or news article you want to print, just choose Print from the File menu—AOL will print whatever text is in the front-most (active) window.

The Directory of Services

Look again at Figure 3-3. In the scroll box of the Members' Online Support window, you'll find a folder representing the "Directory of America Online Services," a searchable database of information on all the services offered by AOL. Information for each service includes the following:

🔺 The service's name.

🔺 Any keywords associated with that service (see sidebar).

🔺 A menu path for access to that service.

🔺 A description of that service.

🔺 A button to take you there.

Figure 3-5: The Directory of Services offers a method of searching all the services America Online has to offer.

Keywords

Keywords are shortcuts to specific destinations within AOL. Without keywords, accessing the Microsoft Knowledge Base, for example, via menus and windows requires that I click the Computing button on the Main Menu, click the Industry Connection, click "Companies Listed A-Z", click the "I-M" button, then double-click the "Microsoft" folder. *Whew!* There's gotta be a better way.

And there is: keywords. The keyword for the Microsoft Knowledge Base is Knowledge Base. Once I know the keyword, all I have to do is choose Keyword from the Go To menu (or type Command-K) and enter "Knowledge Base" into the area provided. Instantly, AOL takes me directly to the Knowledge Base, bypassing all the steps in between.

A list of keywords is available in Appendix A of this book, or within the Directory of Services (which we will discuss in a moment), or by typing Command-K, then clicking the Keyword Help button.

Searching the Directory of Services

One of the most helpful features of AOL's online help is the Directory of Services. This is AOL's answer to the question: "I wonder if they have anything that addresses my interest in..." Are you interested in model airplanes? Search the Directory of Services. How about music, poetry or fine food? Use the Directory of Services.

I was having trouble with Microsoft Word the other day. Couldn't get it to do things I knew it was capable of doing. What to do? Call five friends on the phone and get their voice mail? Call Microsoft long distance and wait as they play bad Seattle radio while I'm on hold?

None of the above. I simply signed on and consulted the Microsoft Knowledge Base. The Knowledge Base is the summation of nearly everything Microsoft knows about its products, including answers from their technical support staff. It's updated periodically and re-leased on CD-ROM. You can subscribe if you wish (if you have a CD-ROM player)—it's only $295 a year.

Or you can use AOL. America Online subscribes to the Knowledge Base and posts it online, complete with a search mechanism to find what you're after. If you forget Microsoft's keyword, use the Directory of Services to find it for you. That's just what I did the other day, and my question was answered within a few minutes (see Figure 3-6).

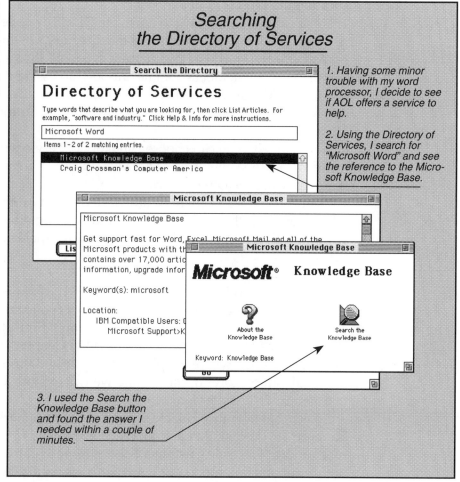

Figure 3-6: The Directory of Services found the Microsoft Knowledge Base for me, and the Knowledge Base had my answer.

Note that the middle window in Figure 3-6 offers the keyword(s) for the Knowledge Base, its location (the menu path that gets you there) and its description. If it isn't what I need, the description saves me the trouble of going there. If it *is* what I need, the keyword and location tell me how to get there quickly.

Locating the Directory of Services

There are at least four ways to get to the Directory of Services.
As shown in Figure 3-3, you'll find the directory's listing in the Members' Online Support window. Since you passed through the free curtain to get to Members' Online Support, accessing the Directory of Services via Online Support is free. It's also in the "Discover AOL" area (keyword: Discover, or click the "Discover AOL" button on the Main Menu).

Alternatively, you can choose Directory of Services from the Go To menu, or use the keyword: Services. If you're not in the free area at the time, accessing the Directory via the Go To menu or via its keyword is on your dime, not AOL's. It's a little faster and more convenient than passing through the curtain, however, so you might wish to use it when you plan to spend only a moment or two there.

Tech Help Live

Let's talk about *rooms* for a moment. At AOL, a room is a place where a number of people gather to talk about a subject of common interest. There are classrooms, for instance, where you'll find a teacher and students (the Online Campus is discussed in Chapter 16, "Education"). There's the Lobby where people go to mingle and meet other people. In fact, AOL offers scores of rooms, and we will explore a number of them in Chapter 12, "People Connection."

Look again at Figure 3-3. Do you see the button marked Tech Live Support? If you click that button, you'll eventually find yourself in a room with at least one Customer Service representative and probably a number of other members, all with questions regarding the service. Conversations in the room are real-time: you don't have to wait for replies. This isn't mail and it's not a message board; it's a room, and like real rooms in real buildings, people in rooms can hold real-time conversations.

There's a lot to be learned here. Not only do you receive answers to your questions immediately, you can "eavesdrop" on questions from other members as well—all at AOL's expense (don't forget that you're still in the free area).

Tech Live help is available weekdays from 9 A.M. to 1 A.M. weekdays, and from 12 P.M. to 1 A.M. weekends. If you need an immediate response, this is the place to find it.

Figure 3-7: A
glimpse of the
Tech Live service.
To get there, use
the keyword:
TechLive.

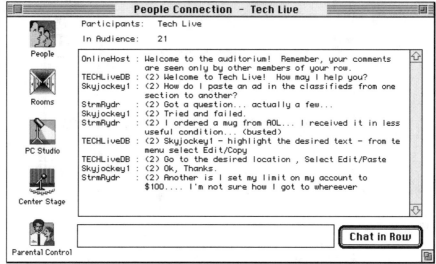

Figure 3-7: A glimpse of the Tech Live service. To get there, use the keyword: TechLive.

Members Helping Members

On my IRS 1040 form, right there next to the word *Occupation*, it says "educator." I write books, teach classes and do some consulting. As an educator, I attend a number of conferences. Most of these conferences are academic, each featuring a number of speakers and seminar leaders.

Reflecting back on those conferences, I must admit that the greatest value I receive from them is not from the speakers or the seminars, it's from the other people attending the conference. My education occurs in the hallways and at lounge tables. People talking to people—peer to peer—that's where I find the Good Stuff.

America Online is no different. Some of the best help online is that received from other members. America Online knows that; that's why it provides Members Helping Members—a formalized version of peer support (Figure 3-8).

Figure 3-8: To
access Members
Helping Members,
click the push-pin
icon in the
Member Services
window, or use
the keyword:
MHM.

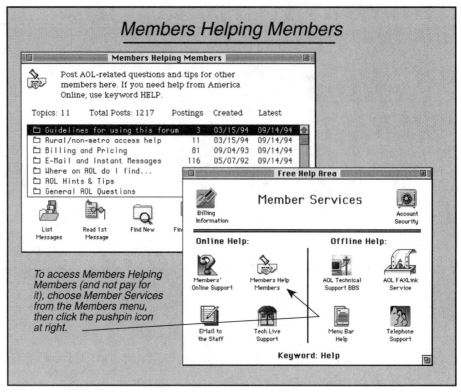

To access Members Helping Members, either click the push-pin icon in the Members' Online Support window, or use the keyword: MHM. Unlike the Directory of Services, you'll pass through the free curtain regardless of how you choose to access this feature. In other words, it never costs you a dime to use Members Helping Members.

Message Boards

Members Helping Members is a *message board*. Though we'll discuss message boards in Chapter 13 ("Clubs & Interests"), the subject is worth a brief mention here as well.

Throughout AOL you'll see little push-pin icons. This is AOL's way of identifying message boards. A message board is analogous to the bulletin boards you see hanging in the halls of offices and academic institutions. People post things there for other people to see: postcards, lost mittens, announcements and messages. America Online's message boards are exactly the same (though you might not see lost mittens on AOL's boards...).

Look again at Figure 3-8. Note how AOL's boards are organized by using folders. The bulletin board analogy weakens a bit here, but AOL's boards get a *lot* of messages (the Members Helping Members board pictured in Figure 3-8 has 1,313). Unless they're organized in some fashion, 1,313 messages posted on a single board would be chaotic and overwhelming. The solution is folders.

You can read all the messages in a folder, browse through them (viewing only their subjects, rather than the messages themselves), or specify only those messages that have been posted since a specific date. This is a very convenient message-reading system and is described in detail in Chapter 6.

For the time being, let's select a folder and read its messages. I chose the AOL Hints & Tips folder and found the series of messages pictured in Figure 3-9.

Figure 3-9:
TABarrett needed
help with her
stuck windows.
Kathy4648 was
there to help.

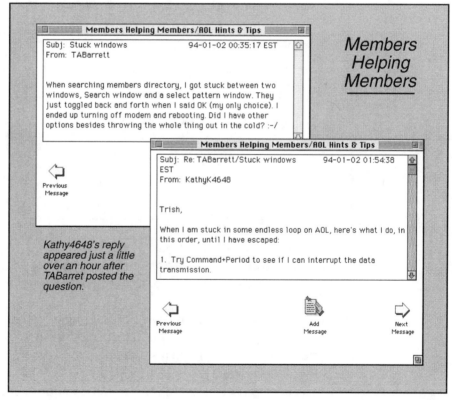

Kathy4648's reply
appeared just a little
over an hour after
TABarret posted the
question.

The Value of Member Help

Look at the last message pictured on Figure 3-9. Not only does Kathy4648 offer a solution to TABarrett's problem, Kathy offers four other solutions as well. This is superb help, and it came from another member. The full text of the message from Kathy4648 appears in Figure 3-10.

Figure 3-10: Kathy4648 offers not one, but five solutions to a problem.

Kathy4648's Message

```
Subj:   Re: TABarrett/Stuck windows    94-01-02 01:54:38 EST
From:   KathyK4648


Trish,

When I am stuck in some endless loop on AOL, here's what I
do, in this order, until I have escaped:

1.   Try Command+Period to see if I can interrupt the data
transmission.

2.   Try Command+Q to quit AOL.

3.   Turn off the modem, forcing an interruption.

4.   Force the program to quit (Command-Option-Escape).

5.   Restart.

Kathy
```

Note another small detail: Kathy4648 must have looked up TABarrett's profile, as she addresses her message to "Trish." That's a nice touch. Kathy didn't have to do that, but it makes her message all the more personable.

I'm reminded of community again. Visiting a big city a few months ago, I was struck by the isolation that seemed to surround everyone I passed on the street. Perhaps it's a defense mechanism for dealing with high population density, but it seemed that everyone was in a cocoon, oblivious to everyone else. No one smiled. No one ever looked anywhere but straight ahead. Thousands of people jostled together yet none were talking. An incredibly lonely place.

On the other hand, in the little Oregon town where I live, there are no strangers. People stop on the street and say hello, swap some gossip and perhaps offer advice.

America Online is more like my little Oregon community. I spent years on other services and never felt like I belonged. I never got mail, I never contributed to a message board, and I never knew where to find help. It was like a big city to me and I was always anxious to leave. At AOL I'm walking the street in a small town on a sunny day and everyone is smiling. The first day I arrived at AOL, I got a letter from Steve Case. People like Kathy4648 go out of their way to offer assistance. This is my kind of place. I'm at home here.

Guides

Guides are members chosen by AOL to serve as real-time assistants. Guides are like Members Helping Members, except there's no waiting. Have a question? Ask a Guide.

I recall an art gallery in Amsterdam. There were a number of Rembrandts there, hanging on the wall just like any other picture. No glass cases or protective Lexan—just those radiant Rembrandts, emancipated and free. A gentleman in uniform stood near. He wasn't a guard; the uniform wasn't that severe. He was a guide. He was a volunteer. He got to spend his days in a room full of the Rembrandts he loved and at the same time share his interest with other people. He explained the Rembrandts to us in a fatherly way, exhibiting a proprietorial regard for his fellow countryman's legacy.

Which is precisely what AOL's Guides are. They're members just like the rest of us—experienced members, with particularly helpful online personalities—but members all the same. They remain politely in the background, leaving us to our own explorations, silent unless spoken to. If we need help, however, Guides are always nearby, ready with friendly advice and information. If you have a question—any question at all—about AOL, its services or its policies, ask a Guide.

Like the guide in Amsterdam, you can identify Guides by their appearance: their screen names have the word "Guide" in them. If Figure 3-9's Kathy4648 was to be a Guide (she should be), she would probably be "Guide Kathy," or something like that.

Figure 3-11: A stop
by the Lobby for
some help from
Guide MO.

A Night in the Lobby

```
7/24/92 3:19:37 PM Opening "Chat Log 7/24/92" for recording.
MajorTom      : Hi all!
Guide MO      : Hey MajorTom :)          ◄─────────
Lthrneck      : ::::getting out ostrich feather:::::
Guide MO      : Nononononono!!!
Lthrneck      : ::::TICKLE, TICKLE:::::
Guide MO      : ::giggling::
Guide MO      : Hey Cantoni!! :)
Cantoni       : Hi MO!
Guide MO      : Hiya NyteMaire :)
NyteMaire     : Hiya MO :)
CountStixx    : Maire!!!!   {}{}{}{}{}{}  ◄─────────
NyteMaire     : {{{{{{{Count}}}}}}}} **
LovlyVix      : Nyte {}{}{}{}{}{}{}{}{}{}{}{}{}
NyteMaire     : {{{Vix}}}}
LovlyVix      : How are you Nyte?
NyteMaire     : Getting crazy, and you? ;)
LovlyVix      : Pretty good Nyte :)
MajorTom      : Anybody know of a utility to convert JPEG to TIFF?
Guide MO      : Let me check the libraries for you, T :) I always use Photoshop :)
PC Kate       : <--trying to type while holding ice pack on face. :)
Lthrneck      : ACK Kate, what happened?
Guide MO      : Kate :( Dentist??
AFC Borg      : Is the ice pack inside or outside the paper bag?
PC Kate       : Lthr, had 3 hours of oral and sinus surgery yesterday.
                They say I should be able to eat again next Friday.
GWRepSteve    : Alchemy would probably be the converter to use, MajorTom...
Lthrneck      : Ouch! Kate!! {}{}{}{}{}{}{}
Lee123        : awww Kate.    * to make it better.....◄─────
LovlyVix      : <--needs to go to dentist for Kates new diet :)
PC Kate       : Vix, works real well... lost just under five pounds  in 2 days. :)
LovlyVix      : Perfect ...that would put me just where I want to be, Kate :)
Guide MO      : MajorTom - I 'm sorry - I don't see what you need offhand,
                though I know we must have it here :/  ◄──────
Guide MO      : I'll check later and email you, if that's any help.
MajorTom      : Thanks Guide. Appreciate it. I have a Plus. Can't run PhotoShop.
Guide MO      : Ok - I just wrote a note to myself -
                I'll check for you when I get off shift at 9 and email you :)
MajorTom      : Great! Thanks for the help. G'Night all!  ◄─
Guide MO      : Night MajorTom :)
```

*To help you follow
what's going on,
my part of the con-
versation appears
in bold.*

*These are hugs
for a new arrival
in the Lobby.*

The asterisk is a kiss.

Chagrin.

*I got an answer the
next day.*

Figure 3-11 is a little hard to follow if you're not used to AOL's so-called "chat rooms." Though chat rooms are discussed in Chapter 12 ("People Connection"), a little explanation seems in order here as well. Twenty-one people were in the room when I visited. Many were just watching (lurkers), but others seemed to be old friends. The room was full of "smileys" (turn your head counterclockwise 90 degrees and :) becomes a smile) and hugs. Smileys are discussed in Chapter 13, "Clubs & Interests," and Chapter 20, "Ten Best." The entire illustration is a "chat log" (see your File menu for the Logging command).

Chat rooms can be intimidating to the first-time visitor. Don't be shy. Jump right in with a Hello, look for the Guide's name, and ask your question. More important, note that I received one immediate answer to my question (from GWRepSteve, a member) and another the next day from Guide MO. I got just what I needed (*Alchemy* worked perfectly, and it's available online), and it only took 10 minutes.

Guides are on duty from 9 A.M. until 6 A.M. (Eastern time), 7 days a week, 365 days a year. To find a Guide, choose Lobby from the Go To menu, type Command-L, or select the People Connection icon from the Departments screen. If you need a Guide quickly, use the keyword: GuidePager.

Members

All of this talk about Guides and Members Helping Members might give you the impression that members play a significant part in the operation of AOL, and you're right. Members are much more than AOL's source of income: they're contributors (most of the files in the data libraries discussed in Chapter 5, "Computing," are submitted by members), they're assistants, and, of course, they are the heart of the online community.

Since members play such an important role at AOL, it behooves us to spend a few pages discussing them: how to find them, the member profile and how to be a better member yourself.

The Member Directory

America Online offers you the opportunity to post a voluntary member profile. Though I'll talk about profiles in a moment, the operative term in the previous sentence is "voluntary." America Online values the individual's privacy, and if you wish to remain secluded in the online community, you may do so. Those members who have completed a profile are listed in the Member Directory.

You can search for a member by real name, screen name or profile. You might see a screen name online and wonder who is behind it: Search the directory. You might wonder if a friend is signed up with AOL: Search the directory.

One of the more interesting things you can do with the directory is to search for people with interests similar to yours. Once you've found them, you can send them mail (I discuss electronic mail in Chapter 4) and, perhaps, strike up a friendship. It's all part of the electronic community.

I, for instance, enjoy the beauty of my state. I live just 13 miles from the Mount Hood National Forest, where hundreds of square miles of virgin forest, lakes, trails and meadows await the explorer. Thinking I might find someone to share my interest, I search the Member Directory for members in my locality by using Oregon as my criterion (Figure 3-12).

Figure 3-12: Much to my delight, 256 other Oregonians have posted their profiles. I'll send them some mail and see if they want to explore the forest someday.

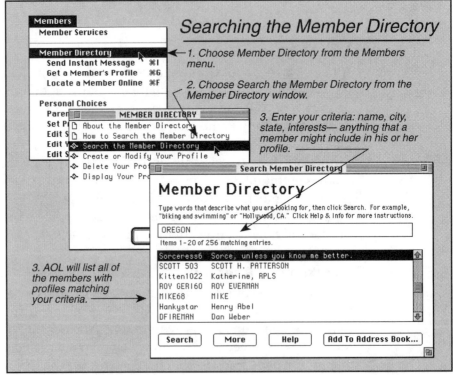

Actually, Figure 3-12 is misleading. My search for "Oregon" omitted those members who used the state's two-character abbreviation ("OR") in their profiles. It also didn't include those members who have elected to omit their profiles. My guess is that there are thousands of AOL members from Oregon, many more than pictured in Figure 3-12. To access the Members Directory, choose Members Directory from the Members menu, then double-click Search the Members Directory option.

Member Profiles

As I mentioned a moment ago, member profiles are optional. If you elect not to complete a profile, your name won't show up in searches like the one described above.

If that's your preference, you cut yourself out of a number of opportunities to become involved in the online community. If you elect to post a profile (or if you're already posted a profile and want to edit it), AOL provides a couple of ways for you to do so.

Look again at the menu pictured in Figure 3-12. Note that one of the options listed there is "Edit Your Online Profile." While this is one way to get the job done, a better way is to go through Member Services. You've got to be signed on in either case, but Member Services is free and choosing Edit Your Online Profile from the Members menu is not. Moreover, the Member Services route offers a few options that aren't available from the Members menu. You can also use the keyword: Profile. Both routes pass through the free curtain.

Once you choose either one of these methods, you'll see the window pictured at the bottom of Figure 3-3. Note the button labeled Accounts & Billing. Click it and follow the path identified in Figure 3-13.

Figure 3-13: You can access your member profile by using the keyword: Profile; by choosing Edit Your Online Profile from the Members menu; or by using Member Services (keyword: Help).

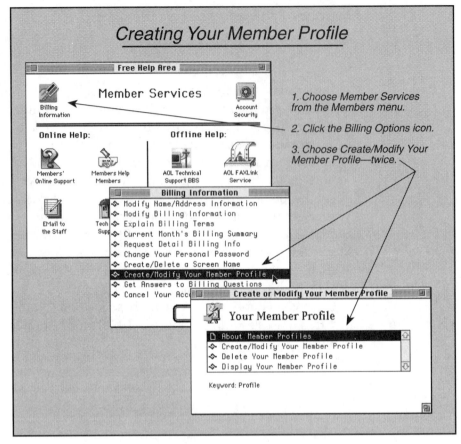

The profile inquiry consists of four screens, each with a few questions about you. Take your time answering these (it's free, after all), and soon you'll have a profile as sterling and poetic as mine (Figure 3-14).

Figure 3-14:
MajorTom's profile
reveals all of my
secrets.

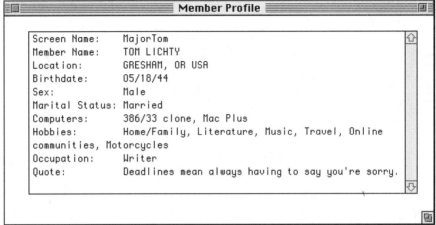

```
Member Profile

Screen Name:      MajorTom
Member Name:      TOM LICHTY
Location:         GRESHAM, OR USA
Birthdate:        05/18/44
Sex:              Male
Marital Status: Married
Computers:        386/33 clone, Mac Plus
Hobbies:          Home/Family, Literature, Music, Travel, Online
communities, Motorcycles
Occupation:       Writer
Quote:            Deadlines mean always having to say you're sorry.
```

Moving On

We've come a long way since the heavy-metal band took the stage at the beginning of this chapter. I hope your journey has been confidence-building for you. America Online offers more help—and more *kinds* of help—than any software I've known. It's online, it's off-line, it's Jay Levitt and the Customer Relations Department, it's Members Helping Members, and it's Guides. Everyone at AOL—members included—helps someone else sooner or later. That's comforting. Not only is AOL a community, it's a *considerate* community, where no one remains a stranger for long.

And now's the time to become a member of that community. The best way to do that is to send electronic mail to someone. Mail is the heart of the AOL community, and we'll explore it thoroughly in the next chapter.

Electronic Mail

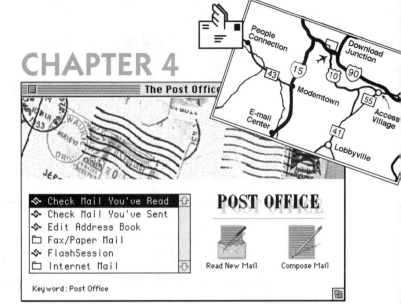

People my age remember the days when the phrase "the mail" meant only one thing. If you wanted to mail something, you handed it to the postman, you dropped it in a mailbox or you took it to the post office. There was no UPS, no fax, no FedEx, no e-mail and no Internet. There was only "the mail"—the US Postal Service—and a first-class postage stamp cost 3 cents.

The fast-moving information age we live in today requires alternatives such as package delivery, overnight letters, facsimile, voice mail and e-mail. Each has its place. Each offers something the others do not. Electronic mail offers immediacy, convenience, multiple addressing and automated record-keeping. Moreover, it's cheap—perhaps the least expensive of the bunch—and ecologically responsible. E-mail has all the makings of a darling, and it is just now entering its prime.

What Exactly is Electronic Mail?

Electronic mail (e-mail for short) is simply mail prepared on a computer and sent to someone else who has access to a computer. There are lots of private e-mail networks—computers wired together and configured to send and receive mail. America Online is one of these. Many of these networks (including AOL) are connected to the Internet (the Internet is discussed in Chapter 14, "The Internet Connection;" Internet mail is discussed later in this chapter), and you can send mail to (and receive mail from) the people across these networks.

The frontispiece is of the AOL Post Office greeting screen. Most of the e-mail commands and resources can be accessed via this screen, or via the Mail menu. Use the keyword: PostOffice.

Most e-mail systems share a number of common characteristics:

- Messages are composed of pure ASCII text. Fancy formatting, graphics and special characters aren't accommodated within messages. AOL for the Macintosh is one of the rare exceptions; a matter I'll discuss later in this chapter.

- Because they're usually simple text, messages can be sent between dissimilar computers. You can communicate with people using PCs, Amigas, mainframes—even terminals (there are thousands on the Internet), which aren't really computers at all.

- The addressee must be known to the mail system.

Additional features are offered by some e-mail systems, including AOL.

- Messages can be replied to or forwarded to anyone, including people connected to networks outside of AOL. This includes commercial services such as Prodigy and CompuServe.

- Files can be attached to messages. In most cases, files are specific to a particular computer or operating system, so the receiving computer must be compatible with the sending computer in order to open the file. On the other hand, files can contain anything: graphics, formatted text, even sound and animation.

- Messages can be addressed to multiple recipients. "Carbon copies" can be sent to people other than the addressee, and "blind" carbon copies (copies sent without the other addressees' knowledge) can be specified as well.

- Messages need not be composed while you're online. Likewise, received messages need not be read while you're online. Any incoming message can be filed for later retrieval and read offline at your convenience. If you choose to reply, you can compose your reply offline as well. You need to sign on only to send and receive mail, a process that rarely consumes more than a couple of minutes online.

Why Use E-mail?

Nothing matches the convenience, immediacy and ecology of electronic mail. Composing a message amounts to nothing more than typing it; mailing a message is accomplished with a single click of the mouse; and AOL files a copy for you, automatically, on the host computers in Virginia. Archaic inconveniences such as envelopes and stamps are never required, and fax funny paper—an ecological disaster if ever there was one—never enters the picture. Indeed, paper of any kind is rarely used when mail is sent electronically.

America Online's e-mail service is an outstanding example of this communication medium. It does all the things e-mail should do and adds enough features to make a mail carrier want to resign. You can compose mail off-line, send (and receive) it when you're away from your computer, address it to multiple recipients, send carbon copies (and blind carbon copies), attach files (to mail addressed to other AOL members), reply to mail received and forward mail to others at AOL or on the Internet. Mail can also be faxed or, if the recipient is really in the dark ages, even sent via the US Mail.

America Online obediently holds your mail until you're ready to read it, announces its availability every time you sign on and never sends you junk mail.

Perhaps best of all, about all you'll ever pay for this service is a nickel—maybe a dime if you're really pedantic. America Online doesn't charge extra for e-mail , even that sent to or received from the Internet. It's not exactly a return to the 3-cent stamp, but it's close.

A Circular Exercise

Before we get to the details, here's a little exercise just to show you how e-mail works. This exercise is somewhat futile: sending mail to yourself is a little like narcissism—a little less vainglorious perhaps, but no less futile. Nevertheless, do it just this once. Nobody's looking.

▲ With America Online up and running, sign on. Leave the In the Spotlight screen showing and choose Compose Mail from the Mail menu. An Untitled Mail window will appear (see Figure 4-1).

Figure 4-1: This window appears whenever you're about to compose some mail. AOL has already identified you as the sender; it's now waiting for you to identify the recipient.

Untitled 1

Address Book

To:

cc:

Attach File

Subj:

File:

☐ **Return Receipt**

Send Later

Send Now

Help

🔺 The insertion point is now flashing in the To text box, where you insert the screen name of the recipient. Type in your screen name. This is the futile part of the exercise—sending mail to yourself—but the rewards are immediate, and there will be no guessing as to whether the mail ever made it to the addressee.

No Accounting for Case

America Online screen names are not case-sensitive. MajorTom works no better than majortom. This is really comforting: I used to be obsessed with such details, worrying that imperfectly addressed mail would end up in electronic limbo somewhere. My anxieties were needless (as most are). Even if you misspell a screen name, AOL will notify you that there's no match for the address you've typed. There's no "dead mail" room at AOL.

🔺 In the subject text box, enter the word "Test" (without the quotes).

🔺 Type something into the message text box. This is the narcissistic part. Don't overdo it. People will talk.

🔺 Click the Send button.

Instantly, a voice announces "You've got mail!" There's a particular comfort in that. Mail moves around the AOL circuit quite literally at the speed of light. You'll never wonder again if your mail will get to its destination by next Thursday. It gets there the instant you send it.

Note also that two things have happened: (1) The mail icon on the In the Spotlight screen has changed, and (2) a tiny mailbox now flashes in the upper right corner of your screen (Figure 4-2).

Figure 4-2: You've got mail! You get two doses of visual indication and one aural prompt every time mail is waiting for you at America Online.

 In the upper-right corner of your screen, a tiny mailbox flashes.

And in the Welcome window, a hand holds up a wad of envelopes for you to open.

🔺 By now, the Untitled window has closed and you're back at the In the Spotlight screen. Click the "You have mail" icon.

🔺 The New Mail window appears (see Figure 4-3). This window is a little redundant when you only have one piece of mail waiting, but soon you'll be a Popular Person and dozens of entries will appear here every time you sign on.

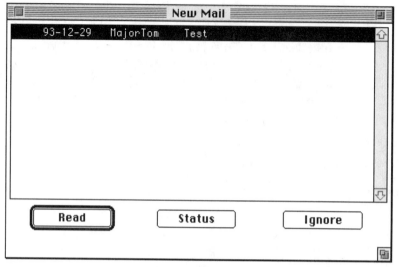

📌 Double-click the entry, which represents the mail you sent a moment ago.

📌 The message window appears, with your message therein (see Figure 4-4).

Figure 4-4: The
mail is received.
Note that you can
forward, reply to
or save this mail
by simply clicking
the appropriate
icon.

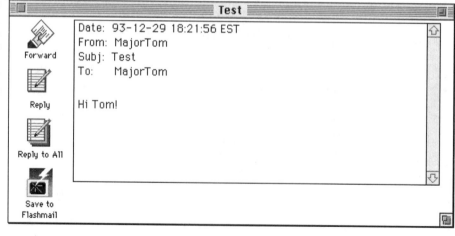

It's probably best for you to toss this mail now, before anyone sees what you've been up to. To throw it away, click its close box (or choose Close from the File menu). I just wanted you to see how simple, fast and easy the process really is. That's the whole idea—above all, e-mail should be convenient, global and inexpensive, and AOL certainly makes it so.

The Mail Menu

Nearly all day-to-day mail activities are performed using the Mail menu. (Some prefer AOL's Post Office screen—see the frontispiece—but we'll discuss the Mail menu here.) The single exception is the FlashSession, which we'll discuss in Chapter 19, "FlashSessions & the Download Manager." FlashSessions aren't for everybody, however: indeed, most seminormal people conduct all of their mail activities using the Mail menu (Figure 4-5) exclusively.

Figure 4-5: The mail menu handles most of your daily e-mail activities.

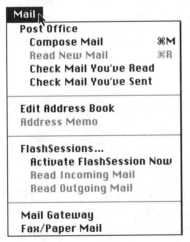

Composing Your Mail

The first option on the Mail menu is Compose Mail, which you choose whenever you want to send mail to someone. This option is available whether you're online or off; you can compose mail off-line and send it later—a feature I'll discuss in a moment.

When the Compose Mail command is issued, AOL responds with an Untitled Mail Form (review Figure 4-1). Note the position of the insertion point in Figure 4-1. It's located within the To field of the window. America Online, in other words, is waiting for you to provide the recipient's screen name. Type it in. (If you don't remember the screen name, you can use your Address Book, which I'll discuss later in this chapter.)

You can send mail to multiple addresses if you wish. Simply include multiple screen names in the To field, separated by a comma and a space. You can place multiple names there (I have never discovered the maximum, but it must be large: Note that the field is actually a scroll box). If you want to send mail to Steve Case and Tom Lichty, type "Steve Case, MajorTom" (without the quotes) in this box.

Press the Tab key and the cursor jumps to the CC (carbon copy) field. Here you can place the addresses of those people who are to receive "carbon copies" of your mail. Carbon copies (actually, they're called courtesy copies now—carbon paper being a thing of the past) are really no different than originals. Whether a member receives an original or a copy is more a matter of protocol than anything else. Note: Use only screen names in the To and CC fields. Do not put members' real names here.

Blind Carbon Copies

As is the case with the traditional "cc:" at the bottom of a business letter, the addressee is aware of all carbon copies. This is a traditional business courtesy.

On the other hand, you might want to send a copy of a message to another person without the addressee (or addressees) knowing you have done so. This is known as a "blind" carbon copy. To address a blind carbon copy, place the recipient's address in the CC field, enclosing it in parentheses. The parentheses are the trick. No one but the recipient of the blind carbon copy will know what you've done. The ethics of this feature are yours to ponder; its use, after all, is voluntary.

Press the Tab key to move the insertion point to the Subject field, and enter a descriptive word or two. Note: The Subject field must be filled in—AOL won't take the message without it.

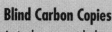 Press the Tab key again. The insertion point moves to the message text area. Type your message there (see Figure 4-6).

Figure 4-6: The completed message is ready to send. Click the Send Now icon (if you're online) or the Send Later icon (if you're not).

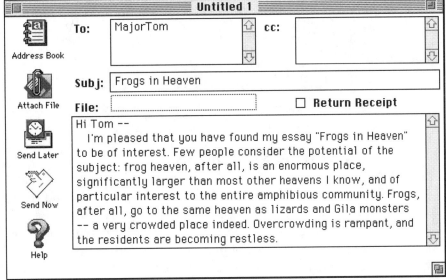

It's subtle, but note that the Send Now icon in Figure 4-6 is dimmed: this message is being prepared off-line (see sidebar).

Preparing Mail Off-Line

Consider preparing mail when you're off-line and the meter isn't running. You can linger over it that way, perfecting every word. When you complete a message, click the Send Later icon. The next time you sign on, AOL will note that you have mail waiting to be sent. To send it, choose Read Outgoing Mail from the Mail menu, then click the Send All button. If you neglect to send it while you're online, AOL will remind you of your forgetfulness when you attempt to sign off (Figure 4-7). Your mail will get sent, in other words, unless you positively don't want it to.

Figure 4-7:
America Online
always reminds
you to send mail,
even if you forget.

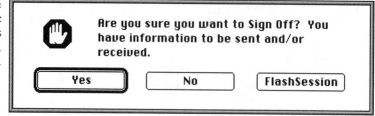

Alternative Mail Sources

Occasionally, you might want to send a text file as mail. Perhaps it's a file you created with AOL's New Memo command (File menu), or a text file from a word processor, or one that you captured online. Regardless of the source, you can send a text file as mail (rather than as a file) by choosing Address Memo from the Mail menu.

When you do, AOL furnishes the Compose Mail window (again, review Figure 4-1) and places a copy of your text file in the message area for you. All you have to do is supply the name of the recipient and send the mail on its way.

The Address Memo command is especially useful for those who prefer to use a word processor to compose messages. Word processors feature spelling checkers and productivity tools that AOL's Compose Mail utility doesn't offer. If you prefer to use your word processor, be sure to save the word processing document as text only, then use the Address Memo command to send it as mail.

A Pain in the Neck

Because there's no eye contact or voice intonation in e-mail messages, sometimes it's necessary to punctuate your conversation with textual "smileys," as they're called. Smileys clarify the sender's intention when it might otherwise be misinterpreted. The phrase, "Just as I thought, Billy Joe: There are no forks in your family tree," could be interpreted as slander. Follow it with a smiley, however, and most members will understand your attempt at depraved humor: "Just as I thought, Billy Joe: there are no forks in your family tree. ;-)"

The semicolon-hyphen-close parenthesis combination at the end of the sentence above is a wink. Turn your head 90 degrees counterclockwise and you'll see a little "smiley face" with its right eye winking. It's a pain in the neck, but it's better than making enemies.

Below are some of the more common smileys. Some people use them more than others, but most everybody does occasionally.

:-) Smile
;-) Wink
:-D Laughing out loud (also abbreviated LOL).
:-(Frown
:-/ Chagrin
{} Hug (usually plural: {{{{}}}} Why hug just once?)

These are the smileys I see most often online. There are scores of others. I've seen :-# (lips are sealed), :-& (tongue tied), :-[(pout), :-* (kiss) and :-O (yell). But my favorite is :-p (sticking out tongue). See Chapter 20, "Ten Best," for more smileys.

All of this is a little like those inane yellow smiley faces that punctuated the '70s, but it's justified here. Misinterpretation of text is easy; smileys help clarify the meaning. Go ahead: Smile at someone today. :-)

Checking Mail You've Sent

Occasionally you might want to review mail you've sent to others: "What exactly did I say to Billy Joe that caused him to visit the Tallahatchee Bridge last night?"

Even if you don't file your mail (a subject addressed later in this chapter), AOL retains everything you send for at least one week. You can review any sent mail by choosing Check Mail You've Sent from the Mail menu. America Online responds by displaying a listing of all the mail you've sent recently. Choose the mail you want to know about from that list, and click the Read button to review what you've sent (see Figure 4-8).

Figure 4-8: You can reread any mail you've sent by using the Check Mail You've Sent command.

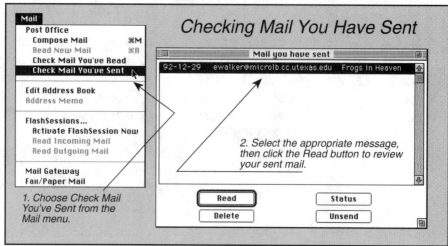

Online Only

The Check Mail You've Sent and the Check Mail You've Read commands are only available when you're online. This mail is stored on AOL's machines, not yours; you have to be online to access data stored there.

As you're reading your sent mail, you can select and copy it, then paste it into other documents (see the Copy & Paste sidebar if you're not familiar with this process). This works especially well for reminder notices, clarifications and nagging. It could save you some typing as well: You might need to send a message that's a near-duplicate of one you sent four days ago. Rather than retyping text from the old message, reopen it using Check Mail You've Sent under the Mail menu, copy the sections you need, and paste them into a new message window.

Copy & Paste

If you're not yet familiar with your Mac, here's a brief lesson in copying and pasting: Select mail messages by clicking somewhere within them and choosing Select All from the Edit menu. To copy the selection, choose Copy from the Edit menu. This puts the selected text on the Mac's Clipboard—its internal memory—where it's ready for use elsewhere. To paste text into another document, Open that document (File menu), click the mouse at the location where you want the text to go, then choose Paste from the Edit menu.

Buttons in the Mail You've Sent Window

A number of buttons appear across the bottom of the Outgoing Mail window pictured in Figure 4-8; each serves a specific purpose.

The Read Button

Select a piece of mail from the list, then click the Read button to read that message. This function was discussed a few pages back.

The Status Button

The Status button tells you when the recipient (or recipients, if the mail was sent to more than one address) read the message. This is a great way to see if someone has read a message you've sent. This only applies to mail sent to another AOL member, however: if the mail was sent to an Internet address (Chapter 14, "The Internet Connection," discusses the Internet), there's no way for AOL to know if the mail was read. The Status button will return "Not applicable" under these conditions.

The Unsend Button

The Unsend button allows you to retrieve mail you have sent from the mailboxes of all recipients, as well as from your Mail You Have Sent list. To unsend a piece of mail, highlight the mail you wish to unsend and click the Unsend button. Certain conditions, however, will disable this feature:

- If any addressee has an Internet mail address.

- If any recipient has read that piece of mail (except you, even if you were on the addressee list).

⚠ If any recipient was a fax or US Mail address.

⚠ If you close the Outgoing Mail window with an unsent message showing, it will be permanently deleted from the AOL archives: It won't show up on your Outgoing Mail list when you check it again. If you want to modify or save an unsent message, double-click it while it's still showing, then either modify it (and resend it if you wish) or copy and paste it into some other document. Then you can Unsend it.

The Delete Button

This button simply removes the selected piece of mail from your Outgoing Mail list. It does not affect the message's destiny: AOL will still deliver it. It's really a feature for people who get lots of mail and prefer to keep their "Check Mail You've Read" lists short.

Reading New Mail

The second option on the Mail menu—Read New Mail—refers to mail you've just received. I don't use this menu item. To me, mail is like Christmas morning: I can't wait to get to it. Immediately after hearing that I have mail, I click the You Have Mail icon (pictured in Figure 4-2) and start unwrapping my presents.

Nevertheless, there are those who don't share my enthusiasm. That, I suppose, is why AOL provides this menu option. When it's chosen, America Online presents the New Mail window (Figure 4-9).

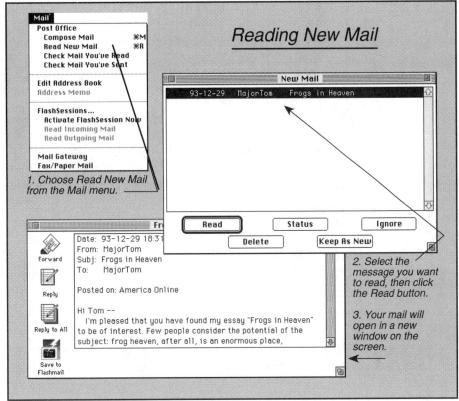

Figure 4-9: Reading
new mail can be
accomplished with
the You Have Mail
button in the
Welcome window,
by pressing
Command-R, or by
choosing Read
New Mail from the
Mail menu.

Though Figure 4-9 shows only one unread piece of mail, a number of pieces might appear here. If more than one shows up, they'll appear in the order in which they were received at AOL. The oldest mail will be at the top, the most recent at the bottom. In other words, to read your mail in chronological order from oldest to most recent, read your messages from top to bottom.

Buttons in the New Mail Window

A number of buttons appears across the bottom of the New Mail window pictured in Figure 4-9. They can be confusing at first, so a discussion of their use is in order.

Read

This button displays the selected piece of mail on the screen for reading. It's the default button: Double-clicking an entry on the list does the same thing.

Ignore

This option will move a piece of mail directly into your Mail You Have Read list without your having to read the mail, in effect "ignoring" that piece of mail. If the sender issues a Status check, he or she will see the word "Ignored" beside your screen name. Be sure that's what you want the addressee to see if you use this command.

Status

This is the same as the Status button in the Mail You Have Sent window mentioned earlier. In this context, it tells you when (and if) other recipient(s) of a particular piece of mail have read (or ignored) it. Again, this button will return "Not applicable" if the mail was delivered to an Internet address.

Keep as New

Clicking this button will return the selected piece of mail to your New Mail list after you've read it. The mail is, however, still considered read as far as other members' Status checks are concerned. In other words, if someone checks the status of a piece of mail that you read then kept as new, they will see the time you read the mail, regardless of whether you kept it as new or not.

Delete

This feature allows you to permanently remove a piece of mail from your New Mail mailbox. It will not appear on the Mail You Have Read list either (I'll discuss the Check Mail You've Read command in a moment). Status checks performed by other members on deleted mail say "Deleted." Compare this button with the Ignore button mentioned earlier.

Printing & Saving Mail

You can print or save any piece of mail that occupies the front-most (active) window by choosing the appropriate command from the File menu. If you choose Print, AOL will display the standard Macintosh Print dialog box. Click the OK button to print.

If you choose Save (or Save As—in this context they're the same command), AOL responds with the traditional Macintosh Save As dialog box. Click the Save Mail as Text box, give your mail a name and put it wherever you please. It will be saved as a standard text file and you will be able to open it with not only AOL's software, but any word processor (or text editor).

Alternatively, you can select and copy any mail appearing on your screen. Now you can open any text file on your disk (or start a new one via the New Memo command under the File menu) and paste your mail into that file.

You can also paste copied AOL text into other Macintosh applications' files if you wish. There are a number of ways to file mail, and I'll describe some of them in the Gorilla Food section of this chapter.

Remember Size

Those of you more fortunate than I might find the placement of AOL's windows to be restricting. My tired old Mac Plus has a tiny, 9-inch screen. To my benefit, the defaults for size and placement of AOL's windows have been determined with 9-inch Mac screens in mind. In other words, if you have a larger screen, a few of AOL's windows may congregate in the upper left corner. If that is your predicament, you'll be happy to discover the Remember Size command under the Windows menu (see Figure 4-10).

Figure 4-10: The Remember Size command lets you permanently relocate (and resize) windows to suit your screen.

If you have a large-screen Mac and want to permanently relocate a window, simply situate the window to your satisfaction, then choose Remember Size from the Windows menu. From that moment on, the window will pop back into your preferred position and size, every time it's used.

Forwarding Mail

Once you have read your mail, you can forward it, reply to it or throw
it out. Each of these options is accomplished with a click of the mouse.
To forward a piece of mail, simply click the Forward icon pictured in
Figure 4-9. America Online will respond with the slightly modified
Compose Mail window that appears at the top of Figure 4-11.

Figure 4-11:
Forwarding mail is
as easy as clicking
an icon, identifying
the recipient and
typing your
comments.

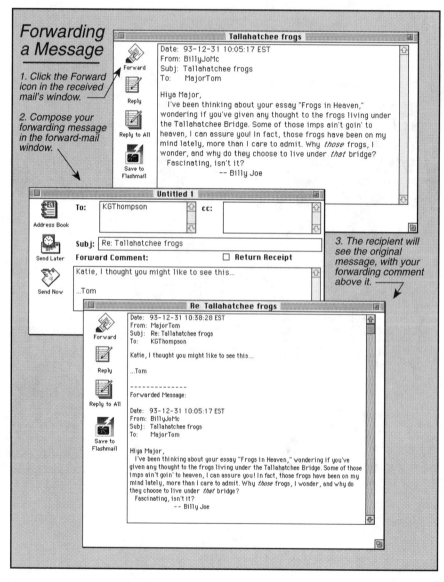

The top window pictured in Figure 4-11 is where you enter your forwarding comment and the address of the person who is to receive the forward. The new recipient then receives the forwarded mail with your comment preceding it. America Online clearly identifies forwarded mail by including a line at the top of the message that declares it as forwarded mail and identifies the person who did the forwarding (see the bottom window in Figure 4-11).

Replying to Mail

You'll probably reply to mail more often than you forward it. Actually, all the Reply icon does is call up a Compose Mail window with the To and Subject fields already filled in with the appropriate information (see Figure 4-12). Aside from these two features, a reply is the same as any other message. You can modify the To and CC fields if you wish, and discuss any subject that interests you in the message text. You can even change the Subject field or remove the original recipient's screen name from the To field, though this somewhat defeats the purpose.

Figure 4-12: The reply window. The Subject and To fields are already completed for you; all you have to do is provide the message.

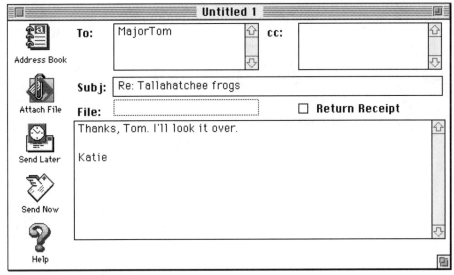

Replying to All

Look once again at the lower window in Figure 4-11. Note that there are two reply icons, including one marked Reply to All. Reply to All allows you to reply to everyone who was sent a message, including any carbon copy addressees. In other words, you have your choice of replying only to the original sender (Reply button) or to everyone who receives a message (Reply to All button).

Note: Reply to All does not necessarily reply to blind carbon copy addressees. The rule here is, Reply to All replies to all whose screen names are visible in the Mail window. If you don't see a name (which would be the case if someone received a blind carbon copy), that person will not receive your reply.

Replying with a Copy of the Original

Some people get lots of mail. Steve Case, for instance, gets hundreds of pieces a day. For Steve's benefit, I always include a copy of his original message when I reply. I do this to help him remember the subject of our discussion. Rather than copy and paste his message into a Reply window, I use the Forward button. Remember that forwarded mail includes a copy of the original message along with your comment. This little trick also works when you want to reply to a very old message the sender might not recall.

Because a copy of the original message gets sent with the reply, using the Forward button is an inefficient way of handling mail. More significantly, AOL has to store much more data. America Online's storage problems, however, are not our concern. The people at AOL are gonna love me for telling you about this.

Checking Mail You've Read

We all forget things now and again: "What did I promise to get my mother for Valentine's Day?" That's why AOL provides the Check Mail You've Read option under the Mail menu. When you choose this command, AOL responds with the Mail You Have Read window (see Figure 4-13).

Figure 4-13: The
Mail You Have
Read window lists
all of the mail you
have read, just in
case you forget.

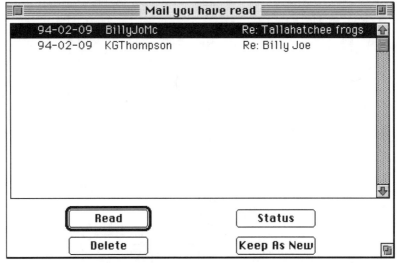

There are no surprises here. Double-click any message in the window to reread it; click the Status button to see when you read it (and when any other addressees, if any, read their copies). Reread mail can be forwarded and replied to just like any other mail.

The Address Book

America Online provides an address book just like the address book next to your telephone. In effect, AOL's book is a cross-reference, listing people's real names and their corresponding screen names. My recommendation is that you use the Address Book, even if you only have a name or two to put there now. Eventually you'll have scores of entries in your book, and you will be glad they're there.

Adding a Name to the Address Book

No one memorizes screen names. Screen names are eccentric composites of letters and numbers like "MikeQ4506," which AOL's sign-on software cooks up for each new member, or something clever like "DerringDo," which the member creates later when AOL's default screen name becomes insufferable. Either way, most screen names are eminently forgettable. That's why AOL provides an Address Book.

Of course, before you can use the Address Book you have to put some names there. It's easy. Online or off, choose Address Book from the Mail menu and AOL will provide the Address Book Editor window pictured in Figure 4-14.

Figure 4-14: The
Address Book
Editor window
allows you to
create, modify and
delete members'
names and screen
names.

To add an entry to your Address Book, click the Create button. America Online will provide the editing form pictured in Figure 4-15.

Figure 4-15: The
Address Book
editing form.

Name: McCallister, Billy Joe

Accounts: BillyJoMc

OK   Cancel

Place the person's real name in the Name field, then place their AOL or Internet address in the Accounts field. The next time you choose Address Book from the Mail window, the name will appear there (see Figure 4-16).

Figure 4-16: The
Address Book
now contains the
new entry.

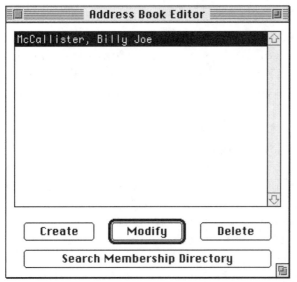

Now you are ready to use the Address Book whenever you prepare mail. Look again at Figure 4-1. Do you see the icon in the upper left corner marked Address Book? If your Address Book is current, you can use it to look up people's addresses and plug them into the To and CC fields of the Compose Mail window. Whenever a Compose Mail form is displayed on your screen, all you have to do is click that icon. From then on, it's only a matter of clicking the mouse.

Multiple Accounts

If you look again at Figure 4-15, you'll notice there's room for multiple addresses in the Accounts field. In fact, the word "accounts" appears, not "account." You might wonder why.

Imagine that you're participating in an online discourse of frog heaven with three other esteemed theologians. Nearly every piece of mail on the subject has to be sent to all three of them. In this situation, you might want to create an entry in your Address Book called Froggers and list all three addresses—with commas between each address—in the Accounts field. Once you have done so, all you have to do is select Froggers from your Address Book to send them mail.

Gorilla Food

Okay, you e-mail Thunder Lizards, here's your raw meat. Read this section and you'll take your place among the e-mail illuminati. Mortals will climb mountains to seek your wisdom; the masses will genuflect as you pass by; your aura will illuminate the northern sky.

Mail-Filing Strategies

A while back I mentioned that e-mail to me is like packages on Christmas morning. I look forward to it with great anticipation. I descend into a pit of depression if a voice doesn't say "You've got mail!" when I sign on. Consequently, I have developed a cadre of online friends and correspond with them regularly. This means that I get a lot of mail.

I send and receive 20 or more pieces of mail a day. With that much mail coming in, finding a place to file that mail is critical. I need fast, convenient, electronic access to it. I copy and paste messages frequently, so a paper filing system just won't do. I am also an environmentalist, another reason why paperless e-mail appeals to me. My e-mail filing system is the bedrock of my online activities.

You might be facing the same need. Because of the Christmas-morning quality of AOL's e-mail system, lots of people get lots of mail, and lots of people need to be thinking about a filing system. Now's the time to bring the subject into the open.

Saving Everything as Flashmail

Though I'll discuss FlashSessions in Chapter 19, you've no doubt noted the Save to Flashmail icon in the received mail window (review Figure 4-4, if necessary). If you click this icon, AOL files your mail in a file with your screen name on it. It's normally found in the Online Mail folder inside the America Online folder on your hard disk. There will be a file there for each screen name on your account.

Mail saved this way can be reviewed online or off by choosing Read Incoming Mail from the Mail menu. It remains available for review until you delete it. (AOL adds a Delete button to the reviewed mail's window when mail is accessed this way.)

This method is extremely convenient, but it has a few flaws:

- It's effective only if you keep a small number of messages on file. Mail stored this way can't be categorized, and the list eventually becomes too long for convenient access (or for the software's 28k limit).

△ While filing mail you've read this way is easy, filing mail you've sent isn't (unless you send carbon copies to yourself).

△ Incoming mail from FlashSessions (I'll discuss FlashSessions in Chapter 19) is filed here, and mixing new FlashSession mail with old mail can become confusing and troublesome.

Nevertheless, if you don't intend to file much mail, if you carbon-copy yourself when necessary, and if you don't intend to use FlashSessions, this might be the most convenient method of them all.

The Online Mail Folder

I mentioned the Online Mail folder a few paragraphs back. America Online's Installer program creates this folder on your hard disk when you install the software. This is a potential location for mail storage. It is never more than a folder away from the America Online application itself, so you won't spend much time searching for it, and it consolidates all of your mail into one place for convenient backup.

This folder has to be organized in some way. Probably the simplest strategy is to save all your mail in your Online Mail folder as it arrives, piece by piece. Every time you read a new piece of mail, choose Save As from the File menu and save the mail in the folder. While this might work if you don't get much mail, it regresses to anarchy after a dozen or so files have accumulated. A Finder screen of such a scenario appears in Figure 4-17.

Figure 4-17: A file-based mailing system can become confusing when mail starts to accumulate.

Online Mail		
Name	Size	Kind
About bees' knees	2K	AOL
Customer Service re...	11K	AOL
Donny Beck 6/3	10K	AOL
Frogging in Alabama	3K	AOL
Nessie	8K	AOL
NM Sunset.GIF	18K	GIFC
Old stuff	7K	AOL
Steve Case 4/02	7K	AOL
SteveC re chapter 3	4K	AOL
Stock info	2K	AOL
To Tom deBoors	8K	AOL
To Tom Williams	12K	AOL
Travel tips for NM	4K	AOL
Vases.PICT	84K	docu
Weather for 7/12	3K	AOL

A Single-File Strategy

Note: All of the strategies mentioned from here on require an under-standing of the Macintosh Cut, Copy and Paste commands. If you are not familiar with these commands, either review the note on page 87 or buy a copy of *The Little Mac Book*. If you're new to the Mac, this book is invaluable.

If your mail is infrequent, a single file might prove beneficial. In-stead of a Mail folder, try a Mail file instead. (Use the New Memo command under AOL's File menu to create a new file.) Each time you receive a piece of mail, read it, then select and copy it. Use the Open command under the File menu to open your Mail file, scroll to the bottom, paste and save. You can store 50 or more pieces of mail this way before the file becomes so large that it's unwieldy. Advantages to this method include the following:

- Only one file needs to be managed; only one file must be opened to access all your past mail; only one file needs to be backed up.

- Mail appears in chronological order.

- Comments and replies appear in context—there's no need to search your disk for the mail that provoked SuzieQ to say "You yahoo! I hope your stack overflows!" If you've been consistent, the offend-ing statement is nearby—probably just above Suzie's malediction.

- On the other hand, AOL limits the size of text files to about 28k. If your Mail file exceeds this amount, AOL won't be able to store it. This is a severe limitation.

File the Header Too

Most of the filing strategies described here rely on the storage of not only received mail, but mail you've sent as well. All you need to do is copy each piece of mail you send and paste it into the appropriate file. Here's a tip: Choose Check Mail You've Sent from the Mail menu and open the mail to be copied from there. Mail retrieved this way contains AOL's header informa-tion—date, time, CCs and blind CCs—the retention of which should be considered a necessity in any mail filing system. If you simply copy text from the message field of a Mail window before you send it, your file won't contain all this information.

A Date-Based Strategy

Alternatively, consider a date-based strategy. This method is essentially the single-file strategy with a file for each month of activity. A greater volume of mail can be accommodated this way, and old material can easily be copied to a floppy for archiving (see Figure 4-18).

Figure 4-18: The date-based strategy accommodates a greater volume of mail.

Online Mail		
Name	Size	Kind
01/93	7K	AOL
02/93	4K	AOL
03/93	2K	AOL
04/93	8K	AOL
05/93	12K	AOL
06/93	4K	AOL
07/93	4K	AOL
08/93	3K	AOL

A People-Based Strategy

I receive too much mail for the single-file method, and I never remember dates. The strategy I use is people-based. Inside my Mail folder are dozens of files, each named after a person with whom I regularly correspond (see Figure 4-19).

Figure 4-19: The list of files in my Mail directory, arranged and sorted by name.

Online Mail		
Name	Size	Kind
Arbuthnot, Carey	2K	AOL
Beck, Donny	11K	AOL
Case, Steve	10K	AOL
Cramer, Sue	3K	AOL
deBoors, Tom	8K	AOL
Johnstone, Ralph	8K	AOL
Larson, Victoria	7K	AOL
Lau, Raymond	7K	AOL
Levitt, Jay	4K	AOL
Prevost, Ruffin	2K	AOL
Rittner, Don	8K	AOL
Ryan, Kathy	12K	AOL
Stoll, Cliff	4K	AOL
Williams, Tom	4K	AOL
Woodman, Elizabeth	3K	AOL

Each person's file contains all the messages I've sent to and received from that person in chronological order. Again, I include mail I've sent as well as received, as discussed in the sidebar.

Searching Text Files

At the moment, my Online Mail folder contains over 2mb of data, representing thousands of pieces of mail. Just yesterday, a reader sent me a piece of mail saying, "Thanks, Tom." That's all it said. It was sent by someone with the AOL screen name GeorgeD12. No offense intended, George, but I get a lot of reader mail, and I had no idea why I was being thanked.

I really hate to throw away mail like that. Maybe I did something really nice for George. Maybe George sent the mail to the wrong person. Maybe he meant to tell me to jump in a lake. I had to know.

The solution is a text-searching program. Each text-searching program does essentially the same thing: I tell the program what to look for and where to look and it looks inside of every file for whatever I'm after. Many of them conduct their work in the background while I work on something else. I told my favorite program of this type—Search Files by Robert Morris—to look for the word "George" in my Online Mail folder, and I went back to work on my manuscript. Sure enough, a few minutes later (yes, minutes, not seconds: Most of these programs amble rather than scramble) my Mac beeped and there was a list of all files with the word "George" in them. Sure enough, GeorgeD12 was there in my FANMAIL file. I had forwarded a message for him to a member whose screen name he didn't know. He didn't want me to jump in a lake after all.

A number of these programs are available online at AOL. Use the keyword: FileSearch, then the criterion: Text Search. Pay the shareware fee if you find a shareware program that's useful to you.

A Subject-Based Strategy

If your online mail relates better to a number of subjects, this might be a better method for you. Perhaps you use AOL to plan your travels. You might have developed some acquaintances in the Travel Club. You might be receiving confirmations from EAASY SABRE, AOL's travel reservations service. Or you might be clipping articles from Wine & Dine Online, the excellent restaurant, food and wine forum. If this is the case, you might develop a number of files for each of your destinations.

These strategies can be combined, of course, and they aren't the only ones. There are no doubt scores of others. What I'm trying to do is convince you of the importance of filing your mail. Decide upon a method, set it up to your satisfaction, and maintain it faithfully. You'll become a better citizen of the e-mail community if you do.

Formatting Messages

Version 2.0 of the AOL software introduced the ability to format mail messages, including font, size and style, among others. Version 2.5 added color to the list. Prior to that, those of us who were fond of emphasis in our messages had to show it without italics. Traditionally, emphasis was expressed by surrounding italicized text with asterisks. A message like "Yes, I *know* that Billy Joe. *Everybody* knows that. But look: Four wrongs squared, minus two wrongs to the fourth power, divided by 5, *do* make a right" was e-mailed as "Yes, I *know* that Billy Joe. *Everybody* knows that. But look: Four wrongs squared, minus two wrongs to the fourth power, divided by 5, *do* make a right." Somehow, the emphasis was lost in the translation.

Lament no more. Now, assuming both sender and receiver are using Macintoshes, and assuming that they are both using Version 2.0 (or later) of the AOL software, messages can be as emphatic as you like.

To change the typographical attributes of a block of e-mail text, simply select the text and choose the appropriate attribute from the Edit menu (see Figure 4-20).

Figure 4-20: E-mail
font, size, style
and color can be
set with these Edit
menu commands,
but only for other
AOL members
using Macs.

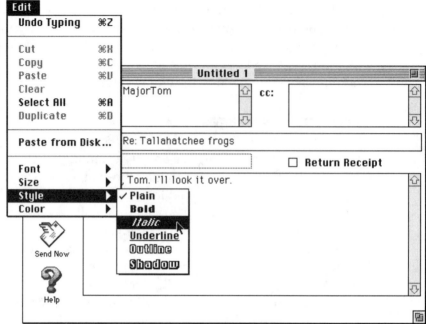

Internet Mail

As much as Steve Case and his fellow shareholders would prefer it, not
everyone is a member of AOL. Some receive their mail via the Internet
(which we'll discuss in Chapter 14, "The Internet Connection"); others
prefer AOL's competition (which, as you might suppose, this book
doesn't discuss).

We're still 10 chapters away from Chapter 14, so discussing Internet
mail is somewhat premature. But this is the mail chapter after all, and
e-mail is a big part of the Internet, so an Internet e-mail discussion
follows.

For the time being, understand that the Internet is a worldwide
interconnected network of networks, each of which is similar to AOL.
Something like 30 million people use the Internet, and you can send
mail to (or receive mail from) any one of them via AOL.

Common Fonts

The sender and the receiver must not only share Version 2.0 or later of the AOL software (or Version 2.5 if you want to use color), they must also share common fonts. If you include text attributed with the San Francisco font in a message, the recipient's Macintosh must have San Francisco installed as well. If a font is sent that's not available on the recipient's machine, the font will not appear and the effect will be lost.

On the other hand, most Macintoshes have Geneva, Monaco, and Chicago installed. These are system fonts and, for the most part, can't be removed. In particular, Geneva is an excellent font for electronic mail. It's not only easy to read on the screen, but most every Mac has it.

Another consideration is that of font anarchy. A message that's riddled with different fonts in different sizes and different styles is not only hard to read, but it looks more like a ransom note than a message—and you know how people feel about ransom notes.

With that said, go ahead and have fun with fonts. Wax poetic with Chancery or toss in a Dingbat (or a Wingding) for fun. Whisper in 7-point italics; shout in 18-point bold. Purplize your prose; paint your journalistic efforts yellow. Do this with friends, however—friends whose Macs are configured with the necessary fonts (and AOL software that's as least as recent as yours).

For more formal communication, my recommendation is to stick with 12-point Geneva, using 12-point Geneva bold and 12-point Geneva italics where appropriate. You can be pretty sure that your formatting will make it to the recipient's screen (assuming the recipient is using a Mac), your messages will be easy to read, and you won't be mistaken for a felon.

Internet Addresses

To identify an Internet addressee, the format PAUL_WILLIAMS@OREGON.UOREGON.EDU is used. Everything to the left of the at sign (@) in an Internet address is the user's name (PAUL_WILLIAMS, in the example). Internet user names aren't subject to the 10-character limit AOL screen names are, so they can become quite elaborate. Everything to the right of the @ sign is the addressee's domain—the name of the network the addressee is using (OREGON.UOREGON.EDU in the example—a computer network at the University of Oregon). Our domain is AOL, which is known as aol.com on the Internet. My Internet address, then, is the combination of my screen name, an @ sign, and AOL's domain name—or MAJORTOM@AOL.COM. Note that Internet addresses appear in all lowercase letters: That's the way it always is on the Internet.

The Directory of Internet Users

Users come and go on the Internet like nighttime talk-show hosts. There are 30 million of them, after all, and thousands come and go every day. Keeping a directory of them would be nearly impossible.

"So what," you say. "There are well over 30 million telephone users in this country and they're all listed in directories." Your point is well taken, but the telephone system is composed of a number of coordinated authorities (the baby Bells), each charged with the responsibility of publishing phone books. Not so with the Internet. No one's charged with the responsibility of maintaining Internet member directories. Those that exist are produced voluntarily, and these volunteers all have lives beyond their spare-time member directories.

In other words, there's no accurate, up-to-the-minute, all-inclusive Internet membership directory. There are a few online directories, but they're more like a Who's Who of Internet users than a comprehensive directory. In other words, you must have the exact address for someone you intend to address via the Internet. You'll have to obtain those addresses from a source other than AOL or the Internet: There's no Internet membership directory to consult.

Here's a tip: Keep a written record of your important Internet addresses. Don't just put them in your AOL address book (you might need an address when you're away from your machine, and AOL's software stores your address book on your hard disk), and don't trust them to memory (few people remember the alphabet soup of Internet addresses accurately). If you carry an old-fashioned (hardcopy) address book with you, that's the best place to keep your Internet addresses.

Sending Internet Mail

Internet e-mail is composed and sent conventionally. To address an Internet user, simply place the recipient's Internet address in the To field of the compose mail form (see Figure 4-21).

Figure 4-21:
Sending mail via
the Internet
requires entries in
the To, Subject
and Message
fields. You can't
leave any of
them blank.

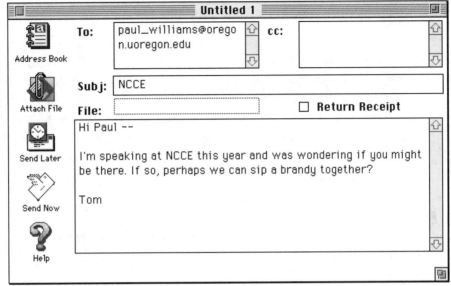

Once you click the Send Now icon (or once you run a FlashSession containing outgoing Internet mail), your outgoing mail is added to the queue of outgoing Internet mail at AOL. America Online uses a "store and forward" strategy for delivering Internet mail: outgoing mail is queued for a period of time, then AOL establishes its Internet connection and sends the mail as a batch. It also receives any incoming Internet mail during the same connection period before it breaks the Internet link.

Undeliverable Mail

Because of the complexity of Internet addresses, you might occasionally misaddress a piece of Internet mail. Fortunately your fallibility has been anticipated in the form of the Internet "postmaster." Should you include a nonexistent domain or user name, the postmaster will intercede and send the mail back to you. It's no problem, really, as the postmaster sends back the body of the message as well (see Figure 4-22). All you have to do is select and copy the message text, paste it into a new mail window, enter the proper address and re-send the mail. Your mail won't end up in some kind of Internet dead letter box: The Internet postmaster always delivers.

Daemons

Look at the sender's address in Figure 4-22. Isn't that a vicious sounding word: daemon? My dictionary defines the word as a "subordinate deity." In this context, however, a daemon (pronounced demon) is an innocuous little Unix program—one that's usually transparent to the user—which is anything but a deity, subordinate or not. Macs have daemons too (though we don't call them that); perhaps the most familiar example is the PrintMonitor—the background program that spools the print output from your applications to your printer.

Figure 4-22: At top, a misaddressed Internet mail message looks as good as any other, but a few minutes later I receive the "User unknown" message pictured in the center window. Note the inclusion of my message's text in the postmaster's message in the bottom window. When I later copy and paste the mail into a new mail window (and fix the address), the mail will be delivered satisfactorily.

Undeliverable Internet Mail

Subj: NCCE
Date: 94-01-03 10:13:37 EST
From: MajorTom
To: pd_williams@oregon.uoregon.edu

Hi Paul --

I'm speaking at NCC
might be there. If so

Tom

Though the message at left looks acceptable, the user name is incorrect. The mail is undeliverable.

A few hours later, the mail is returned from the Internet postmaster. Note that the body of the undelivered message is included in the postmaster's message.

Noting the "user unknown" message, I recheck Paul's address, find the error, and re-send the mail to the proper address.

Subj: Returned mail: User unknown
Date: 94-01-03 12:06:45 EST
From: MAILER-DAEMON@mailgate.prod.aol.net
To: MajorTom

----- Transcript of session follows -----

While connected to oregon.uoregon.edu [128.223.32.6] (tcp):
>>> RCPT To:<pd_williams@oregon.uoregon.edu>
<<< 553 unknown or illegal user:
pd_williams@OREGON.UOREGON.EDU
550 pd_williams@oregon.uoregon.edu... User unknown

----- Unsent message follows -----

Hi Paul --

I'm speaking at NCCE this year and was wondering if you might be there. If so, perhaps we can sip a brandy together?

Tom

Sending Mail to Other Commercial Services

To reach a few of the more common Internet-connected commercial services, use the address formats shown in Figure 4-23.

Figure 4-23: Use these address formats to reach users on other commercial services.

Service name	Example
AppleLink	name@applelink.apple.com
AT&T Mail	name@attmail.com
CompuServe	12345.678@compuserve.com
Delphi	name@delphi.com
GEnie	name@genie.geis.com
MCI Mail	name@mcimail.com
NBC Nightly News	nightly@nbc.com
Prodigy	name@prodigy.com
The White House	president@whitehouse.gov, or vice-president@whitehouse.gov

Note: CompuServe addresses must show a period (rather than CompuServe's traditional comma) between the fourth and fifth numbers. That's because AOL separates the addresses of multiple recipients with commas. If AOL encounters a comma in a CompuServe account number, it will try to send the mail to two addresses.

Internet Mail Trivia

Actually, this isn't trivia at all. I was trying to attract your attention with a sidebar. If you're an Internet mail user, this is Really Important Stuff:

 The maximum message length for outgoing Internet mail is 28k, or about 15 pages of text. If you must send a message longer than that, use a word processor to cut your mail into pieces.

 If you use a word processor to prepare outgoing Internet mail, be sure to save the file in a text-only format (most word processors offer this option) before using AOL's Address Memo command. The text-only file format will strip all character and paragraph formatting from your message. Don't try to send formatted word processing files as e-mail over the Internet.

 Don't use any special characters (like copyright symbols or the "smart quotes" offered by some word processors) in Internet mail. If a character requires the use of the Option key, it's off-limits. Likewise, don't use any of the formatting commands under AOL's Edit menu (font, size, style, color): the Internet will strip your message of all formatting before it's sent.

 Don't use the Attach File button for outgoing Internet mail. The Internet simply doesn't accommodate attachments.

 Some of the services listed in Figure 4-23 charge their members for Internet mail, both incoming and outgoing. Keep that in mind when sending mail to these people: they might not appreciate the gesture.

 America Online doesn't charge you anything extra for Internet mail, sent or received. If you're counting your blessings, add that to the list.

 If you're going to use Internet mail frequently, go to your local bookstore and buy a copy of *A Directory of Electronic Mail !%@:: Addressing & Networks* (see the bibliography). You'll be a better citizen of the Internet community if you do.

Receiving Internet Mail

Internet mail is received like any other AOL mail: it's announced when you sign on and you can read it by clicking the You Have Mail icon on the In the Spotlight screen. The only way you'll know it's Internet mail is by looking at the sender's address, which will be an Internet address.

You'll also see the Internet "header" at the end of the message. Reading Internet headers is a little like reading the Bible in its original Hebrew: enlightening perhaps, but not requisite to effective use of the medium.

A few notes regarding received Internet mail:

 If you want to give your Internet address to someone else (it's very impressive printed on your business cards), remove any spaces, change everything to lowercase, and follow it with @AOL.COM. As I mentioned earlier, my Internet address is MAJORTOM@AOL.COM. Steve Case's Internet address is STEVECASE@AOL.COM.

Use Internet Mail Appropriately

Don't send e-mail to fellow AOL members using their Internet address. In other words, don't send mail to majortom@aol.com when you can simply send mail to majortom. Tagging an AOL member's address with "@aol.com" forces the mail to go all the way out on the Internet and bounce around in cyberspace for a couple of hours before it returns. It also makes it difficult for the recipient to reply without doing the same. If the addressee is an AOL member, his or her screen name is the best address for efficient mailing.

America Online's maximum e-mail message length is around 28k. (It's actually more than that but AOL reserves a small overhead space for forwarding comments.) If someone on the Internet sends you a message longer than that, AOL will cut it up and deliver it to you as multiple pieces of mail. Use a word processor to re-assemble the pieces.

America Online offers plenty of help with Internet e-mail, including a message board and an avenue for communication with the AOL Internet staff. Use the keyword: MailGateway to explore this feature.

Attaching Files to Messages

Understand that we've finished our discussion of Internet mail. This is a new topic. As I mentioned a few pages back, you can't attach files to Internet mail.

Also understand that we're not talking in the abstract here: Files are files. On the Mac, files can include text, graphics, data, sound, animation, even programs. Any of these files can be attached to a piece of e-mail. When mail is received with an attached file, the file is then downloaded in its native format, which is astounding.

File transmission requires elaborate protocols and error checking. Not a single bit, nibble or byte can be displaced. Most other telecommunications services require you to decide upon one of many cryptic protocols with names like XModem and Kermit. You also have to determine the number of data bits, stop bits and the parity setting your system needs. All told, of the 50 or so potential configurations for file transfer, usually only one of them will work in a given situation.

Forget all of that. You need not become involved. America Online handles it all invisibly, efficiently and reliably. If you want to send a file, all you have to do is click the Attach File icon (review Figure 4-1) and AOL will take care of it from there.

Tip: If you're a traveler and you take your PowerBook with you on the road, send e-mail to yourself, attaching important files that you've constructed while away from the office. America Online will hold them for you until your return. If something untoward should happen to your data while you're on the road, you can download your files when you return. It's cheap insurance.

Figure 4-24 follows a telecommunicated file from beginning to end. The journey spans half a continent—from Oregon to Mississippi—but only costs pennies.

Use Attached Files Appropriately

Before the recipient can do anything with an attached file, it has to be downloaded, saved and (usually) viewed with some kind of program other than AOL itself. This is something of a nuisance for the recipient. In other words, don't send attached files when a simple e-mail message will do.

You might be tempted, for instance, to send a word processing file instead of a conventional message to another member. Perhaps the message is long, or you want to format it, or you just prefer your word processor over AOL's text editor. Resist the urge. America Online can handle e-mail messages up to 28k in length (about 15 pages), no one expects fancy formatting when it comes to e-mail, and you can always send unformatted word processing files by copying them and pasting them into a Compose Mail window. Attached files should never be sent when simple messages will do.

Figure 4-24:
Sending an MG
across the country
is as easy as
clicking a mouse.
(Illustration by Rich
Wald. Keyword:
File Search, then
use the criterion:
Classic Cars.sit.)

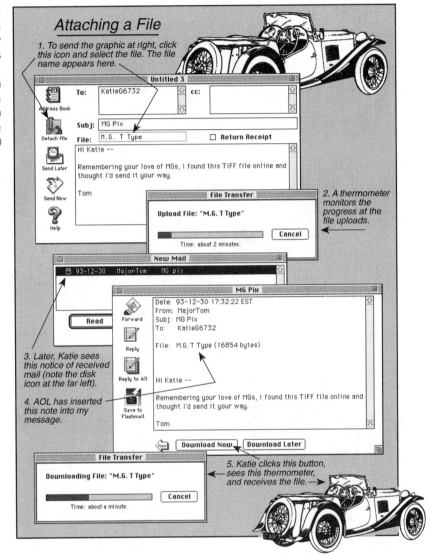

Figure 4-24:
Sending an MG
across the country
is as easy as
clicking a mouse.
(Illustration by Rich
Wald. Keyword:
File Search, then
use the criterion:
Classic Cars.sit.)

Attaching a File

1. To send the graphic at right, click this icon and select the file. The file name appears here.

2. A thermometer monitors the progress at the file uploads.

3. Later, Katie sees this notice of received mail (note the disk icon at the far left).

4. AOL has inserted this note into my message.

5. Katie clicks this button, sees this thermometer, and receives the file.

Attaching a Single File

You can attach a single file or multiple files to e-mail messages. Furthermore, you can compress these attached files (I'll discuss file compression in a moment) to reduce transmission time.

To attach a single file to an e-mail message, click the Attach File icon in the message's window. America Online will respond with the sequence of windows pictured in Figure 4-25.

Figure 4-25:
Attaching a single
file amounts to
little more than
clicking an icon
and locating the
file on your disk.

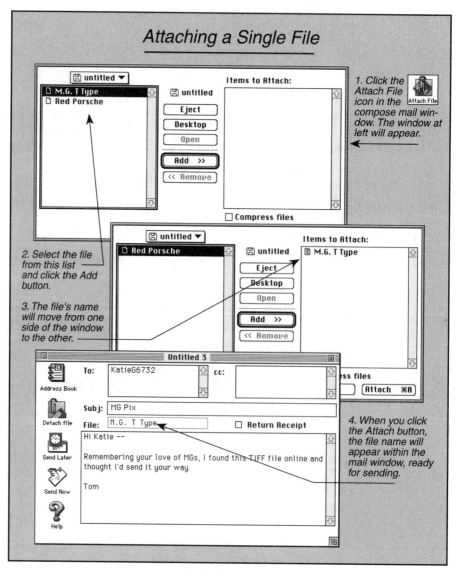

When you click the Send Now icon pictured in the bottom window of Figure 4-25, you trigger the sequence of events pictured in Figure 4-24. America Online will hold the mail and the file until the addressee is ready to read the mail and download the file. If you address the mail to multiple recipients—even if they're receiving carbon copies or blind carbon copies—each will be afforded the opportunity of downloading the file.

And downloading files attached to received mail is optional. Though the MG Pix window pictured in step 4 of Figure 4-24 offers both Download Now and Download Later buttons, the recipient might elect to ignore them both. (Keep that in mind if you ever receive mail with attached files you don't want.)

Attaching Multiple Files

You can attach more than a single file to an e-mail message if you wish, in the form of a StuffIt archive. StuffIt (discussed in detail in the next chapter) is a tool for compressing (and decompressing) files. Your AOL software is capable of unstuffing files that have been compressed using StuffIt, and it's capable of stuffing files as well (see Figure 4-26).

Figure 4-26: By stuffing multiple files into a single StuffIt archive, AOL can attach multiple files to one e-mail message.

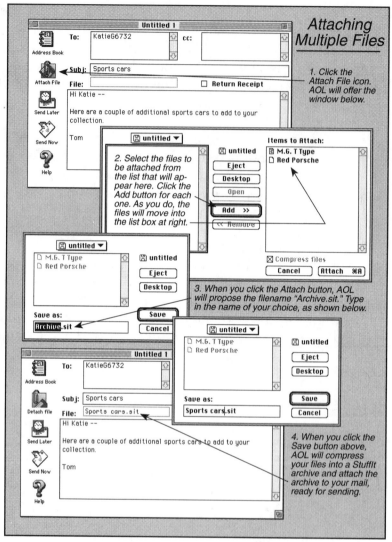

The events pictured in Figure 4-26 all occur within the AOL software: You don't need additional software to create the archive or to unstuff it.

Not All Computers Are Macs

The feature that provides for the attachment of multiple files depends on StuffIt, which is Macintosh software. While StuffIt archives are commonplace in the Macintosh universe, they're black sheep everywhere else.

If the recipient isn't using a Macintosh, don't use the multiple-file attachment feature, and don't compress single files. Send your files one at a time, without compression. This will take more effort and no doubt more online time. While you're waiting for the upload to conclude, use the time to reflect on your wisdom in choosing Macintosh.

The important concept to understand is that your AOL software makes an intermediary file—the StuffIt archive (with the .sit extension) pictured in step 4 of Figure 4-26. Remember that StuffIt archives may contain multiple files. The archive is the (single) file that's actually sent; it isn't broken out into its individual components until the recipient downloads and unstuffs it. It's a bit like mailing a number of Christmas presents in a single box: when the recipient opens the box each present emerges independently, but until then it's a single package.

The AOL software unstuffs (decompresses) files attached to e-mail with the .sit filename extension automatically. The software usually makes a new folder and places the individual (unstuffed) attached files within that folder, leaving the recipient with both the StuffIt archive and the folder on his or her disk.

This is much harder to explain than it is to do. Before you actually send multiple files to another member, find a couple of small (under 10k) files on your disk, attach them to a piece of mail, then send the mail to yourself. Participate in the process from start to finish, walking through the steps pictured in Figure 4-26. This will all make sense when you do.

You Can Stuff a Single File Too

If you look carefully in the top window of Figure 4-25, you'll note a little check box labeled "Compress files." Though this box is automatically checked when you select multiple files, you might want to turn it on if you're selecting just one.

In fact, you should compress every file you send, unless it's small—say, under 5k—or if it's headed for a machine that's not equipped with AOL's Macintosh software. Compressing files cuts down on uploading and downloading time. Compressing files not only benefits you, but the recipient as well.

E-mail Alternatives

The world is not a perfect place. No one can always correctly predict the weather, computers don't always address envelopes reliably, and some people still aren't online. What if you want to communicate with these heathens? You could write them a letter, but that requires paper, an envelope, a stamp and a trip to the mailbox. You could phone them, but an answering machine will probably take the call (and your money as well, if it's long distance). You could try telepathy or ask Scotty to beam you there, but these are emerging technologies and you know how reliable they are (remember *The Fly?*).

Paper Mail

Instead, use AOL to send 'em a letter. All you have to do is prepare normal e-mail and include a special address (see Figure 4-27). A few days later, a real paper letter in a real paper envelope will arrive at your specified destination, looking for all the world like you typed it yourself. The cost for this service is somewhere between the cost of a first-class stamp and a long-distance phone call; and it's no more difficult than sending e-mail. This brings such a convenience to communicating that it almost eliminates procrastination.

Speaking of procrastination, when was the last time you wrote your mother?

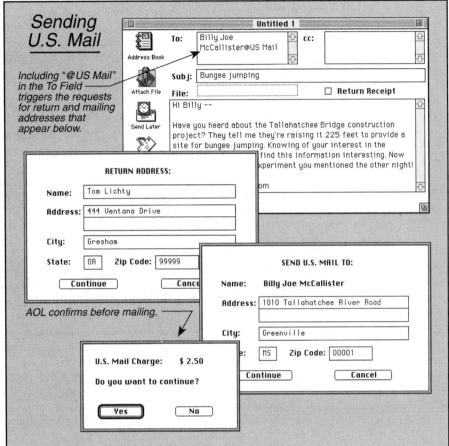

Figure 4-27:
Sending a message
via US Mail
involves
completing return
and mailing
address forms
before
confirmation.

Note that the only difference between sending regular e-mail and sending US Mail is the address. If AOL sees @usmail in an e-mail address, it automatically triggers the address request dialogs you see pictured in Figure 4-27.

Note: Zip codes are required, and AOL verifies that they match the cities in both the return and mailing addresses. If they don't, you will receive an "invalid US Mail address" error and be sent back to the offending entry.

Sending a Fax

Perhaps your mother owns a fax machine (doesn't everyone?). You can save a few cents and a few days over paper mail by sending her a fax instead. Again, AOL stands ready to serve, even if you don't own a fax machine yourself. The process is no more complicated than sending paper mail—or e-mail for that matter (see Figure 4-28). Again, an @ sign in an address triggers the dialog. Within a few minutes of sending fax mail, AOL sends e-mail to you confirming the transmission of the fax message.

Figure 4-28: Fax mail differs little from normal e-mail.

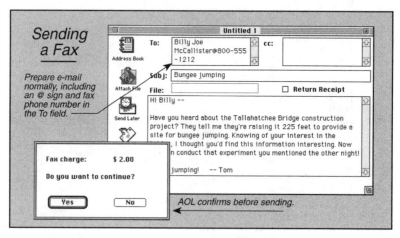

The Fine Print

Fax and paper mail can be sent to multiple addresses. Complete the To field just as you would for e-mail, separating the recipients' names with commas. You'll be charged for each address, however.

- All charges are billed to your AOL account.

- Paper mail requires zip codes.

- Fax addressee names cannot exceed 20 characters, including spaces and punctuation. Paper mail addressee names are limited to 33 characters.

- You can't attach files to fax or paper mail messages. Both services are plain text only.

- Both fax and paper mail messages wrap to 70 characters on a line. Fax pages contain a maximum of 60 lines. Paper mail messages contain 40 lines on the first page (to make room for the address) and 53 lines on all others.

- Forced page breaks may be declared: Type ">>> PAGE BREAK <<<" (without the quotes) on a line by itself. This works for both fax and paper mail.

- Paper mail is limited to four pages. Fax mail is limited to 24k.

- Include your real name (not your screen name) in the text of both fax and paper mail.

- In either case, you'll receive a confirmation identifying all charges before AOL sends your mail (refer again to Figures 4-27 and 4-28). If, after reviewing the charges, you decide you don't want to send the mail or the fax, you can cancel at that point. You will also receive a confirmation (via e-mail from AOL) that your fax has been transmitted a few minutes after you click the Send button.

Moving On

As it has been described, AOL's e-mail facility is impressive work. It holds your mail for you, even after you've read it. It allows you to send courtesy copies. It provides access to the Internet, fax and the US Post Office. Best of all, it rarely costs you any more than your monthly AOL membership fee.

Jay Levitt

Fully one-third of AOL's business is e-mail. AOL handles *half a million* pieces of mail a day—few post offices have that volume—and we all simply assume that each message will make it from sender to receiver without a hitch.

Which it does, thanks to Jay Levitt. Jay is AOL's Mail Guy. Few people are more pivotal to the service than the person in charge of the mail. Jay Levitt is so important that his screen name is "Jay." Even Steve Case doesn't have a first-name screen name. Jay does. In a little office less than 10 feet from the "engine room" of AOL, he sits surrounded by computer screens: a Mac, a PC, an HP workstation, a terminal and two PDAs (Personal Digital Assistants: palmtop computers that many feel will become e-mail's hingepins in the upcoming years). He plays these terminals like a keyboard musician at a rock concert—the fingers of his left hand a blur as they tap out commands to display instantaneous mail volume, while the right hand tickles one of the two mainframes that are dedicated to his imperative. All the while he carries on a conversation with me, popping witticisms like Victor Borge on a good night.

The rock musician analogy isn't far off the mark (though I doubt that you'd ever find him in leather and chains), for Jay Levitt is in his early 20s. *Just a kid!* Kid or not, he's a scholar, a prodigy and a gentleman. Most of all, he's one of the finest friends I made at AOL. Few could do as well.

But e-mail isn't everything AOL has to offer. America Online is also composed of departments—14 of them to be exact. We'll begin our departmental exploration with the Computing Department, the subject of the next chapter.

The Colossus of Memnon was erected in the 14th century B.C. by the Egyptian king Amenhotep III. The Colossus is composed of two seated stone figures each measuring 38 feet high. If they ever stood up, they would tower over every structure in Washington, DC, including AOL's four-story office building a few miles away. While King Kong was satisfied with only one Faye Wray in the palm of his hand, it would take six Faye Wrays to fill a Colossus hand—and there are four of them.

In size, the colossus of departments at AOL is Computing & Software. All other departments pale in comparison—mere King Kongs, pebbles in the sandals of a colossus like the Computing Department. Exploring a colossus takes a while, but that's what we'll do when you turn the page....

Computing

If you love your Macintosh, if it beckons with an alluring radiance whenever you're in the same room with it, and if you needlessly optimize your hard disk and reorganize your folders, you're going to love this department. The Computing Department is the consummate carnival for Macintosh maniacs. It's an opiate, a tabernacle, a jubilation. You'll spend a lot of time here.

In fact, even if you're *not* a Macintosh fanatic, The Computing Department might still become one of your mainstays. There are thousands of files here—fonts and graphics in particular—that will appeal to even the casual Macintosh user. If you need help with either your Mac or the software you run on it, The Computing Department is ready to oblige. And there are some invigorating forums here, ranging from the fundamental to the existential. This place is as rife with opportunity as a sunny Saturday in August, and you can enjoy it any day of the year.

The Computing Department's main window serves as this chapter's frontispiece graphic. To reach the Computing Department, use the keyword Computing.

Figure 5-1: The ultimate Mac software toy store: The Computing Department offers a boundless universe of resources.

The Beginners Forum

There's so much great stuff here, it's hard to know where to begin. I suppose starting at the beginning is appropriate, and the beginning, in this case, is the Beginners Forum (keyword: Beginners). The Beginners Forum offers a Handy-Dandy Help Manual, text "maps" of AOL (updated monthly), many step-by-step help files, and the forum's Handy-Dandy Chart of Command-key shortcuts. Also included are uploading and downloading instructions and all of AOL's online help files in text format.

Figure 5-2: One of the practice files available for downloading in the Beginners Forum. Explicit instructions are available in the forum for the downloading and viewing processes. (Shameless self-promotion courtesy of the forum leader.)

Need more? A section called Frequently Asked Questions is full of (what else?) frequently asked questions (and the answers). Message boards offer an opportunity to ask questions of the forum's staff and get personalized step-by-step help. There's a library of files hand-picked for the beginner, and a section called Help Me I'm Lost! that stands ready to help anyone who's feeling overwhelmed by the sheer magnitude of the service.

Life's Ups & Downs

If you like to laugh, check out "I Laughed So Hard I Cried," featured in the Beginners Forum. Forum leader Sandy Brockmann posts her personal library of Funny Stuff here, much of which is her own. Consider the following example:

BRICKLAYER'S ACCIDENT REPORT
Gentlemen:

I am writing in response to your request for additional information in block #3 of the accident reporting form. I put "poor planning" as the cause of my accident. You said in your letter that I should explain more fully and I trust that the following details will be sufficient.

I am a bricklayer by trade. On the day of the accident, I was working alone on the roof of a new six-story building. When I completed my work, I discovered that I had about 500 pounds of bricks left over. Rather than carry the bricks down by hand, I decided to lower them in a barrel using a pulley, which was attached to the side of the building at the sixth floor.

Securing the rope at ground level, I went up to the roof, swung the barrel out and loaded the bricks into it. Then I went back to the ground and untied the rope, holding it tightly to ensure a slow descent of the 500 pounds of bricks. You will note in block #11 of the reporting form that my weight is 155 pounds.

Due to my surprise at being jerked off the ground so suddenly, I lost my presence of mind and forgot to let go of the rope. Needless to say, I proceeded at a rather rapid rate up the side of the building.

In the vicinity of the third floor I met the barrel, which was now proceeding in a downward direction...

Well, you get the idea. I cut the story off because I want you to visit the forum. Find the story for yourself (it's #7 in the series) and read the whole thing. Keep smiling! :-)

Forum Leader Sandy Brockmann (AFL SandyB) expresses the forum's credo this way: "Most of all, though, the Beginners Forum is a place to get warm, caring, efficient help. There is no question that can't be asked in the Beginners Forum. We know what it's like to be new online; we know that to most it feels like a chasm just waiting to swallow us up. Yet we're told it's a new and exciting world—a world full of friends, fun and information. But still there's that chasm we're facing and (almost) to the person, the newcomer online faces that fear of feeling dumb. The Beginners Forum acknowledges those feelings and helps each user through them—with warmth and information."

Figure 5-3:
Whenever people ask me where to begin on AOL, I tell them to begin their journey at the Beginners Forum.

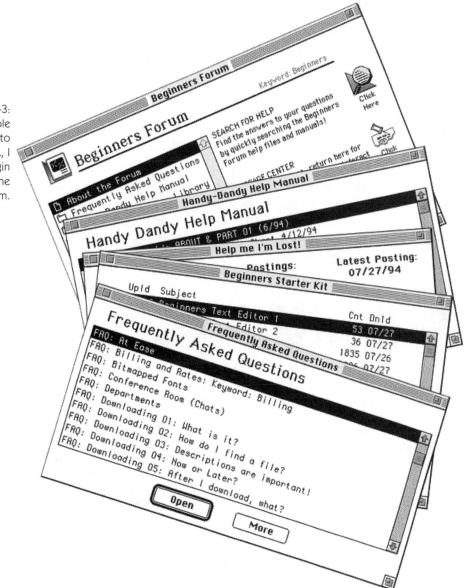

Industry Connection

Even hairy-chested Macintosh users need help with their software or hardware now and again. There are a number of methods:

- Worry at the problem, trying solutions as they come to mind. This usually solves problems within a week.

- Look up the solution in the manual (if you remember where you put it). This usually takes half a day.

- Call the customer support line that's offered by the publisher or manufacturer. This usually involves 20 minutes on hold (listening to a bad radio station playing commercials for stores in a city 3,000 miles away), then a call back, which usually gets through within a couple of days.

- You could sign on to AOL, type in the publisher's keyword, and post your question. Within 24 hours, you will not only receive a response from the vendor you're trying to reach (Figure 5-4), but two or three others from fellow users who have had the same experience.

Figure 5-4: Dr Bear had a problem Wednesday morning. By two that afternoon he had a response.

The Industry Responds

Subj: 2.03 on Plus and SE   10:08:11 EDT
From: Dr Bear1

I am regularly getting co-processor not installed errors when using the speller. Any ideas?

Subj: Speller problems reply   13:55:53 EDT
From: WPMac

Are you running system 6.0.7 on these machines? I would suggest using 6.0.5 and keeping your inits to a minimum. It's possible the program is running out of memory when it tries to load the speller. How much memory do you have on these machines and how much is available to WordPerfect?

- Dave Nielsen
WP Corp, Macintosh Problem Resolution

No Place for Vilification

Look again at Dr Bear's question in Figure 5-4: He identifies the software version he's using, the model of machine and the specific wording of the error message. This is accomplished in a two-sentence, 14-word posting. He is concise, specific and nonantagonistic.

If we all communicated problems—no matter how frustrating and agonizing—this effectively, we might always receive prompt, courteous responses like Dave Nielsen's. Requests for industry support are not the place to demonstrate theory or try to prove expertise; nor are they opportunities for vilification.

Prepare your question in advance, before you sign on. Spend a few moments scrutinizing it for brevity and courtesy. Sign on and post your message only after it has passed this kind of inquisition. You can prepare a message off-line, away from a message board, by choosing New Memo from the File menu (or press Command-N). Then, after signing on and finding the message board you want, just copy the text of your new memo and paste it into the form used for posting messages on the board.

The service that provides this solution is AOL's Industry Connection (Figure 5-5). Hundreds of vendors currently maintain message boards on AOL, and every one of them is checked every day—often more frequently than that—by the appropriate vendor. Not only is excellent vendor support to be found here, but so is peer support, libraries of accessories and updates, announcements from the industry and tips from other users.

Figure 5-5:
Hundreds of
companies offer
support via
America Online.
These are a few of
the companies
beginning with A.

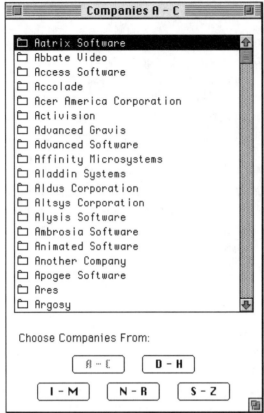

Allow me a few examples. The Berkeley System's library of files, for instance, offers more than 40 modules for its popular After Dark screen saver. Most of these modules are free, a few are "postcardware" (send the author a postcard from your city), and the rest are shareware costing less than $10. A screen saver is a utility that darkens or alters your screen after a certain period of time has elapsed. The Aldus and Quark Forums stand ready to serve desktop publishing users. The Claris Forum had four libraries of files the last time I checked, each containing more than 30 entries. WordPerfect Corporation even offers a suggestion box. Microsoft has recently expanded its online support—always a superior alternative to calling Redmond long distance. There are no surcharges for these services. They're yours for the cost of the connect time only.

Figure 5-6: Here
are four of the
major vendors
offering online
support for their
products. In the
background is "Mr.
Melty," an After
Dark screen saver
module that I
downloaded from
the Berkeley
System's Forum. It
"melts" my screen
until the image
completely
disappears.

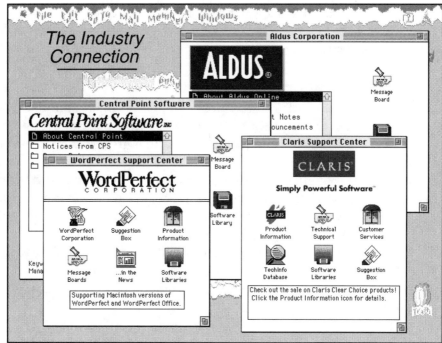

Figure 5-6: Here are four of the major vendors offering online support for their products. In the background is "Mr. Melty," an After Dark screen saver module that I downloaded from the Berkeley System's Forum. It "melts" my screen until the image completely disappears.

In the days when I was active as a computer consultant, I used to tell my clients that online support is the best kind of support money can buy (perhaps that's why I'm no longer a consultant). Humbling as it might seem, no matter how complex or peculiar your problem, someone else has probably experienced it before. Chances are, someone reading the boards will see your posting and reply. This is peer support—people helping people—almost the definition of the online community. Contribute to that community: Post questions when you've got them, and post replies when you have answers.

The Forums

Perhaps the busiest forums on AOL are in the Computing Department. This industry is a moving target, and those who try to keep it in their sights seek information with eagerness that borders on the fanatic. The Computing Department offers forums for every level of computer enthusiast, from beginners to developers, and those forums are extremely popular.

I think it's appropriate, then, that we steal a peek at a few. I want you to see the breadth of this department, to expand your horizons. Perhaps you'll discover something that interests you in the process.

The Music & Sound Forum

What good is a Macintosh if it doesn't make sounds? How long does it take to tire of Simple Beep and Wild Eep? And isn't it time you changed the "Welcome" sound that greets you whenever you sign on to AOL?

Whether you're a professional musician, a sound hobbyist, or just curious, the Macintosh Music & Sound Forum (keyword: MMS) is always rewarding. Guests, files and a wealth of MIDI (musical instrument digital interface) tracks await the explorer here.

One area of significant activity is the sound library, where TV and movie sounds abound, and replacement sounds for your AOL software are among the most popular downloads (see Figure 5-7).

Figure 5-7: You can change your America Online sounds whenever you please. There are scores of alternatives in the Macintosh Music & Sound Forum.

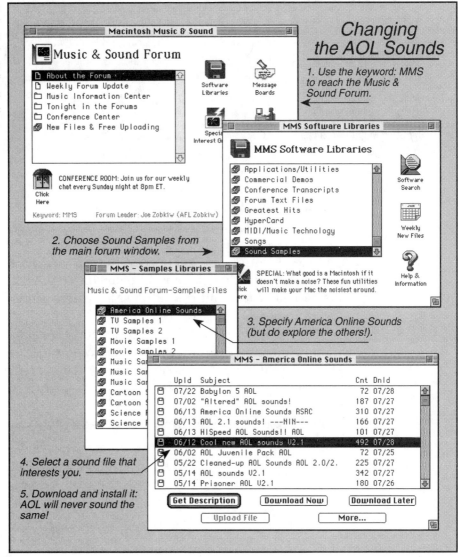

Changing
the AOL Sounds

1. Use the keyword: MMS to reach the Music & Sound Forum.

2. Choose Sound Samples from the main forum window.

3. Specify America Online Sounds (but do explore the others!).

4. Select a sound file that interests you.

5. Download and install it: AOL will never sound the same!

> **SndPlayer**
>
> Once you've downloaded a sound from the Music & Sound Forum, you'll want to hear it and (if you like what you hear) install it in your system. For that you need a utility, and the utility most Macintosh users use is SndPlayer by David Lambert of Dejal Userware in Auckland, New Zealand. This utility not only plays Macintosh sound files but sound files formatted for the PC as well. It's relatively inexpensive shareware and available in the MMS libraries. Find it quickly by using the keyword FileSearch, then specifying the criterion SndPlayer.

The Utilities Forum

Macintosh Thunder Lizard users are fond of the bumper sticker that reads, "He who dies with the most utilities wins!" Thunder Lizard users collect Control Panels, Function Keys, INITs and Extensions like baseball cards, and they do most of their collecting here. The forum meets formally every Saturday at 11 P.M. (Eastern time).

Just the other day I discovered a little program that automatically issues the Macintosh "Shut Down" command after a predetermined amount of inactivity (Figure 5-8). In Chapter 19 (where we'll discuss FlashSessions and the Download Manager), it becomes readily apparent that once a FlashSession has concluded (usually some time in the middle of the night), it would be nice if someone (or something) would turn off the Mac. This little utility does just that.

Figure 5-8: I found this little shutdown utility in the Utilities Forum. The utility is called Downer, by Roman Software in Corvallis, Oregon (all the good stuff comes from Oregon). It's a shareware ($2) Control Panel device, and it takes about two minutes to download.

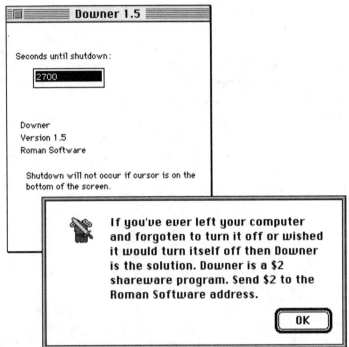

These kinds of programs aren't readily available for sale through traditional retail channels. The wealth of shareware and freeware programs found on AOL offers you bargains, productivity enhancements, honest-to-goodness application software (for a fraction of what a commercial program would cost) and fun and games (see sidebar). The Utilities Forum is an ideal vehicle for the distribution of shareware and freeware. To get there in a hurry, use the keyword MUT.

What Is Shareware?

Two major channels exist for the distribution of computer programs and data. The traditional commercial channel involves publishers, distributors and retailers. Each must make a living, thus each adds a bit to the cost of the product. There's a considerable distance between the people who use the material and the people who actually create it.

The alternative distribution method is referred to as *shareware*. The shareware method is usually a direct connection between the user and the person who created the program. Shareware programs and data are posted on telecommunications services like AOL where they can be freely downloaded whenever we, the users, please. Shareware can also be distributed among individuals or through users' groups without fear of incrimination. Every piece of shareware I have ever seen avidly encourages this kind of distribution.

Shareware is usually complete. If you download a shareware program, you get the complete program—not a "crippled" version—and (usually) documentation as well. You can try it out for a few weeks before you decide to buy. If you decide to keep it, the author usually requests that you send money. Since the money is sent directly to the author—no publishers, distributors or retailers are involved—shareware can theoretically cost much less than commercially distributed software. The author's share is all you pay for shareware, and the author's share is a very small portion of the total cost of the software distributed through commercial channels.

The shareware model also provides a direct channel for communication between user and author. If you have a complaint or a suggestion for improvement, send e-mail to the author. Chances are you'll get a reply. This is a significant feature: To whom do you send mail if you think your car or your refrigerator can be improved? And do you really think they will ever reply?

While most shareware authors request financial remuneration, a few others simply give their material away (freeware), or request a postcard from your city or town (postcardware) or a donation to a favored charity.

The shareware concept only works if users pay, and payment is voluntary. Sadly, only about 10 percent of the people who use shareware programs actually pay for them. This is undoubtedly the biggest fault in the shareware concept. The potential that shareware offers is especially rewarding for us the users, but only if we honor the honor system that's implicit in the shareware concept. In other words, if you use shareware, pay for it, and encourage others to do the same.

The Graphic Arts Forum

Where would the Mac be without graphics? It stands to reason, then, that the Graphic Arts Forum is one of the most popular Macintosh forums available on AOL. This is the place for discussions of Art, Graphics, Design, 3D, Animation, Video, Architecture, Engineering, Computer-Aided Design or Drafting, and all related topics. To get to the forum, use the keyword MGR.

The Online Home Companion

Everyone has a favorite forum. Mine's the Online Home Companion, nestled comfortably (where it's been for years) in the Macintosh Graphic Arts Forum. The Companion is a place for onliners who are looking for the eclectic, the humorous and the comfort of friends.

Any topic is welcome at the Online Home Companion, as long as the topic *isn't* computers. When it was originally created, the forum's founders said, "This is a coffee break, a lunch break, the office party, happy hour. It's a place to play, to laugh, to think and to share. It's a park bench, a blanket under a spreading tree—a place to be free."

But it's not a place for computer talk.

The forum defies description, but I guarantee it's worth the visit. Use the keyword MGR, then double-click the Online Home Companion entry in the list box.

Discussion's one thing; the graphics themselves are another. And this forum is rife with them—more than 10,000 at last count—ranging from aeronautics to zucchinis. Most are color; many are 24-bit, resplendent in more than 16 million colors per image. Best of all, they're all free: All you pay for is the connect time required to download them.

The Online Graphics Viewer

The Graphic Arts Forum is also a showcase for AOL's new online viewer technology. Appearing first in Version 2.5 of AOL's Macintosh software, the online viewer allows you to not only see your graphics as you download them (I'll discuss downloading in a moment), it also allows you to preview them *before* they're downloaded (see Figure 5-9).

Figure 5-9: The online graphics viewer lets you preview images before you elect to receive them, then observe their progress as they're downloaded. (The image is of the planet Jupiter just after the comet Shoemaker-Levy 9 impacted the planet in July 1994.)

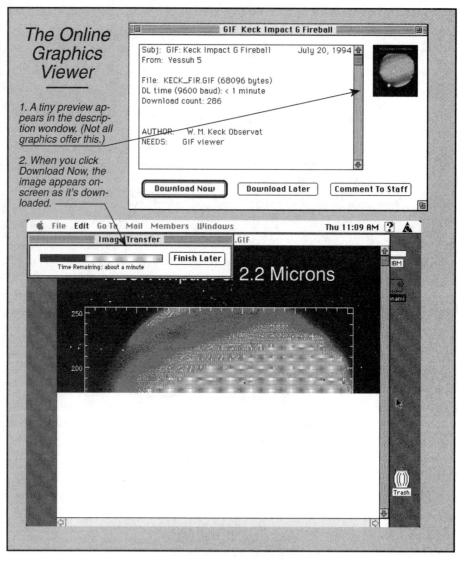

The Online Graphics Viewer

1. A tiny preview appears in the description wondow. (Not all graphics offer this.)

2. When you click Download Now, the image appears on-screen as it's downloaded.

The preview function is a godsend. The tiny image that's sent while you're reading the file description is usually enough for you to determine whether you want to spend time downloading the image or not. Though it's not available for all images (more images offer it each day), when it is available, it's exactly what you'll need.

Even if a preview isn't available, the online viewer exposes the image in stages as it's downloaded. Should you decide you don't need the image, simply stop the download (there's always a button on the screen for that) and move on to something else.

Downloading Preferences

Enough can't be said in favor of the online graphics viewer, but it does have one flaw: It slows downloads somewhat. Not much if you have a fast Mac, but just a bit nonetheless.

If the viewer isn't to your liking, you can always turn it off. Choose Preferences from the Members menu, then choose Graphics Viewing Preferences and turn Auto-View Graphics off.

Not all graphics respond to the viewer, by the way. Occasionally you'll find one that not only won't preview, but it won't display as it's being downloaded either. Don't fret, the graphic will no doubt be accessible later, though you might need a graphics viewing program other than AOL to view it.

The graphics viewer isn't just for use online. It will open any ART (AOL's proprietary graphics format), PICT (the Mac's native graphics format), JPEG (more about JPEG later) or GIF (graphic interchange format) file on your disk. Just choose Open from the File menu. It will save in these formats as well, regardless of the file's original format. Just choose Save As from the File menu.

There are a number of other forums in the Computing Department. Check out the Business, Desktop Publishing, Hardware and HyperCard Forums. The Macintosh Games Forum (keyword: MGM) is a big favorite: The *RoboWar* strategy game that I'll discuss in a moment is found there. The Computing Department is a feast for the Macintosh appetite. If you ever get the hunger, there's a forum here waiting to sustain you.

Tim Barwick

Tim Barwick gazes at the woods outside his window, just a few minutes from downtown Washington, DC. Red squirrels scamper up deciduous trees, reveling in the springtime sunshine. The forest's contrast to the rush hour chaos on Route 7 a half-mile away somehow reflects Tim's contrast to the hubbub at AOL. Originally a member, then a forum leader, then the Department Head of the Computing Department, now the Manager of the Product Development team, Tim personifies contrast. The contrast is heard rather than seen: a native of England, Tim speaks with an old-world elegance that hardly conforms to the frenzied, neological industry he helps shape.

As Manager of Product Development, Tim serves as liaison between the members and the people who write the software that's installed in our computers. Tim, in other words, is the staple in the customer-satisfaction recipe.

Tim's old-world heritage is reflected in his management philosophy: he is champion for the rank and file. His philosophy is reflected in today's AOL software. "I know it's corny," Tim says, "but customer satisfaction is paramount. We listen to our users, and many of the features we now offer are the result of end-user suggestions." The shape, the feel—the spirit of the service didn't result from a white paper drafted by directors or advisory committees. AOL is our progeny. Tim Barwick sees to that.

Downloading Files

The most popular aspect of the Computing Department is its extensive collection of software. All it takes is a browse through the libraries: the number of times a file has been downloaded is shown beside each file's name, and most of those numbers exceed 100. Let's say there are 60,000 files in the Computing Department. A hundred downloads for each of 60,000 files equals 6,000,000 downloads. *Six million!* But that's just the Computing Department. More than 20,000 files reside elsewhere within AOL, spread across the service like flowers in a meadow. Members graze this meadow, downloading bouquets of files and smiling. People must be on to something here. It might be appropriate, then, to spend a few pages discussing downloads: what they are, where they are and how to get one for yourself.

What Is Downloading?

Simply put, downloading is the process of transferring a file from AOL's host computer to a disk in your computer. Files can be programs, Control Panels (the Downer utility pictured in Figure 5-8 is a Control Panel), fonts, graphics (many of the graphics in this book have been downloaded), sound, animation and, of course, text. In fact, this whole book has been downloaded: Using attachments to AOL's electronic mail, I uploaded the manuscript to AOL (more about uploading later), and the publisher downloaded it. (Attachments and e-mail are discussed in Chapter 4.)

A Downloading Session

Perhaps the best way to explain downloading is to download a file for you and explain the process as it's happening. With all this talk about 60,000 files, how do you find the good stuff? Frankly, the best strategy is to buy a copy of *The Mac Shareware 500* (see sidebar) and refer to it when you're in the mood for something new. The book comes with enough shareware on disk to pay for itself, and it's *the* reference for Macintosh shareware.

The Mac Shareware 500

The trouble with shareware is there's so *much* of it. If you downloaded every utility, graphic and font that sounds interesting, you would spend the rest of the century online. Even reading descriptions can become laborious.

We need to know what's good and what's better; we need to know what's compatible with our machines; we need to know where to find shareware online; and we need to know what the shareware fees are. What we need is a guide. Someone who has seen it all and is willing to share opinions with us.

Would I bring it up if such a service wasn't available online? The Mac Shareware 500 Forum is based on the book of the same name by Ruffin Prevost and Rob Terrell. As the title suggests, the book lists 500 shareware packages available online, ranks each one, specifies their prices, and identifies things like compatibility, version numbers and the authors' names and addresses.

The forum serves as an adjunct to the book. It offers message boards (so you can hear what others have to say), new additions, opportunities to meet the authors online, and a library containing all 500 packages featured in the book. If you download shareware, this is the place to start. Use the keyword Mac500.

Finding a File

Before you can download a file, you've got to find it. This could be a horrendous task were it not for AOL's searchable database of online files. The database is only a keyword away.

A Begin by typing Command-K (for keyword) and entering the keyword FileSearch (Figure 5-10). There are lots of other ways to find files for downloading on AOL, but this is the best.

Figure 5-10: The keyword FileSearch takes you directly to a database of files stored on America Online. There, criteria can be entered as described in the text.

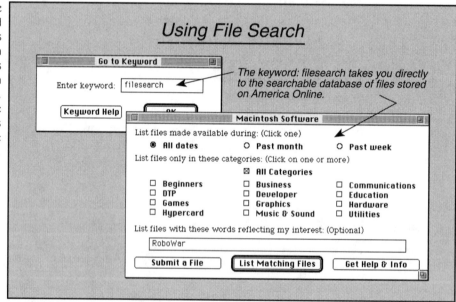

A Lots of references emerge once the search is completed (Figure 5-11). *RoboWar* is a popular game. If you want to search for RoboWar, use the criteria "RoboWar AND Harris" (programmer David Harris wrote the game). That will filter out most of the supporting RoboWar files.

Figure 5-11: I can
read a file's
description before
I download it.

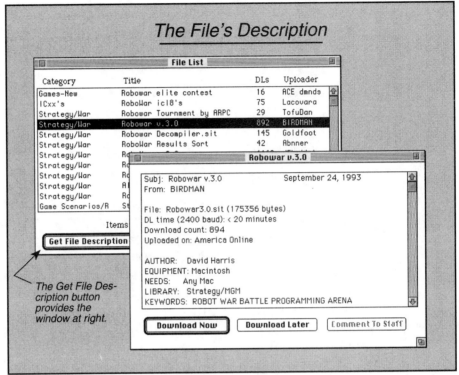

Figure 5-11: I can read a file's description before I download it.

The Get File Description button provides the window at right.

🔈 When I click the Get File Description button, AOL provides a complete description of the file (see Figure 5-11). This intermediary step is critical. There are lots of things I need to know about this file before I choose to download it.

The Online File Database

Use of the keyword FileSearch is a convenient way to search all of AOL's libraries with one command. The keyword cuts across forums and departments to provide access to all the files currently available online. This method also assigns the file-searching task to the host computer rather than to your Mac, and the host computer searches very quickly—rarely taking more than a few seconds to search the more than 60,000 files available.

Look again at the Macintosh Software dialog box pictured in Figure 5-10. Two categories of check boxes are provided, allowing you to specify only those files that have recently been uploaded (the "past week" option is great for finding only new files), or only those files that fit certain criteria.

More important, a text box is also available within the Macintosh Software dialog box. Here you can specify your own criteria. Words entered here are matched against key search words appearing in the following areas:

- The person who uploaded the file.

- The file's name.

- The subject line.

- Keywords assigned to the file.

There are three special words you can use in a match phrase: *and, or* and *not*. Each of these words modifies how the next word in the phrase is used. I might receive dozens of matches to the search phrase "clock," most of which would be clock graphics, not desk accessories. The search phrase "clock *and* DA," on the other hand, narrows the search. (The *and* modifier is the default. By the way, whenever more than one word appears in a search phrase, AOL assumes there's an *and* between them. Thus the phrase "clock and DA" is the same as the phrase "clock DA.")

Perhaps I want a calendar as well as a clock. Here's where the *or* modifier comes in. The phrase "clock *or* calendar" finds either one.

The *not* modifier excludes material matching the following criterion and narrows the search. The phrase "clock *not* graphics" would provide a listing of all clock files that aren't graphics.

Combining modifiers can be unclear. The phrase "clock or calendar and DA" is ambiguous. Do I mean "clock, or calendar and DA," or do I mean "clock or calendar, and DA?" The solution is found in the use of parentheses. The phrase "(clock or calendar) and DA" says "look for a clock or a calendar, excluding everything but desk accessories from either category." It pays to be specific.

- When the File Search dialog box opens, I enter my criterion: "RoboWar" (refer to Figure 5-10). In this case, I know the name of the file I want to find. That's not always the case, and AOL can accept myriad search criteria to deal with the alternatives.

Reading a File Description

Let's look at RoboWar's file description in its entirety (Figure 5-12).

Figure 5-12: A wealth of information is found in file descriptions.

> *Subj: Robowar v.3.0*   *September 24, 1993*
> *From: BIRDMAN*
>
> *File: Robowar3.0.sit (175356 bytes)*
> *DL time (2400 baud): < 20 minutes*
> *Download count: 894*
> *Uploaded on: America Online*
>
> *AUTHOR: David Harris*
> *EQUIPMENT: Macintosh*
> *NEEDS: Any Mac*
> *LIBRARY: Strategy/MGM*
> *KEYWORDS: ROBOT WAR BATTLE PROGRAMMING ARENA*
> *--------------------------------------*
>
> *RoboWar 3.0 Instructions*
> *c 1993 David Harris*
>
> *I. Introduction*
>
> *Welcome to RoboWar. In this game, you will pit armored robots against each other in gladitorial combat or build your own robots to vie for championship in the arena! Only clever design and skillful implementation will bring your robot to the top. May victory go to the strongest!*
>
> *Features of RoboWar include animated combat, sound effects, a unique programming language (RoboTalk) with an assembler and interpreter, color graphics on Macs with color monitors, and a complete robot development factory with a Drafting Board, Hardware Store, Icon Editor, and Recording Studio.*
>
> *+++*
> *Found virus free using CP AntiVirus (w/ 22 Apr 93 Sig) - AFL Rod*

🔥 The Subject, From and File lines are all searchable criteria. If I wanted to see all the files submitted by Birdman, I could specify "Birdman" in the search phrase pictured in Figure 5-11. This is especially valuable when you want to find all the files submitted by your favorite graphic artist. Note that the File line not only includes the file's name, but its version number and size as well.

🔥 The file date is used when you specify "Past month" or "Past week" in the Macintosh Software dialog box.

🔺 The download time is AOL's best guess as to how long it will take to download the file. This time is estimated based on the baud rate at which you're currently connected. If you're connected at 9600 baud, the estimate is based on that baud rate. *This number is only an estimate.* If you signed on during a peak usage period (around 9 P.M., Eastern time, is a peak usage period), this number might be slightly optimistic. If you're signed on at 4 A.M., this number will be pessimistic. I downloaded *RoboWar*, which AOL estimates as a 20-minute download, in 17 minutes during a mid-morning session at 2400 baud.

🔺 The download count is a rough indication of the file's popularity. While this might not be too significant for a new posting like *RoboWar 3.0* (at least it was new at the time I downloaded it), it's an indication of the popularity of files that have been around for a while. If you're looking for a graphic of a cat, for instance, and 40 files match your search criteria, you might let the number of downloads (review Figure 5-11) direct you. Often, however, the number of downloads is more reflective of the catchiness of a file's name or description than of its content.

🔺 The Equipment and Needs lines are critical: If your Mac isn't up to the task, or if you need special software, it's nice to know *before* you download the file. For instance, you will need System 7 (or later), a movie player and the QuickTime Extension to view any of the scores of QuickTime movies posted on AOL, and the Equipment and Needs lines inform you of this.

🔺 Keywords are those that provide matches when you enter your own search criteria. Read these. They offer valuable insight as to how to word your search phrases. *Note:* In this context, a keyword is a word assigned to a shareware file that is used to help categorize and describe it for easy search and retrieval. These are separate from and can't be used by AOL's navigational keyword function (accessed by typing Command-K or choosing Keyword from the Go To menu), which lets you move quickly from one place in AOL to another.

The description itself is provided by the person who uploaded the file. RoboWar's description, for instance, indicates that the game includes sound, graphics, a programming language and more. (It *doesn't* indicate that RoboWar also includes a complete user's manual, which appears as part of the program's extensive help files.)

Before being posted, each file uploaded to AOL is checked for viruses by one of the forum's personnel. File descriptions not only tell you what virus detection software was used to check the file, but also which version of that software was used.

File descriptions can be saved for later reference. Simply choose Save from the File menu before you close the description window. America Online will ask where you want to store the description, which it will store in ASCII text format. All the text that you read on your Mac's screen is formatted this way, and it can be read off-line (after you've saved it to a separate file) on any word processor or the AOL software itself (just choose Open from AOL's File menu).

Using the Fastest Local Access Number

As I mentioned in Chapter 1, AOL employs the services of a variety of long distance services. When you first sign on to AOL, the host computer consults its database of telephone numbers in your locale and assigns one of them as your primary AOL calling number. It will also assign you an alternate number in case the first number is busy or having problems.

The most effective way to judge downloading efficiency is to use a modem with indicator lights. One of them should be marked "receive data" or "RD." This light will stay continuously lit or almost so during an efficient download. Inefficient downloads are indicated when this light flashes on and off like a digital clock that needs to be set. Usually this condition is caused by a heavy load on the host computer. Calling back at a different time of day usually solves the problem.

If calling back at a different time of the day doesn't solve the problem, try the alternate number. Here's how:

- If the sign-on screen isn't showing, choose Set Up & Sign On from the Go To menu.

- Click on the button marked Setup.

- Two major segments dominate the Setup screen, marked First Choice and Second Choice. If these two numbers are rated at the same speed (9600 baud, for example), try reversing the numbers and services. *Be sure to reverse them both!* Failure to swap both numbers *and services* (if they're different, and be sure to reverse them—along with the numbers—if they are) is one of the most common errors people make when they fiddle with this screen.

- Sign on again and try out your setup.

Remember, the description's downloading time is an estimate. However, if your downloads reliably exceed this estimate, you might have a problem. If neither calling back at a different time of day nor swapping services improves your downloading time, send an e-mail message (I discuss e-mail in Chapter 4) to Customer Support. Sometimes they're aware of a service problem in your area and can set your mind at ease.

The Downloading Process

Once you've read a file's description, you might decide to download it. This is the easy part: all you have to do is click on the Download Now button. (The Download Later button is discussed in Chapter 19, "FlashSessions & the Download Manager.")

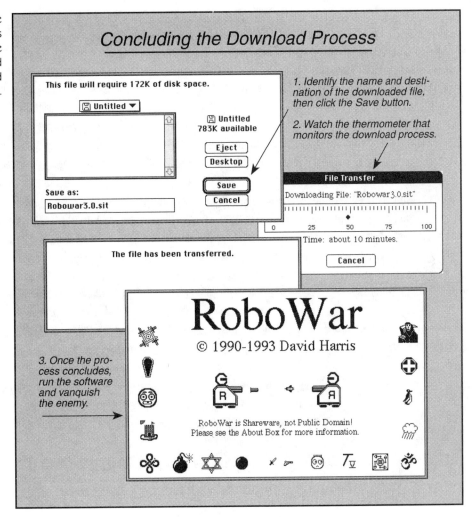

A Remember that downloading is the process of transferring a file from AOL to a disk in your computer. In other words, you're going to have to decide where to put the file. The destination can be either a hard disk or a floppy, and that's the next decision you'll be asked to make (Figure 5-13). Choose a disk and a folder, then click on the button marked Save.

Figure 5-13: The download process is automatic once you've determined the file's name and destination.

Concluding the Download Process

This file will require 172K of disk space.

Untitled ▼

Untitled
783K available

Eject

Desktop

Save

Cancel

Save as:
Robowar3.0.sit

1. Identify the name and destination of the downloaded file, then click the Save button.

2. Watch the thermometer that monitors the download process.

File Transfer

Downloading File: "Robowar3.0.sit"

0   25   50   75   100

Time: about 10 minutes.

Cancel

The file has been transferred.

3. Once the process concludes, run the software and vanquish the enemy.

RoboWar
© 1990-1993 David Harris

RoboWar is Shareware, not Public Domain!
Please see the About Box for more information.

When you click on the Save button, the downloading process progresses predictably, monitored by the onscreen thermometer pictured in Figure 5-13. When the download is completed, you'll be notified both aurally ("File's done!") and visually (see the message pictured in the third window from the top in Figure 5-13).

File Names & Destinations

Look again at Figure 5-13 and note the proposed file name. If you want to use a file name other than the one proposed, all you have to do is select the proposed name (if it isn't selected already) and start typing. I don't recommend this, unless the proposed file name conflicts with one already on your disk. The file's documentation, for instance, might refer to the file by name; if you change the name, the reference might be unclear. Forum discussions might refer to the file's original name; and if you go searching for an update to the file, you'll need to refer to it by its original name. Some programs, especially fonts, Control Panels and Extensions (most anything stored in the System Folder), require that their names not be changed for any reason. So use the original name unless you have a good reason not to.

I also recommend you download to floppy disks rather than your hard disk. Have a few formatted floppies at your side, and specify one when you encounter the dialog pictured at the top of Figure 5-13. I suggest this strategy for two reasons related to safety: (1) Downloaded files might conflict with your Mac. It's *very* rare, but these conflicts could corrupt the disk that contains the file. (2) Downloaded files could contain a virus. As I mentioned a moment ago, AOL's files are checked for viruses before they're posted, but new viruses are dreamed up every day, and one could conceivably sneak through. Though this potential is also remote, it's better to be safe than sorry. I'll show you how to find virus-detection software online in a moment.

Saving to floppies imposes only a slight penalty on downloading time. Though floppy disks are slower in reading and writing than hard disks, the primary limiting factor by far during the downloading process is baud rate. The additional time required to download RoboWar to a floppy—a 175k file—is about 10 seconds.

File Formats

The number of potential file formats for downloaded files is staggering. Fortunately, some standards and conventions relieve the situation.

File name extensions are the realm of DOS files (files used by IBM-PCs and clones). Nearly every DOS file name consists of up to eight characters, a period and a three-character file name extension, such as RoboWar.sit. Though this is stifling (eight characters is hardly enough for a properly descriptive file name), the three-character extension is particularly useful. All you have to do is look at a DOS file's name to see what kind of file it is. DOS file names ending in .PM5 are PageMaker files; those ending in .TXT are text files; and those ending in .TIF are TIFF graphic files.

This convention is finding its way into the Macintosh community as well, and for good reason: Unlike DOS files, Macintosh file names don't identify their formats. Though this might not seem significant when you're viewing file icons on the Mac, there are no file icons when you're reading file descriptions online. That's why most online file names include extensions, even if they're Mac files.

The chart pictured in Figure 5-14 identifies some of the common Macintosh file name extensions and their meanings. File format compatibility differs from program to program. PageMaker, for instance, reads nearly all these formats. Excel, on the other hand, can only read TXT and Excel formats. Read your software documentation to determine which formats are of use to you.

Figure 5-14: File name extensions for some of the most common Macintosh file formats you'll find on America Online.

Filename Extensions

Textual formats

TXT	Unformatted ASCII text
MW	MacWrite
DOC	Microsoft Word

Graphic formats

TIFF	Tagged-image file format
GIF	Graphic interchange format
PAINT	MacPaint (also PNT)
PICT	Macintosh PICT
EPS	Encapsulated PostScript

Compressed formats

SIT	StuffIt (AOL unstuffs automatically)
JPEG	Joint Photographic Experts Group
SEA	Self-Extracting Archive
ZIP	PK Zip (primarily IBM)

Other formats

PM5	PageMaker version 5
XLS	Excel worksheet
XLC	Excel chart
QT	Macintosh QuickTime (multimedia)

File Compression & Decompression

Look again at Figure 5-14. Three compressed formats are identified there and they require further explanation.

Why compress files? There are three good reasons: (1) Compressed files are much smaller than their uncompressed counterparts and thus take significantly less time to download; (2) Compressed files require less storage on a disk; (3) Compressed files are often stored in an "archive," a collection of several files all compressed into a single file (the archive). Archives are a convenient way of grouping multiple files for storage and downloading.

Amazingly, compressed files can be as small as 20 percent of the original; yet when they're decompressed, absolutely no data is lost. I don't know how they do that. Smoke and mirrors, I suppose.

Figure 5-15: The original image on the left measures 21,394 bytes. The image on the right was compressed to 9,111 bytes (43 percent of the original), then decompressed for printing. No data was lost; both pictures are identical. (Graphic enhancement by David Palermo using Adobe PhotoShop.)

Figure 5-15 indirectly identifies a problem common to all compressed images: They're useless until they are decompressed. The compressed image in Figure 5-15 couldn't be included in the illustration until it was decompressed. In other words, you must have decompression software before you can use compressed images. That's the bad news. The good news is that you already do: It's part of the AOL software in your Macintosh.

StuffIt

A shareware program called *StuffIt* is responsible for a great deal of the file compression encountered in the Macintosh environment. StuffIt can compress ("stuff") a single file or a multitude of files into a single file—the archive. StuffIt archives are identified by a .sit file name extension.

Like all archives, StuffIt archives must be decompressed ("unstuffed") before use, and incredibly, that happens automatically when you use AOL. If stuffing is done with smoke and mirrors, automatic unstuffing must be done with smoke and mirrors and eyes of newt. Whatever the technique, it works, and we're the beneficiaries.

When your AOL software downloads a file with .sit at the end of its file name, it makes a note to itself to unstuff the file immediately after you sign off. When the unstuffing process concludes, the original .sit file remains on your disk (probably in a separate folder), along with all the files (and folders, if there are any) that comprise the archive. An *unstuffed* copy of the file will also appear on your disk, ready for use.

To Stuff or Not to Stuff

The automatic unstuffing feature can be disabled if you want. As mentioned before, you might prefer to download to a floppy disk rather than your hard disk. Automatic unstuffing might create files that exceed the floppy's capacity. To avoid that problem, you can override automatic unstuffing and do it yourself later. To disable automatic unstuffing, choose Preferences from the Members menu, then choose Downloading Preferences. You can also use the same command to configure your Mac to automatically delete .sit (stuffed) files after they're unstuffed. Preferences are discussed in Appendix E.

The Preferences command also allows you to configure AOL's software to automatically delete the original archive. Though you might want to activate this preference in deference to disk space, I recommend leaving it turned off. Once the download is complete (and once the AOL software has decompressed it), copy the archive to a floppy and store the floppy somewhere, *then* delete the archive from the disk to which it was downloaded. This strategy provides an archived backup of your downloaded data, ready for recovery should something catastrophic happen to the working copy on your Mac.

America Online not only gives you the unstuffing part of StuffIt, it gives you the stuffing part as well. You can use your AOL software to unstuff any file with the .sit file name extension: Just choose Open from AOL's File menu, find the file on your disk, and "open" it. If you want to stuff your own files, follow the directions in Chapter 4 that describe attaching files to e-mail. You can do this while you're off-line. It makes no difference who you identify as the e-mail recipient, because after AOL stuffs the file, simply *don't send the mail* (just close its window and say No when AOL asks you if you want to save it).

You're also welcome to acquire a copy of StuffIt for yourself. It's available online: Use the keyword FileSearch, then search for "StuffIt." You'll find a number of files meeting the criteria; the one you want is named *StuffIt Lite*. StuffIt Lite is shareware: If you like the program, pay the person who wrote it and you can use it indefinitely with a clear conscience.

A more elaborate version of StuffIt—StuffIt Deluxe—is available commercially from Aladdin Systems, Inc. StuffIt Deluxe offers more features and better support, but StuffIt Lite remains available as shareware. It's nice to have the choice.

Raymond Lau

StuffIt author Raymond Lau wrote the program in 1987 when he was 16 years old. Ray writes, "A friend, who had both a PC and a Mac, asked me one day why, with PackIt III, then standard [for the Mac], you couldn't easily skip files when decompressing like you can with the IBM programs. StuffIt was originally written as a utility for our own use... Its name, as well as its original trash chute icon, was meant as a play on words and images."

Only Ray Lau knows how many shareware copies of StuffIt have been registered, but you can be sure that it's in the tens of thousands. Courtesy of his StuffIt royalties, Ray is now finishing up his undergraduate work at MIT, where he plans to continue graduate studies in— naturally—computer science.

Compact Pro

This wouldn't be a democracy without competition, and StuffIt's primary shareware competition is *Compact Pro*, by Bill Goodman. Compact Pro archives can span multiple floppies (making it an effective alternative to backup software) and support data encryption (in the versions distributed in North America). If you're going to invest in compression software for the Macintosh, don't neglect to include this software in your library.

Self-Extracting Archives

There are other forms of file compression, the most common of which is the *self-extracting archive*. A prime example of a self-extracting archive is *Disinfectant*, by John Norstad. Disinfectant is virus protection freeware, intended to detect and (optionally) disinfect your Mac of any computer viruses. You should have this software. To locate it online, use the keywords File Search, then the criterion Disinfectant. Once you have it, use it.

Look at the top window in Figure 5-16. I've just downloaded Disinfectant33.sea to a blank floppy disk and you're seeing that disk's window. Note that the file name concludes with the .sea extension. Files with this extension are self-extracting archives. Rather than depend on software on your disk for decompression, .sea files decompress themselves. Disinfectant uses Compact Pro for this; others use StuffIt. Either brand of compression software can be used to create a self-extracting archive. Normally, AOL's software will automatically decompress .sea files at sign-off. If it doesn't, all you have to do is double-click the .sea file's icon to decompress it manually.

Figure 5-16: The Disinfectant self-extracting archive decompresses itself when I double-click its icon. The decompression software is embedded in the archive; no local decompression software is required.

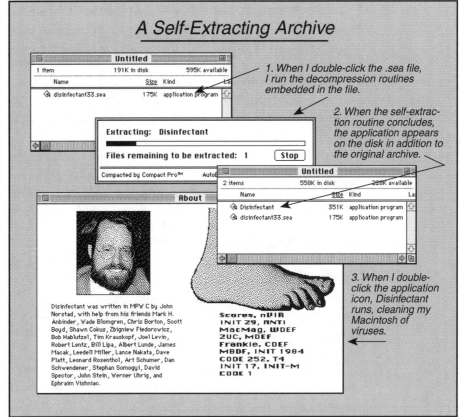

Note the two Untitled windows pictured in Figure 5-16. The top one shows a single file—the archive Disinfectant33.sea—on my floppy. After the archive is decompressed, two files appear on the same floppy: the original (compressed) archive and the (decompressed) Disinfectant application. Note the *size* of the files pictured in Figure 5-16. The original archive measures 175k. The decompressed Disinfectant application measures 351k, more than twice the size of its original archive.

PKZIP

While StuffIt is the file compression standard for Macintoshes, a program called PKZIP is the standard for IBM-PCs and clones. Instead of being stuffed and unstuffed, .zip files are "zipped" and "unzipped." A number of files that are suitable for use on either platform—graphics, mostly—were originally constructed on a PC and are zipped rather than stuffed. (This is beginning to sound like a recipe for baked turkey:

"First stuff, then zip the carcass, then bake at 350 degrees for four hours....")

Zipped files won't decompress themselves automatically, nor are they self-extracting archives. You have to unzip them before you can use them. Amazingly, the Mac AOL software can probably do that. Just choose Open from the File menu, find the zipped file on your disk, and double-click its file name. Not all zip files decompress this way, but most do.

JPEG

The newcomer on the block of graphics file compression formats is JPEG, formulated by the Joint Photographic Experts Group to establish a "lossy" compression standard. All of the other file compression methods I have mentioned are "loss-less," meaning no loss in information is encountered in the compression process. *Lossy* formats lose some data in the compression process, which is never regained.

Lossy compression would never do for text: dropping a character or two here and there would be catastrophic. On the other hand, lossy compression for bit-mapped graphics (the kind produced by scanners, in particular) isn't much of a problem. After all, who will notice of a bit of information $1/300$ inch across is light blue or dark blue? In fact, most files subjected to lossy compression techniques are hard to tell from the original.

If you're willing to accept some minor data loss, you can achieve compression levels much higher than loss-less compression. While GIF compression, for example, might reduce a given file's size to 30 percent of the original, JPEG compression could reduce it to 10 percent—even less if you're willing to accept slight visible distortion.

Your AOL software will open JPEG files. Just choose Open from the File menu. It will save graphics files in this format too (but read the sidebar).

Once Is Enough

Your AOL software will save graphics in the JPEG format as well as open them. Since some loss of information is involved, however, you don't want to repeatedly open, then save JPEG files. If you intend to make changes to a graphic, make them all *before* you save the graphic using the JPEG format. A JPEG save should be your last save for any particular image.

Uploading Files

With all this talk about downloading, it's easy to forget that before a file can be *down*loaded, it first must be *up*loaded. Pursuant to its community spirit, AOL depends on its members for most of its files—members like you and me. Uploading isn't the exclusive realm of AOL employees and forum staff, nor is it that of the supernerds. Most of the files you can download from AOL—I'd guess over 90 percent—have been uploaded from members, using Macintoshes just like yours.

Earlier I defined downloading as "the process of transferring a file from AOL's host computer to a disk on your computer." Uploading is just the reverse: the process of transferring a file from a disk on your computer to AOL's host computer. Once received, it's checked for viruses and the quality of its content, then posted. The process rarely takes more than a day: Upload a file on Monday and you'll probably see it available for downloading Tuesday morning.

The Uploading Process

Begin the uploading process by visiting the forum where your file seems to fit. If it's a graphic, post it in the Graphic Arts & CAD Forum. If it's poetry, post it on the Writers Club. Once you're in the forum, select the library that's the most appropriate place for your file (if there's more than one library in the forum) and click on the Upload File button. (Some forums have an icon marked Submit a File; use this icon if it's available.)

Recently, I uploaded a magazine article to the Writers Club. When I clicked on its Upload button, I received the Upload File Information form pictured in Figure 5-17. You'll encounter this form every time you upload a file to AOL.

Figure 5-17: You'll
be asked to fill out
the Upload File
Information form
for every file you
upload to America
Online.

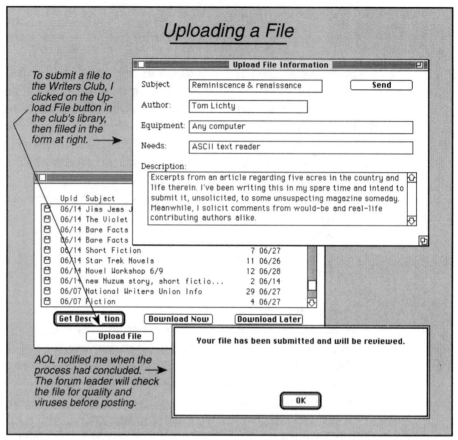

The Upload File Information Form

All too often, uploaders fail to complete the Upload File Information form adequately. After all, this form "sells" your file to other members, and what you have to say about it determines whether a member will take the time to download it. Here are some hints for creating accurate, useful and compelling descriptions of files you upload:

🔺 The Subject field should be (1) descriptive, and (2) catchy, in that order. Look at the window in the foreground of Figure 5-17. Do you see how the subjects are listed there? The subject line is your headline: If you want members to read your story, hook 'em with a really great subject line.

A. The Equipment line should identify any special equipment required to access the file. A color graphic requires a color Macintosh; Mac Pluses and SEs won't do.

A. The Needs line is where you specify the particular software application or program that's required to access your file. A GIF file, for instance, requires some kind of GIF conversion program.

A. The Description field is where you get specific. Here you differentiate your file from others that might be similar. If you're submitting a program, you should include the version number. Be specific and persuasive: you're selling your file here. Think about what you would want to read if you were considering downloading the file. Make it sound irresistible.

If you're submitting a number of related files, or if your file's size exceeds about 20k, stuff it using StuffIt. This saves downloading time and is the polite way to offer your material. Archives should generally be smaller than 800k, so they'll fit on a single floppy disk. America Online only accepts StuffIt archives for Macintosh files. As I mentioned before, StuffIt is available online.

Concluding the Uploading Process

America Online's by-now familiar thermometer will keep you entertained while the upload is underway, followed by the dialog box pictured at the bottom of Figure 5-17.

The time spent uploading your file will be credited back to you. Though you might not see the credit before you sign off, it will appear soon thereafter. To check your billing information, click on the Departments button in the sign-on window, click on Members Online Support, click on Billing Information, then click on Check Current Bill (or simply type the keyword Billing). There you should see a note crediting your account with any time you have spent uploading files. The billing area is free, so you won't be charged for whatever time you spend online checking your account's billing information.

Tips From Tim

Earlier in this chapter I mentioned Tim Barwick, the AOL staffer charged with the responsibility of maintaining the Computing Department. A few weeks ago, I sent him a message asking if he had any tips for uploaders. His response appears below. He's quoting my questions ahead of his replies; my questions are surrounded by chevrons (<< >>).

> Date: 16:58:01 EDT
> From: Tim Barwick
> Subj: Uploading
> To: MajorTom
>
> Tom, in answer to your uploading questions.
>
> <<Any hints? Specifically, any hints about keywords, descriptions, titles, etc.? Any hints about file size?>>
> In general, keywords, descriptions and titles will be adjusted by the online staff. They'll bring them into line with the forum's look and feel. Any tips about functionality or especially neat features are very helpful.
> <<The member stuffs, right?>>
> Yes the member stuffs the file before uploading. We accept both StuffIt and StuffIt Deluxe archives.
> <<Once the file is sent, does the Forum Leader look it over before it's added to the library? Is this process standardized? How do you check for viruses? Do you always check for them?>>
> Every file is checked for viruses before being released. The program that was used to check the file is listed at the bottom of the file description.
> <<What does the uploader get out of the deal?>>
> Credits [to screen names] are given for uploading. We also feature the best uploads in the Software Center so the member gets recognition from their peers of having contributed a 'top' file.
> <<When are files removed? Under what conditions?>>
> Files are removed when an update is issued. We'll also remove files if the uploader requests we do so. Let me know if you have any other questions on uploading, Tom.
>
> :D-Tim

Moving On

This has been a long chapter steeped in technicalities. We've explored the largest department on the service and peeked at a few of its forums. We've downloaded files, archived files, unstuffed files and uploaded files. We've even explored criteria phrases for the searching of online databases. For making it this far, you deserve a gold star.

You also deserve a break from technicalities—a break that I offer in the next chapter. We're about to explore Today's News, another extremely effective use of the online medium.

Best of all, you won't have to wait for "film at 11," or the morning paper, or even news on the hour: AOL's news is available whenever you want it, and it's never stale. It's as current as news can be, and it's only a page away....

CHAPTER 6

Today's News

Eighty years ago, people got their news from newspapers. At best, newspapers offered the news once a day—a small inconvenience considering the urgency with which events occurred back then. Radio emerged 70 years ago, offering the potential of immediate, "on the scene" coverage. But there were no pictures, and you had to be listening when the news was broadcast or you missed it. Forty years ago, television brought pictures, but even today you're at the mercy of TV scheduling if you want the latest.

Have you considered online news? It's immediate (updated perpetually), it has pictures, and it's available at your convenience: there's no broadcast schedule that must be observed. (There are no commercials either!)

America Online is aware of its prerogative, and a recent redesign of the service (see the frontispiece and use the keyword: News) emphasizes the potential.

Top Stories

Look again at the frontispiece above. That list of stories you see at the left of the window is always current and changes as events change. These are the stories that lead the news; the online "front page." To read any of the stories featured there, simply double-click the headline (see Figure 6-1).

Today's News offers not only the news, but sports and weather that's diverse, practical, and always up to the minute.

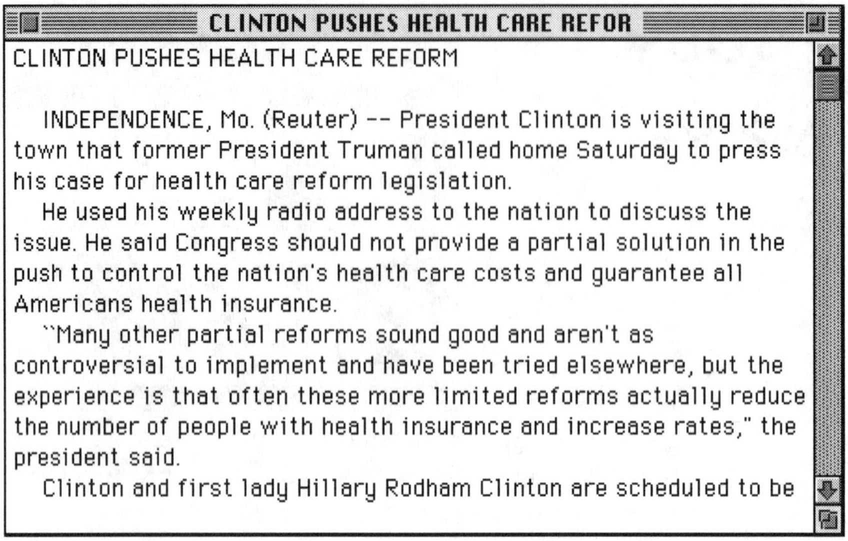

CLINTON PUSHES HEALTH CARE REFOR

CLINTON PUSHES HEALTH CARE REFORM

INDEPENDENCE, Mo. (Reuter) -- President Clinton is visiting the town that former President Truman called home Saturday to press his case for health care reform legislation.
He used his weekly radio address to the nation to discuss the issue. He said Congress should not provide a partial solution in the push to control the nation's health care costs and guarantee all Americans health insurance.
``Many other partial reforms sound good and aren't as controversial to implement and have been tried elsewhere, but the experience is that often these more limited reforms actually reduce the number of people with health insurance and increase rates," the president said.
Clinton and first lady Hillary Rodham Clinton are scheduled to be

Figure 6-1: By double-clicking the sixth lead story pictured in the frontispiece, the complete text of the story is displayed. I can now read, save or print it.

Saving Articles

Whenever an article appears on your screen in the front-most window, it's available for saving on a disk. To save an article (news or other-wise—I'm talking about any article, at any time), just choose Save from the File menu. You'll see a standard Macintosh file-save dialog box, where you can change the article's suggested name and determine its location. (This saving procedure goes for graphics also—see "Down-loading" in Chapter 5, "Computing.")

Saved articles are pure text and can be opened with any word processor. You can open saved articles with AOL's software as well—whether you're online or off—by choosing Open from the File menu.

Keeping a Log

While articles like those pictured in Figure 6-1 are informative, invaluable, and often fascinating, reading them online is not. I prefer to absorb information like that at my leisure, when the online clock isn't running.

The solution is found in AOL's Log feature. When a log is turned on, all text appearing on your screen is recorded on your disk. You can zip through an online session without delay, letting articles flash across your screen with the tempo of an MTV video. Then, when you've accessed what you need, sign off and review the log. Any word processor will open a log file, as will your AOL software: just choose Open from the File menu.

Now that I've read the paragraph above, I feel compelled to make a disclaimer: some things such as portfolios offer their own saving routines; others, such as the EAASY SABRE gateway (discussed in Chapter 11) may have to be copied and pasted into a new document for saving. Generally speaking, the logging feature logs articles—AOL text files—for later review.

To start a log, choose Logs from the File menu, click System, then click Open. America Online will display a standard file-open dialog box complete with a suggested file name and location (Figure 6-2). Change what you want, then click Save. From then on, all the text you see onscreen will be saved on your disk.

Figure 6-2: Log files capture on-screen activity to disk for later review.

A Few Notes Regarding Logs

To capture the complete article in your log you must double-click (open) the article's headline while you're online and allow AOL to complete the article's transmission to your Mac (be sure it's complete: If the More button is active, there's more to follow). When the beachball cursor stops spinning, transmission is complete. You don't have to read it online—you don't even have to scroll to the end of it—you just have to receive it in its entirety.

Log files are limited in size to about 26k. This is roughly 15 pages of text. When AOL reaches that limit, it will open another log file and name it #2, then #3 and so on until your logging session ends.

You can always suspend or stop a log by returning to the Log's window (refer again to Figure 6-2) and clicking the appropriate button. Do this when you're browsing material that you don't want to appear in your log.

If you look carefully at the center window in Figure 6-2, you will note three types of logs. The System log is the one that captures articles such as those discussed in this chapter; it doesn't capture chats and instant messages (discussed in Chapter 12, "People Connection").

Printing Articles

You can print any article that appears in AOL's front-most window. This is best done off-line, when the clock's not running. Again, use the File menu. Choose Print and you'll see your Mac's standard printing dialog box. Make any changes that are necessary to the print configuration and click OK. America Online will print the article to your Mac's currently selected printer. (Refer to your Macintosh manual for a complete description of Macintosh printing procedures.)

Searching the News

Look again at the frontispiece for this chapter. In the upper right corner of the window you'll see an icon labeled "Search News." This is an extremely powerful tool.

It's powerful because it searches not only the world news, but also business, entertainment, sports and even weather. If you know of a subject that's in the news and you want to know more, click this icon.

Look at Figure 6-3. Searching for the word Virus, AOL finds 14 stories in the news, ranging from computer viruses to President

Clinton's Health Plan. Along the way, AOL even found a business item ("Gilead Sciences Announces Fiscal 1995 First Quarter..."). Since my true interest was in the International Anti-(Computer) Virus competition in Holland, I narrowed my search by using the criteria: Computer Virus and conducted the narrower search (four "hits") pictured in the lower window of Figure 6-3.

Figure 6-3: Using the criterion Virus, I receive 14 "hits" in an America Online news search. By specifying Computer Virus, I narrow my search to 4 hits, a much more manageable number.

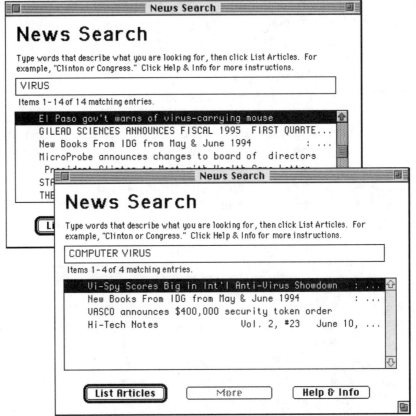

Specifying effective search criteria for AOL's database searches takes a bit of practice and a working knowledge of Boolean operators. You'll find a discussion of database searches in Chapter 13, "Clubs & Interests."

No Criteria

Here's a little trick you might find revealing: conduct a news search with no criteria whatsoever. Leave the criteria field (where the words Virus, and Computer Virus appear in Figure 6-3) empty, then click the List Articles button.

This tells AOL to search for anything, and it will find every article in today's news. Typically, you'll see two to four thousand of them: an indication of the extent of the Today's News Department. America Online subscribes to the Reuters and Associated Press, among others. Few news sources are this extensive.

U.S. & World News

America Online's top stories and News Search features access every news article on file in the Today's News Department—3,200 of them on the day I researched this chapter. If you prefer a more structured approach to your daily news, use the buttons arrayed across the bottom of the Today's News window.

The leftmost of those buttons is labeled "U.S. & World," leading you to an organized presentation of the day's world news (see Figure 6-4). Use the keyword: USNews if you want to access this feature directly.

Command-Period

Some of the articles offered by AOL are lengthy. And sometimes after reading the first few sentences of an article, you will find it's not what you're after. What do you do? Wait while the beach ball cursor spins on your screen, mocking your impatience?

Indeed not. You use the AOL command that means STOP! It works nearly everywhere on AOL and it's especially useful when long articles or lists threaten to make morning molasses out of your Quicksilver Quadra.

This important command is, of course, Command-period. It started with the original Macintosh software as an option to stop printing. Over the years it expanded to include long retrieves, interminable recalculations and everything else in the Macintosh environment that needed interruption now and again.

Now it applies to AOL as well. Whenever you want to interrupt something, press Command-period. It works for long articles, ponderous downloads, dreary mail and ceaseless searches. It's especially valuable when a sluggish sign-on sequence portends a noisy line and a need for redialing. It inspires a feeling of omnipotent power, and it will become your best online friend. Keep it in mind.

Figure 6-4: The U.S. & World News feature structures world news into regions to facilitate browsing. By selecting the "Russia/CIS" entry in the main U.S & World News window, I'm presented with a half-dozen associated news stories.

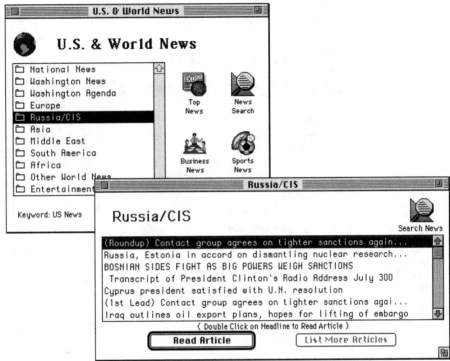

The buttons across the bottom of the Today's News window (review the frontispiece) are analogous to the sections of your daily newspaper. They're especially useful if you're just browsing the news, with no particular interests in mind other than a general subject area.

Business

Don't confuse today's business news with the Personal Finance Department found elsewhere on AOL. The business news offered in the Today's News Department is just that: the news—today's most recent business news from around the world. Investing advice, stock market timing charts, mutual funds and analysis are all discussed in Chapter 10, "Personal Finance."

Like the US & World News area, the Business News area brings a coherent structure to an expansive number of news articles, with categories ranging from Media & Leisure to High Technology (see Figure 6-5).

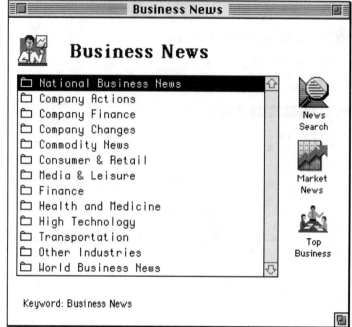

Market News

Look again at Figure 6-5. Do you see the icon labeled Market News?
This is the direct route to AOL's equivalent of the stock market charts
of your daily newspaper (see Figure 6-6). All the information you
expect in your newspaper is here, with one significant difference:
AOL's stock market information is current and updated constantly
during periods of stock market activity.

Figure 6-6:
America Online's
Market News
rarely trails the
NYSE ticker by
more than 20
minutes during
trading. To get
there in a hurry,
use the keyword:
MarketNews.

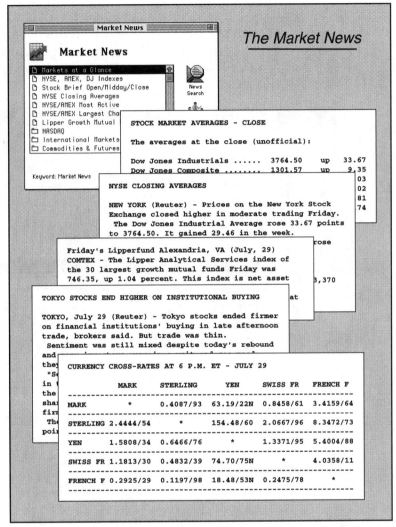

The Market News

Market News

- Markets at a Glance
- NYSE, AMEX, DJ Indexes
- Stock Brief Open/Midday/Close
- NYSE Closing Averages
- NYSE/AMEX Most Active
- NYSE/AMEX Largest Cha
- Lipper Growth Mutual
- NASDAQ
- International Markets
- Commodities & Futures

News Search

Keyword: Market News

STOCK MARKET AVERAGES - CLOSE

The averages at the close (unofficial):

Dow Jones Industrials ...... 3764.50   up   33.67
Dow Jones Composite .... 1301.57   up   9.35

NYSE CLOSING AVERAGES

NEW YORK (Reuter) - Prices on the New York Stock
Exchange closed higher in moderate trading Friday.
The Dow Jones Industrial Average rose 33.67 points
to 3764.50. It gained 29.46 in the week.

Friday's Lipperfund Alexandria, VA (July, 29)
COMTEX - The Lipper Analytical Services index of
the 30 largest growth mutual funds Friday was
746.35, up 1.04 percent. This index is net asset

TOKYO STOCKS END HIGHER ON INSTITUTIONAL BUYING

TOKYO, July 29 (Reuter) - Tokyo stocks ended firmer
on financial institutions' buying in late afternoon
trade, brokers said. But trade was thin.
Sentiment was still mixed despite today's rebound

CURRENCY CROSS-RATES AT 6 P.M. ET - JULY 29

	MARK	STERLING	YEN	SWISS FR	FRENCH F
MARK	*	0.4087/93	63.19/22N	0.8458/61	3.4159/64
STERLING	2.4444/54	*	154.48/60	2.0667/96	8.3472/73
YEN	1.5808/34	0.6466/76	*	1.3371/95	5.4004/88
SWISS FR	1.1813/30	0.4832/39	74.70/75N	*	4.0358/11
FRENCH F	0.2925/29	0.1197/98	18.48/53N	0.2475/78	*

Top Business

If you look again at Figure 6-5 you'll see an additional icon on the right, "Top Business." Click this icon to reveal the business news "lead stories:" the top stories—not of the day, but of the moment (Figure 6-7).

Figure 6-7: A select number of the day's key business news stories are featured in the Top Business section.

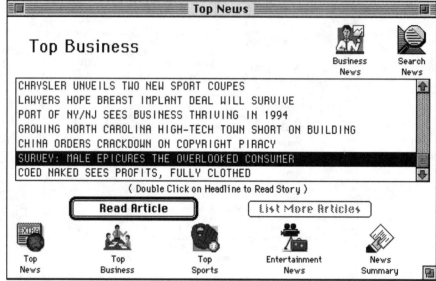

Male Epicureans

With a full-time medical student for a wife, I've become the chef and houseboy at home, a complete role reversal for both of us after 20 years of conjugal conventionalism. I was intrigued, then, when I saw the "Male Epicures the Overlooked Consumer" headline pictured in Figure 6-7. The story (quoted below) tells me I'm far from alone. I never thought of myself as an "overlooked consumer," but I'm willing to be patronized the next time I step into a cooking store.

"SURVEY: MALE EPICURES THE OVERLOOKED CONSUMER

"NEW YORK (Reuter) - Picture this — a kitchen, pots simmering on the stove. Someone is chopping ingredients for a gourmet meal. Expect this to be a woman?

"Wrong. Chances are very good that the chef, and the purchaser of the wine, the china and the espresso machine, is a man.

"A recent study shows men, either as part of families or alone, are in large numbers buying household goods and foods and consider themselves knowledgeable and interested....

"Although women are consistently targeted by advertisers and marketers as the primary household purchaser, men are shopping, cooking and giving parties, the statistics show.

"According to Shifrin Research, a public opinion research firm, men who enjoy food and wine—epicures—make up 30 percent of the adult male population.

"And, according to the survey for *Food and Wine* magazine, men who like to cook at home and eat in restaurants appear to be as involved in buying food as women in general...."

You see? It's about time people start taking us seriously. Now, anyone for macaroni and cheese?

Entertainment

Can you recall an occasion when you purchased a product and were pleasantly surprised when you got more than you bargained for? If you're interested in news from the entertainment field, AOL might be just one of those events.

I say this because without fanfare, the Entertainment section of Today's News is primarily composed of articles from *Variety*, the preeminent industry magazine that profoundly influences people in the entertainment capitals of our nation.

It's posted each day on AOL. All you have to do is click the Entertainment button in the Today's News window (Figure 6-8).

Figure 6-8: The
Entertainment
section of Today's
News features
news of the
entertainment
industry, most of
which is drawn
from *Variety*
magazine.

This is one of AOL's best-kept secrets. Variety magazine is the entertainment industry's Bible, and now you know where to find it.

There's Much More

Don't confuse the Entertainment and Sports sections of the Today's News Department with the Entertainment and Sports Departments themselves. America Online offers much more than is described here for entertainment patrons and sports fans. This chapter discusses today's entertainment and sports news; the Sports and Entertainment Departments are discussed in Chapters 8 and 9 respectively.

Sports

The button marked Sports at the bottom of the Today's News window leads you to Sports News (keyword: SportsNews), pictured in Figure 6-9.

Figure 6-9: Sports News offers not only the top stories, but routes to the sports discussion boards, sports headlines, and various topical sports news areas.

Most of the buttons that surround the window pictured in Figure 6-9 change with the season, but two remain where you see them: Top Sports (a compilation of the lead sports stories of the hour) and Highlights. Clicking the Highlights icon takes you to the Sports Highlights section where, among other things, you'll find Sports Headlines.

I mention Sports Headlines because I want to share a strategy with you. There's a lot of sports news on AOL. You probably won't have the time to read every story. If you're like me, you have a few stories you're following and you want to know about them first.

For this you should use News Search. No matter where you are, use the keyword: NewsSearch, and search for the subjects—sports or otherwise—that interest you.

But that's a somewhat monochromatic strategy. Following one or two sports stories to the exclusion of others ignores the abundance of sports events that transpire every day. Many of these might interest you as well.

Here's my strategy: click the Highlights icon pictured in Figure 6-9, then examine the Sports Headlines (Figure 6-10). The headlines are extensive and ideal for browsing. Once you find a headline that intrigues you, use News Search to find (and read) the story behind the headline.

Figure 6-10: In conjunction with America Online's News Search facility, Sports Headlines offers an effective method for pursuing the sports news of your choice.

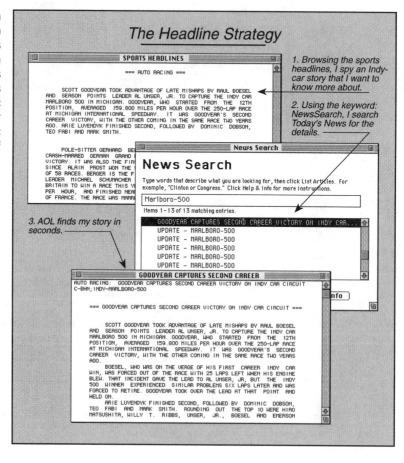

Weather

Naturally, AOL is resplendent with weather information. This is where the online medium really excels. America Online's weather is not only always up to the minute, it's also graphic and colorful.

The primary Weather window (see Figure 6-11) offers access to the day's weather news (check here before traveling or when the weather is particularly interesting), forecasts (updated continuously and organized by state), and boards (lots of experts hang out here: post questions freely); it also offers a route to the color weather maps, and that's where the fun begins.

Figure 6-11: Sometimes the best things come in simple packages: though not a stellar production, America Online's primary Weather window offers a wealth of current weather information, including maps.

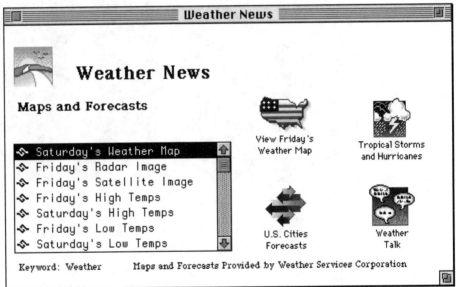

The maps are provided by Weather Services Corporation, which provides forecasting and consultation services for *USA Today*, among others. Those colorful weather maps on the back page of *USA Today* are derived from the same data that's available on AOL when you use the keyword: Weather.

The precipitation, jet stream and tropical outlook maps are released between 10 a.m. and 11 a.m. (Eastern time) each day; the temperature bands for the next day will be available between 6 p.m. and 7 p.m. (see Figure 6-12).

Figure 6-12: You'll have to imagine it here, but each of these maps displays in 16 colors and downloads in less than a minute. To get to them quickly, use the keyword: WeatherMaps.

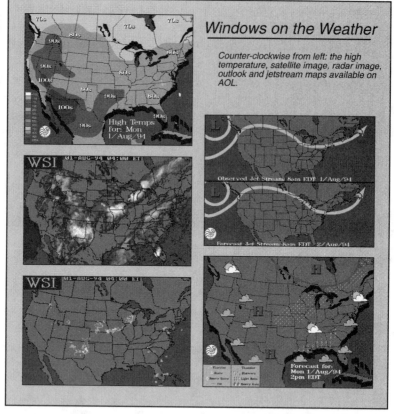

No special software is required for viewing these maps: simply double-click any listing, read the description if you wish, then click the Download Now button. If you're using Version 2.5 (or later) of the AOL software, the maps will be displayed on-screen as they're downloaded. None of them take more than a minute to download at 9600 baud; they'll display satisfactorily even if you don't have a color monitor (or printer); and the files are always available for viewing after you've downloaded them (even after you sign off) by choosing Open from the File menu.

For a detailed description of the downloading process, read Chapter 5, "Computing," and review Figures 5-9 and 5-13.

Moving On

The online medium is a newcomer to the dissemination of the daily news. We've developed the habit of seeking the news in our papers or broadcast media.

The online medium, however, boasts immediacy, comprehensiveness and independence. America Online's news is updated constantly, it never needs to cater to time or space constraints, and there are no advertisers to oblige. More people are discovering this inherent advantage every day. If you follow the news, try this medium for a month and compare.

The list of those who embrace the online medium for the dissemination of news includes the broadcast and print media themselves—many of which appear on AOL. There are so many, in fact, that they now have their own department, the Newsstand, where publications as diverse as CNN, NBC, TIME and even the Gray Lady herself—*The New York Times*—have found a home. It's a diverse and stimulating place, and we begin its exploration on the next page. . . .

CHAPTER 7

The Newsstand

I alluded to the online medium's superiority for the dissemination of journalistic material in the previous chapter. Immediacy was the primary benefit cited there, but the online medium has another significant journalistic benefit: capacity.

Most magazine readers value the printed medium, but if you're like me, you've given up on filing past issues. After a few months, most of my magazines go into the trash. Naturally I regret trashing them soon thereafter, for it's then that I decide to review something I saw in that issue that just contributed to the landfill over the hill.

I have good news, periodical patrons: You can trash those magazines without guilt, because AOL now has the Newsstand, where you can read current issues, save articles, download files and even talk to the editors online. Perhaps best of all, most of AOL's online publications provide database access to past issues. Chances are, if you search for a subject of interest, it's there. That's what I mean by the benefit of capacity.

Macworld Online

There's so much great stuff in the Newsstand, it's hard to know where to begin. One thing I know we all have in common is our Macs; thus Macworld Online (see Figure 7-1) is probably a place to begin.

The Newsstand is AOL's answer to the problem manifest in that stack of magazines in the garage. The Newsstand is not only horizontally comprehensive (lots of publications), it's vertically comprehensive as well (most back issues are searchable). To get there, click the Newsstand button on the Main Menu, or use the keyword: NewsStand.

Figure 7-1:
Everything but the
ads: nearly all the
current issue of
Macworld is
online, plus past
issues and
software libraries.
Use the keyword:
Macworld to
get here.

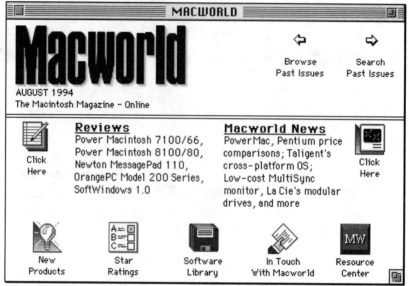

I visit Macworld once a month without fail, and every time I contemplate a purchase—hardware or software—I consult the reviews. A few months ago I researched the availability of a triple-speed CD-ROM drive. A brief search of past issues produced a product announcement of just the device I needed (Figure 7-2).

Figure 7-2:
Searching past
issues of
Macworld,
America Online
found an article
describing the CD-
ROM drive I
eventually
purchased.

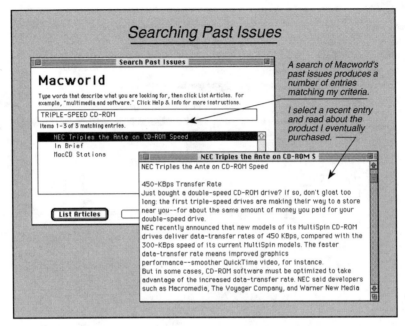

While the ability to search past issues is a primary feature of Macworld Online, hundreds of news stories, reviews and files are also available—all searchable, and all in a form that you can use for inclusion in documents of your own. In addition, a special section called "In Touch With Macworld" features message boards that put you in touch with Macworld's editorial staff, and a library of files offers indices to past issues, macros and programs (Figure 7-3).

Figure 7-3: Articles, product reviews, a library of software (including AreaCodeFinder, which is pictured here) and a one-on-one forum with the editors rounds out Macworld Online.

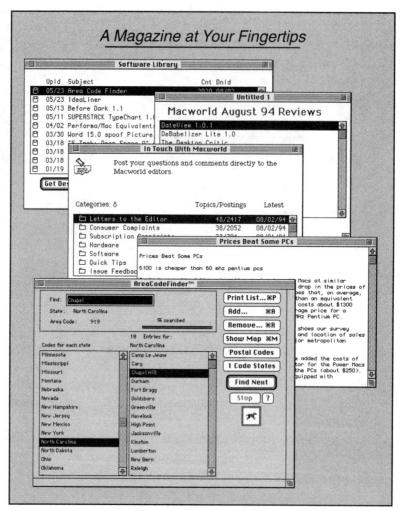

TIME Online

Now here's a bold experiment: *TIME* magazine not only posts its latest issue before it reaches many (non-virtual) news stands, it also posts stories online from its international editions—stories that aren't available in the domestic version of the magazine. The people at *TIME* even post stories that fail to make either edition due to space or time constraints. TIME Online (see Figure 7-4) is the only place you'll find these stories.

Figure 7-4: TIME Online is an experiment in which the world's oldest and largest news magazine plugs into the world's newest and fastest-growing medium.

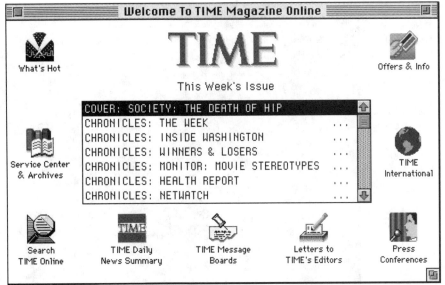

The text of the current issue appears online each Sunday by 4 p.m. (Eastern time). The text of the stories that appear in *TIME*'s international editions appears each Wednesday.

TIME versus CLOCK

Veteran AOL members have no doubt noted one significant change in the service. The keyword: Time no longer produces the online clock. Lots of people depend on that clock to tell them how long they've been online, but when TIME came online, the keyword was reassigned to the magazine. If you want the online clock, use the new keyword: Clock.

There's more. Each evening at 8 p.m. (Eastern time), TIME Online posts a feature called TIME Daily, where *TIME*'s view of the day's late news is offered, along with pointers to message board topics. Pictures from the magazine are available in the Daily News Summary archives, as is the current cover for the magazine (see Figure 7-5).

Figure 7-5: TIME
magazine's covers
are available each
week in GIF and
JPEG formats.
Your America
Online software
will open them for
viewing.

You can search past issues, of course, and send letters to the editors.
WHAT'S HOT lists the best of TIME Online's articles and messages,
and TIME Press Conferences are real-time online interviews with
newsmakers, authors, moviemakers and *TIME* staffers.

This is online journalism at its best. It represents an optimistic
alliance between print and electronic media, and it's only available on
AOL via the keyword: TIME.

@times

Don't confuse *TIME* magazine with *The New York Times*. *The Times* is a newspaper; *TIME* is a magazine. About the only thing they share in common is America Online.

One of the great strengths of *The Times* is its cultural coverage and criticism. For decades, readers have relied on *The Times* critics for guidance in choosing everything from books to videos. Now, with @times, thousands of *Times* reviews—movies, videos, books—are available in one place (see Figure 7-6).

Figure 7-6: @times offers, among other things, the creme de la creme of *The New York Times*: its entertainment and arts features. To get there in a hurry, use the keyword: @times.

Look for *The New York Times* Best Seller List here, along with *The Times* weekday book, video, and movie reviews. @times also features the top international and domestic news, business and sports stories. These stories appear before they're printed in the paper: articles from the next day's newspaper begin appearing after 11 p.m. Sunday to Friday nights and after 9 p.m. on Saturdays.

Data on Demand

Screens such as that pictured in Figure 7-6 are abundant with graphics and interface components. Think of it: in the Newsstand alone, there are scores of publications, each with a screen as complex as that offered by @times.

If all these visual effects were stored on the AOL host computer and fed downline every time you visited a section of the service, AOL would seem as slow as the building of the pyramids. On the other hand, if all of these components were stored on your disk, your AOL folder would be as vast as the inside of Pharaoh's tomb.

There's a compromise, and it's called Data on Demand (or DOD, among AOL's cognoscenti).

Here's the trick: only a few of AOL's special graphics are stored in your AOL folder when you first install the software. When you initially visit an area such as @times, the additional components for that area are downloaded—automatically—to your disk. The download occurs only once—during the first visit to an area—and it's accompanied by a notification similar to that pictured in Figure 7-7.

Figure 7-7: A DOD download occurs the first time you visit an area such as @times.

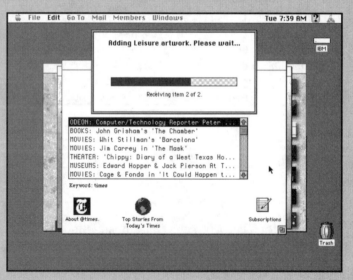

The theory is that each of us visits an abridged number of areas on the service—no one visits every one—so each of us accumulates an Online Database file (that's its name; it's in your AOL folder) that's customized to our personal interests. It's an effective solution to a somewhat unappeasable problem.

Chicago Online

When I first visited AOL's headquarters, the staff was particularly optimistic about a newly launched service called Chicago Online. At that time, Chicago Online represented two significant strategies that made the inauguration of the Newsstand auspicious and that today offer a glimpse into the future of online journalism.

The first strategy is that of a stand-alone, municipal communications service. Chicago Online is a parochial service, optimized for the people of Chicago, by the people of Chicago. It has its own message boards, chat rooms, news, sports and weather (plenty of the latter, actually). In a way, Chicago Online is like a local newspaper. The nation has *USA Today* and *The Wall Street Journal*, and Chicago has the *Chicago Tribune*. The nation has AOL and Chicago has Chicago Online. Neither precludes the need for the other. Nearly every community in the country has its own newspaper; we might someday all have our own little online areas as well. After all, local communications channels are as much a part of the community as national ones. America Online knows that, and that's why they're testing the waters with Chicago Online (see Figure 7-8). (For additional evidence of the potential of this alliance, visit the Mercury Center, an online publication of the *San Jose Mercury News*. Use the keyword: Mercury to get there.)

Figure 7-8: Chicago Online offers a potential glimpse of future telecommunications and a banquet of sustenance for the online appetite as well.

The second strategy is that of the strategic alliance. Chicago Online is the product of an alliance between the *Chicago Tribune* and AOL. The *Tribune* gains a communications channel that's significantly more bilateral (and less costly) than a daily newspaper, and AOL gets a test bed for another avenue in the electronic community. Perhaps best of all, we all get to observe the formative moments of a new communications medium. Ecologically speaking, the "electronic newspaper" (or something like it) will soon be a necessity, and this alliance represents the exploration of that potential by two of the most progressive representatives of the electronics and newspaper industries. There's lots of hope here, for all of us.

But enough existentialism. *The Chicago Tribune* is no lightweight when it comes to information, after all. There's a wealth of practical information for us outlanders. Check out Gene Siskel's Flick Picks (and Dave Kehr, Roy Leonard, and Sherman Kaplan's reviews), Ed Curran's *Technogadgets* and the *Chicago Tribune Cookbook Online*. Chicago Online isn't a half-hearted experiment in alternative media, it's a mature, expansive and resourceful communications medium. Give it a half-hour of your time. It will reward you eloquently.

Moving On

There are scores of publications in the Newsstand. Many cater to specific interests, others serve more general needs. Be sure to check out *Bicycling Magazine, New Republic, Omni, Smithsonian, WIRED* (mentioned in Chapter 14, "The Internet Connection"), *Popular Photography, Saturday Review, Worth,* and any others that appeal to you. This place is a quarry of priceless literary nuggets, and you pay nothing extra for access to it.

For many, literature is a staple of life. Sports, then, is no doubt its condiment. Shall we sprinkle a bit of it on AOL? Turn the page. . .

Sports

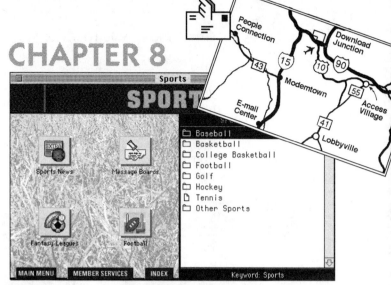

CHAPTER 8

A friend of
mine brought a smile to my face when she related a story about her
boyfriend. In something of a reversal of stereotypes, *she* is the computer
fanatic of the two; until recently, he had no interest whatever in the
subject.

He does, however, have a keen interest in sports. She discovered the
Sports Department on the first day she signed on to AOL. Grabbing
him by the hair (I'm taking some creative license here, but I kind of like
the reverse Cro-Magnon image), she sat him down in front of the
screen and made him explore the department with her. In minutes he
was using the mouse, typing messages and downloading files. He had
never used a computer before, and now she can't get him away from it.

Ah, but now who will slay the giant mastodon and protect the cave
from the wily saber-toothed tiger?

The News

I discussed Sports News in Chapter 6, "Today's News," so I won't
spend much time on the subject here. Note, however, that the Sports
News icon in the upper left corner of the Sports Department's main
window (see Figure 8-1) leads to the same categories of sports news
that appear in the scroll list in the main window. In other words, if
you're here to browse the news, save yourself a mouse click or two and
browse the stories from the main Sports window rather than from the
Sports News icon.

The Sports Department offers sports news, sports message boards, sports files and
Fantasy League games. To get there, click the Sports option on AOL's Main Menu, or
use the keyword Sports.

On the other hand, the Sports News icon does lead to the news-searching mechanism discussed in Chapter 6. If you're seeking information on a specific subject and you're not in the mood for browsing, use this method of searching AOL's database of current sports articles. Click the Highlights icon.

Figure 8-1: The main Sports Department window and the Sports News window duplicate content.

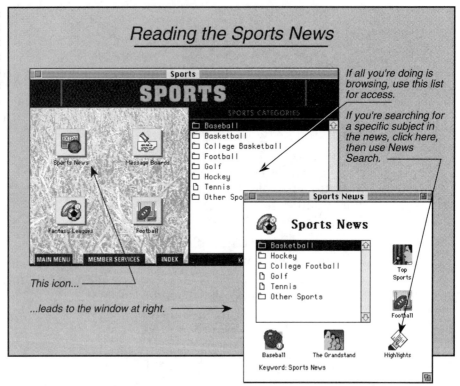

The Message Boards

Sports fans like to talk about their interests with other sports fans. Sports talk is especially rewarding when it's carried on with people who aren't directly within your sphere of acquaintance, especially with people who live all over the country. If this sounds appealing, consider visiting the Sports Department's message boards (Figure 8-2).

Figure 8-2: Don't let the Grandstand moniker fool you. These are the Sports Department's message boards—a feature of the Grandstand perhaps, but not the Grandstand itself. I'll discuss the Grandstand (and how to get there) in a few pages.

Messages on the sports boards are diverse and occasionally unexpected. Consider the thread of messages I found on the Golf board (pictured in Figure 8-3). When was the last time you talked directly to the programmer of your favorite computer game?

Figure 8-3: Now we know what golfers do in the winter: They play golf—on their Macs.

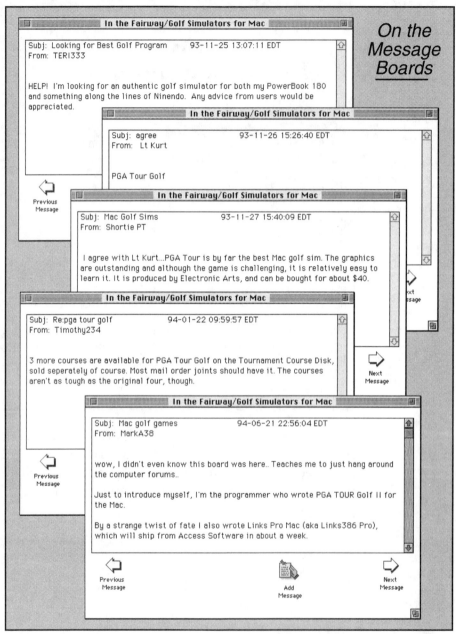

Message boards are wonderful things, but getting to know how to use them effectively takes a little learning. Assistance is provided in Chapter 13, "Clubs & Interests."

The Grandstand

If you enjoy sports, you'll love the Grandstand (use the keyword Grandstand; it's the most effective way of getting there). America Online's homage to the sports enthusiast is current, relevant and vast (Figure 8-4). In the interest of sports widows and widowers everywhere, however, I suggest moderation. The walls of prehistoric caves the world over are riddled with pictographs of smashed keyboards and fractured computer screens. It's not a pretty sight.

Figure 8-4: The Grandstand offers something for every sports enthusiast.

While investigating the Grandstand the other day, I downloaded a Microsoft Excel spreadsheet file that offered plenty of features for World Cup soccer fans (part of which is pictured in Figure 8-5). I also discovered an online club dedicated entirely to baseball cards, providing news, price polls and conferences for baseball card collectors throughout the nation.

Figure 8-5: A quick browse through the Grandstand turns up a picture of a Ferrari 412 T1 uploaded by Nigel Mans, a rendition of the NHL World Cup logo created by Roby Baggio, a World Cup tracking spreadsheet for Microsoft Excel by Stan Nickle, and a little application called NCAA OfficePool by Arlington-Boyd.

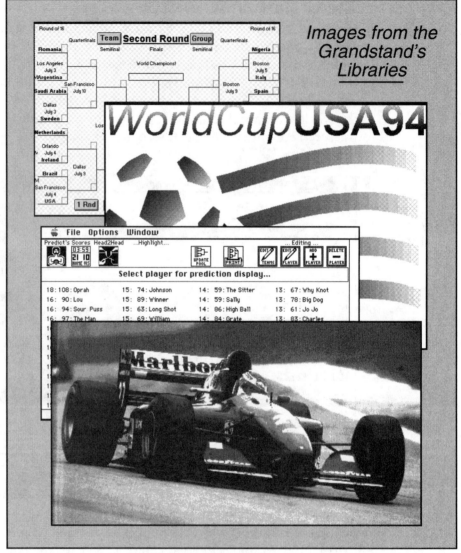

Perhaps the most interesting aspect of the Grandstand is its assortment of fantasy teams assembled by members—make-believe teams made up of real players in the sport. The Grandstand Fantasy Baseball League (GFBL), for example, is modeled after "Rotisserie League Baseball," as described in the book of the same name by Glen Waggoner (Bantam Books). Team owners (that's us—the members of AOL) each draft 23 players from the available talent in the American or

National League. The players' actual big-league performances are used in computing the standings of the GFBL team. Standings (see Figure 8-6), stats, newsletters and other league information are found in the message and library sections of the GFBL, and members watch them fanatically. Double-click any of the folders in the scroll box of the Grandstand's main window to access the leagues.

Figure 8-6: The end-of-July standings of the GFBL National League. Kornbread's Krumbs seem to be pulverizing the competition.

Fantasy Baseball

```
GFBL National League K      Backporch Baseball '94 by UofDWare
07/31/94                 League Standings              Page   1


Team Name        Total  BA    HR    RBI   STL   ERA   WIN   SAV   RAT
---------------  -----  ----  ----  ----  ----  ----  ----  ----  ----
Kornbread's Kru  77.0  11.0  11.0  11.0   9.0  10.0  11.0   3.0  11.0
Legal Eagles     66.0  12.0   5.0   8.0   1.0  12.0   7.0   9.0  12.0
Black Labs       65.5   8.0   6.0  10.0  11.0   9.0   8.0   5.5   8.0
Wolverines       64.5  10.0   7.5   9.0   7.5  11.0   4.0   5.5  10.0
Cunctating Mast  57.0   7.0  12.0  12.0  10.0   6.0   5.0   4.0   1.0
Trolley Dodgers  52.0   2.0   2.0   1.0  12.0   7.0  12.0  10.0   6.0
Hebron Settlers  46.0   1.0   3.0   2.0   3.0   8.0   9.0  11.0   9.0
Master Batters   45.0   5.0   7.5   7.0   7.5   2.0  10.0   1.0   5.0
Hell Razors      43.0   9.0   1.0   4.0   6.0   3.0   1.0  12.0   7.0
P.A.'s           43.0   6.0  10.0   6.0   5.0   4.0   6.0   2.0   4.0
Clutchers        37.0   4.0   9.0   5.0   2.0   5.0   2.0   7.0   3.0
Team Terrific    28.0   3.0   4.0   3.0   4.0   1.0   3.0   8.0   2.0
```

Moving On

Speaking of games, it's time to move on to the Entertainment Department, where games (along with television, radio, movies, books, music, cartoons, columnists and critics) abound.

Sounds like an interesting place. Turn the page and let's see what it has to offer.

Entertainment

I've made a number of online friends over the years, and I've developed ongoing philosophical discussions with a few of them: it's my brain food and I enjoy it.

The other day a friend and I were discussing some of the significant changes in the American lifestyle over the past 100 years. Our conclusion: three major developments have changed that lifestyle forever: (1) the automobile, (2) the computer, and (3) the media.

That last development is the one that brings us to the subject of this chapter: Entertainment. Imagine entertainment when there were no movies, no videos, no television, no magazines, and very few books! What did those people do with their time? They certainly didn't hang around AOL's Entertainment Department.

That opportunity, it would appear, is uniquely ours. And it's one you're not going to want to miss. This place is rife with the spangles of technoglitter.

What's Hot

You'll want to begin your Entertainment Department visits here. The contents of What's Hot (note its icon in the frontispiece to this chapter) change constantly, listing a practical number of timely entertainment topics (see Figure 9-1).

The Entertainment Department not only offers a banquet of riches for watchers, readers and listeners, it also provides an avenue of communication with the writers, stars and producers. It's an exposition for multimedia habitues, and it's available via the Main Menu or the keyword: Entertainment.

Figure 9-1: As I write this chapter, NBC, CSPAN, Court TV and MTV are What's Hot. (Helen Hunt and Paul Reiser of NBC's *Mad About You* appear in the background. Their graphic is filed in the NBC libraries.)

Critics' Choice

Critics' Choice (see Figure 9-2) is actually a multimedia syndicate, specializing in entertainment reviews. You'll find their reviews not only on AOL, but in newspapers as well. Their mission is to serve as a provident guide to entertainment—a mission they fulfill admirably. Use the keyword Critics.

Figure 9-2: Though there are lots of places to find reviews of books, television, videos and movies online, I prefer Critics' Choice.

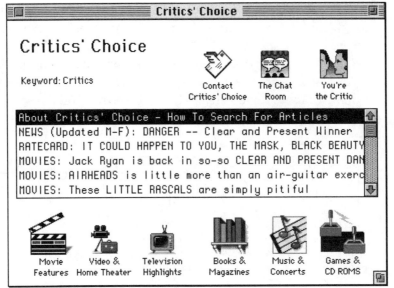

A Review of Online Reviews

While Critics' Choice is AOL's sovereign source of media reviews, you'll find a number of others. *Hollywood Online* (discussed later in this chapter) is one, *The New York Times* and the *Chicago Tribune* (discussed in Chapter 7, "The Newsstand") are a couple of others. The *San Jose Mercury-News* offers reviews as well (keyword: Mercury), and so does *TIME* (keyword: TIME).

The Afterwards Coffeehouse (keyword: art) discusses art, the *Atlantic Monthly* (keyword: Atlantic) and *Saturday Review* (keyword: Saturday) magazines review a wide variety of media, and RockLink (keyword: RockLink) reviews music. Try each one of these services: that's the only way to find the reviewers whose preferences match yours.

The RateCard (third item in the list box in Figure 9-2) is especially convenient if you're intending to see a movie. Reviews from *The New York Times, Playboy, Gannett News Service, Mercury News,* National Public Radio, *Chicago Tribune* and *USA Today* are all summarized in the RateCard, as are the venerable Gene Siskel and Roger Ebert. Though many of these reviewers are found elsewhere on the service, they're all collectively quoted here: a handy feature for moviegoers (see Figure 9-3).

Figure 9-3: The RateCard is a quick way to see what the reviewers have to say about the current crop of movies.

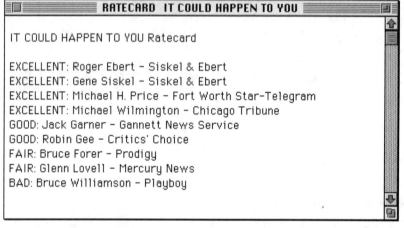

```
RATECARD  IT COULD HAPPEN TO YOU

IT COULD HAPPEN TO YOU Ratecard

EXCELLENT: Roger Ebert - Siskel & Ebert
EXCELLENT: Gene Siskel - Siskel & Ebert
EXCELLENT: Michael H. Price - Fort Worth Star-Telegram
EXCELLENT: Michael Wilmington - Chicago Tribune
GOOD: Jack Garner - Gannett News Service
GOOD: Robin Gee - Critics' Choice
FAIR: Bruce Forer - Prodigy
FAIR: Glenn Lovell - Mercury News
BAD: Bruce Williamson - Playboy
```

The remainder of Critics' Choice offers consummate, relevant reviews of all of today's media (see Figure 9-4). As you examine Figure 9-4, note the Coming Soon feature in the movies section and the Laserdisk Report in the video section. The television section offers descriptions of this week's episodes for nearly all shows; the magazine section describes the feature stories of dozens of popular magazines; the music section offers a gift guide; and the games section offers strategies and tips.

Figure 9-4: The contents of Critics' Choice. Nearly every current attraction is reviewed, and all reviews are searchable.

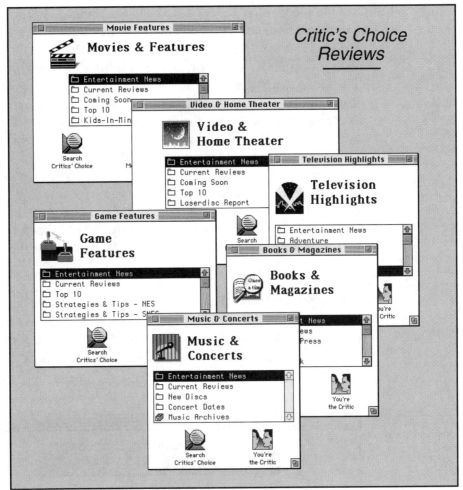

Search Tips

All the reviews in Critics' Choice are searchable—just click any of the search icons pictured in Figure 9-4. Want to see a really great movie? Search for "4STAR." Want to take the kids to a matinee? Search for "MPAAG." Want a review of a Scott Turow novel? Search for "thriller and legal." Searching methods are described in "About Critics' Choice," available from the area's main screen.

Don't forget the Critics' Choice video reviews. If you're like me, you can spend hours in a video store and leave with nothing to show for it. Unless I know what I want before I walk in the door, I become a tremulous enormity of indecision after 10 minutes of video-store browsing. The video store in my town is about the size of Texas. It's hard to browse in a store the size of Texas. Either you know what you want or you're swallowed by the immensity of it all, wandering aimlessly in a labyrinth of racks and little plastic boxes where the exits are known only to the pubescent knaves who staff the place.

Critics' Choice is an operative example of the potential that online services represent today. The Critics' Choice database is vast, and no place gathers the arsenal of reviewers that the RateCard does. Before you buy the popcorn; before you fire up the VCR; before you visit a bookstore or record shop, make Critics' Choice your first stop.

Hollywood Online

Hollywood Online offers all of the things you'd expect from its title: pictures of your favorite stars from the Pictures and Sounds library, cast and production notes in Movie Notes, and talk on the Movie Talk message board (see Figure 9-5).

Figure 9-5: Hollywood Online is a prototype of online multimedia resources—and it's available now via the keyword Hollywood.

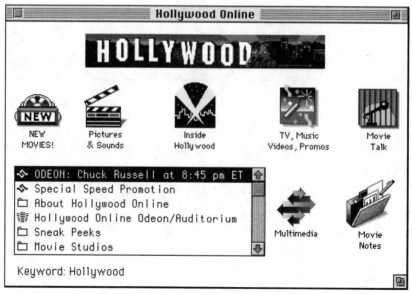

Two other things, however, fascinate me: (1) You can download sneak previews of selected motion pictures before they're released, and (2) multimedia figures heavily in Hollywood Online's contents. Film clips are complete with color, sound and animation; and interactive "kits" provide an opportunity to browse a film's contents, allowing you to replay scenes that interest you and skip those that don't.

Still pictures, posters and sound clips are available here as well, and most of them download in less than two minutes at 9600 baud (see Figure 9-6).

Figure 9-6: Against a backdrop poster from "The Next Karate Kid" starring Hilary Swank, I've pasted clips of Harrison Ford in "Clear and Present Danger," Bridget Fonda in "It Could Happen to You," and Jim Carrey in "The Mask." They're all available in the Pictures & Sounds library of Hollywood Online.

Be sure to check out Joey Berlin's "Inside Hollywood" (Figure 9-7). His long list of credits includes *The Los Angeles Times*, *New York Newsday* and the *New York Post*. He also writes the nationally syndicated newspaper columns "Film Close-Up" and "Pop Talk" for the Copley New Service.

Figure 9-7:
Joey Berlin's Inside
Hollywood is a
must for the
theatre goer.

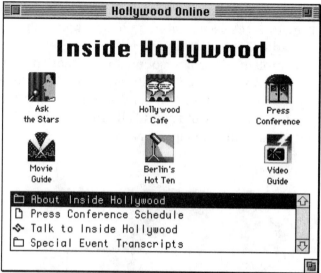

Book Bestsellers

Two features in Book Bestsellers are of particular interest. The first is
the bestseller lists (Figure 9-8), compiled by the trade magazine *Publishers
Weekly* and presented as they appear in *The Wall Street Journal*. These
lists serve as an alternative to the lists that appear in *The New York
Times* (discussed in Chapter 7, "The Newsstand"). Compare them: the
differences are occasionally enlightening.

Figure 9-8: The bestseller lists and reviews found in Book Bestsellers. To get here quickly, use the keyword: Books.

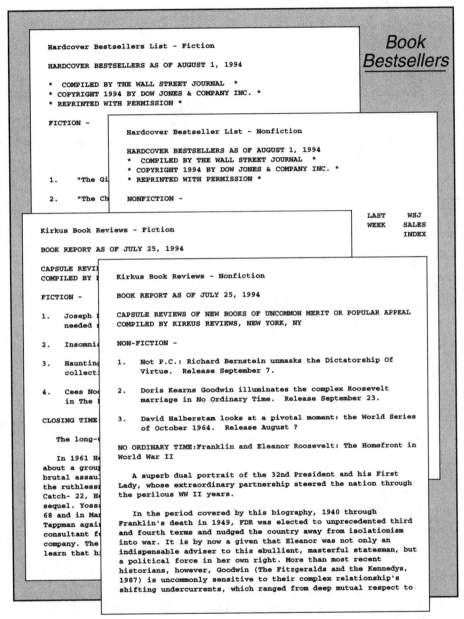

```
Hardcover Bestsellers List - Fiction

HARDCOVER BESTSELLERS AS OF AUGUST 1, 1994

*  COMPILED BY THE WALL STREET JOURNAL  *
* COPYRIGHT 1994 BY DOW JONES & COMPANY INC. *
* REPRINTED WITH PERMISSION *

FICTION -

            Hardcover Bestseller List - Nonfiction

            HARDCOVER BESTSELLERS AS OF AUGUST 1, 1994
            *  COMPILED BY THE WALL STREET JOURNAL  *
            * COPYRIGHT 1994 BY DOW JONES & COMPANY INC. *
1.   "The Gi  * REPRINTED WITH PERMISSION *

2.   "The Ch  NONFICTION -

                                                    LAST    WSJ
                                                    WEEK    SALES
                                                            INDEX
Kirkus Book Reviews - Fiction

BOOK REPORT AS OF JULY 25, 1994

CAPSULE REVI
COMPILED BY    Kirkus Book Reviews - Nonfiction

FICTION -      BOOK REPORT AS OF JULY 25, 1994

1.   Joseph    CAPSULE REVIEWS OF NEW BOOKS OF UNCOMMON MERIT OR POPULAR APPEAL
     needed    COMPILED BY KIRKUS REVIEWS, NEW YORK, NY

2.   Insomni   NON-FICTION -

3.   Haunting  1.   Not P.C.: Richard Bernstein unmasks the Dictatorship Of
     collect:       Virtue.  Release September 7.

4.   Cees No   2.   Doris Kearns Goodwin illuminates the complex Roosevelt
     in The          marriage in No Ordinary Time.  Release September 23.

CLOSING TIME   3.   David Halberstam looks at a pivotal moment: the World Series
                    of October 1964.  Release August ?
     The long-
               NO ORDINARY TIME:Franklin and Eleanor Roosevelt: The Homefront in
  In 1961 H    World War II
about a grou
brutal assau      A superb dual portrait of the 32nd President and his First
the ruthless   Lady, whose extraordinary partnership steered the nation through
Catch- 22, H   the perilous WW II years.
sequel. Yoss
68 and in Ma      In the period covered by this biography, 1940 through
Tappman agai   Franklin's death in 1949, FDR was elected to unprecedented third
consultant f   and fourth terms and nudged the country away from isolationism
company. The   into war. It is by now a given that Eleanor was not only an
learn that h   indispensable adviser to this ebullient, masterful statesman, but
               a political force in her own right. More than most recent
               historians, however, Goodwin (The Fitzgeralds and the Kennedys,
               1987) is uncommonly sensitive to their complex relationship's
               shifting undercurrents, which ranged from deep mutual respect to
```

The second feature is the reviews, compiled by Kirkus Reviews of New York. These reviews appear before the books become available at book stores and libraries. Kirkus hires independent reviewers, so the reviews are often more diverse than those appearing in *The Times*. Again, compare for yourself, and—if you are a true literati—give thanks that AOL offers alternatives such as this.

Don't forget the Book Bestseller boards! This is the place for your reviews—often the most incisive of all.

Cartoons

Let's take a little survey. What's the first section you read when you pick up the Sunday paper? If you're like me, you read "the funnies" before anything else. Often they're the *only* thing I read, depending on how dreary the world has been that week.

America Online is particularly rich in cartoons, and you don't have to wait until Sunday morning to enjoy them. A number of nationally acclaimed cartoonists contribute to AOL each week including:

- Charles Rodriguez, who produces cartoons regularly for *MacWEEK* magazine; his work has appeared in *Stereo Review* and *National Lampoon* as well. His "CompuToons" are computer-related and available only on AOL.

- Mike Keefe, a nationally syndicated cartoonist based in Denver. Mike and his cartoons are featured in Chapter 19, "FlashSessions & the Download Manager."

- Peter Oakley, who began drawing pictures on his Macintosh Plus in 1987 using MacPaint software. He now lives in Seattle, where he's a full-time cartoonist drawing for a number of publications, including AOL's own "Modern Wonder" cartoon series.

The Cartoonist's Life

The cartoonist's life seems like an easy one. All you have to do is sketch a funny picture, then send it off to a magazine and wait for a big check to come back in the mail.

Peter Oakley knows better. On the subject of the cartoonist's life he writes, "The truth is that magazine cartooning is extremely competitive, there are hundreds of remarkably talented cartoonists out there, and few of us are what you would call famous. And because I am doing something new, there was considerable resistance to 'computer-generated' cartoons in the traditional pen-and-ink cartoon market. Of course, the most comfortable home for these cartoons is on the computer, and so it was just a matter of time before they would show up on a telecommunications network. [America Online] is the first national network to host a regular cartoon feature, and I am glad 'Modern Wonder' has found a home here."

Figure 9-9: Three 'toons from the Cartoon Forum: "Heavy Fog," by Theresa McCracken; "Whistle," by Charles Rodriguez; and "Crash and Burn," by Peter Oakley. New cartoons are posted weekly in the Entertainment Department.

As you might assume by looking at Figure 9-9, cartoons from members are available as well, and there's a lively discussion on the Toon Talk message board involving all who find an interest in cartooning.

Columnists & Features Online

Columnists & Features Online is the best way to read provocative newspaper columnists and communicate with them online (see Figure 9-10).

Figure 9-10:
Columnists &
Features Online
offers current
material as well as
an extensive,
searchable library.
Use the keyword:
Columnists.

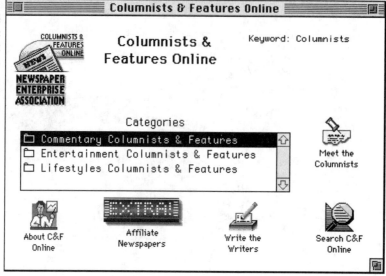

The Newspaper Enterprise Association (NEA) syndicates distinguished writers and political columnists to newspapers nationwide, including the 29 (a number that's sure to grow) featured on AOL (see Figure 9-11).

Figure 9-11: A sample of the columnists available via America Online, assembled for bilateral discourse via Columnists & Features Online.

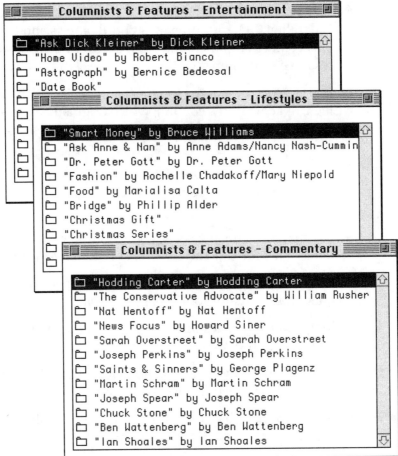

The text of each column appears the same day it is released to the newspapers and remains online for a week. After that, past columns are posted in the library and can be searched using standard AOL criteria. Some of the columnists include:

▲ Hodding Carter III, State Department spokesman for Jimmy Carter's administration, offers sharp opinions on today's issues from the perspective of a respected insider and noted partisan of strong, active government.

▲ "The Conservative Advocate" by William Rusher. Written by the former publisher of *National Review*, "The Conservative Advocate" jabs and lampoons liberals and the left, mixing humor and political commentary in this popular voice of the American right.

- "Environment" by J.D. Hair. The president of the National Wildlife Federation, J.D. Hair offers insightful reports and timely accounts of current environmental concerns, covering all aspects of natural resource protection.

- Nat Hentoff. One of the foremost authorities on the First Amendment, Nat Hentoff's column, which originally appears in *The Washington Post*, examines how legislative decisions affect our basic freedoms to speak, write, think and assemble.

- "Saints And Sinners" by George Plagenz. A personal look at family values and spiritual issues from an ordained minister and news veteran.

- Ian Shoales. Amusing social commentary from this popular National Public Radio and *San Francisco Examiner* humor columnist.

- Martin Schram. Politics with a liberal perspective from this frequent commentator for CNN's *The Capital Gang*.

- Joseph Spear. An advocate for the average American, Spear offers witty, insightful political commentary.

- "Home Video" by Robert Bianco. Up-to-the-minute reviews of home video releases from this *Pittsburgh Post-Gazette* journalist.

- "Smart Money" by radio personality Bruce Williams. Gives incisive answers to personal finance questions.

- "The Tax Adviser" by George Smith. Advice for year-round tax planning from an experienced CPA.

- "Wheels" by Peter Bohr. Advice on keeping your car in shape from this contributing editor to *Road & Track*.

- "Ask Anne & Nan" by Anne B. Adams and Nancy Nash-Cummings. Household hints from two expert problem-solvers and National Public Radio personalities.

- Dr. Peter Gott. Medical advice from this practicing physician and patients' rights advocate.

- "Fashion" by Rochelle Chadakoff and Mary Martin Niepold. Trends and tips on the latest fashions, plus interviews with leading designers.

- "Food" by Marialisa Calta. Witty observations and easy-to-prepare recipes from this well-known food journalist.

- "Astrograph" (horoscope) by Bernice Bede Osol. What's in the stars for you? You'll find it in "Astrograph," one of the most popular astrology columns in America.

Horoscopes

Mention of Bernice Bede Osol's "Astrograph" column reminds me that horoscopes play a transcendental role in the Entertainment Department. Daily horoscopes for each of the astrological signs are posted each week; you're welcome to consult them before you do anything rash. Use the keyword: Horoscope to access this area quickly.

Figure 9-12: That's my horoscope you're reading there. Let's see...it appears as if today would be a good day to call my broker (a Capricorn) and buy 654 shares of AOL stock...

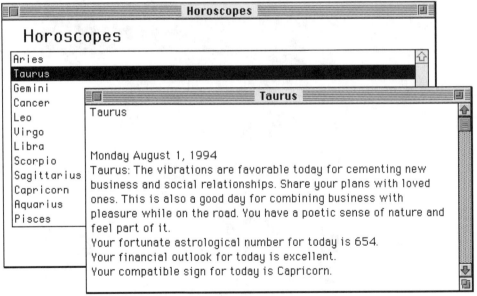

The Grateful Dead Forum

In Chapter 1, I mentioned my preference for classical music. Stephen King might do his writing while rock and roll plays at 120 decibels, but I write to Mozart. I'm not a purist, however. As an Oregonian and a former "radical" of the '60s, I confess a liking for the Grateful Dead. The Dead are especially fond of Oregon, and they exhibit that fondness with an annual visit to Eugene, a Mecca for Deadheads if there ever was one.

Two years ago while I was writing the first edition of this book, the Grateful Dead was just another board on the RockLink Forum. It was a crowded board—its messages always numbered around 500—but just a board nonetheless. The other day when I looked in on the Dead I discovered they had a forum of their own (Figure 9-13). Something peculiar is going on here. This band is older than color TV, yet it provokes one of the most active areas on AOL today.

Figure 9-13: The Grateful Dead Forum defies rational interpretation. (Text significantly edited by the author.)

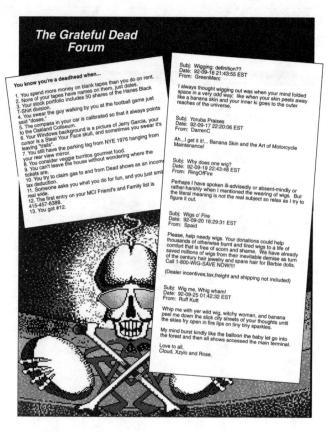

The Trivia Club

One of the most active chat rooms on AOL (we'll discuss chat rooms in Chapter 12, "People Connection") is the Trivia room. This is one of the two places where trivia addicts get their fix.

The other is the Trivia Club (keyword: Trivia), where the Trivia Teaser (see Figure 9-14) is offered each day. Free time is awarded once a month to the highest three scorers in each trivia game. The Club's library has profiles of some great triviots, sounds for use in the chat room games, and graphics of some of the staff and players.

Figure 9-14: You've gotta be fast to win in the Trivia Club's Trivia Teaser. The correct answer was posted in just over two minutes after the question was published.

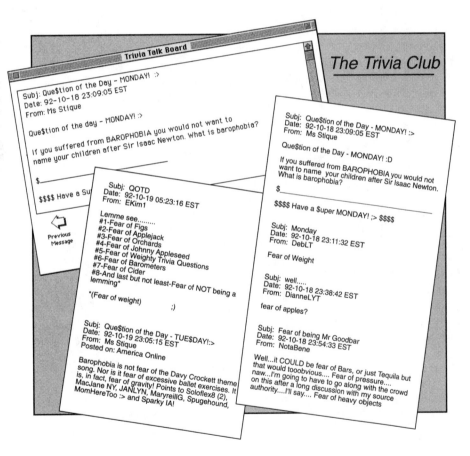

Moving On

From the trivial to the profound, we now make the not inconsiderable transition to the world of the Personal Finance Department. Lots of people subscribe to AOL for financial purposes alone, and AOL rewards them with relevant (and current) information, and advice from professionals and fellow investors alike. Grab your checkbook and turn the page. . .

Personal Finance

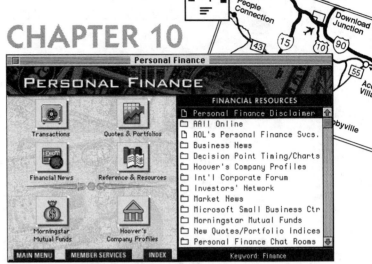

Have you ever seen those little radios that pick up weather reports? I use one every day. It's tuned to the local National Oceanic and Atmospheric Administration (NOAA) station, which broadcasts nothing but the weather 24 hours a day. These gadgets are the ideal information machine: always current, always available and nearly free. Now if I could only find a similar source for financial information.

Aha! What about AOL? If there ever was a machine for instant financial news, this is it. Unlike television or radio, AOL's market information is available whenever you want it: There's no waiting for the six o'clock news or suffering through three stories (and four commercials) that you don't want to hear before they get around to the one you do. Unlike newspapers, AOL's financial news is always current. It's not this morning's news, it's this minute's news. It's current, it's always available and it's almost free.

I wonder if Ted Turner knows about this?

Your Personal Stock Portfolio

Let's begin this chapter with a financial exercise. This one is risk-free, but nonetheless, quite real. A portfolio of investments is a fascinating thing to follow and nourish, even if it's only make-believe. And if you want to add some real punch to it, AOL offers a brokerage service. You can invest real money in real issues and realize real gains (or real losses).

The Personal Finance Department is an anchorage for investors in the sea of financial bedlam. There's financial data here in plenty, and it's pertinent, precise and never more than 15 minutes old. Click the Personal Finance button on the main menu, or use the keyword: Finance.

Whether you intend to invest real cash or funny money, join me as we create a personal portfolio of stocks and securities.

Quotes & Portfolios

Begin the journey by clicking the Personal Finance button on the Main Menu or by typing Command-k and entering the keyword: Finance. America Online responds by transporting you to the Finance Department (see Figure 10-1).

Figure 10-1: America Online might be the perfect financial information machine: it's always current and it's available 24 hours a day.

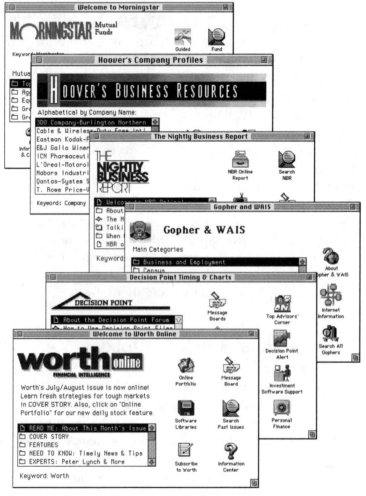

A wealth (pun intended) of financial information awaits you here, as does opportunity. You cannot only seek counsel on your investments, you can actually buy them here and maintain a portfolio as well. And that, for the moment, is our focus. Click the icon labeled Quotes & Portfolios, and let's invest our surplus cash (see Figure 10-2).

Figure 10-2: The Quotes & Portfolios window allows you to access market news, look up an issue, build a portfolio and actually buy and sell issues. It's available from the main window of the Personal Finance window, or use the keyword Quotes.

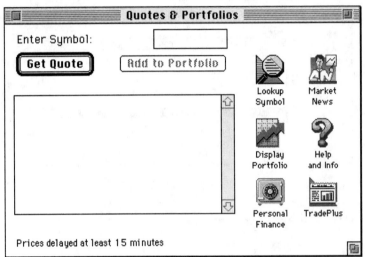

The Quotes & Portfolios section of the Personal Finance Department is a comprehensive financial information service equaled by few others in the telecommunications industry and available on AOL without surcharge. The only thing you pay when you're visiting here is your normal connect-time charges. America Online is connected to the financial centers of the world via high-speed telephone lines, providing financial information updated continuously during market hours on a 15-minute (minimum) delay basis.

Finding a Stock Symbol

America Online is waiting for us to enter a stock symbol. Stock symbols are those abbreviations you see traveling across the Big Board in a stockbroker's office. What shall we buy? Since it's something that we all have in common, let's look up AOL. America Online is a publicly traded issue, after all, so we should offer a reference to it here.

But what's AOL's symbol? Hmmm . . . Let's try the Lookup Stock Symbol icon. When you click that icon and follow the path pictured in Figure 10-3, we discover that AMER is the symbol for America Online.

Figure 10-3: Don't know the symbol for an issue? Let America Online look it up for you.

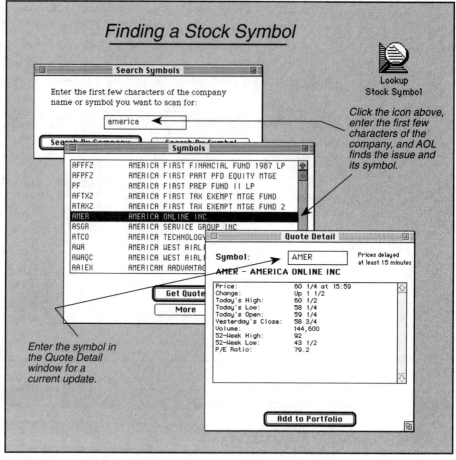

Once you have the symbol, enter it into the box indicated in Figure 10-3 and click on the Get Quote button. The results are pictured in Figure 10-3's scroll box.

Building the Portfolio

Note the current price, then click on the Add to Portfolio button. America Online responds with the dialog box shown in Figure 10-4.

Figure 10-4: Enter
the current price
and the number of
shares, then click
OK. The
"investment" will
be added to your
portfolio.

Stock symbol: AMER

Number of shares: 100

Purchase price: 55 1/4

**Leave both "Number of shares" and
"Purchase Price" blank to exclude from
portfolio value calculation.**

[OK] | Cancel]

Since this is only make-believe, buy as many shares as you'd like. Don't worry: AOL doesn't share your portfolio with anyone, and you won't be charged any special fees for this exercise; it's a private matter between you and your computer.

My portfolio consists of the AOL investment I've just described, plus additional investments in Apple Computer, IBM (no favorites here) and Intel (an Oregon company; it pays to invest locally). Whenever I want to know how my portfolio is doing, I use the keyword: Portfolio, and view the window pictured in Figure 10-5.

Figure 10-5: My
"fantasy portfolio"
includes shares in
Apple Computer,
America Online,
IBM and Intel. If
only it was real. . .

Stock Portfolio

Total portfolio value: $17,018.75 (+706.25)

Symbol	Qty.	Curr. Price	Change	Purch. Price	Gain/ Loss	Value
AAPL	100	29 3/4	−1/2	45 7/8	−1,612.50	2,975.00
AMER	100	55 1/4	−1	12 5/8	+4,262.50	5,525.00
IBM	50	44 1/8	−3/8	92 3/4	−2,431.25	2,206.25
INTC	100	63 1/8	−1 1/8	58 1/4	+487.50	6,312.50

[Details]   [Remove]   [Save Portfolio...]

Charting the Portfolio

One of the little-known features offered by AOL is its ability to save portfolios on a disk, providing fuel for electronic spreadsheet programs like Microsoft's Excel (see Figure 10-6).

Figure 10-6: By saving my portfolio and using Excel's data parsing feature, I can graph my portfolio's performance over time. If you're an Excel user, read the sidebar for instructions.

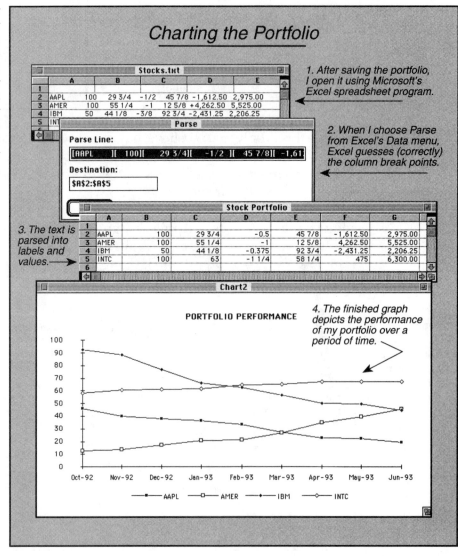

To save a portfolio, click the Save Portfolio button in the Portfolio window (again, refer to Figure 10-5). America Online will then guide you through a standard Macintosh file-save procedure. The file is saved as ASCII text, but most standard spreadsheet programs have parsing features that can convert ASCII text into spreadsheet cells for easy graphing.

Graphing Instruction Manual

Though this is not an Excel manual, so many readers have written asking me to explain the charting procedure that I'll explain it—briefly—here:

1) Open a historical worksheet of your portfolio's investments' prices over time. If such a worksheet doesn't already exist, make a new one. The leftmost column of this worksheet should contain the issues' stock symbols; each column to the right thereafter should contain dates and selling prices for your investments. The topmost row should be reserved for dates, which you will enter. These instructions tell you how to save the current selling prices.

2) Use Excel to open the portfolio text file you saved via the instructions in the text. The data displayed will probably have to be parsed: Excel usually opens portfolio files without parsing.

3) Select the cells in column A representing your issues. Don't select any of the cells to the right, or above or below these cells.

4) Choose Parse from Excel's Data menu. Excel will guess where to parse the data. It's always right. Click OK.

5) Select the column of information representing the current prices for your portfolio and copy them.

6) Use the Window menu to switch to your historical worksheet and paste the data into the appropriate cells. Enter the date in the blank cell above the data you've just pasted.

7) Save the worksheet before you quit. If you wish, use traditional Excel charting methods to construct the chart shown in Figure 10-6.

The TradePlus Gateway

Though you can pretend all you want, eventually you're going to want to make some investments, and that's what TradePlus is for. To get there, click the TradePlus icon displayed in Figure 10-2. Eventually you'll enter the gateway displayed in Figure 10-7. Interestingly, there is no keyword (at the moment) for this service.

Figure 10-7: The TradePlus gateway. It's here that you can buy and sell investments online.

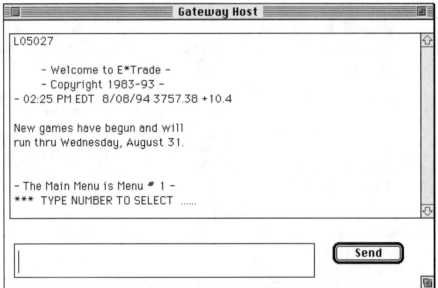

TradePlus is the home for the market investor. During trading hours, TradePlus tracks NYSE, AMEX and NASDAQ advances, declines and volume; Dow Jones indices (price, change, high, low); Standard & Poor's Index (put volume, call volume, ratio); most active issues; and percentage gainers and losers. TradePlus also monitors stock, options and commodities prices—all continuously updated on a 15-minute delay basis.

Gateways

The TradePlus gateway is only one of a number of gateways offered by AOL. The word, however, begs for definition. A gateway is a passage to another computer system, independent of AOL. Once you "enter" a gateway, AOL becomes passive and all communication occurs with the remote system. Most of these systems are textual (rather than graphical) and offer a menu-based interface similar to that pictured in Figure 10-7. America Online's graphical interface—utilizing the mouse, pull-down menus and windows—isn't very common in the online universe. Thousands of machines use the TradePlus system, and few offer the graphical potential your Mac does. The TradePlus system has to serve them all, so its interface is structured around the lowest common denominator—the textual interface. You'll return to the AOL interface as soon as you exit the gateway; don't let the seemingly antiquated nature of the textual interface bother you.

You can buy and sell stocks online via TradePlus as well. The brokerage firm of Quick & Reilly offers discounted commissions and insures accounts up to $2.5 million. You will be assigned a personal broker and an automated portfolio management account. The portfolio management system maintains all your personal records and automatically updates your portfolio every time you buy or sell. Brokerage records are available online 24 hours a day, 7 days a week.

And, except for the commission you pay if you buy and sell real stocks online, all of this is free. You pay only your normal connect-time charges to AOL.

The Bulls & Bears Game

Regardless of whether you choose to invest real money, you're always welcome to participate in AOL's Bulls & Bears game. (The game is available via the Transactions button in the main Personal Finance window, or use the keyword: BullsAndBears). Players invest $100,000 in game money in stocks or options of their choice. The game automatically maintains your portfolio, reflecting trading activity and current prices. Each month, contestants with the top three best-performing portfolios win free online time. There's no better education for the would-be investor, and the rewards are real, even if the investments are not.

Morningstar Mutual Funds

I began investing a couple of years ago. I located a broker—Dave is his name—with whom I found mutual trust, and in whom I found a kindred soul. Trading through him has never been stressful.

As I would expect, Dave is extremely knowledgeable about the market—especially mutual funds and bonds, which is where I've done most of my investing. I asked him one day where he got his information. "Morningstar," he said. "It's an interdictory association," he said obliquely. That evening I looked up the meaning of the word "interdictory" and felt that I was right privileged to walk among the ranks of the plutocracy.

Then I peeked around AOL and found Morningstar there, complete with User's Guide and Guided Tour (see Figure 10-8). The plutocracy had come to the proletariat and the plutocrats didn't even know. Now I read Morningstar just as Dave does—and I don't tell him that I do. Kindredness warrants cynicism when my money's involved.

Free of Extra Charges

Most commercial online services offer some of the news and finance features found on AOL. None offers them all, however, and none offers them at the price AOL charges: nothing beyond the normal connect-time charges. This is unique to AOL. In this industry the word "premium" usually translates to "extra charge." Aside from sending the occasional fax or piece of mail via the US Post Office (which is discussed in Chapter 4, "Electronic Mail"), you will rarely find an extra charge for any of the services AOL offers. With all the money you save, perhaps you can invest in the stock market or buy a small business. If you do, AOL stands ready to help—at no extra charge, of course.

Figure 10-8:
Morningstar offers
data, publications
and software for
analysis of more
than 3,800 mutual
funds, closed-end
funds, variable
annuities, variable
life, variable
universal life,
Japanese equities,
and American
Depository
Receipts. Use the
keyword:
Morningstar.

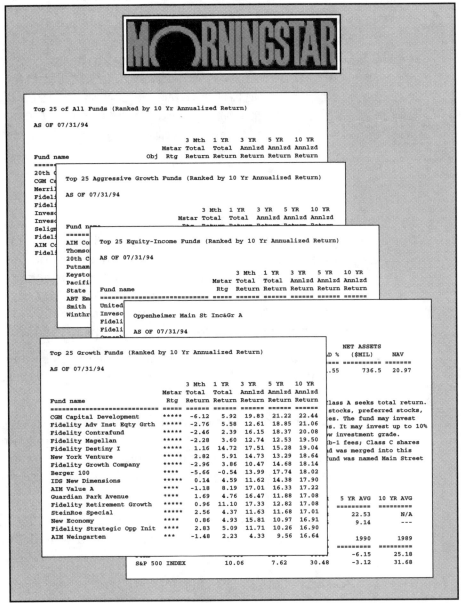

Top 25 of All Funds (Ranked by 10 Yr Annualized Return)

AS OF 07/31/94

Top 25 Aggressive Growth Funds (Ranked by 10 Yr Annualized Return)

AS OF 07/31/94

Top 25 Equity-Income Funds (Ranked by 10 Yr Annualized Return)

AS OF 07/31/94

Oppenheimer Main St Inc&Gr A

AS OF 07/31/94

Top 25 Growth Funds (Ranked by 10 Yr Annualized Return)

AS OF 07/31/94

Fund name	Mstar Rtg	3 Mth Total Return	1 YR Total Return	3 YR Annlzd Return	5 YR Annlzd Return	10 YR Annlzd Return
CGM Capital Development	*****	-6.12	5.92	19.83	21.22	22.44
Fidelity Adv Inst Eqty Grth	*****	-2.76	5.58	12.61	18.85	21.06
Fidelity Contrafund	*****	-2.46	2.39	16.15	18.37	20.08
Fidelity Magellan	*****	-2.28	3.60	12.74	12.53	19.50
Fidelity Destiny I	*****	1.16	14.72	17.51	15.28	19.04
New York Venture	*****	2.82	5.91	14.73	13.29	18.64
Fidelity Growth Company	*****	-2.96	3.86	10.47	14.68	18.14
Berger 100	****	-5.66	-0.54	13.99	17.74	18.02
IDS New Dimensions	*****	0.14	4.59	11.62	14.38	17.90
AIM Value A	****	-1.18	8.19	17.01	16.33	17.22
Guardian Park Avenue	****	1.69	4.76	16.47	11.88	17.08
Fidelity Retirement Growth	****	0.96	11.10	17.33	12.82	17.08
SteinRoe Special	*****	2.56	4.37	11.63	11.68	17.01
New Economy	****	0.86	4.93	15.81	10.97	16.91
Fidelity Strategic Opp Init	****	2.83	5.09	11.71	10.26	16.90
AIM Weingarten	***	-1.48	2.23	4.33	9.56	16.64

S&P 500 INDEX   10.06   7.62   30.48

NET ASSETS
D %   ($MIL)   NAV
.55   736.5   20.97

lass A seeks total return.
stocks, preferred stocks,
es. The fund may invest
s. It may invest up to 10%
w investment grade.
b-1 fees; Class C shares
d was merged into this
fund was named Main Street

5 YR AVG   10 YR AVG
22.53   N/A
9.14   ---

1990   1989
-6.15   25.18
-3.12   31.68

Hoover's Handbook

Morningstar isn't the only investor's reference available on AOL. If your investing interests exceed mutual funds and bonds, investigate the Hoover's Handbook (keyword: Hoovers). The Hoover's Handbook searchable database includes profiles of more than 900 of the largest, most influential, and fastest-growing public and private companies in the world. The voice is lively and interesting; the data is pertinent to every investor; and the price—free of surcharges to AOL members—is as affordable as old clothes used to be.

The Decision Point Forum

Now we're getting serious. The Decision Point Forum provides a platform and materials to help you learn, refine and profitably utilize technical analysis skills and market timing information. You're encouraged to assimilate information and opinions, then arrive at your own conclusions. There are no magic systems here, only aids that help you make your own decisions. And there are plenty of them:

- The buy/sell signals generated by the forum's timing models are summarized in the Decision Point Alert, updated each week on Saturday mornings.

- Each market day the forum posts chart tables of the 150 stocks and 160 mutual funds that they're following. Featured are four proprietary timing models that can help you identify stocks that might be in the beginnings of a new trend. Two-year charts are provided for the stocks and funds in this portfolio.

- There are message boards, where you can post questions and exchange ideas with other members regarding the technical condition of the market and the stocks you own or follow.

- There is a vast collection of chart libraries (see Figure 10-9) containing files of stock, mutual fund, and market indicator charts. These are updated each week.

Figure 10-9: The Decision Point Forum is the home of America Online's stock market charts. There are hundreds of them here, and they're all available for downloading and viewing with your America Online software.

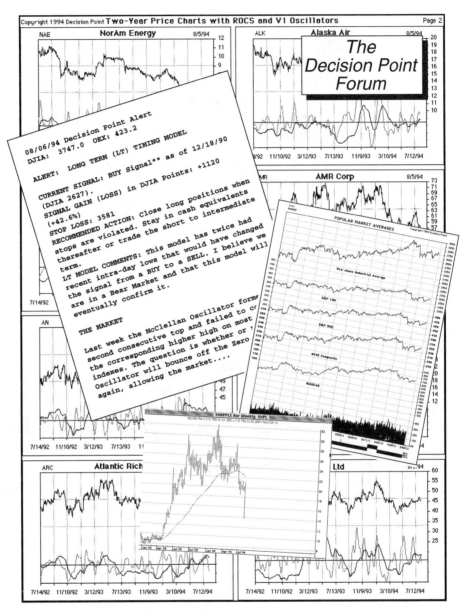

- A collection of historical data files of market indicators and indexes is available for download in the database libraries so that you can construct your own charts. This data is also updated weekly.

- A collection of essays/articles covering various subjects is available in the reading libraries. Of particular importance is the "Timing Model Documentation"—a thorough explanation of how to use the timing models found elsewhere in the forum.

- The Top Advisors' Corner features comments by prominent stock market advisors.

- The Investor's Resource Center lists sources of investing information, products and services.

If you're a serious investor—or if you've considering investments in the stock or mutual funds markets, the Decision Point Forum should be a frequent stop in your AOL journey.

***Worth* Magazine**

No serious investor should conclude an AOL journey without exploring the articles of Worth Online, the electronic version of *Worth* magazine, the magazine of financial intelligence. Here you can download current and past articles written by such Wall Street experts as Peter Lynch, Graef Crystal, Gretchen Morgenson, Bob Clark, Jim Jubak and John Rothchild. It's available in the main Personal Finance window, or by using the keyword: Worth.

Real Estate Online

If I'm ever again in the market for real estate, this is the first place I'll go for information. Real Estate Online, AOL's real estate forum, offers tips on buying a home, information on mortgage loans, property listings in all 50 states and a comprehensive collection of articles for reading (see Figure 10-10).

Figure 10-10: Real Estate Online offers everything a home buyer (or seller) will ever need. In a 15-minute visit, I found more than a dozen articles for reading, a library of Macintosh programs—including a mortgage loan analysis spreadsheet for Excel—and an alert regarding changes in FHA loan limits.

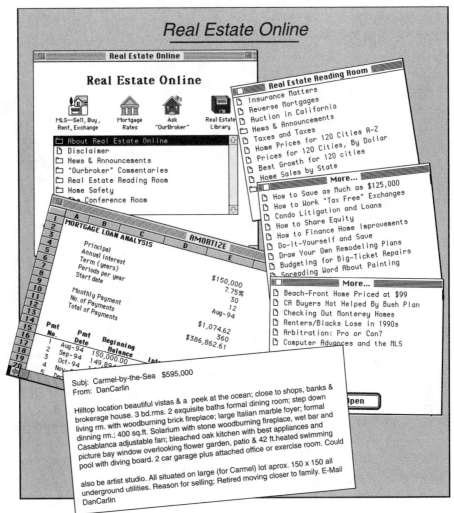

The person responsible for this wealth of information is Peter G. Miller, author of six real estate books, two of which were on the top-ten best-selling nonfiction book list during the summer of 1992. Miller's forum features weekly commentaries, home prices and trends in all fifty states, current mortgage rate listings and a board featuring properties for sale. You'll find handy financial programs in the library, and an "Ask Our Broker" board where you can obtain answers to those sticky real estate questions that simply can't be asked of brokers or agents who are involved in a transaction. Few personal transactions equal the monetary significance of buying or selling a home, and the real estate forum is one of the few unbiased sources of information available. It's as near as your computer (keyword: Real Estate).

Moving On

It's a disservice to the Personal Finance Department to end this chapter here. There's much more than I've described, and I don't want you to misinterpret my emphasis. I've tried to present the diversity of features offered by the department, not a listing of its best stuff.

If you're interested in personal finance, take the time to explore the Tax Forum (its Resources are invaluable if you do your own taxes), Your Money (where you set your financial goals and then methodically pursue them with the resources provided), the International Corporate Forum (where you can participate in conferences with some of the world's biggest institutional investors), and the Investor's Network (an open forum where you can confer with other investors—people just like yourself).

Too much time in the Personal Finance Department, however, can lead to information overload. By now you probably need a break. How about a respite: a cruise perhaps, or a journey to a land where no one has gone before. In Chapter 11, "Travel," we'll do just that.

Travel

W ho hasn't indulged in the "If I had a million dollars. . ." fantasy? My favorite is travel: South America, the British Isles, a blue water cruise, the Orient Express. . .

Heck, I'd be happy if someone just gave me a ticket to Tucumcari.

Of course, fantasies require money. That's why they're fantasies. If you want money-optional indulgences, try AOL's Travel Department. Not only can you indulge your fantasies here, you can actually commit them. You can book airline, car and hotel reservations; you can consult with other travelers before you depart; you can even buy a car. This place can really get expensive if you give it a chance. You'd better hide your credit card before you read any further.

As is so often the case, the montage of features in Figure 11-1 is incomplete, and we don't have space here to explore the entire department. If you're a traveler, get to know this department: it will add to the richness of your adventure, and more than likely reduce its cost.

The Travel Department is AOL's all-in-one travel venue. You can learn about your destination here, make your lodging and travel reservations, and even download pictures of it—all without leaving your keyboard. It's a must for the intrepid traveler. Click the Travel button on the Main Menu, or use the keyword Travel.

Figure 11-1: Logos
for a few of the
services you'll find
in the Travel
Department.

The EAASY SABRE Gateway

Here's another example of a gateway, though in this case AOL has
provided a very untextual interface for it. American Airlines's SABRE
reservations system is one of the few centralized travel reservations
systems in America. As such, it's used by travel agents and airline
reservation counters as well as AOL members. When you enter the
EAASY SABRE gateway, you actually log on to the Sabre computer
itself. America Online's host computer remains relatively passive until
you exit the gateway.

Few telecommunication services are as easy to use as AOL. Most are
purely textual: no windows, no pull-down menus, no dialog boxes.
Like many other telecommunications systems, Sabre is textual. In the
rough, it's almost intimidating. It's designed to serve travel agents,

after all, and they attend schools to learn how to use this kind of thing. Respecting the plight of the normal person, AOL overlays a graphical interface on top of the EAASY SABRE system; the result is the only Mac interface for EAASY SABRE. And it *is* easy.

The first time my travel agent found out I was using Sabre, she was incredulous: she had attended school for weeks to become proficient at it, and I was using it with no training whatsoever. She also couldn't believe I was using my standard telephone line to access it, or that I was paying nothing but my normal AOL connect-time charges to use it. Not only is EAASY SABRE easy to use, it's a bargain as well.

Being a professional system, Sabre is in no way abbreviated. Not only can you make airline reservations (on *any* airline, not just American), you can reserve automobiles and hotels as well (see Figure 11-2). Indeed, EAASY SABRE allows you to make reservations on over 350 airlines, reserve a room at over 27,000 hotels, or rent a car at any of nearly 60 car rental companies worldwide. . .all from your computer.

Figure 11-2: The EAASY SABRE graphical interface was developed specifically for the Macintosh edition of America Online and only appears here: you won't find it anywhere else.

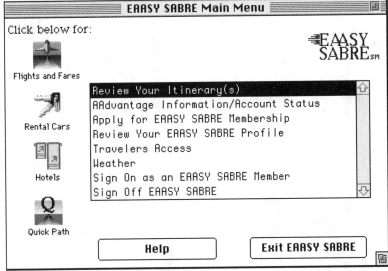

Don't let Figure 11-2 fool you: you don't have to be a Sabre member to poke around the EAASY SABRE system, but becoming a member is easy. You don't have to be Someone Important, and membership doesn't cost a dime.

Finding a Flight

One of my favorite jaunts is a trip to North Carolina in the spring. They have some delectable cuisine there (to say nothing of the mint juleps), it's a comely place, and the natives talk with a lilt that could melt even Jack Palance's heart. (Did I mention that my publisher is there too? And that they usually pay for the trip? It's amazing how a travel allowance can make a place seem suddenly endearing.) Let's use EAASY SABRE to see if there's a flight that will get me there (Figure 11-3).

Figure 11-3: All I have to do is identify where and when I want to travel; EAASY SABRE supplies the how.

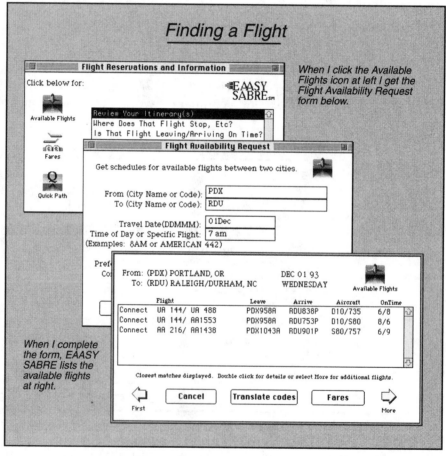

There are four points I should make about Figure 11-3. One, I didn't have to use the airport abbreviations (PDX, RDU) that you see in the middle window. I could have specified Portland, Oregon, and Raleigh, North Carolina, and the system would have supplied the same information. Two, EAASY SABRE found something like nine flights that met my criteria, though only three appear in Figure 11-3's lower window (the First and More arrows reveal the other six). Three, I can see how reliable each flight has been recently by looking at the On Time column. And four, I specified a date of December 1. Who wants to wait till spring?

Finding the Cost

Another 10 minutes on the system reveals the cost of not only the airline tickets, but the car rental and hotel as well (see Figure 11-4). These rates differ drastically (especially for car rentals, all of which offer essentially the same service), and Sabre practically begs you to do some comparison shopping.

Figure 11-4: Let's see: $600 for the flight, $150 for the car and $50 a night for the hotel. North Carolina, here I come!

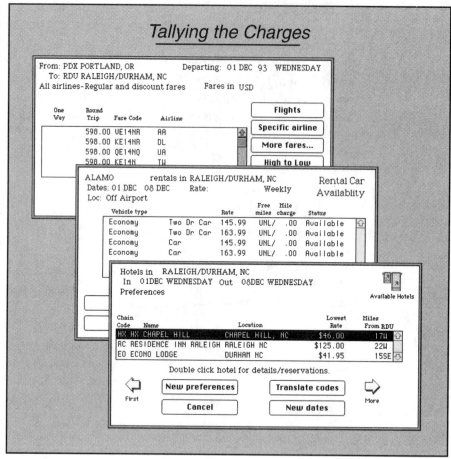

Booking the Reservations

Before you can book reservations, you need to sign up for a "membership" in EAASY SABRE. Though it sounds formal, membership amounts to little more than providing your credit card number and mailing address. As I mentioned before, membership in EAASY SABRE is free. Once you're a member, you simply double-click on any one of the items you see in Figure 11-4 to book it. EAASY SABRE establishes an itinerary for that trip (which you can review and print at any time— look again at the top of Figure 11-3), and within a few days provides confirmation numbers and (in the case of airline reservations) mails the tickets to you.

Not only is membership free, so is browsing the system. You pay only your normal AOL connect charges. Even if you don't plan to go anywhere, no one will tattle if you indulge in a little fantasy traveling. It's a great cure for the wintertime blues; and who knows, maybe you too will visit the beautiful Raleigh-Durham area of North Carolina. Sip a mint julep while you're there: there are none better in the South.

The Travel Forum

As long as we're in a traveling mood, let's check out the Travel Forum. Articles, message boards and a library offer a wealth of information and tips for the domestic or world traveler (see Figure 11-5).

Figure 11-5: The Travel Forum offers packing tips, a list of all the toll-free telephone numbers for hotels and airlines around the country, a Bargain Box and much more.

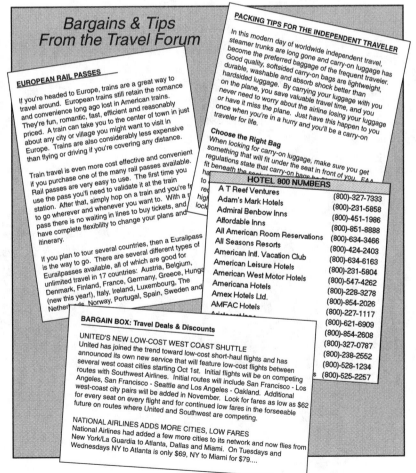

Are you looking for a romantic hideaway for your getaway weekend? Check the cruise message board. If you're looking for the best itinerary for your train trip through Europe, check the World Traveler message board. If you're traveling overseas, check out the U.S. State Dept Travel Advisories, and the Forum's special events with travel experts. In-depth articles cover topics such as "How to find hotel discounts" and "Should I buy trip cancellation insurance?"

Travel plans, perhaps above all else, benefit from peer support. The Travel Forum is where you can solicit the advice of peers and pros alike. No travel plans are complete until you talk to those who have been there. For this purpose, check the Travel Forum's message boards. Lots of people travel, and most who do like to talk about it. Their comments are candid and relevant, and because it's a message board, everything is current.

Getting Bumped

Ever been at a gate, waiting to board a flight, when the agent announces over the loudspeaker that the flight was overbooked and would anyone like to give up their seat? Usually some kind of motivation is included in the announcement, and the motivation is often lucrative. People with time on their hands can profit from these situations, as the (edited) thread of Travel Forum messages below indicate. . .

Subj: How to get bumped   91-05-04 14:12:14 EDT
From: William40

Taking a long trip and you want to get bumped and have the time to enjoy the experience? It's fun. Check all possible routes to your destination. Make a list of all flight segments on all routes. Ask for the load factors on each flight for each flight segment—that is, how many seats have been booked. Divide this number by the total number of seats available on each flight. Airlines always book more reservations than available seats because of no-shows. The number of available seats divided by the number of booked seats is the probability that the flight is oversold. Multiply the probabilities for all of the flight segments for each route and book your reservations on the route which gives you the greatest probability of being bumped. Simple.

More ▷

Subj: bumped   91-05-05 14:52:13 EDT
From: Fred44
It's not so complicated. And it's even more complicated.
Best flights are Fri & Sun night, pre holiday. Thanksgiving is the busiest. William40 idea is interesting and may produce the best mathematical model...but the carrier can substitute a larger or smaller aircraft at any time, for any reason. Therefore this model can fail.
A better way to determine "Actuals" (load) is to call reservations and indicate that you are an airline employee pass riding. The agent will tell you how difficult or easy it will be to get on board. If you are trying to get bumped you want to hear an answer like "impossible." That would be a good indicator.
I've managed to get bumped twice in one day (once from CO and then from AA) but it's not that easy. I wrote a newspaper article on a fellow who got bumped 26 times in one year.
Tip-o-the-wings to ya,
Fred44

Subj: airfare secrets   93-11-06 02:17:12 EST
From: Jeremy12
I used to be an airline ticket agent. One aspect of bumping overlooked here involves the 'history' of each particular flight. Every flight has its own history of no-shows and oversales, differences exist between even two flights on the same route, same airline but different days and times, and time of year. Some flights are authorized to be oversold to even twice their capacity at certain times of year. While it is obvious that holiday periods and weekends usually provide more occasion for bumping, it is not an exact science and formulas are not reliable.

Travelers' Corner

Don't confuse the Travel Forum with Travelers' Corner. Though the two serve similar purposes, there's a subtle but significant difference in their focus.

Arnie Weissmann began planning for an around-the-world journey in the early 1980s. To his frustration, he couldn't find information about his destinations. He knew how he was traveling, he knew what his costs were going to be, he knew what to pack and how to dress–what he needed were friends who were familiar with his destinations to tell him what to do when he got to each one, how to behave, how to find the good stuff, and how to avoid the bad. He needed what the Travelers' Corner calls "destination profiles" (see Figure 11-6). The Travel Forum, in other words, concentrates on planning, transportation and reservations. The Travelers' Corner focuses on what to do once you arrive. You should become familiar with both.

Figure 11-6: The Travelers' Corner offers destination information for thousands of locations around the world.

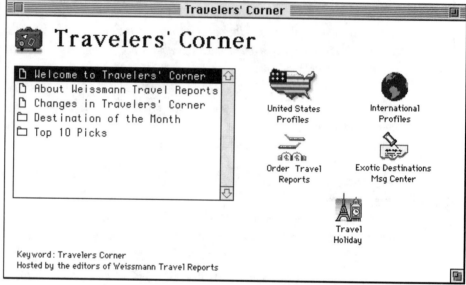

Look also at the Top 10 Picks and Destination of the Month features. If you're ready for travel but not sure of where you want to go, the insights here are invaluable (see Figure 11-7).

Figure 11-7:
IBettyBoop was
considering
Cancun in April.
She posted a
single message
and received not
only the responses
she requested, but
some beneficial
tips as well.

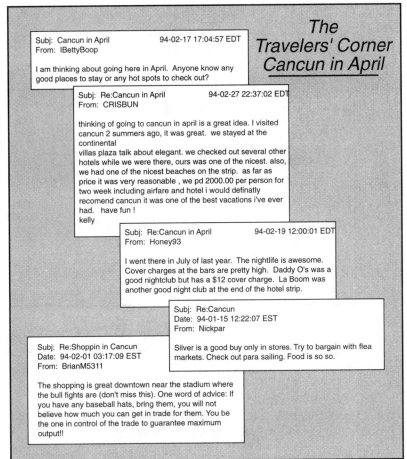

The
Travelers' Corner
Cancun in April

Subj: Cancun in April   94-02-17 17:04:57 EDT
From: IBettyBoop

I am thinking about going here in April. Anyone know any
good places to stay or any hot spots to check out?

Subj: Re:Cancun in April   94-02-27 22:37:02 EDT
From: CRISBUN

thinking of going to cancun in april is a great idea. I visited
cancun 2 summers ago, it was great. we stayed at the
continental
villas plaza talk about elegant. we checked out several other
hotels while we were there, ours was one of the nicest. also,
we had one of the nicest beaches on the strip. as far as
price it was very reasonable , we pd 2000.00 per person for
two week including airfare and hotel i would definatly
recomend cancun it was one of the best vacations i've ever
had. have fun !
kelly

Subj: Re:Cancun in April   94-02-19 12:00:01 EDT
From: Honey93

I went there in July of last year. The nightlife is awesome.
Cover charges at the bars are pretty high. Daddy O's was a
good nightclub but has a $12 cover charge. La Boom was
another good night club at the end of the hotel strip.

Subj: Re:Cancun
Date: 94-01-15 12:22:07 EST
From: Nickpar

Silver is a good buy only in stores. Try to bargain with flea
markets. Check out para sailing. Food is so so.

Subj: Re:Shoppin in Cancun
Date: 94-02-01 03:17:09 EST
From: BrianM5311

The shopping is great downtown near the stadium where
the bull fights are (don't miss this). One word of advice: If
you have any baseball hats, bring them, you will not
believe how much you can get in trade for them. You be
the one in control of the trade to guarantee maximum
output!!

AutoVantage

Somewhere a few pages back I mentioned that most telecommunications services are textual in nature and much more difficult to use than AOL. With AutoVantage, I have an opportunity to show you what I mean. The moment you enter AutoVantage, everything changes. Gone are the attractive windows, menus and dialogs to which you've become accustomed. Even the mouse is essentially inactive. A window appears instead, populated with nothing but text (see Figure 11-8).

Figure 11-8: Textual interfaces aren't much fun and are generally more difficult to learn, but in the case of AutoVantage, it's worth the trouble.

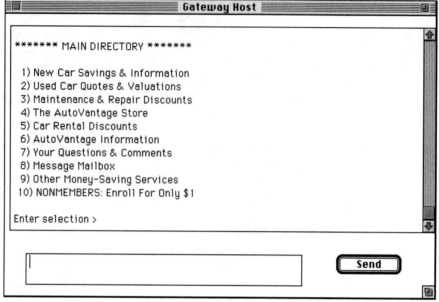

AutoVantage is one of the few premium services (one for which an extra fee is charged) available to AOL members: its annual fee of $49 entitles you to the following:

🔺 New car summaries that detail a model's features, the pros and cons of buying the model, specifications, available options, sticker and dealer prices, and road test highlights.

🔺 Used car pricing onscreen, instantly, from the vast nationwide used car AutoVantage database. This service gives you the estimated selling and trade-in prices, an overview of the model, bargaining tips and recall history for any car up to 20 years old.

🔺 New cars at a discount. AutoVantage will arrange for you to purchase a car at a local dealer. On the average, a member who purchases a car this way saves $2,000, though savings vary, of course, with make and model.

🔺 Locate nearby service centers online. AutoVantage members are able to access a list of all participating service centers within a 50-mile radius. Each listing highlights the address, phone number, contact name and discount offer made by the servicing agency. You can search by type of service, type of car needing service or the service center name.

◭ Prenegotiated national discounts. Savings of 10 to 20 percent off the local price on virtually everything from oil changes, tune-ups and transmissions to auto glass and body repair.

Figure 11-9: "Psst: Hey Buddy! Wanna buy a used Camaro?" Before you do, check out AutoVantage.

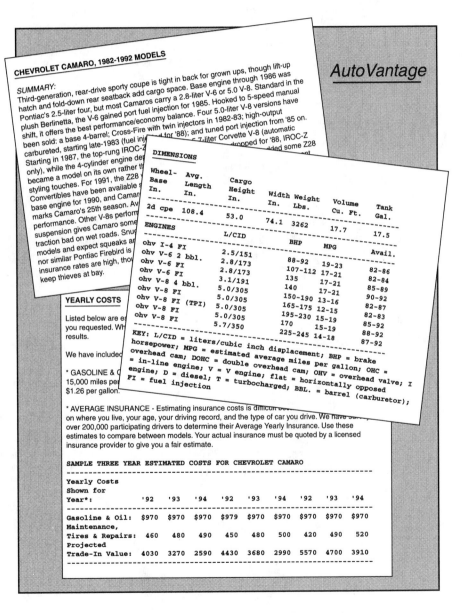

CHEVROLET CAMARO, 1982-1992 MODELS

AutoVantage

SUMMARY:

Third-generation, rear-drive sporty coupe is tight in back for grown ups, though lift-up hatch and fold-down rear seatback add cargo space. Base engine through 1986 was Pontiac's 2.5-liter four, but most Camaros carry a 2.8-liter V-6 or 5.0 V-8. Standard in the plush Berlinetta, the V-6 gained port fuel injection for 1985. Hooked to 5-speed manual shift, it offers the best performance/economy balance. Four 5.0-liter V-8 versions have been sold: a base 4-barrel; Cross-Fire with twin injectors in 1982-83; high-output carbureted, starting late-1983 (fuel inj____ for '88); and tuned port injection from '85 on. Starting in 1987, the top-rung IROC-Z ___ 7-liter Corvette V-8 (automatic only), while the 4-cylinder engine de____ ___ dropped for '88, IROC-Z became a model on its own rather th__ ___ ___ded some Z28 styling touches. For 1991, the Z28 ___ Convertibles have been available s____ base engine for 1990, and Camar___ marks Camaro's 25th season. Av____ performance. Other V-8s perform___ suspension gives Camaro some___ traction bad on wet roads. Snu___ models and expect squeaks a___ nor similar Pontiac Firebird is ___ insurance rates are high, tho___ keep thieves at bay.

DIMENSIONS

Wheel-Base In.	Avg. Length In.	Cargo Height In.	Width In.	Weight Lbs.	Volume Cu. Ft.	Tank Gal.
2d cpe 108.4	53.0		74.1	3262	17.7	17.5

ENGINES	L/CID	BHP	MPG	Avail.
ohv I-4 FI	2.5/151	88-92	19-23	82-86
ohv V-6 2 bbl.	2.8/173	107-112	17-21	82-84
ohv V-6 FI	2.8/173	135	17-21	85-89
ohv V-6 FI	3.1/191	140	17-21	90-92
ohv V-8 4 bbl.	5.0/305	150-190	13-16	82-87
ohv V-8 FI	5.0/305	165-175	12-15	82-83
ohv V-8 FI (TPI)	5.0/305	195-230	15-19	85-92
ohv V-8 FI	5.0/305	170	15-19	88-92
ohv V-8 FI	5.7/350	225-245	14-18	87-92

KEY: L/CID = liters/cubic inch displacement; BHP = brake horsepower; MPG = estimated average miles per gallon; OHC = overhead cam; DOHC = double overhead cam; OHV = overhead valve; I = in-line engine; V = V engine; flat = horizontally opposed engine; D = diesel; T = turbocharged; BBL. = barrel (carburetor); FI = fuel injection

YEARLY COSTS

Listed below are e___
you requested. Wh___
results.

We have included ___

* GASOLINE & ___
15,000 miles pe___
$1.26 per gallon.

* AVERAGE INSURANCE - Estimating insurance costs is difficult be___ on where you live, your age, your driving record, and the type of car you drive. We have su___ over 200,000 participating drivers to determine their Average Yearly Insurance. Use these estimates to compare between models. Your actual insurance must be quoted by a licensed insurance provider to give you a fair estimate.

SAMPLE THREE YEAR ESTIMATED COSTS FOR CHEVROLET CAMARO

Yearly Costs Shown for Year*:	'92	'93	'94	'92	'93	'94	'92	'93	'94
Gasoline & Oil:	$970	$970	$970	$979	$970	$970	$970	$970	$970
Maintenance, Tires & Repairs:	460	480	490	450	480	500	420	490	520
Projected Trade-In Value:	4030	3270	2590	4430	3680	2990	5570	4700	3910

Premium services are scarce on AOL. So are textual interfaces. Nonetheless, AutoVantage might well pay for itself through the money you'll save on regular maintenance and service, and it certainly pays for itself the first time you buy or sell a car—it's probably the second-largest financial transaction of our lives (for the largest—real estate—see Chapter 10, "Personal Finance"), and most of us know very little about the business. If all this makes you a little nervous (and it should), investigate AutoVantage. It helps to even the score.

Your Wallet Is Safe at AOL

All of this talk about premium services, buying cars and booking airline tickets may make you a little squeamish: "Does my AOL membership obligate me for anything beyond the standard monthly fee and connect charges?" No, not at all. All of the additional-expense items I've discussed in this chapter are voluntary—not at all requisite to membership in AOL. This is the Travel Department, after all, and most travel is discretionary. . .and an additional expense.

Pictures of the World

Before I conclude this chapter, I must call your attention to Pictures of the World (keyword: Pictures). Carl and Ann Purcell are freelance photographers whose work appears in newspapers and magazines around the world. In a word, their work is magnificent. It's especially radiant when it's displayed on a high-resolution color screen. I'm not the only one with this opinion: when I last checked the Pictures of the World forum, nearly 3,000 people had downloaded the Purcell's image of the Golden Gate Bridge!

Figure 11-10: The perfect scene for the conclusion of the travel chapter. The couple with the dog in the moonlight is one of thousands of images available in the Pictures of the World forum.

America Online is sprinkled with spangles of magnificence, like evening gowns at the Academy Awards. But unlike the Academy Awards, you have to look around to find AOL's spangles. Pictures of the World is one of them.

Moving On

The Travel Department is one of the most utilitarian features AOL offers. A few hours spent here can save you hundreds of dollars and hours of frustration once you're on the road. Visit this place before your next vacation. As Karl Malden says: "Don't leave home without it."

Planning, however, is one thing. There's a lot to be learned from spontaneous experiences as well, especially those involving a lively exchange of views and experiences among people of widely varying backgrounds and interests. People Connection is the real-time headquarters of AOL, and it's a journey of sorts itself. Like all journeys, however, it's best to travel prepared. Your tour guide for People Connection begins on the next page. . .

People Connection

People Connection is the real-time headquarters of AOL. This is not the home of message boards and e-mail: communication here is as immediate as a telephone conversation. Unlike telephone conversations, however, with People Connection any number of people can be involved.

People Connection is the heart of the AOL community. It is here you make the enduring friendships that keep you coming back, day after day. Here, in a "diner," you can order a short stack and a cup of coffee, and talk over the weekend ahead. You can also sip a brew in a "pub" after a long day on the job. There are "events" here as well, where you can interview eminent guests and hobnob with luminaries.

Doesn't that sound like a community to you? This isn't couch-potato entertainment, this is *interactive* telecommunication—where imagination and participation are contagious and the concept of community reaches its most eloquent expression.

It sure beats reruns.

Proving that AOLers do exist in real life, a photo of seven members at the Las Vegas AOL gathering in January 1994. Top row (L to R): Trevayne, NealnJanet (2 people). Bottom row (L to R): WaterLily, CaNurse, Vrroom, Kunphuzed.

This photo (along with thousands of others) appears in the Gallery, a feature of People Connection. To get to People Connection, click the People Connection button in the Main Menu window.

A Haven for Shy People

America Online is a haven for shy people. Shy people usually like other people, and they're likable themselves; they just don't do well with strangers. Most shy people want to make friends—and all friends were once strangers—but they aren't very adept at doing it.

This is why shy people like AOL. Nobody can see them online, nobody seems to notice if they don't talk much, and if they're uncomfortable, they can always escape at any time—just by signing off. Perhaps best of all, if you're a shy person, you can use a *nom de plume* and no one will even know who you are. There's a bit of masquerade ball in People Connection: you can wear the mask of a different screen name and be whatever or whomever you want. There's something comforting yet exciting about those possibilities.

Shy people can begin the AOL journey in a "safe" place like a forum, where no one's the wiser when they read a few forum messages or download a file or two. The next step would be to make an online friend and exchange some mail. Regardless of the path taken, it takes some time to work up the courage to venture into People Connection, since that invariably means ending up in a room full of strangers. This is not where shy people feel their most comfortable.

The irony is that shy folks love People Connection once they become acquainted with it. It's the perfect outlet for years of pent-up sociability. I'm a shy person. It took me months to work up to People Connection. Yet now it's one of my greatest rewards. I go there whenever I have time. You will too, once you get the hang of it.

The Lobby

Unlike the other departments we've explored, a visit to People Connection requires first passing through the "Lobby." The Lobby is one of AOL's so-called *chat rooms*, where real people communicate in real time. No messages are left here. There are no files to download. America Online's Lobby is similar to the lobby of a hotel: it's an area people pass through, often on their way to some other destination. Every so often, people bump into an acquaintance, or just sit there a moment to rest.

Entering the Lobby

To begin our People Connection adventure, choose People Connection from the Department screen, choose Lobby from the Go To menu, use the keyword Lobby, or press Command-L. No matter which method you use, you will soon find yourself in the Lobby (see Figure 12-1).

Figure 12-1: The
Lobby screen
seems empty just
after I enter.

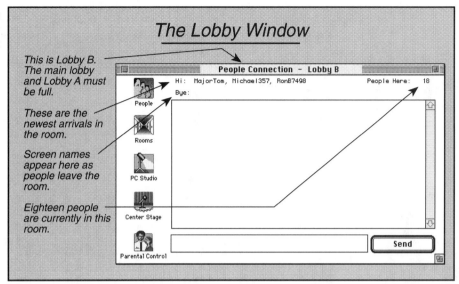

The Lobby Window

*This is Lobby B.
The main lobby
and Lobby A must
be full.*

*These are the
newest arrivals in
the room.*

*Screen names
appear here as
people leave the
room.*

*Eighteen people
are currently in this
room.*

People Connection - Lobby B

Hi: MajorTom, Michael357, RonB7498   People Here: 18
Bye:

People

Rooms

PC Studio

Center Stage

Parental Control

Send

Note that the chat room window pictured in Figure 12-1 says that
you are in Lobby B. When I entered the Lobby, AOL routed me to
Lobby B. This happens whenever traffic on the system is heavy. When
the main Lobby reaches capacity (rooms are considered filled when
they contain 23 members), AOL places people in the secondary lobby—
Lobby A. It too must have filled by the time I arrived, so I got placed in
Lobby B. Note that it was also approaching capacity, so new arrivals
were about to be routed into yet another lobby. This isn't uncommon.
There are often a dozen or more lobbies in operation at any one time.
America Online will run out of letters in the alphabet if this keeps up.

People in a room can see when others enter it by watching the text at
the top of the window following the word "Hi." Since mine is the first
name on the list, I was the most recent arrival. Departing members'
names appear after the word "Bye." I just got here; no one has left since
I arrived.

Finally, note that there is no text in the main (conversation) portion
of the window other than the announcement telling me where I am.
The only true conversation appearing here occurs after my arrival, and
I have just walked in the door. That situation changes the moment I
speak (see Figure 12-2).

Figure 12-2: No matter how shy you're feeling, say hello when you enter a room.

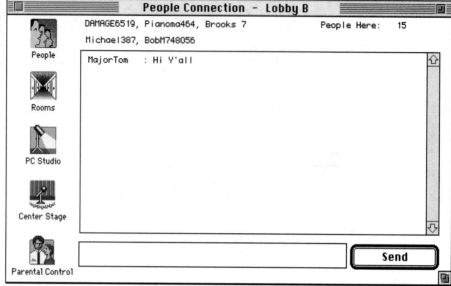

Look again at Figure 12-2. This lobby is active today. People are rushing through it with hardly a pause. By the time I've said hello, in a matter of seconds, three more people have arrived and six have left. America Online's lobbies are something like a hotel lobby just after a large meeting has let out: people are scurrying everywhere. (This is particularly true during periods of heavy usage. The session pictured occurred on a Sunday morning. America Online is almost always busy on the weekends.)

Seconds later, a conversation has begun (see Figure 12-3).

Figure 12-3: Catchy
screen names
come in handy
when you first
enter a room.

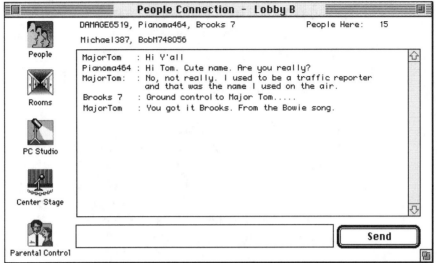

Though I became immediately involved in a conversation, don't feel obligated to do so yourself. It's perfectly all right to say hello, then just watch for a while. In fact, I recommend it: it gives you a chance to adapt to the pace of the conversation—to get to know who is in the room and what they're like. Lobbies are good for this. They're lobbies, after all. It's perfectly natural for people to sit in a lobby and watch other people.

Guides

To carry my hotel lobby analogy a bit further, you might find a "concierge" there—a *Guide*—to answer your questions. Like a real-life hotel concierge, AOL's Guides are chosen for their knowledge of the territory and their friendly personalities. Watch the conversation for a while. No doubt you'll soon see someone with the word "Guide" in his or her screen name. More likely, a Guide will welcome you to the room.

Take a moment to look back at Figure 3-11. Do you see the Guide there? She welcomed me the moment I walked into the room and went out of her way to be of assistance. This is the way all Guides tend to be.

Guides are on duty from 9 A.M. to 6 A.M. (Eastern time), seven days a week. Since I already discussed them in Chapter 3, "Online Help & the Members," I won't go over their function again. But if you would like to review that section, turn back to that chapter (see page 67).

Exploring Other Public Rooms

As is the case with hotel lobbies, you won't want to stay in AOL's
lobbies indefinitely. Lots of other rooms await you, where conversations are more focused and residents less transitory. These rooms can
be great fun; all you have to do is find the one that suits you best.

The Event Rooms Guide

Room exploration should not be done randomly. The method I recommend is to become familiar with the event rooms before you enter
them. To do this, click the PC Studio icon. It's the "spotlight" icon
pictured in Figure 12-3. The PC Studio window opens with its selection
of options. Double-click What's Happening This Week, then double-
click Event Rooms Guide (see Figure 12-4).

Figure 12-4:
Become familiar
with the Event
Rooms Guide
before you spend
time in People
Connection.

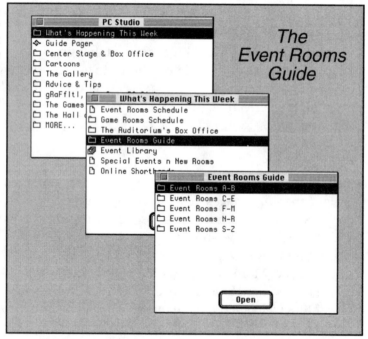

Many of the rooms available on AOL at any particular moment are
spontaneously created by members. While spontaneous rooms can
sometimes be entertaining and fun, they lack the focus found in the
regularly scheduled event rooms. Event rooms are populated by hosts

and regulars—people who have developed an online camaraderie and whose patter is familiar and neighborly. Hosts keep the conversation on track and offer a familiar "face" to anyone who visits. Hosts and regulars aren't cliquish, however; you're never made to feel unwelcome in one of AOL's event rooms. At this writing, 33 event rooms are listed (a number that's sure to change), ranging from the Best Lil Chathouse to Parents R US (see Figure 12-5). Shall we drop in on one?

Figure 12-5: Thirty-three event rooms are scheduled this week. Double-click any one for a description.

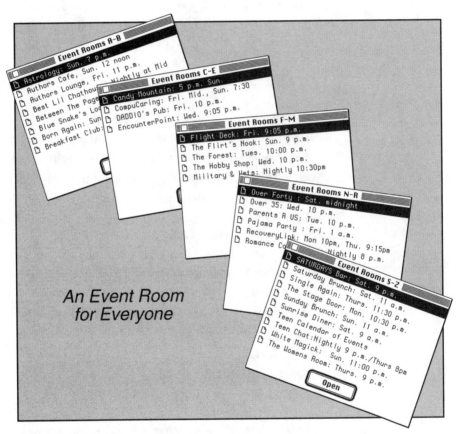

One of my favorites is the Authors Cafe, which meets every Saturday at 1 P.M. (Eastern time). You never know who'll turn up—familiar writers visit it regularly. America Online is a favorite haunt for writers, partly because of the Writers' Club (keyword: Writers) and partly because of its unique chat rooms such as the Authors Cafe. The morning I visited, Tom Clancy dropped by, unscheduled and unannounced.

The log of his appearance appears below. Typical of a chat room, smileys and shorthand abound. The symbol :) is a smile and :(is a frown (turn your head 90 degrees counterclockwise); and "LOL" means "laughing out loud." These can be modified with semicolons (winks) or D's (open-mouth smiles).

D P Gumby:	Hi Tom!! :)
Tom Clancy:	Good morning, Gumby
Tom Clancy:	and Rosey
D P Gumby:	Hey Tom..... you should think about joining us at the Allentown Bash!
Tom Clancy:	when's the party?
D P Gumby:	We've got about 100 onliners coming to the Bash.... it's gonna be a blast! :)
D P Gumby:	August 21-23.... in Allentown PA!
Tom Clancy:	busy then—doing something with Johns Hopkins
Tom Clancy:	their summer camp for kids with cancer
ROSEY DAWN:	Got any new books close to being released, Tom???
Data Dump3:	<— showing a prospective customer the service :D
Tom Clancy:	sorry, Rosey, no. I just came to terms with Putnam for #7, which I now have to write :(
Gleeful:	Hiya Prospective Customer..;D
Data Dump3:	Mornin' Tom :D
D P Gumby:	I'll be first in line for it, Tom! :)
ROSEY DAWN:	Oh well, anticipation makes it even better!
Tom Clancy:	hello, Dump
Gleeful:	lol Tom...you sold it and you haven't written it yet?? :D
Tom Clancy:	that's normal
ROSEY DAWN:	Heck, Glee—I'd *buy* it too — just knowing Tom is going to write it
Tom Clancy:	the advance money is the literary equivalent of a gun to the head
Gleeful:	Tom...doesn't that put a lot of pressure on you tho???
D P Gumby:	I think, based on past performance...we can assume it'll be a good investment on behalf of the publisher
Tom Clancy:	pressure....what do you think?
Tom Clancy:	they pay you $XM, and you have to deliver a product, from inside your head, that's worth $XM

ROSEY DAWN: What's in your head, Tom, is worth at least $XXXXX

D P Gumby: Or more! :)

Tom Clancy: thanks, ma'am, I'd like to think so

Gleeful: awww Tom...You'll be just fine...just ask us..we know..D

Data Dump3: Sheesh Tom, I would hate to run around w/ a price on my head....let alone in it!!! ;D

Tom Clancy: don't worry, all writers are scared at this stage

Tom Clancy: we're SUPPOSED to be insecure, but not as badly as actors are

D P Gumby: That's a good point, Tom.. i do a lot of theater.. and it's awfully frightening sometimes!!

Tom Clancy: I speak a lot, and I always get stage fright

D P Gumby: they say the best of them do, Tom...

Tom Clancy: there's no dishonor in it, it happened to Olivier, too

Tom Clancy: it's a thoroughly crummy way to earn a living, but you do it because you love it, and because you have to do it

Gleeful: Have to Tom??

Tom Clancy: yeah, it's my mission in life, it's what I do

Rich OO: Money is a great motivator. :)

Gleeful: Tom...do you give a lot of talks??

Tom Clancy: quite a few, yes

Rich OO: Tom..I always draw a blank til the speech is over,,,I have no idea what I've said. :)

Gleeful: Are books usually the subject or something else, Tom?

Tom Clancy: me, too, Rich

Tom Clancy: Glee, I just get up there and ramble

Tom Clancy: All my speaking money goes to my kids' school

Gleeful: Good place for it to go.;D

ROSEY DAWN: Will you run for President, Tom????

GATEWAY: You have my vote, Tom!

Tom Clancy: Rosey, do I LOOK that STUPID?????

Gleeful: See ya'll later!! I have an appt to keep..;D

Gleeful: Tom..it was nice to meet you..:D

AFC Doug: <— off to jump out of an airplane. :D

Tom Clancy: don't forget the chute, pal

D P Gumby: Time for me to run... see y'all later! Take care, Tom!

The Event Rooms Schedule

The Event Rooms Schedule is posted in the PC Studio along with the Event Rooms Guide. Look again at the center window in Figure 12-4: do you see the schedule there? Double-click it to view it. The week's schedule is pictured in Figure 12-6.

Figure 12-6: The seven-day Event Rooms Schedule. Use this schedule along with the Event Rooms Guide to plan your visits.

The Event Rooms Schedule

Day	Time	Event	Host
Mon.	8:00 PM	Romance Connection	RCLisa,RC Koala,RCDreamer
	9:00 PM	LaPub Happy Hour	PubTend EM
	9:00 PM	Teen Chat	
	9:00 PM	POWs Left Behind	Vets Jerry
	10:00 PM	RecoveryLink	SuziPooh, GabeCT
	10:30 PM	The Stage Door	Dale Lyles
	10:00 PM	LaPub	PubTend BB
	12:00 AM	Best Lil Chathouse	MadamLynn
	12:00 AM	LaPub Late Nite	PubTendAnn
Tue.	8:00 PM	Romance Connection	RCSoftie,RCdeLune,RCLovebug
	9:00 PM	Teen Chat	Sweet6Teen, Monopoly8
	9:00 PM	LaPub Happy Hour	PubtendWAR
	9:00 PM	New Member Lounge	NML Cactus
	10:00 PM	The Forest	Alandra
	10:00 PM	Parents R US	Forevermom
	10:00 PM	LaPub	PubTend RS
	11:00 PM	Between The Pages	MizChiff2
	11:00 PM	Blue Snakes Lodge	Blue Snake
	12:00 AM	Best Lil Chathouse	MadamShena
Wed.	8:00 PM	Romance Connection	RC Lucy,RC Susie/RCAmore
	9:00 PM	Teen Chat	DrCatalyst
	9:00 PM	The Dorm	Odysseyll
	9:00 PM	LaPub Happy Hour	PubTendAla
	9:05 PM	EncounterPoint	Heelslovr
	10:00 PM	Hobby Shop	Grashopper
	10:00 PM	Over 35	Tamira
	10:00 PM	LaPub	Pubtend WD
	12:00 AM	Best Lil Chathouse	MastrSofty
Thu.	8:00 PM	Teen Chat	WarwickTO,Avante
	8:00 PM	Romance Connection	RC Lucy,RC Johnny
	9:00 PM	LaPub Happy Hour	Pubtend T
	9:00 PM	The Womens Room	EvaS
	9:00 PM	New Member Lounge	NML TJ
	9:15 PM	RecoveryLink	SuziPooh & GabeS
	10:00 PM	LaPub	PubtendSen
	11:00 PM	Movie Madness	MizChiff2
	11:30 PM	Single Again	Pacaba
	12:00 AM	Best Lil Chathouse	Mastr Trev

Day	Time	Event	Host
Fri.	8:00 PM	Romance Connection	RCWitchDr/RC Softie
	9:00 PM	LaPub Happy Hour	PubTend Mo
	9:00 PM	Teen Chat	Vaprok,Orca13
	9:05 PM	Flight Deck	MileHigh
	9:00 PM	New Member Lounge	NML Lisa
	10:00 PM	LaPub	PubTend LS
	10:00 PM	Daddios Pub	Daddio
	11:00 PM	Authors Lounge	SteveGlasr
	12:00 AM	LaPub Late Night	PubTend Aeo
	12:00 AM	Best Lil Chathouse	MastrVGogh,MastrSkeev
	12:00 AM	CompuCaring	Heels lovr
	1:00 AM	Pajama Party	PJ Johnny
	9:00 AM	Sunrise Diner	Alandra
Sat.	11:00 AM	Saturday Brunch	Laila1
	12:00 PM	Authors Cafe	MizChiff2
	8:00 PM	Romance Connection	RCSkeeve,RC Lisa
	9:00 PM	Saturday's Bar	Tomw19
	9:00 PM	New Member Lounge	NML Densa
	9:00 PM	LaPub Happy Hour	PubTend TD
	9:00 PM	Teen Chat	Esprit2,DrCatalyst
	10:00 PM	LaPub	PubTend GF
	11:00 PM	Best Lil Chathouse	MastrDwagn,MadamTiggy
	12:00 AM	LaPub Late Night	PubTend Aeo
	12:00 AM	Over Forty	Jo1040X
Sun.	9:00 AM	The Breakfast Club	Open
	11:00 AM	Sunday Brunch	Wrenchy
	5:00 PM	Candy Mountain	Odysseyll
	6:30 PM	Bible Chat	Pet Sounds
	7:00 PM	Astrology	Jo Bringe,Erlic
	7:30 PM	CompuCaring	Heels lovr
	8:00 PM	Romance Connection	RC FiFi,RCWitchDr,RC Lucy
	9:00 PM	New Member Lounge	NML Iguana
	9:00 PM	Born Again	Patoby
	9:00 PM	LaPub Happy Hour	PubTend Mo
	9:00 PM	Teen Chat	Odysseyll, DanW190
	9:00 PM	The Flirts Nook	The Flirt
	10:00 PM	LaPub	Pubtend Fox, Pubtend WD
	11:00 PM	White Magick	Cerridwynn
	11:00 PM	Best Lil Chathouse	Mastr BOO, MadameRose
	12:00 AM	LaPub Late Nite	PubTend AV

There are three things I need to mention about the schedule in Figure 12-6:

🔺 This schedule is subject to change. By the time you read this book, the schedule you see in Figure 12-6 will probably be out of date. Check it for yourself. Print it if you wish (choose Print from the File menu when the schedule is on the screen). Don't rely on Figure 12-6 as the final word.

▲ No matter how current it might be, the Event Rooms Schedule lists only those events in the People Connection Department and not those scheduled by individual forums or clubs. The Ten Forward Lounge, for instance, is the Star Trek Club's chat room, and it isn't mentioned in the Event Rooms Schedule at all. Consult individual clubs (see Chapter 13, "Clubs & Interests," for a discussion of clubs) for their chat rooms and schedules, or use the keyword TITF (Tonight in the Forums) to see what's about to happen.

▲ Note the names of the hosts in Figure 12-6. Each of the Event Rooms is hosted, and that is a matter of significance. The hosts' duties include keeping the conversation going, selecting topics, aiding members who have questions (not to the degree that the Guides do, but aid nonetheless), and making sure all members have an enjoyable time—including the shy ones. Events rooms are sponsored by AOL; each room and its host have to go through a trial period before the room is added to the schedule. Though a number of rooms are simply opened by members (and don't appear on the schedule), you can be assured of certain standards of behavior when you visit an event room, and most of the credit for this goes to the host.

Finding Other Rooms

You can always tell which other rooms are available at any particular moment by clicking the Rooms icon at the left side of any chat window (review Figure 12-2 for Lobby B's window). When you click that icon, you'll see the window pictured in Figure 12-7.

Figure 12-7: A
Public Rooms list
appears whenever
you click the
Rooms icon in a
chat window.

Seventeen rooms are listed in Figure 12-7 and the More button (at the bottom of the window) is active. In fact, more than 35 rooms were available when I visited. Note that the lobby is filled to capacity (again, 23 is the maximum for a room: must have something to do with the fire marshal), so there must be other lobbies hidden beneath the More button. I can go into any room by double-clicking it, or I can get a list of all the people in a room (without going in) by selecting the room, then clicking the People button at the bottom of the screen.

The Active Public Rooms window in Figure 12-7 only lists the *active* public rooms—rooms with people in them. Often, public rooms are available and no one is in them. A listing of these rooms is available by clicking the Available Rooms button (see Figure 12-8).

Figure 12-8: The Available Public Rooms window lists only those available rooms that are currently unoccupied.

Three Kinds of Rooms

People who are new to AOL often have trouble understanding the three kinds of rooms AOL has to offer. Each serves a different purpose. Entering one without an understanding of what's inside is a bit like opening meeting room doors in a large hotel: some might welcome you enthusiastically, others might make you feel unwelcome, and still others might be engaged in conversations that are of no interest to you whatsoever.

- *Public rooms* are created and named by AOL to reflect their conversational focus. Some of these are hosted; some are not. So far, public rooms are all we've discussed.

- *Private rooms* are created and named by members. Their names never appear on any of the lists you can see. I'll discuss private rooms in a few moments.

- *Member rooms* are named and created by members (see Figure 12-9). Member rooms are rarely hosted, though Guides might occasionally visit them. Conversations in member rooms are usually unmonitored and topics range from the sublime to the scurrilous.

Figure 12-9:
Member rooms are
created by
members and are
not hosted. You
can create one of
your own
whenever you
wish using the
Create Room
button.

Note that Figure 12-9 contains a Create Room button. Anyone who wishes can create a member room—to talk about a specific topic, or no particular topic at all. You can create your own member room (in which case its title will appear in the window pictured in Figure 12-9), or, if an existing member room topic appeals to you, highlight the room and click the People button (see the bottom of the window in Figure 12-9). You can tell a lot about a room by seeing the names of the people who are there.

Parental Control

We've discussed it before: AOL is a community. On a political level, communities range from socialism to anarchism. But in this country we think of something in between. There *is* a government, after all, but it's not authoritarian; people do pretty much as they please, within certain bounds.

Our politics are reflected in our families: we seek a balance between despotic authority and profligate anarchy. Parents struggle with this balance: equanimity is elusive. Nowhere is this more evident than in matters of censure.

Every parent adopts a personal level of censorship: that's as it should be. Recently, however, the media have offered their assistance: all motion pictures are rated, many television cable companies offer selective channel blocking, a rating system is emerging for video games, and AOL offers a feature called *Parental Control* (keyword: Parental Control).

Parental Control can only be used by the master account. The master account is the permanent screen name that was created during your first sign-on to AOL. Parental Control enables the master account holder to restrict—for other names on that account—access to certain areas and features available online. It can be set for one or all screen names on the account; and once it is set for a particular screen name, it is active each time that screen name signs on. Changes can be made only at the master account level, and therefore, only by the person who knows the master account's password.

Figure 12-10:
Using my master
account—
TLichty—I am
able to control
access to
selective areas
within the
service for all
my other
accounts.

Parental Control

To restrict or block a screen name from using a feature, select the check box that is across from the screen name and under the area you wish to restrict.

Screen Name	Block Instant Messages	--- People Connection ---		Block Conference Rooms
		Block All Rooms	Block Member Rooms	
T Lichty	☐	☐	☐	☐
MajorTom	☐	☐	☐	☐

[Cancel] [OK]

Refer to Figure 12-10: the master account holder can set any or all of the following four Parental Control features:

- *Block Instant Messages* turns off all Instant Messages to and from the screen name. (We'll discuss Instant Messages later in this chapter.)

- *Block All Rooms* blocks access to People Connection.

- *Block Member Rooms* only blocks access to the member-created rooms within People Connection.

- *Block Conference Rooms* blocks access to the special-interest rooms found throughout AOL, such as the classrooms in Learning and Reference, the technical forums in Computing and Software, and the NeverWinter Nights role-playing game in Games and Entertainment.

The Parental Control feature is an elective, not an imperative. Use it if you want; ignore it if you wish. That's a level of intervention that accommodates any parental attitude, and that's the way most of us prefer to have it.

The New Member Lounge

If you're new to chat rooms, you should start at the New Member Lounge. It meets every evening at 9:00 P.M. (Eastern time). Before you enter this or any room, however, it helps to know some of the basic protocol.

- If you intend to stay in a room for a while, say hello when you enter.

- Don't type in uppercase. That's shouting.

- Speak when spoken to, even if you say nothing but "I don't know."

- Use a screen name containing your first name or a nickname. Talking to "TLic7563" is like talking to a license plate. "MajorTom" allows people to call me "Major," "Tom" or "T."

- Keep a log of your first few chat room visits by choosing Logging from the File menu (logs are discussed in Chapter 6, "Today's News "). Review the log off-line when your session has concluded. You'll learn a lot about chats this way.

- Learn your shorthands and smileys, if for no other reason than to figure out what people are doing when they type something like "{{{{{{{{{{{{**}}}}}}}}}}}}" or "ROFLWTIME." To find shorthands online, choose Online Shorthands from the What's Happening This Week window pictured in Figure 12-4. Smileys are also discussed in Chapter 4, "Electronic Mail," and in Chapter 20, "Ten Best."

- There are no stupid questions. Guides, hosts and members love to help. If you're made to feel stupid or unwelcome in a room, visit another.

Private Rooms

Private rooms are the same as public rooms except that they don't appear in any of the rooms windows. Private rooms can hold as many as 23 people and are established by members. There's no way to see a list of private rooms. You'll never know about a private room unless you create one of your own or someone invites you into theirs.

Look again at Figure 12-9. The Private Room button pictured there allows you to create or visit a private room. When you click this button, AOL asks you for a room name. If you enter a name and the room already exists, AOL takes you into that room. If it doesn't exist, AOL creates it and takes you there. If you create a room, the only people who can enter it are those who know its name.

Online Conference Calls

Consider the private room as an alternative to the conference call. We don't tend to think of them that way; but private rooms are essentially mechanisms whereby people from around the country can hold real-time conferences. America Online's private rooms are much less expensive than the phone company's conference calls, and participants can keep a log of the conversation for review once the conference has concluded (see Chapter 6, "Today's News," for a discussion of logs). Conferences are often more productive when participants have to write what they say (makes 'em think before they speak) and when vocal inflections don't cloud the issue.

To hold a private-room conference call (or to simply meet some friends for a chat in a private room), tell the participants the name of the room and the time you want to meet beforehand, then arrive a few minutes early and create the room. Instruct the participants to enter the Lobby (Command-L gets you there in a hurry) when they sign on, click the Rooms icon, click the Private Room button, then type in the name of your room. Try it: it's in many ways superior to a conference call—and cheaper to boot.

Chat Room Technique

It's easy to participate in an online chat. All you need to do is read other members' comments and type your responses, then press the Enter key (or click the Chat window's Send button) when you want to send your own comment. But if you plan to spend a lot of time chatting online, here are a few techniques that might come in handy while you're visiting a chat room.

Cut & Paste

Remember that AOL's windows can be resized and relocated anywhere on the screen. First, size the chat window down to leave a small open area on your screen. Now choose New from the File menu and size the resulting Untitled window to fit the open area (see Figure 12-11). Use the Untitled window as a scratch pad. Make notes and jot responses there. If you want to send a note as a chat comment, copy it from the Untitled window, paste it into the comment box and click Send.

Figure 12-11: Two windows on my screen: at top, Lobby A; below, Untitled 1, where I'm scribbling notes that can be copied later to the top window. I can also use the Untitled window to paste material copied *from* Lobby A for saving later to disk.

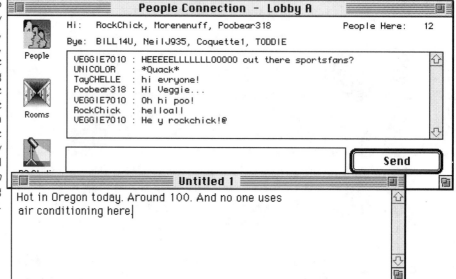

Getting Information About People in a Room

You can find out about anyone in a chat room by clicking the People icon in the upper left corner of the room's window (review Figure 12-3 for this icon). The People in this Room window will open to list—you guessed it—all of the people in the room (see Figure 12-12).

Figure 12-12: Want to know who's in your room? Click the People icon.

If you want to know more about a specific person, select the name and click the Get Info button pictured in Figure 12-12. If that person has completed a profile (discussed in Chapter 3, "Online Help & the Members"), everything they want you to know about them will appear on your screen.

The Gallery

If you want to know even more about a person, check out the Gallery (keyword: Gallery). Members can send their photographs to a scanning service and the electronic result is posted in the Gallery, or they can post scans of their own. There's a search button, so you don't have to look through long listings. Steve Case is there; so am I. Printed gallery photos make great trading cards: "I'll trade you one Steve Case for two MajorToms...."

Sending an Instant Message

Look again at Figure 12-12. See the button marked "Message"? If I wanted to send an Instant Message to MizChiff, I could click that button. Only MizChiff would see it; the other people in the room would be none the wiser. This feature is especially handy, since you will often want to "whisper" privately to someone in a chat room. We'll discuss Instant Messages in a few moments.

Highlighting & Ignoring Members

Investigate the Hilite and Ignore buttons pictured in Figure 12-12. When rooms become full and everyone is talking, it can be difficult to follow what's going on. Often, three or four conversations are going on at the same time. If you wish to exclude a member's comments (or those of all the members in a conversation in which you're not interested), select the member's name in the People in this Room window and click the Ignore button. From then on, that member's text will not appear on your screen.

Conversely, if you want to emphasize a specific member's comments, select the member's name in the People in this Room window and click the Hilite button (note how I've Hilited MizChiff in Figure 12-13). These two buttons are a real boon when chats get busy, yet not every member is aware of them.

Figure 12-13:
MizChiff is the
operator of the
Authors Cafe and I
don't want to miss
any of her
comments. To
emphasize her
text, I clicked on
the Hilite button,
pictured in Figure
12-12.

Chat Room Sounds

As long as we're talking about little-used commands, note that a new item—Chat—appears on your menu bar when you're in a chat room. The Chat menu allows you to change your chat room preferences and send chat room sounds. You can send these sounds just as you send text; people in the room will hear the sound just as they would read the text. All you have to do is double-click the sound from the Select a Sound window. That's the good news. Here's the bad news:

- Only Macintoshes can send and receive chat room sounds. Members using other types of machines will only see the sound's name in the chat room window. (Look again at Figure 12-11: Do you see the word *Quack* there? That's a sound.)

- Both the person sending the sound and those who want to hear it must have the sound installed in their Online Sounds file. America Online doesn't transmit the sound file when you send a sound—sending the actual sound itself would take too long using a modem—but rather a *notification* to play the sound. Members' Macs will play the sound only if they have the sound on file.

Finding & Installing Sounds

Hundreds of sounds are posted in the Macintosh Music and Sound Forum (keyword: MMS). To find them quickly, use the keyword FileSearch, then specify "Chat sound" as your search criteria. Remember, sound files are large—usually at least 5k per second—so they may take a while to download.

If you want to add a sound to your Online Sounds file, use the appropriate utility. I'm fond of Riccardo Ettore's *Sound Mover*, which is included in the Sound Manager shareware package available on AOL. It comes with instructions, or you can contact the author of the program on AOL—his screen name is "REttore." To find Sound Manager, use the keyword FileSearch, then specify "Sound Manager" as your search criteria.

Instant Messages

An *Instant Message* is a message sent to someone else online. Don't confuse Instant Messages with e-mail. Unlike e-mail, both the sender and the recipient have to be online at the same time for Instant Messages to work.

As I mentioned earlier, an Instant Message sent to someone else in a chat room is something like whispering in class, though you'll never get in trouble for it. You'll probably encounter Instant Messages most often when you're in a room. It's then, after all, that other people know you're online. Instant Messages aren't limited to chat rooms, however: they work whenever you're online, wherever you might be.

A moment ago, I suggested a private room as an alternative to conference calls. You might also consider Instant Messages as alternatives to long-distance phone calls. Pam Richardson (my primary contact at Ventana Press) and I need to have a number of discussions nearly every day. Unfortunately, Pam is in North Carolina and I am in Oregon—we're about as far away from one another as we can be without being in different countries. Instead of making long-distance telephone calls across the country and four different time zones, we have agreed on mutual times to go online, and now we "talk" without worrying about the cost. All we pay is our normal connect-time charge. A conversation we had the other day appears in Figure 12-14.

Figure 12-14: The
Instant Message
window contains a
running log of our
conversation in the
upper text box
along with the
response I'm
composing in the
lower one.

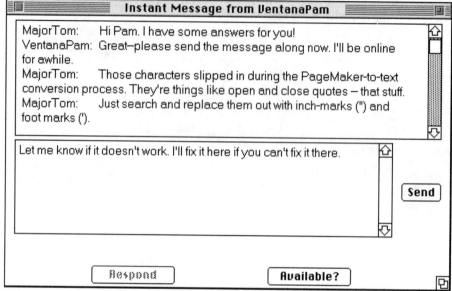

To send an Instant Message, choose Instant Message from the Members menu or type Command-I. Enter the recipient's screen name and your message where appropriate and click Send. After that, a running log of the conversation is maintained in the Instant Message window, as pictured in Figure 12-13.

- Before you send an Instant Message, use the Available? button, pictured in Figure 12-14, or the Locate a Member Online command under the Members menu. If the recipient isn't online when you send an Instant Message, AOL tells you and you'll have to wait for another opportunity. (If a member is not available online, consider sending e-mail instead. Electronic mail is discussed in Chapter 4.)

- You can send sounds in Instant Messages just as you can in a chat room. Use the sound-broadcasting format described earlier, and be sure that the recipient is using a Mac.

Available or Locate?

The Available? button in the Instant Message window does the same thing as the Locate a Member Online command under the Members menu. I prefer the button. Most of the time, if a member is online you're going to want to say hello, right? If you discover the member online via the Locate command and want to say hello, you have to call up the Instant Message dialog box anyway; but in the period of time it takes to produce that box, you might lose your opportunity.

OK, it's a small matter, and locating members online isn't like locating pike: they aren't liable to disappear in a matter of seconds. Nonetheless, it's one less command to learn, and every time you don't use the Available? button, you'll wish you did.

- Figure 12-14's window has been enlarged from the default. Like all of AOL's windows, the Instant Message window can be sized as you please. If you want to change the size of a window permanently, choose Remember Size from the Windows menu after you have sized the window to your satisfaction.

- You cannot receive or send Instant Messages while in a free area such as the Members' Online Guide. America Online closes any open Instant Message windows when you enter a free area.

- Determine where the intended recipient is before sending an Instant Message by clicking the Available? button in the Instant Message window. This feature tells you if the recipient is online, and if so, whether he or she can receive Instant Messages. It also tells you if a member is in a chat room, in which case you might want to go to that room rather than send an Instant Message.

- If the recipient is online but in a free area, in the process of downloading or in some other way unable to receive an Instant Message, AOL tells you—after it unsuccessfully tries to deliver the message.

- Instant Messages are accompanied by a "tinkerbell" sound and the Instant Message window becomes the frontmost window on your screen. The Preferences command under the Members menu allows you to change these options, but most people prefer the high degree of priority Instant Messages receive without changing their preferences.

- You can log Instant Messages (handy for "phone call"-style Instant Messages such as those I exchange with Pam) by choosing Logs from the File menu.

- If you don't want to be disturbed by Instant Messages, you can turn them off at any time by sending an Instant Message to "$im_off" (without the quotation marks, with the dollar sign, and always in lowercase). Include a character or two as text for the message; otherwise AOL will respond with a "cannot send empty Instant Message" error. A single character will do. To turn Instant Messages back on, send an Instant Message to "$im_on."

Virtual Romance

Robin Williams writes wonderful little books for computer users. Her book *The Little Mac Book* (published by Peachpit Press) should be on every Mac user's shelf. Robin is the penultimate romantic: she's charmed by the Byronic, the poetic, the courtly. She writes:

"There was a letter in my mailbox. I didn't recognize the name of the sender. The letter quoted MacBeth, 'Tomorrow and tomorrow and tomorrow creeps in this petty pace from day to day, to the last syllable of recorded time....' The writer complained of a gloomy evening in Atlanta, wet and dark and lonely. I realized this person had probably done a search for users who mentioned an interest in Shakespeare in their bios. So I sent a letter back, which included, 'Hey, lighten up. MacBeth's dysfunctional. I know a bank where the wild thyme blows, where oxlips and the nodding violet grows.'

"We exchanged several other short letters. He was a 24-year-old son of a minister. I was a 37-year-old single mother of three, pure heathen. It was easy to be friends because neither of us expected anything from the other.

"One late night I was hanging around in the lobby. I had only been connected to America Online for about a month, so I was still learning the etiquette and the conventions of online socializing. I heard a tinkling sound, as if someone threw fairy dust at me. On the screen was my first Instant Message, and it was from my friend. We sent a few messages back and forth, then he suggested we go to a private room. I had no idea what a private room was at that time, nor was I aware of what private rooms are generally used for. So I innocently tripped along with him to a room.

"I remember the feeling that night so clearly because it gave me a brief glimpse into the power of virtual reality. Meeting him in the lobby that night was as if I saw him across the

More⟩

floor of a crowded room. He winked at me, nodded his head toward the hallway, and we snuck out and met in the corridor. We tiptoed down the hall and slipped into an empty room. It was very innocent; we chatted about our lives, history, philosophy, religion. I was so involved in this conversation that took place in the computer's nether world of digital bits and analog streams that when my neighbor walked into my room I jumped. I felt like she had intruded on a very personal moment, as if I had been caught in a dimly lit room, holding hands.

"Somehow, over the months, this unlikely relationship took an unexpected romantic turn. When I received a letter telling me how he had reached up with his left hand, reached into his fantasy, and pulled me down beside him, when he said, 'I would trade my loneliness for the warmth of her laughter; she would trade her nightgown for the cloak of a young man's affection,' when I found emotions raging in me that fought between my brain and my heart, I realized there were facets to human nature that this new medium of communication was going to expose in new and different ways. It was going to be an interesting summer."

Center Stage & Rotunda

America Online offers two special chat rooms called *Center Stage* and *Rotunda*. This is the format AOL uses to present special guests or to offer "game shows" for members to play.

Typically, members attending a Rotunda or Center Stage event sit in "rows" of seats in the audience. Each row has a limited number of seats. This is how AOL accommodates a large audience of members without exceeding its own 23-member room capacity. Your chat window contains the text of everything that's happening on stage, along with comments from other members in your row (but not from members in other rows). You can change rows if you like, as long as there's an empty seat in that row, and you can turn off the comments of members in your row if they're distracting.

Provision is usually made to submit questions or comments to the people onstage. The event's host receives your message and (optionally) delivers it to the guest for a response.

Center Stage and Rotunda schedules are posted each day and are available by using the keyword: Center Stage or the keyword Rotunda (see Figure 12-15). There are many other "large-room" events sponsored by individual forums as well. To see their schedules, use the keyword TITF (Tonight in the Forums).

Figure 12-15: The Box Office lists all upcoming Center Stage events. Double-click any one for details.

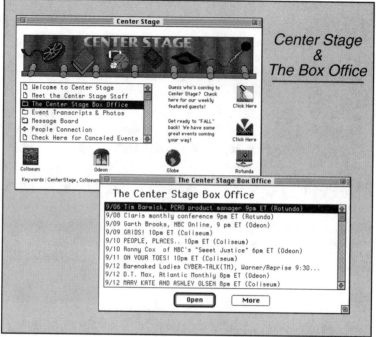

Figure 12-15: The Box Office lists all upcoming Center Stage events. Double-click any one for details.

Rules for the Center Stage game shows are available by opening the Game Show Rules folder pictured in Figure 12-15. Read them before you take part in a game. Game shows are often profitable: winning contestants are awarded free connect time.

The person in charge of Center Stage—AOL's "theater district"—is Amy Arnold. Another team player who has come up through the ranks, Amy recruits the guests who have filled her four auditoria to capacity recently—something that rarely happened before she took over.

As I mentioned a moment ago, the Center Stage feature is often used to present special guests to members. One of those recently featured was Guy Kawasaki. Kawasaki is the former Director of Software Product Management at Apple Computer, and as such was one of the key players in the success of the Macintosh personal computer.

Guy left Apple in 1987 to start his own software company. An author, he's written *The Macintosh Way, Selling the Dream, Database 101*, and *The Computer Curmudgeon*. Formerly he was a columnist for *MacUser* magazine. Portions of his Center Stage transcript appear below.

Marge Hawk: Hi Guy! Welcome to Center Stage!
Mac Way: Hi all!

Marge Hawk: Do you plan on writing a biography?

Mac Way: Who would care about my biography?

Mac Way: I am just a Diligent Oriental who did okay in Silicon Valley.

Mac Way: Not like I am Bill Gates or Steve Jobs.

Question: What would be one thing you would like to change in the computer industry?

Mac Way: Good question. Let me think... Several things come to mind 1) Level of compensation for Apple execs. Nah, too obvious. 2) Software piracy. Nah, too greedy. 3) Assumption that you have to have lots of money to start a company. This is it. I want everybody out there to have the courage and masochism to start new companies and not listen to the prevailing cr** that it takes lots of (vc) money.

Question: Guy, do you recommend living in the Silicon Valley area to young people trying to get into the computer industry?

Mac Way: It is not really necessary. I think the place to start in the business is in field sales. That way you can learn about rejection and what customers want. If you work in the Valley, in the headquarters of companies, you tend to lose touch with customers because you live in the "Tower."

Question: I am an avid PC user and I have recently read your book. Can you give me one good reason why I should buy an Apple?

Mac Way: Sure. You can never have too fast a car, too many silk blouses, or too easy a computer to use. How many apps do you really use? I bet a Macintosh owner can use more.

Question: Guy, Do you think Apple has sold out Mac evangelism and religion in favor of market share, "strategic" alliances and business footholds?

Mac Way: Another good question. I don't think Apple "sold out." I think it just "leased" it for a while. When they need good, ole evangelism for the next computer, they'll get back the feelings. Toward the end of the Apple II, there wasn't much "evangelism" for it either.

Question: Do you think there will ever be an end to the Windows/Macintosh "debate?"

Mac Way: Never. What else do the press and analysts have to write about? You can say you heard it here first. The world can be divided into two groups: 1) those who can do, and 2) those who can't. Those who can't and can write, become press. Those who can't and can't write, become analysts. The best way to make money is to do the opposite of what the press and analysts say. End of sermon.

Question: What are the most underaddressed areas where we need new software?

Mac Way: Telecommunications for mere mortals.

Question: What curriculum/activity would you recommend to someone who wants to develop Mac multimedia software?

Mac Way: A course in personal bankruptcy would help. I just don't believe in MM yet. I think John Sculley read too many issues of Nova. MM is a solution in search of a need, IMHO.

Question: Guy, Many PC users continue to claim that the Mac is underpowered and erratic in its design and short on customer support. Do you think Apple has addressed these challenges with the recent changes at the company?

Mac Way: Yes, but who cares what PC users think? Why should eagles worry about what pigs think of the sky?

Ahem! On that note, perhaps it's best if we wrap up this chapter.

Moving On

Many of those who are new to AOL sidestep People Connection at first. Perhaps it's too intimidating. Perhaps they're shy. Whatever the reason, it's a shame. People Connection is the heart of the AOL community. It is here that you finally stop thinking of AOL as an electronic service and begin thinking of it as people. In the search for community, People Connection is where you find the bounty.

Speaking of bounty, do you have a hobby? Perhaps you have an interest: cooking comes to mind, or bicycling. Hobbies and interests are best enjoyed when there are others around with the same penchant: you can share your ideas with them and hear of theirs.

The trouble is, people with similar interests are sometimes hard to find—but not if you look around AOL. There are nearly a million of us here now, and with numbers like that, there's bound to be a few who share your interests.

The place to investigate is the Clubs & Interests Department, and it's coming up next.

Clubs & Interests

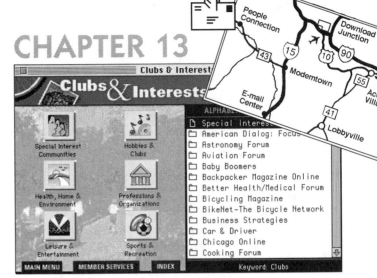

f we were to award prizes to AOL's departments, Clubs & Interests would win the Size Prize. No other department is this large; no other department offers such diversity; no other department represents the potential Clubs & Interests does. If you have an interest, there's probably some place here that serves it (see Figure 13-1).

The Index

Look again at the frontispiece for this chapter. Like all department screens, this one offers a little button at the bottom marked "Index." The Clubs & Interests index is especially important because it serves as a roadmap to the largest department in the system.

That's what indexes are: roadmaps. And like all roadmaps, AOL's indexes are best perused on paper.

Try this: Click the Clubs & Interests Index button, then choose Print Text from the File menu. America Online will offer a standard Macintosh Print dialog box, then you can send the index to your printer. (Be prepared: the Clubs & Interests Index was 19 pages when I printed it!)

Do this for each department on the service, then file the printouts in a three-ring binder with an indexing tab for each department. When you're finished, you'll have a convenient, printed roadmap to the entire service. I've one right here next to my keyboard. It's probably my most frequently used reference.

The Clubs & Interests Department is AOL's gateway to everything from astronomy to wine. African Americans, Hispanics, gays and professional groups all find homes here. It's as multiethnic as Ellis Island and as variegated as a harlequin's tights. Click the Clubs & Interests button on the Main Menu or use the keyword Clubs.

While the size of the Clubs & Interests Department is good for you, it's not so good for me: there's no way I can do this department justice. It's too large for that, and frankly, descriptions of special interests are a bit like puppies at a picnic: lots of dynamic, but they're not necessarily welcome at everyone's plate.

Figure 13-1: A few of the many clubs in the Clubs & Interests Department. There are scores of others.

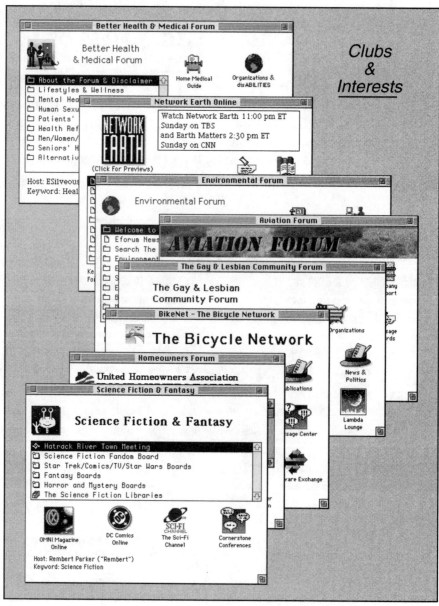

Instead, I'm going to use this department as an opportunity to describe three fundamental AOL tactics: searching online databases, reading message boards and multitasking while downloading.

Clubs Defined

Before we begin our tactical didactic, it might be best if I formally define the word *club*. The Clubs & Interests Department is primarily composed of clubs, after all. We need an example, one that's familiar to all and resplendent with people, goodies and activity.

Nomenclature Evolving

The term *club* is an evolving one at AOL. Only a few months ago, AOL's preferred term was *forum*. Other telecommunications services call them *roundtables* or *bulletin boards*. Club is probably the best description: the term *forum* has formal Roman overtones, the term *roundtable* doesn't include things like libraries of files, nor does *bulletin board*.

Lately, AOL has become especially fond of *cross-pointing*. Look again at the bottom window in Figure 13-1: cross-pointers to OMNI Magazine Online, DC Comics, and the Sci-Fi Channel appear there, none of which are part of the Science Fiction & Fantasy Club per se, but each might be found in a "clubhouse," so each appears here.

Club implies membership, however, and membership usually implies membership fees. Don't worry: there are never any membership fees for AOL's clubs. Join 'em if and whenever you wish; you're always welcome.

The perfect candidate is Wine & Dine Online. You'll find Wine & Dine Online listed in the scroll box of the Clubs & Interests main window, or by using the keyword Wine. This is a particularly refined club, one that every epicure should visit (see Figure 13-2).

Figure 13-2: Wine &
Dine Online offers
articles, folders,
message boards
and a library
of files.

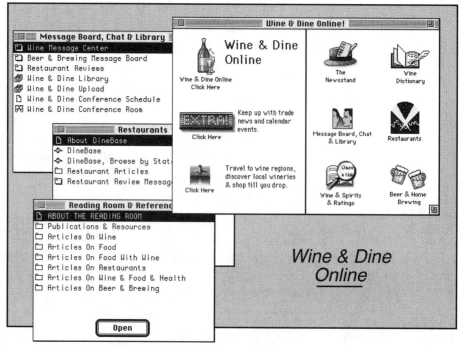

I picked this club because its composition is fairly representative of most clubs on AOL—a little more resplendent than some, perhaps, but representative nonetheless. The primary club window contains nine icons, some of which are detailed in Figure 13-2. What I want you to notice in the illustration are the icons. We see so many of them while we use our Macs that we tend to overlook them; but that's not wise when you're exploring clubs.

Reference Materials

Look carefully at the icons in the subsidiary windows of Figure 13-2. The little page icons with turned-down corners represent *articles*. Double-click article icons to read them. The folder icons hold collections of articles, grouped by subject. The "facing faces" icon is a chat room (which we discussed in Chapter 12, "People Connection"). Icons with pushpins are message boards, and the disk icons represent libraries. Let's discuss these one at a time.

Articles & Folders

Let's begin our exploration of this club by double-clicking the folder labeled "Articles On Wine" (see Figure 13-3).

Figure 13-3: Don't forget to explore folders labeled "More" when they're available.

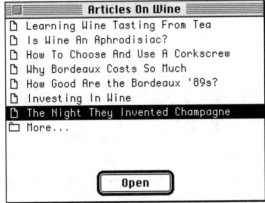

The articles/folders metaphor is repeated here. Seven articles and a folder appear in this window. Double-click any one of them to open it. The article entitled "The Night They Invented Champagne" piques my interest. Let's look it over (Figure 13-4).

Figure 13-4: It's a long story, and good reading—especially if you like champagne.

THE NIGHT THEY INVENTED...

However unromantic, the fact is that it took far longer than one night to invent Champagne, and the capture of bubbles in this very special wine in the early 1700s required a series of coincidences and technical gymnastics. It is worth recounting, because June is one of the most popular times of the year for Champagne (weddings, graduation and all), and because the finest sparkling wines are still made in the traditional Champagne method. It is also important because, more than any other wine, Champagne is made in the winery. If it is true that 70% of the quality of nonsparkling wines is made in the vineyard and 30% in the winery, the inverse is the case for sparkling wine.

The invention of Champagne is the story of monks, a marginal vineyard district whose wines were not selling particularly well, a

The article pictured in Figure 13-4 was written by Craig Goldwyn, editor of Wine & Dine Online and president of the Beverage Testing Institute, Inc. He has published hundreds of articles as the wine critic for the *Washington Post* and the *Chicago Tribune*. A more notable authority is hard to find, and Craig's always available to answer your questions and provide advice. His screen name is "goldwyn."

It Wasn't a Night at All

The story pictured in Figure 13-4 goes on to recount the complete history of Champagne (with a capital C—only the United States uses the term generically).

As it turns out, the Champagne district in northern France isn't the best place to grow grapes. The soil is less than ideal (*champagne* means "chalky white soil"), and the growing season is short—Champagne grapes often don't mature with enough sugar for winemaking. Champagne winemakers of yesteryear would often add cane sugar to feed the yeast.

Unfortunately, the Champagne district is gripped by cold weather by the time the grapes are harvested and the yeast hibernates most of the winter. When things warm up in the spring, the yeast wakes up and conducts a second fermentation, inundating the wine with excessive carbonation. The French called this *vin fou*, meaning "crazy wine."

And they loved it. Parisians traveled 90 miles to obtain it—no small feat in the seventeenth century. The wine was rare too—the bottles kept blowing up in the cellars and the wine that survived was precious stuff indeed.

The local monks, whose livelihood depended on winemaking, tried to prevent the profits from going down the sewers. One of these monks was Dom Perignon at the Benedictine Abbey of Hautvillers. He began to experiment with plugs cut from cork bark, invented a way to tie them down with string, and beefed up the thickness of the bottles. Only then did champagne become a successful commercial product.

Today the most precious champagne of them all—from the prestigious Moet-Hennessy house of spirits—carries his name.

Searching Online Databases

The searchable database is unique to the telecommunications industry. It's a benefit that simply can't be matched anywhere else. Searchable databases are perpetually maintained with not only the latest information but archived items as well. They can be searched without having to leave your keyboard. They arrive in the form of plain text, ready to be included in other documents or printed. Searchable databases are fast, immediate and usually extensive. America Online offers more than 40 of these databases; when you see one (look for the "handshake" icons such as that next to "DineBase" in Figure 13-2), take a few minutes to explore it—it's always worth the time.

Here's an eloquent example: The database of wines offered in Wine & Dine Online is probably the largest of its kind available to the public. Thousands of wines are listed here, along with prices and ratings from the Beverage Testing Institute. This is an excellent tool for cutting through a mystique that prospers on the obscurity of unfamiliar names and the bewilderment of heterogeneous prices.

I need a wine for tonight's dinner. Always the parochial Northwesterner, I'd like an Oregon wine if one's available. Before I go shopping, however, I consult Wine & Dine Online's wine database (see Figure 13-5).

Figure 13-5: Become an instant enologist. Impress your friends with your wisdom and frugality. Look it up on America Online.

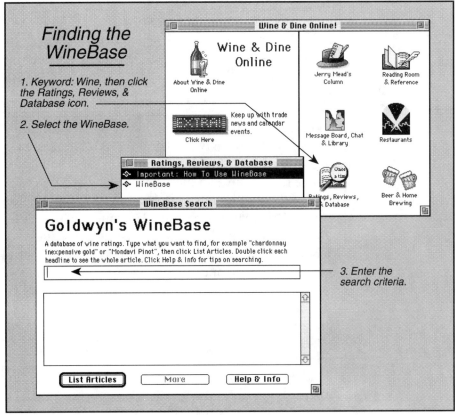

Note the open-book icon in the Wine & Dine Online window of Figure 13-5. That's AOL's way of identifying a searchable database. Significant riches are available here almost instantly. That's a good thing: my dinner guests will be arriving shortly. I type in "Oregon" as a search criterion (see Figure 13-6).

Figure 13-6: A search on the criterion "Oregon" produces 298 wines, far too many from which to make my decision.

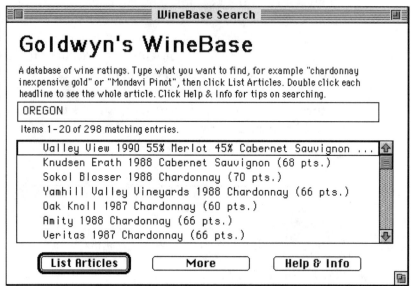

Looking at Figure 13-6, I see that WineBase contains 298 references to the state of Oregon. Note that only 20 references have been downloaded to my Mac, of which 7 appear in the scrollable window pictured in Figure 13-6. Note also that a button marked "More" appears at the bottom of the window. If I wanted to view more choices, I would use this button to see the remaining 278 wines, 20 at a time (see sidebar). By the time I read through that many listings, my guests will have departed in a pique, unfed and without libation, muttering disparaging remarks about AOL and my preoccupation with the Mac.

The "More" Button

Look again at Figure 13-6's window. Do you see the button marked "More?" It's amazing how often this button is overlooked. As discussed in the text, my search based on the criterion "Oregon" was very inefficient. The WineBase found 298 entries matching that search criterion. While I thought I was looking for a product produced in limited numbers, the WineBase surprised me with the breadth of its knowledge of Oregon wines.

Rather than spend my online time listing all 298 entries, AOL chose only to download the first 20 (a safe assumption, since I would probably want to narrow my search), and offer them in Figure 13-6's scrolling window. Since matching entries remained, AOL activated the More button. If I wanted to see more than the first 20 entries, I'd click that button and AOL would send another 20; clicking again would result in another 20 entries and so on.

Don't overlook this button! It's not unique to the WineBase—many AOL windows have one—and if it *is* overlooked, lots of opportunities are missed.

I need to refine my criteria. It's a warm fall afternoon and I'm in the mood for a cool white wine. A chardonnay would be nice (see Figure 13-7).

Figure 13-7: By using the word "and," I'm able to refine the search criteria.

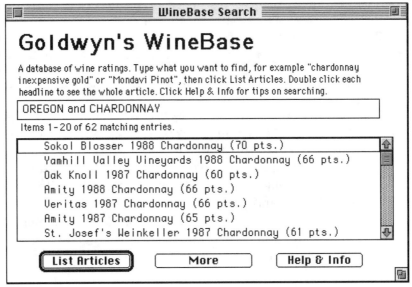

Notice the criteria shown in Figure 13-7. By saying "Oregon *and* Chardonnay," I'm able to exclude all wines that don't meet both criteria. I've narrowed it down to 62 wines, but that's still too many to sift through before my guests arrive. And these are important guests. People I want to please. Only the best will do. WineBase includes references to medals each wine might have won: bronze, silver, gold or platinum. I can exclude the no-medal wines as well as the bronze-medal wines with some *or* criteria (see Figure 13-8).

Figure 13-8: Improper use of *or* criteria is worse than specifying no criteria at all.

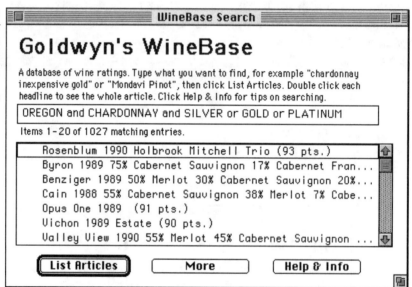

WineBase Search

Goldwyn's WineBase

A database of wine ratings. Type what you want to find, for example "chardonnay inexpensive gold" or "Mondavi Pinot", then click List Articles. Double click each headline to see the whole article. Click Help & Info for tips on searching.

OREGON and CHARDONNAY and SILVER or GOLD or PLATINUM

Items 1-20 of 1027 matching entries.

Rosenblum 1990 Holbrook Mitchell Trio (93 pts.)
Byron 1989 75% Cabernet Sauvignon 17% Cabernet Fran...
Benziger 1989 50% Merlot 30% Cabernet Sauvignon 20%...
Cain 1988 55% Cabernet Sauvignon 38% Merlot 7% Cabe...
Opus One 1989 (91 pts.)
Vichon 1989 Estate (90 pts.)
Valley View 1990 55% Merlot 45% Cabernet Sauvignon ...

[List Articles]   [More]   [Help & Info]

Uh-oh! More than a thousand matches! A mistake has been made. This is a problem similar to an algebraic statement such as "x = 5 plus 2 times 7." What's the value of x: 49 or 19? Do you first add the 5 and the 2, then multiply? Or do you multiply first, then add? WineBase has the same problem. It seems to be interpreting my criteria as "Oregon and chardonnay and silver—or gold, or platinum."

The solution is the same as the solution for mathematical expressions—parentheses. The answer to the statement "x = 5 plus (2 x 7)" is specific, as are the criteria in Figure 13-9.

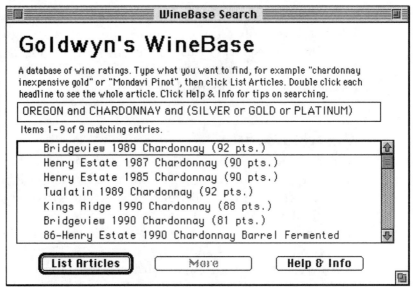

Figure 13-9: That's more like it. Nine wines is just the right number from which to choose. I'll take the list to the store and be back by the time my guests arrive.

Actually, the selection of wines at the shop I frequent is especially comprehensive. I suspect they will have all nine of the wines listed in Figure 13-9. Rather than pick one at random, I'll poll the database further. A double-click on Bridgeview 1989, for instance, produces the description pictured in Figure 13-10.

Figure 13-10: The database record for a single wine reveals its price, awards and ranking.

```
Bridgeview 1989 Chardonnay (92 pts.)

WINE TYPE: White
PRICE AT THE WINERY: $11.95/750 ml (Moderately-Priced)

BRAND NAME: Bridgeview
VINTAGE: 1989
VARIETAL (GRAPE TYPE): Chardonnay
SPECIAL DESIGNATION: Barrel Select
WINERY IS IN: Oregon USA
CASES PRODUCED: 1,200 cases

REVIEWED BY: The American Wine Competition portion of the World Wine Championships
Conducted by the Beverage Testing Institute Inc.

DATE REVIEWED: 12/90
SCORE (50-100): 92
AWARDS: Gold Medal

WineBase version 2.2, available exclusively on America Online
(c) Copyright by BTI
```

Reviewing all nine listings takes about 10 minutes. Indeed, the whole process only required about 15 minutes from sign on to sign off. Our dinner guests will be astounded with my enological expertise and entranced by my erudite conversation. Naturally, I'll take all the credit, though WineBase properly deserves it.

Message Boards

Not all clubs feature databases, and not all members require access to one. Fortunately, there's much more to AOL's clubs than databases. These are clubs, after all. People gather in clubs to discuss subjects of mutual interest and to learn more about their field. They might conduct some database research while they're online as well; but people make a club, and people make AOL's forums.

America Online's message boards are the electronic analog of the old familiar cork board and pushpins. Message boards (call them "boards") are especially appropriate to online clubs. One of the unique advantages clubs offer is convenience: you can drop in any time of the day or night, read the messages and post your replies.

Most of us visit our favorite clubs every time we sign on, and anxiously read all the messages posted since the last time we visited. The feeling is remarkably immediate, and withdrawal sets in after about three days absence. In other words, boards are addictive—but that's part of the fun.

Reading Messages

One of my favorite clubs in the Clubs & Interests Department is the Cooking Club (keyword: Cooking). These folks like their food, and their library of recipes (The Kitchen Closet) ranges from elegant appetizers to tantalizing desserts. The Cupboard offers articles and reviews of cookbooks and cooking software, and The Kitchen (a chat room, a topic we discussed in Chapter 12) opens each Sunday evening at 8:00 P.M. (Eastern time) for a cooking class, new recipes and lively camaraderie. (This is an especially nonthreatening chat room by the way. If you're new to chat rooms you might try this one first: there's very little aggression among people who spend their Sundays sipping sherry and discussing soufflés.)

Editing the Go To Menu

Once you've found a club to your liking, you might want to visit it every time you sign on. Rather than navigate a stack of menus or type a keyword, give the club a place on your Go To menu. Items at the bottom of the Go To menu are under your control; you can add or delete any one you please. The only requirement is that the item must have a keyword.

Let's say you've become an active participant in the Cooking Club. To add it to your Go To menu, follow the procedure illustrated in Figure 13-11.

Figure 13-11:
Adding menu
items is
accommodated
via the Edit
Favorite Places
command.

Note that there are a total of ten positions that you can customize on the Go To menu, and that mine only has six active. You don't have to have all ten positions filled if you don't want to, nor do you have to use those that AOL initially provides. You can change any item (select it and type over), or delete items (select the item, then use the Delete—or Backspace—key on your keyboard). Changes made to the Go To menu are unique to that computer, by the way, and not to any particular screen name. They won't appear when you're using another machine.

Once a club has been added to the Go To menu, all you have to do to get there is choose it from that menu. My Go To menu contains the names of the places I like to check every time I'm online. By choosing each one in order, I never neglect to visit places I'm likely to forget.

But I'm getting ahead of myself. I've chosen this club because it's an excellent example of message boards. In fact, it has three of them. Everyone eats food, after all, and most of us who eat it aren't shy when it comes to talking about it. For this discussion, we'll examine the Cooking Club's recipe-exchange board, The Cookbook (see Figure 13-12).

Figure 13-12: Type the keyword Cooking to open the Cooking Club's main window, then double-click The Cookbook to visit the board.

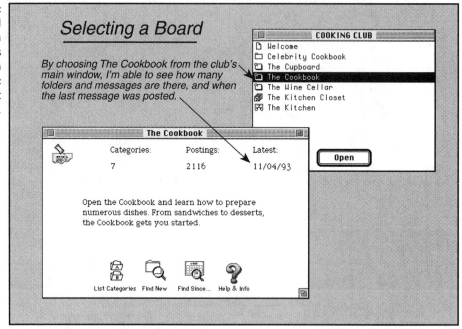

Four icons appear across the bottom of The Cookbook window: List Categories, Find New, Find Since and Help & Info. We'll examine each of these, beginning with the one marked List Categories. Since this is a complex board—it's a cookbook after all, and cookbooks are typically large and organizationally complex—a click on Figure 13-12's List Categories icon produces a list of categories (the top window in Figure 13-13), each of which is followed by a list of *topics*. The Desserts category, for instance, is further subdivided into more specific topics (Frozen Marshmallow Salad, Lisa's Strawberry Crepes, and so on). Note that Figure 13-13's top window offers no Create Topic icon: these categories were established by the forum leader and can't be changed. The second window offers a Create Topic icon, and its topics represent the specificity that's typical of the members' interests. In this board, the categories are the staff's creation; the topics belong to the members.

While this is a little anarchistic, it's also democratic; and that's the way message boards should be. If you feel like making a comment that's off the subject, use the Create Topic icon to make a new folder for it.

Figure 13-13: The seven categories posted on The Cookbook's recipe board are followed by seven member topics. Each topic folder contains a number of individual recipes.

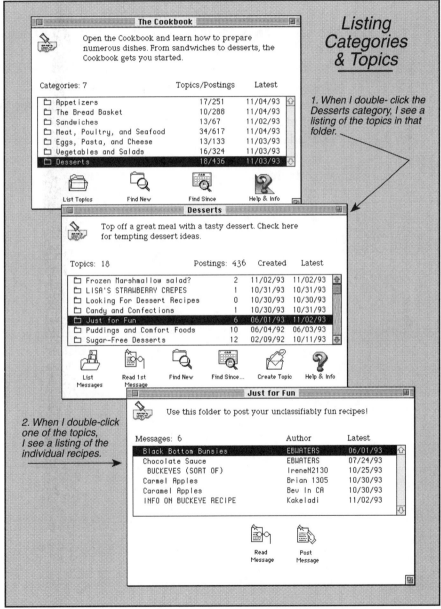

The bulletin board metaphor is distorted a bit here. Individual messages aren't normally posted on boards; *folders* are posted on boards (the messages themselves are inside the folders). Look again at the top window in Figure 13-13: this board is currently holding over 2,000 messages. If all 2,000 were posted independently, the board would be a mess. You would never find a thing. The board's nested folders are merely organizational tools intended to help you locate topics of interest to you.

To read the messages placed in a folder, double-click the folder. By double-clicking the Just for Fun topic folder in Figure 13-13's center window, we reveal the six recipes listed in the Just for Fun window at the bottom of that illustration.

To read all of the messages in a folder, double-click the first one, then use the Next Message icon (see Figure 13-14) to sequentially display the rest.

Figure 13-14: Once you have read the first message in a folder, click the Next Message icon to read the remaining messages in the order of their posting.

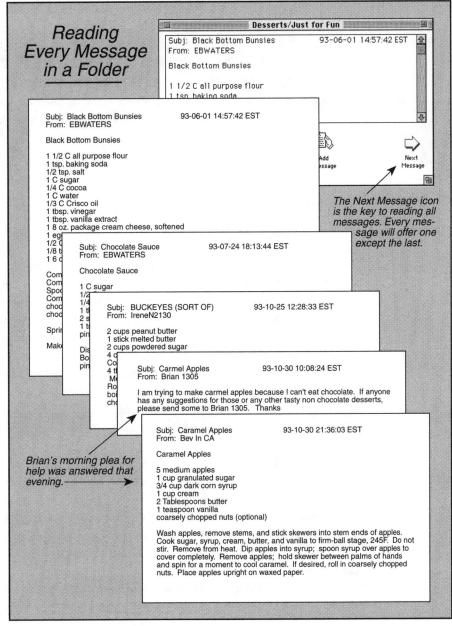

Reading Every Message in a Folder

Desserts/Just for Fun

Subj: Black Bottom Bunsies   93-06-01 14:57:42 EST
From: EBWATERS

Black Bottom Bunsies

1 1/2 C all purpose flour
1 tsp. baking soda

Add Message

Next Message

The Next Message icon is the key to reading all messages. Every message will offer one except the last.

Subj: Black Bottom Bunsies   93-06-01 14:57:42 EST
From: EBWATERS

Black Bottom Bunsies

1 1/2 C all purpose flour
1 tsp. baking soda
1/2 tsp. salt
1 C sugar
1/4 C cocoa
1 C water
1/3 C Crisco oil
1 tbsp. vinegar
1 tbsp. vanilla extract
1 8 oz. package cream cheese, softened
1 eg
1/2 C
1/8 t
1 6 c

Com
Com
Spoo
Com
choc
choc

Sprin

Make

Subj: Chocolate Sauce   93-07-24 18:13:44 EST
From: EBWATERS

Chocolate Sauce

1 C sugar
1/2
1/4
1 t
2 s
1 t
pin

Dis
Bo
Co
pin

Subj: BUCKEYES (SORT OF)   93-10-25 12:28:33 EST
From: IreneN2130

2 cups peanut butter
1 stick melted butter
2 cups powdered sugar
4 c
4 t
Me
Ro
boi
cho

Subj: Carmel Apples   93-10-30 10:08:24 EST
From: Brian 1305

I am trying to make carmel apples because I can't eat chocolate. If anyone has any suggestions for those or any other tasty non chocolate desserts, please send some to Brian 1305. Thanks

Subj: Caramel Apples   93-10-30 21:36:03 EST
From: Bev In CA

Caramel Apples

5 medium apples
1 cup granulated sugar
3/4 cup dark corn syrup
1 cup cream
2 Tablespoons butter
1 teaspoon vanilla
coarsely chopped nuts (optional)

Wash apples, remove stems, and stick skewers into stem ends of apples. Cook sugar, syrup, cream, butter, and vanilla to firm-ball stage, 245F. Do not stir. Remove from heat. Dip apples into syrup; spoon syrup over apples to cover completely. Remove apples; hold skewer between palms of hands and spin for a moment to cool caramel. If desired, roll in coarsely chopped nuts. Place apples upright on waxed paper.

Brian's morning plea for help was answered that evening.

Log Those Messages

Reading messages is one of the most time-consuming activities AOL offers. Rather than read messages online, save a log of them (I discussed logs in Chapter 6, "Today's News") as they download to your Mac. Let them scroll off your screen as fast as they can; do not try to read them while you're online. When you have finished the session, sign off, open the log (choose Open from AOL's File menu) and read it at your leisure. You can always add messages to boards by signing back on again.

Browsing, Finding & Reading Messages

I need to take a side trip here. The verbs *browse, find* and *read* have particular, unequivocal meanings when it comes to message boards; it's important that you understand how to use them. Think of a public library: you might go to the library simply to pass the time. You walk in and browse, picking up a book here and there as different titles strike your fancy. On another day, you might visit the library with a specific title already in mind, in which case you go straight to the card files and find that particular book. Regardless of how you come across a book, you eventually want to sit down and read it, page by page.

America Online attaches the same meanings to these verbs. Look again at the Desserts window at the center of Figure 13-13. Six icons parade across the bottom of the window, representing variations on the three verbs we're discussing.

The List Messages icon displays the folder's message subjects, authors and dates, not the messages themselves (see the Just for Fun window at the bottom of Figure 13-13). The List Messages feature is like browsing through the books in a library: they're similar concepts. The leftmost icon (List Messages, in this case) is the default: if you double-click a folder, you'll see the list that appears in the lower window of Figure 13-13.

Clicking the Read 1st Message icon produces a window displaying the first message in the folder (see the top window in Figure 13-14).

The Subject Line

As you read through this section, note the role played by the messages' subject lines. A subject line like "Comment" doesn't illuminate its contents very well. Alternatively, the subject line "Chocolate Sauce" clearly summarizes the content of the message and intrigues the reader. Spend a moment thinking about subject lines when you post your own messages; they're significant.

This might be a board you read often. You might visit it every time you sign on. If you do, you can go right to the Find New icon, which displays only those messages posted since you last visited (see Figure 13-15).

Figure 13-15: Only new messages appear when you click the Find New icon. You can read them, add to them, or list all of the messages in the folder.

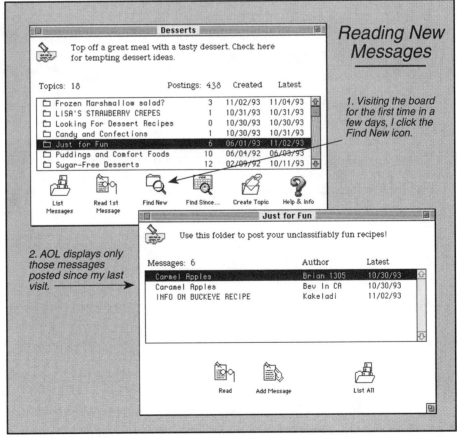

Note the Add Message icon at the bottom of Figure 13-15. This is how you add messages to the folder. All you need to do is click the icon, enter the subject and text of your message, then OK your effort. Your message will be added to the folder immediately. I'll discuss this further in a moment.

Your Personal Date

Your personal "date of last visit" is marked the instant you visit a board. This implies two things: (1) No matter how many (or how few) messages you read while visiting a board, none of the messages posted prior to that visit are displayed when you next click the Find New icon; and (2) If anyone (including you) posts a message on a board while you're reading, that message will appear when you next click the Find New icon.

Note that I'm talking about *boards* here, not folders. If a board contains 600 messages in 24 folders and you read one message in one folder, none of the remaining messages will show up the next time you click the Find New icon, in any folder on the board. This is a significant subtlety. Don't let it trip you up.

Most boards contain hundreds of messages. No matter how interested in the subject you might be, it's doubtful you'll want to read every message the first time you visit a board. Or maybe you've been away from the board for a few months and don't want to be deluged with all the messages posted since your last visit. These are two of the reasons why AOL provides the Find Since icon (see Figure 13-16).

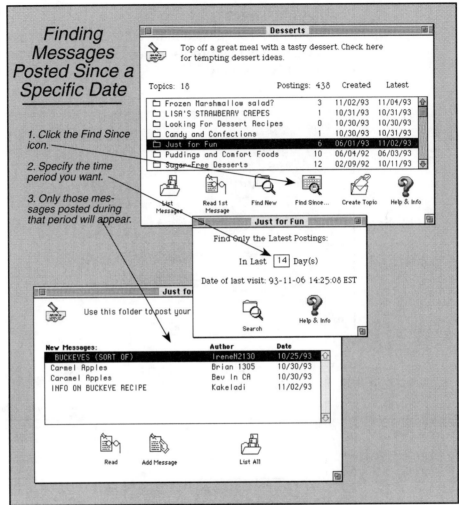

Figure 13-16: The Find Since icon allows you to specify the extent of a message list.

It took me months to figure out just how the List Messages, Find and Read icons work. I hope this little discussion saves you the trouble. Regardless, find a board that interests you and start reading its messages. Start with just one or two folders, read the last week's worth of messages, and become familiar with the subject and the people. When you feel confident, post your own messages. It is at that moment—when you have joined the fray—that message boards start to get really interesting. This is part of the fun; don't deny yourself the opportunity.

Posting Messages

A moment ago, I suggested that you post your own messages. It might help if we review that process. There's not much to it: take a look at Figure 13-17 to see how.

Figure 13-17: Posting your own message is as simple as clicking an icon.

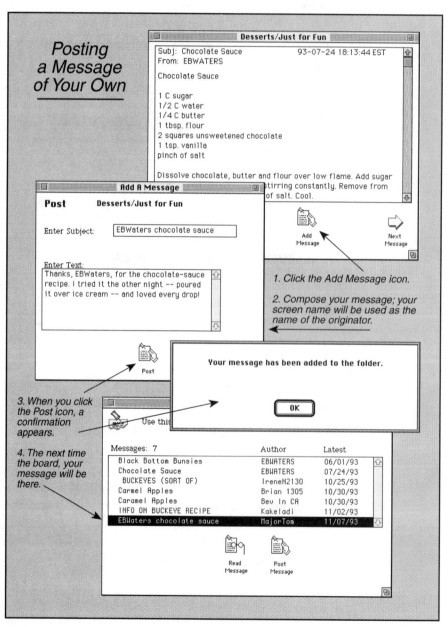

Online Etiquette

If you want to be heard, if you want replies to your messages, and if you want to be a responsible online citizen, you should comply with a few rules of telecommunications etiquette. Since Emily Post and Miss Manners haven't yet spoken on the subject (now that I think about it, Emily Post *has* spoken on the subject, and we'll discuss her in the next chapter), we'd best discuss it here.

- Post messages only when you have something to say, phrase the subject header effectively, and be succinct. The best messages have provocative headers and pithy prose. If your message fills more than a screen of text—if it requires a trip to the scroll bar to read—edit it.

- Stick to the subject. If the folder you're participating in is entitled "Weasels in Wyoming," don't discuss armadillos in Arizona.

- If your message wanders, summarize before responding. You might quote a previous posting (do so in brackets: "When you said <I really prefer Macintosh> were you talking about apples or Apples?"). This will help others stick to the topic.

- Don't post chain letters, advertisements or business offers unless the board was created for it. And never send junk mail to unsuspecting recipients.

- HEY YOU! CAN YOU HEAR ME??!! (Did I get your attention? Did you like the way I did it?) All caps are distracting, hard to read and arrogant. Use all caps only when you really want to shout (and those occasions are rare). For emphasis, place asterisks around your text: "I *told* you he was a geek!"

- Do not issue personal attacks, use profanity or betray a confidence. If criticism is specifically invited, remember that there is no vocal inflection or body language to soften the impact and remove the potential for misinterpretation. E-mail is a better forum for criticism than boards are.

- For the same reason, subtleties, double entendres and sarcasm are rarely effective.

- Avoid emotional responses. Think before you write. Once you've posted a message, you can't take it back.

- Remember your options. Some replies are better sent as mail than as messages. If you're feeling particularly vitriolic, send mail to the perpetrator. This saves face for both of you.

Posting effective messages is something of an art. Messages like "Me too" or "I don't think so" don't really contribute to a board. Before you post a message, be sure you have something to say, take the time to phrase it effectively and give it a proper subject header.

Threaded Boards

Some boards offer *message threading*: messages arranged so that you can elect to read responses to a specific message. Compare this with the Read 1st Message command pictured in Figure 13-14. Reading the first message displays the first message on a board with the option to read all of the remaining messages on the board as well.

Threaded message boards allow you to choose to read only the replies to a specific message. This is especially appropriate where the subject of a specific folder is likely to be broad and its messages are numerous and varied. To examine a threaded board, let's visit the Pet Care Club (keyword: Pets). A number of veterinarians from universities and private practices visit this board regularly, some of whom are on the board's staff. If you have pets—dogs, cats, reptiles, birds, even farm animals—this is a club you will want to visit often (see Figure 13-18).

Figure 13-18: The Pet Care Club offers boards for not only dogs and cats, but for farm animals, fish—even for reptiles.

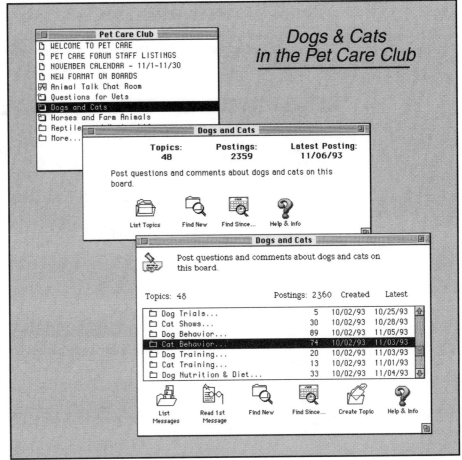

Until now, threaded boards look just like unthreaded boards. But look what happens when I double-click the folder labeled "Cat Behavior" (Figure 13-19).

Figure 13-19:
Threaded boards
offer a Responses
column and a List
Responses icon at
the bottom of
the window.

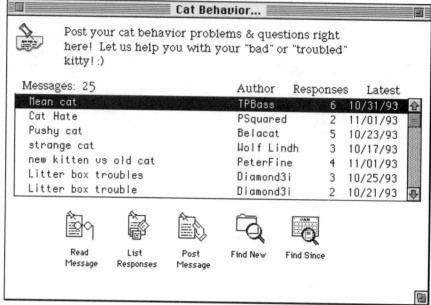

Look carefully at Figure 13-19: a Responses column appears, identifying the number of responses that have been posted to any particular message. A new List Responses icon appears at the bottom of the window as well.

Now watch what happens when I double-click the "Mean cat" posting (Figure 13-20).

Figure 13-20: Note
how the list of
responses to the
"Mean cat"
message provides
me with the
opportunity to
post a reply or
reread the original
message in case
I've forgotten
a detail.

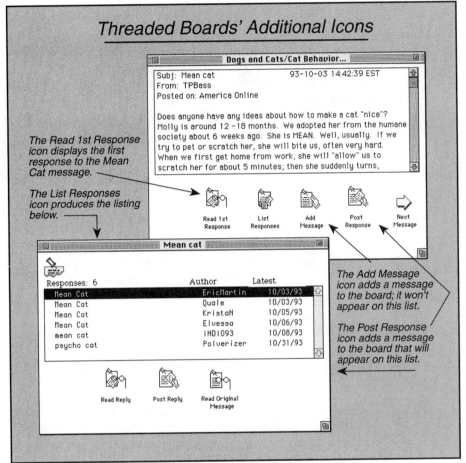

The Read 1st Response and List Responses icons are new to the
message window, as is the Post Response icon. When I click the List
Responses icon I see a listing of only the responses to the "Mean cat"
message. This provides a method by which I can stick to the "Mean
cat" subject, and not wander all over the board.

Proper Replies

Be sure you post replies to messages properly. Look at the upper window in Figure 13-20: two reply icons appear there—Add Message and Post Response. The Add Message icon simply adds a message to the board; the added message is posted independently and not identified as a response to any other message. A message posted via the Post Response icon will appear as a response in a list of responses, similar to those pictured in the lower window of Figure 13-20. It's not just a matter of semantics; it's an organizational imperative. Give consideration to your replies on threaded boards: post them where they're most appropriate.

Not all boards are threaded. Some lend themselves to threading, some don't. Some of my favorites aren't threaded and I'm glad: threading discourages the kind of browsing that favored boards merit. Don't look upon an unthreaded board as old-fashioned or anarchistic. Welcome them, and celebrate their diversity.

Libraries

Libraries are collections of computer files, and the libraries in Clubs & Interests are especially bountiful. For the sake of discussion, I have chosen the Star Trek Club (keyword: Trek). This is a particularly imaginative club, offering not only libraries of information, but simulations as well. "Starfleet Online" (a role-playing chat room spinoff of the Star Trek Club) meets every evening except Saturdays and "boldly goes where none have gone before."

Libraries consist of files, and files are available for downloading to your computer. The library in the Star Trek Club contains text files, graphics files and even a few animations. Text and graphics files are usually generic and can be viewed with the appropriate software on any type of computer. Animation files are more computer-specific. If you're not sure whether you have the appropriate hardware or software needed to use a file, double-click the file's name to get a description of it. Under the headings "Needs" and "Equipment," you'll find out what you need to take advantage of that particular file.

Though downloading was discussed in Chapter 5 "Computing," a review seems in order here. Figure 13-21 describes the process.

Figure 13-21: A quick glimpse of the file downloading process. Downloading is discussed in Chapter 5, "Computing."

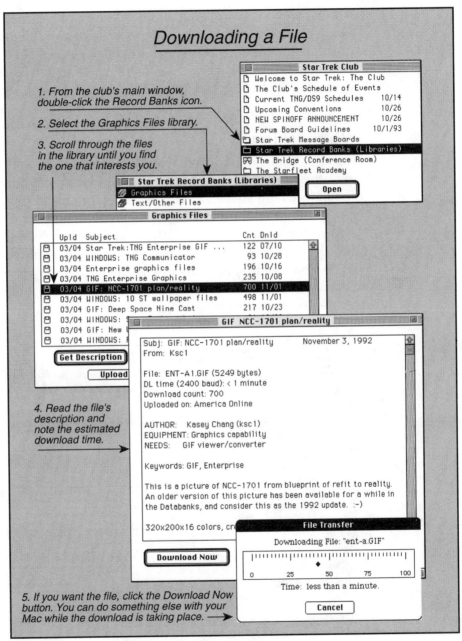

Downloading a File

1. From the club's main window, double-click the Record Banks icon.

2. Select the Graphics Files library.

3. Scroll through the files in the library until you find the one that interests you.

Star Trek Club
- Welcome to Star Trek: The Club
- The Club's Schedule of Events
- Current TNG/DS9 Schedules 10/14
- Upcoming Conventions 10/26
- NEW SPINOFF ANNOUNCEMENT 10/26
- Forum Board Guidelines 10/1/93
- Star Trek Message Boards
- Star Trek Record Banks (Libraries)
- The Bridge (Conference Room)
- The Starfleet Academy

Open

Star Trek Record Banks (Libraries)
- Graphics Files
- Text/Other Files

Graphics Files

Upld	Subject	Cnt	Dnld
03/04	Star Trek:TNG Enterprise GIF ...	122	07/10
03/04	WINDOWS: TNG Communicator	93	10/28
03/04	Enterprise graphics files	196	10/16
03/04	TNG Enterprise Graphics	235	10/08
03/04	GIF: NCC-1701 plan/reality	700	11/01
03/04	WINDOWS: 10 ST wallpaper files	498	11/01
03/04	GIF: Deep Space Nine Cast	217	10/23
03/04	WINDOWS:		
03/04	GIF: New		
03/04	WINDOWS:		

Get Description

Upload

4. Read the file's description and note the estimated download time.

GIF NCC-1701 plan/reality

Subj: GIF: NCC-1701 plan/reality   November 3, 1992
From: Ksc1

File: ENT-A1.GIF (5249 bytes)
DL time (2400 baud): < 1 minute
Download count: 700
Uploaded on: America Online

AUTHOR: Kasey Chang (ksc1)
EQUIPMENT: Graphics capability
NEEDS: GIF viewer/converter

Keywords: GIF, Enterprise

This is a picture of NCC-1701 from blueprint of refit to reality. An older version of this picture has been available for a while in the Databanks, and consider this as the 1992 update. :-)

320x200x16 colors, cre

Download Now

File Transfer

Downloading File: "ent-a.GIF"

0   25   50   75   100

Time: less than a minute.

Cancel

5. If you want the file, click the Download Now button. You can do something else with your Mac while the download is taking place.

Nearly every club at AOL offers a library of files, and many of the libraries are searchable. While the essence of any club might be colloquy and networking, the availability of an elegant library adds considerable value to the experience. Where would a club like the Star Trek Club be without Star Trek goodies?

Multitasking

America Online offers three ways to download files: (1) You can simply click the Download Now button and sit in front of your machine like a fossil, watching all the excitement the thermometer provides; (2) You can queue files for downloading and wait until the end of your online session (or for another part of the day) and download then. This is a function of the Download Manager, which we'll discuss in Chapter 19; or (3) You can do something else with your Mac while the download concludes in the background, like write that letter you owe to your mother or pay the bills (see Figure 13-22).

Figure 13-22: In the foreground I'm using Quicken to pay my household bills. My America Online software is downloading a graphic in the background. Neither process interferes much with the other, even on a slow machine.

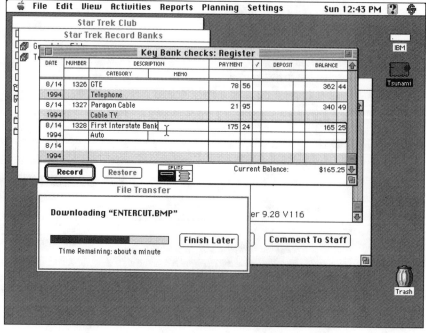

The process of doing more than one thing at a time with your computer is known as *multitasking*, and it might come as a surprise to you (many veteran AOL members are ignorant of this feature) to discover that your AOL software offers true multitasking capabilities: start a download, then go off and do something else with your Mac.

Here's how it's done:

- Ideally, start the software you intend to use during the download before you sign on. I started Quicken, for instance, before I began the online session pictured in Figure 13-22.

- If you haven't done so already, start your AOL software. It isn't important which software starts first. The AOL software, however, must occupy the frontmost window in order for you to sign on.

- Sign on, locate the file you want to download, and start the downloading process by clicking the Download Now button pictured in Figure 13-21.

- Mouse to the Application menu (it's the AOL triangular logo in the upper right corner of your screen when you're running the AOL software) and choose the other application you want to use. If that application isn't already running, choose the Finder from the Application menu and run your application via the Finder.

- Use the other application normally. When the download concludes, AOL's software will let you know by announcing it ("File's done!") and by flashing its Application menu icon on the menu bar. It does this even when it's running in the background.

- When the download has concluded, use the Application menu to return to the AOL software and continue your online session.

Multitasking seems a bit magical to me, and at first I didn't trust it, but it works. In three years I've never had a download go bad or a file become corrupted because of a multitask problem. In fact, I'm writing this sentence as a download is underway.

With all of that said, a few caveats are in order:

- You must be running System 7 or later on your Macintosh. If the truth be known, it's the System—not the AOL software—that provides the multitasking capability. Systems earlier than 7.0 didn't provide it. To see which version of the System you're using, choose About This Macintosh (or About the Finder) from the Apple menu when you're in the Finder.

- You can't multitask within the AOL software itself. You can't, for instance, visit a chat room or send an Instant Message while you're downloading a file from the Star Trek Club. Everything (except the thermometer's Cancel button) within the AOL window is inactive during a download.

- Some software doesn't tolerate multitasking very well, especially software that relies heavily on disk activity or your computer's central processing unit. Games are notoriously unfriendly to the multitasking environment.

- If you've got them, watch the lights on your modem. If the Receive Data (RD) light goes out or flickers badly while you're multitasking, you're asking too much of your Mac. Run a FlashSession instead.

SeniorNet Online

My disclaimer at the beginning of this chapter notwithstanding, there's one club that I must mention. SeniorNet (the parent organization to SeniorNet Online) grew out of a research project begun in 1986 at the University of San Francisco to determine if computers and telecommunication could enhance the lives of older adults—in this case, adults who are 55 or older.

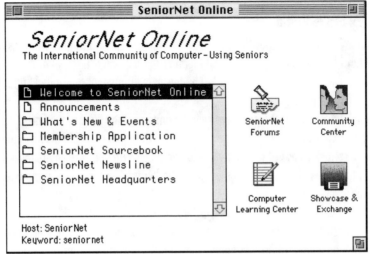

Figure 13-23:
SeniorNet Online is
home to over
5,000 SeniorNet
members
worldwide. Use
the keyword
SeniorNet.

Though access to SeniorNet Online is afforded to any AOL member, those who qualify for and join SeniorNet receive a number of other benefits, including

- Unlimited SeniorNet Online access.

- Discounts of 25 to 50 percent on selected magazines and books .

- Significant discounts on computer hardware and software.

- *Newsline*, SeniorNet's quarterly newsletter. Each issue includes step-by-step computer workshops, computer product reviews, computer tips and other articles of interest to computer-using seniors.

- Discounted admission to the national SeniorNet conference. The 1993 conference was held in Hawaii.

SeniorNet Online's boards are especially well spoken and appropriate to the membership. Topics range from wellness to writing, and hundreds of postings appear every day. When I last visited, over *twenty thousand* messages were available. This might be the most active forum on AOL.

The History of the World

Peeking at the SeniorNet libraries the other day, I happened across this gem from History teacher Richard Lederer. Richard has pasted together the following "history" of the world from certifiably genuine student bloopers collected by teachers throughout the United States. Read carefully: you might learn something!

"The inhabitants of ancient Egypt were called mummies. They lived in the Sarah Dessert and traveled by Camelot. The climate of the Sarah is such that the inhabitants have to live elsewhere, so certain areas of the dessert are cultivated by irritation. The Egyptians build the Pyramids in the shape of a huge triangular cube. The Pyramids are a range of mountains between France and Spain.

"Without the Greeks, we wouldn't have history. The Greeks invented three kinds of columns—Corinthian, Doric and Ironic. They also had myths. A myth is a female moth. One myth says that the mother of Achilles dipped him into the River Stynx until it become intolerable.

"Achilles appears in the Iliad, by Homer. Homer also wrote The Oddity, in which Penelope was the last hardship that Ulysses endured on his journey. Actually Homer was not written by Homer but by another man of that name.

"Socrates was a famous Greek teacher who went about giving people advice. They killed him....

"In midevil times, most of the people were aliterate. The greatest writer of the time was Chaucer, who wrote many poems and verses and also wrote literature. Another tale tells of William Tell who shot an arrow through an apple while standing on his son's head.

"The Renaissance was an age in which more individuals felt the value of their human being. Martin Luther was nailed to the church door at Wittenberg for selling papal indulgences. He died a horrible death, being excommunicated by a bull....

"It was an age of great inventions and discoveries. Gutenberg invented the Bible. Sir Walter Raleigh invented cigarettes. Sir Francis Drake circumcised the world with a 100-foot clipper....

"Delegates from the original thirteen states formed the Contented Congress. Thomas Jefferson, a Virgin, and Benjamin Franklin were two singers of the Declaration of Independence. Franklin had gone to Boston carrying all his clothes in his pocket and a loaf of bread under each arm. He invented electricity by rubbing cats backwards and declared, 'A horse divided against itself cannot stand.' Franklin died in 1790 and is still dead."

Surely you know more now than you did a few minutes ago, even though I've cut more than half of the article in the interest of brevity. If you want it all, snoop around in the SeniorNet libraries. There's great reading to be found there.

Moving On

America Online's Clubs & Interests Department might seem vast, and it is. But AOL's clubs are analogous to the range of clubs in any community, real or virtual: they're just the clubs in that community. One community does not equal a universe, no matter how large.

There are thousands of other online communities beyond those offered by AOL, scattered around the surface of the earth like cloves in an orange pomander. This universe of communities and the clubs within them is wired together via a protocol called the Internet, and the Internet's features—clubs and all—are available to any AOL member free of any charges beyond AOL's normal rates.

The Internet is vast and it can be intimidating. But not if you have a good guide. And you do. Just turn the page...

The Internet Connection

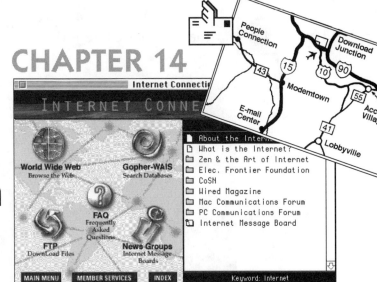

I saw television for the first time in 1954. We lived in a small town at the time, and the nearest station was over 100 miles away. The TV man—a shaman in his time—erected an immoderate antenna atop our roof and left us with a round, grainy black-and-white picture in our living room that would change our lives forever. We received one channel.

Years later, another TV guru—this one more closely connected with snake oil than shamanism—took away our antenna and replaced it with a magic cable. We received 35 color channels and started paying for the privilege.

Yet another TV man visited our home years later—more intellectual than the others, he dressed in a white lab coat and used words like "azimuth" and "latitude"—and planted a microwave dish in our backyard. Now we have more channels than the summer sky has stars, and the content of most of these channels is about as stratospheric.

I'm warming up to a discussion of the Internet. Before America Online, your computer was like a one-channel television set: functional and perhaps even entertaining, but a relic nonetheless. Connecting to AOL is not unlike connecting your TV to the cable: an ocean of opportunity is suddenly available, inconceivably vast at first, but finite nonetheless.

The Internet Connection is your gateway to the universe of online information. Why stay home when you can cruise the InfoBahn? Use the keyword Internet to get there.

Figure 14-1: The InfoHighway RestStop is an ongoing, informal forum in AOL's People Connection. The graphic was created by OddManOut, who says "If you...enjoy good palaver, then you're welcome at the RestStop." Press Command-L (for the Lobby), then check the active rooms for the InfoHighway RestStop.

Now imagine connecting your computer not just to AOL, but to thousands of other computer networks, many with forums, e-mail and thousands of files to download. It's not unlike the wonder you might feel while gazing at summer stars—each a sun, many with planets—except the Internet's stars are attainable. The Internet takes you there.

A Superset of AOL

The Internet, then, is a superset of AOL. It's everything AOL is—forums, mail, files to download, chats—only bigger. Much bigger. AOL is less than 5 million people in less than 5 countries; the Internet is as many as 50 million people in over 100 countries. No one owns it, it has no central facility and there are no assigned Guides or Terms of Service. And there's no Steve Case. An advisory committee is at the helm, but its concerns are primarily technical, and its members are all volunteers.

Now that I read the previous paragraph, I hasten to add that there's no "it," either. The Internet isn't a singular entity. It's comprised of scores of independent networks—some military, some academic, some commercial—all interconnected. Indeed, these *inter*connected *net*works are the very basis of the Internet name.

Nouns & Adjectives

If you're going to live in the neighborhood, you're going to have to speak the language. Used as a noun, the Internet is referred to as "the Internet." One would never say "Send me a message on Internet;" it would have to be "Send me a message on *the* Internet."

Used as an adjective, the article is dropped. It's "Internet mail," not "the Internet mail."

If you really want to speak in the vernacular, just call it "the Net," and refer to yourself as a "netter." That'll keep 'em guessing.

Military Preparedness

The best way to define the Internet is to examine what it was: like democracy, the Internet is best understood by observing its past.

Most importantly, the Internet began as a military contrivance. Most Net users know this, but many have never grasped its significance. The Internet's early military credentials have more to do with what it is today than any other factor.

The Internet is a collection of millions of independent computers, or hosts. Most hosts are in turn connected to other computers via different kinds of networks, forming domains. Hosts are identified to one another on the Internet by their domain names (actually, they're identified to one another by the numeric equivalents of domain names). AOL's domain name is aol.com. The whole thing is called the Domain Name System, and you can find out more about domain names in the "Internet Addresses" section a little later in this chapter.

Using leased high-speed telephone lines (not modems), each domain is wired to at least one other domain on the Net, and often more. The slowest of these telephone lines operates at 56 kbps—more than five times faster than a 9,600-baud modem. Many of these domains maintain a constant connection to the Net. They don't sign on and off as we do with AOL, they're online all the time.

A simplified map of this arrangement might look like that pictured in Figure 14-2.

Figure 14-2: The Internet extends around the globe as a web of independent domains interconnected round-the-clock by dedicated, high-speed telephone lines.

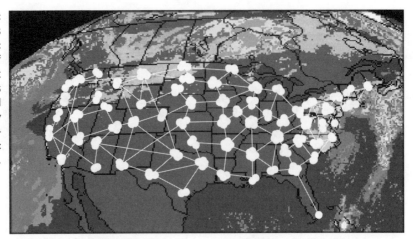

Don't interpret either Figure 14-2 or 14-3 literally. I drew the white lines, and they're not intended to represent literal Internet or AOL nodes (especially since all I've included is the US mainland—a politicocentric decision if there ever was one). It would take a map the size of a picture window to display all of these nodes. While there might be such maps somewhere, this isn't their place. The image of the continent is from the GEOS satellite. Use the keyword Weather, then investigate the color weather maps.

Compare the Internet strategy with that of AOL. America Online consists of a host computer system (in Virginia) and thousands of client computers (our Macs). While the Internet strategy looks like a web, the AOL strategy looks more like a star (see Figure 14-3).

Figure 14-3: America Online's star-like network consists of a host computer and thousands of intermittently connected clients.

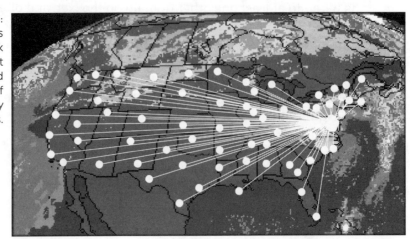

Now the military part: look again at Figure 14-3. If Ace Excavation were to dig up a fiber-optic cable in Vienna, Virginia, most of us would be without AOL—a disheartening experience. On the other hand, if a backhoe unplugged a domain in the Internet, communications would simply be routed around it. Indeed, a large percentage of the Net's domains could be eliminated, and the Net would still function.

Forever prepared, the Defense Department commissioned the Advanced Research Projects Agency (ARPA) to configure a computer network that would accommodate just such a possibility. This happened in the late 1960s; the network was called the ARPANET.

Academic Anarchy

By the early 1980s, educators discovered the value of sharing research information and computing resources through interconnected computers—especially supercomputers, which are precious as platinum. The educators weren't interested (much) in security; their interest was access. Their computers held vast amounts of data and true to form, they wanted to share that information objectively, without bias, with anyone in the community who wanted access.

ARPANET was a possible answer, but there were fundamental differences in the military and academic attitudes. The academic community elected instead to develop its own network which it called NSFNET—named for the National Science Foundation, the academics' primary source of funding. Significantly, NSFNET used the same networking strategy ARPANET used: interconnected domains randomly distributed around the globe. Most of these computers were at colleges and universities; none were subject to any form of central control. The result could have been dysfunctional anarchy, but by definition a computer network implies some form of universal protocol: electronic standards that define how computers communicate. The result is best described as *consensual anarchy*, whereby everyone marches to his or her own drum, but all agree on a common route for the parade.

And that's how the Internet is today: an agglomeration of independent domains drawn from ARPANET and NSFNET (both now phased out), each owned by organizations that are independent of one another, interconnected by high-speed data lines and not subject to any form of central control. There's no central data storage, either. Data are scattered about the Net like dyed eggs on Easter Sunday: hidden in faraway places, waiting for discovery. It amazes me that the thing even exists—it's one of the few working models of functional anarchy today, and it works extremely well.

WIRED Magazine

WIRED is the "magazine of the digital generation"—covering interactive media, the networking community and the toys of technology. Started in early 1993, *WIRED* has quickly ascended to the vanguard of the literary aristocracy. Its design is precocious, its content acerbic, its language offensive. The information age has few perspectives that can match *WIRED*'s insight, candor or irreverence, and none can match them all.

Best of all, *WIRED* is available online at AOL. Only past issues are available—you'll have to visit your newsstand for the latest edition—but *WIRED*'s content isn't so timely that it becomes obsolete in a month or two. If this chapter interests you and you're not yet a *WIRED* devotee, read this magazine. Use the keyword WIRED.

Until recently, military and academic users comprised most of the Internet community. It might have been an anarchistic community, but it was also a very exclusive club. Things have changed. Commercial accounts were allowed access in the early 1990s, opening the door to millions of everyday computer users like you and me. Now all of us with AOL accounts are offered Internet access. And there's no extra charge.

Internet Addresses

Before we go any further, we need to discuss Internet addresses. I touched on them briefly in Chapter 4, but they deserve more than that. They're really not much different from the addresses at the US Post Office, though rather than being sent to you at your home, Internet mail is sent to your *domain*. Domain or domicile, they're the same thing: they're the places where you receive mail.

International Top-Level Domains

When my friend Kyoko writes to me from Japan, the address she places on the envelope goes from the specific to the general: she starts with my name and ends with "USA," in the format *name/address/city/state/usa*.

International Internet addresses are exactly the same. At the far right you'll find the name of the country. This is called the *top-level domain*. Figure 14-4 identifies the abbreviations for some common international top-level domains.

Figure 14-4:
Country abbreviations are the top-level domain of international Internet addresses.

Abbreviation	Country
au	Australia
at	Austria
ca	Canada
dk	Denmark
fi	Finland
fr	France
de	Germany
it	Italy
jp	Japan
no	Norway
uk	United Kingdom
us	United States

Perhaps the most well-known example of an international top-level domain is

USERNAME@WELL.SF.CA.US.

indicating a user on the Whole Earth 'Lectronic Link (the WELL) in San Francisco (sf), California (ca), USA (us).

Note that the segments of Internet addresses are separated by periods. It's always that way. (Well, *almost* always. The Net's an anarchy, after all, and you will occasionally see other address formats. They're rare, however, and assuredly the exception to the rule.)

US Top-Level Domains

At the risk of sounding politicocentric again, most domains are within the United States, and the "us" top-level domain is typically omitted for activity within this country, just as it is for paper mail that's to stay within our borders. Instead, top domains for US users typically identify the type of system they're using. Figure 14-5 identifies the common US top-level domains.

Figure 14-5: US top-level domains identify the nature of the user's affiliation.

Abbreviation	Affiliation
com	business and commercial
edu	educational institutions
gov	government institutions
mil	military installations
net	network resources
org	other (typically nonprofit)

My Internet address, as mentioned in Chapter 4, is MAJORTOM@AOL.COM. Anyone looking at my top-level domain can determine that I'm affiliated with a commercial organization—in this case, America Online.

Domain Names & Computer Names

To the immediate left of the top-level domain is the name of the location of the host computer and associated network domain that's actually connected to the Internet. Thus, a domain name such as UOREGON.EDU implies that there's a network named "uoregon" somewhere, and it has a direct line to the Internet.

Many institutions—especially educational ones—have more than one local area network (LAN). Most of my academic associates work at the University of Oregon, but the U of O has at least seven satellite networks connected to the University's central mainframe. One of those networks is located within a building called Oregon Hall, and the users on that network add to the string their identifier, oregon.uoregon.edu, which identifies the Oregon Hall (oregon) LAN, which is connected to the University of Oregon domain (uoregon), which is an educational institution (edu).

User Names

Most Internet activity takes the form of e-mail, and e-mail is sent to individuals. The format PDWILLIAMS@OREGON.UOREGON.EDU is used to identify an individual. Everything to the left of the at sign (@) in an Internet address is the user's name. Internet user names aren't subject to the 10-character limit that AOL screen names are subject to, so they can become quite elaborate.

Most people on the Net use their first initial and last name as their Internet name. This format is usually unique (at least to the domain), and it's not gender-specific (an issue which many Net users prefer to avoid). Spaces aren't allowed (so you'll often see underscores in their place: FRED_MORGAN@MIT.EDU), and Internet addresses are not case sensitive. None of this should make a whit of difference to you, as your screen name (minus any spaces) automatically becomes your Internet user name. Your domain (sounds regal, doesn't it?) is aol.com.

The World Wide Web

Cultivated in UNIX and nurtured by computer professionals, the Internet became a variegation of disjointed fragments: USENET, Gopher, WAIS, Telnet and mail. The Internet almost seemed to take pride in its incoherence. Now that the Net has evolved from its experimental stage, coherence, convenience—even hospitality—are not only appropriate, but essential.

Apparently, the scientists at CERN—the European Particle Physics Laboratory in Geneva, Switzerland—agree, for in 1989 they set out to advance the Internet an order of magnitude up the evolutionary ladder. The result of their endeavors—introduced in 1990—is the *World Wide Web*, a department store-like gathering of FTP, Gopher, Telnet, WAIS gateways, e-mail and newsgroups. It's like a department store in that the Web puts all of these things under one roof, in familiar, convenient surroundings. If you can use a mouse, you can use the Web. Indeed, the Web is so obliging it might become your only use of the Internet (other than e-mail) from now on.

Hypermedia

The Web's cosmos is comprised of *hypermedia*. In my experience, the use of polysyllabic buzzwords usually indicates that the words' true meanings are obtuse and opaque. "Hypermedia" is no exception, but it's the heart of the Web, and an understanding of hypermedia is pivotal. Perhaps Figure 14-6 will help.

Figure 14-6:
Hypermedia
provides a
nonlinear pathway
to the infinite
potential of the
World Wide Web.

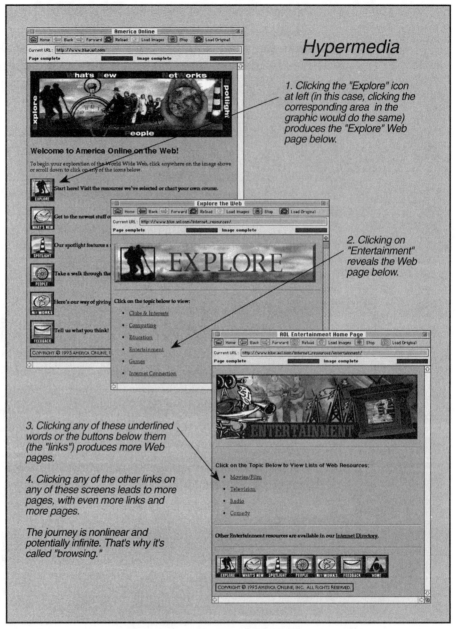

Each Web *page* consists of text and graphics (and more—like sound and video—if it's a really ambitious page), usually marked with *links* (*hyperlinks*, actually), or areas on the page that, when clicked, lead to something else. Links can produce more Web pages, graphics, sounds or videos: there's no limitation other than the capability of your hardware and the designer's imagination. The path shown in Figure 14-6 is only one of an infinite number of paths we could have explored. A click on the Spotlight or What's New buttons on AOL's Welcome page would fork to other paths, just as fertile and just as infinite as the one in the illustration. Indeed, the Web is a vast cosmos of resources, linked almost capriciously. This, perhaps, is why it's called the World Wide Web.

Nomenclature

So far, we've defined the *World Wide Web*, *page* and *link*, but there are a few other terms that require interpretation before we continue:

 A *Web browser* is software designed to browse the World Wide Web. Your AOL software contains a Web browser; you don't need anything else to browse the Web.

 URL is the Uniform Resource Locator, or the address for each article of text, and each graphic, sound or video on the Web. There are millions of them, thus their addresses are lengthy and specific. URLs can be typed directly into the text field just below the menu bar in AOL's Web window. They can be pasted there too, which is probably a better idea.

 HTTP is HyperText Transfer Protocol. Appearing below a URL, http tells the browser to expect a hypertext Web document.

 HTML is HyperText Markup Language, the programming language that's used to create Web pages.

Hot Lists

As you explore the Web, you'll discover pages you'll want to return to; when you return, you won't want to type URLs from the keyboard. That's what the *Hot Lists* feature is for.

I've enlarged a section of the AOL screen in Figure 14-7 to identify the menus and windows that you need to know about with regard to Hot Lists. If you want to "mark" a page by adding it to your main Hot List, simply select Add to Main Hot List under the Services menu and it will appear in your Main Hot List. You can create a new hot list by selecting New Hot Lists in the same menu and giving it a name.

To add pages to a hot list other than the Main Hot List, just do this:

1. Open the hot list you want the page in.

2. Copy the URL from the page.

3. Click on the New Item button in the hot list window.

4. Fill in the name and paste in the URL (see Figure 14-7).

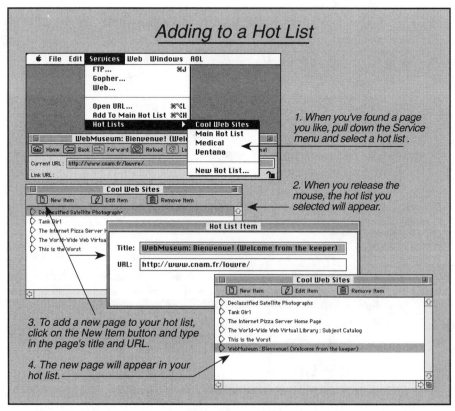

Figure 14-7:
Adding pages to
Hot Lists is simple.

To open a Hot List window, pull down the Services menu to Hot Lists and select a Hot List, whether you're online or off. To go to one of the places in a Hot List, just double-click it.

Browsing

This is not a place to become mired in procedural details. As the AOL software presents it, the Web really requires little explaining. It's a place for leisurely browsing, like an art gallery (try the French Louvre's Web Museum at HTTP://WWW.CNAM.FR/LOUVRE/) or the shelves of books in a public library (try the World Wide Web Virtual Library at HTTP://INFO.CERN.CH/HYPERTEXT/DATASOURCES/BYSUBJECT/OVERVIEW.HTML). Be prepared for wandering and wondering at all of the remarkable rewards the Web has to offer. Add pages in your hot list when you find places you want to return to, and surf the sea of the Internet the way the people at CERN intended. This is the Internet at its best; it will bring you back time after time.

Mailing Lists

Internet mailing lists are something of a cross between Ed McMahon and Rush Limbaugh (a vivid, if not particularly adept, analogy if there ever was one).

Mailing lists are like Ed McMahon in that they arrive in your mailbox frequently and seemingly unbidden. They're like Rush Limbaugh in that they accept material from listeners (subscribers in this case) and broadcast those contributions to everyone else on the list.

Shameless Plug

This chapter's description of mailing lists and the Web is necessarily abbreviated. Other Internet features will be abbreviated in this book as well. This is a tour of AOL, after all, not the Internet. If you want to become acquainted with the Net and AOL's gateway to it, read my *America Online's Internet*, also available from Ventana Press. Use the keyword AOL Store, or look for it at your local bookstore.

Think of AOL's message boards. Mailing lists, like boards, are where people discuss issues of a common interest. There are thousands of lists, and the issues range from ablation to zymurgy.

Lists are often called *reflectors*: mail you send to a list is broadcast (reflected) to everyone else who subscribes to the list. Conversely, you will automatically receive—as Internet mail—every message sent to the list by each of the other subscribers.

In that way, mailing lists are similar to the AOL address book feature. Using an address book, you can associate a number of screen names with a single address book entry; when you select that entry, multiple screen names are plugged into the To (or CC) field of an outgoing mail form. An Internet mailing list is the same way: mail sent to it is received by every subscriber to the list. One name represents many.

America Online offers a direct line to its Internet mailing list feature, just use the keyword MailingLists (see Figure 14-8).

Figure 14-8: The keyword MailingLists provides access to Internet mailing list information, including a searchable database of lists currently available.

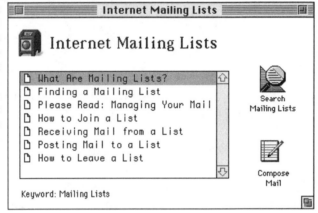

Subscribing to a good mailing list can be entertaining, stimulating, enlightening and overwhelming. You should subscribe to one, just for the experience. Before you do, however, understand a few mailing list basics:

- It's not unusual for a list to generate a prodigious volume of mail. For this reason, it is important that you manage your mail box to avoid losing your mail. Your AOL mailbox is limited to 500 pieces of mail, including both read and unread mail. Unread mail disappears five weeks after the date it was sent. Read mail disappears one week after the date it was sent—even sooner when the mail load at AOL is heavy. If your total mailbox mail count (both read and unread) exceeds 500 pieces, the AOL system will start to delete excess mail, starting with read mail and then unread mail.

- Don't subscribe to a mailing list unless you plan to read it.

🔺 When reading a list's description, be sure to take note of how to "unsubscribe" in case you change your mind about receiving it.

🔺 If you subscribe to any mailing lists, sign on regularly to read your mail and clear your mailbox.

🔺 Some lists are "moderated," some are not. Moderated lists are comparable to AOL's hosted chat rooms in that their content never strays too far off the subject and rarely becomes offensive. Unmoderated lists embody the anarchistic nature of the Internet and can become quite idiosyncratic and incautious.

🔺 America Online offers a searchable database of lists (review Figure 14-8). Again, the keyword MailingLists will take you there. Don't be surprised if the subject you have in mind isn't listed. Do spend some time exploring the database: it searches the list descriptions by content rather than by keyword. A search using the criterion "flying," for instance, produces all the lists with the word "flying" in their descriptions, including "high-flying" and "flying by the seat of your pants." While searches like this can drift off the subject quickly, you never know what you'll unearth.

Newsgroups

Newsgroups are similar to mailing lists in that they're a free exchange of ideas, opinions and comments, usually confined to a specific field of interest. You visit a newsgroup, read the messages that are there, reply to those that inspire a response, post new messages when you have a new topic to propose, and come back another day to see what responses you've provoked.

Unlike mailing lists, no mail is involved with newsgroups. Most activity occurs while you're online, including reading and responding to postings. Thus, some will say that newsgroups are more immediate, more interactive and more conversational than mailing lists. News–groups or mailing lists: for most it's a matter of preference. You will probably want to dabble in both of them for a while.

The Official AOL Tour Guide

Figure 14-9: The
America Online
Newsgroups
screen. To reach it,
use the keyword
Newsgroups.

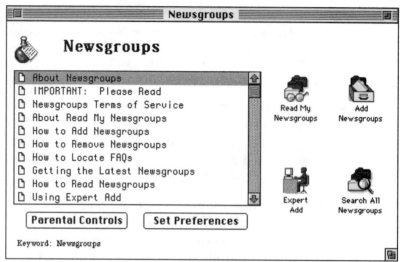

Figure 14-9: The America Online Newsgroups screen. To reach it, use the keyword Newsgroups.

At the moment, over 18,000 newsgroups flood the Internet. This figure is more than quadruple the 4,000 mentioned in Adam Engst's *Internet Starter Kit* (copyright 1993), and that figure is more than double the 1,500 mentioned in Ed Krol's *The Whole Internet* (First Edition, copyright 1992). If the number of newsgroups keeps doubling every year, we'll have more than half a million of them by the turn of the century.

Because newsgroups are an Internet resource, AOL's own internal Terms of Service (TOS) don't apply. There are guidelines, however, and AOL's USENET Newsgroups TOS is a codification of these guidelines. The USENET TOS is always available in the list box at the keyword Newsgroups, where it's called "IMPORTANT: Please Read" (review Figure 14-9). Read it. Doing so might save you considerable newsgroup face, and AOL doesn't charge for the time when you do.

Getting Help

As I mentioned earlier, space considerations forbid the description of operational details for AOL's Internet features here. I have another book for that. Fortunately, however, help is never far away when you're using AOL's Internet features. A number of methods are available for accessing help, either from AOL, from other members, or from the Internet community at large.

Online Help

Nearly every Internet window on AOL offers a potential for online help. Figure 14-10 offers a sampling.

Figure 14-10:
Help topics
abound at the
Internet
Connection.

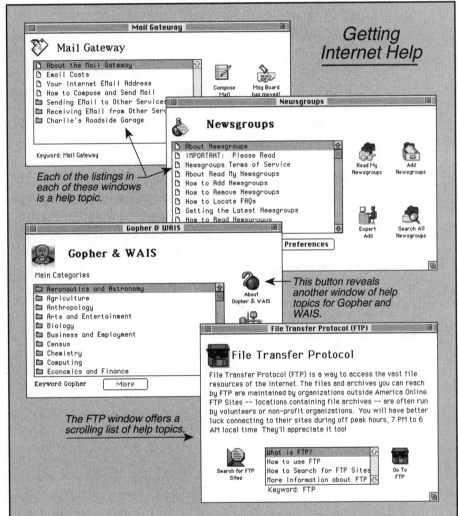

The good news is that because the newsgroup help files are stored at AOL (and not on your hard disk), they can be changed whenever the Internet staff wants to change them. These help files, in other words, always reflect changes made in response to suggestions from users or changes in the Net itself.

The bad news is that you have to be online to access them, and for that you pay.

Here's a tip: print 'em. Whenever a help window is open, all you have to do is choose Print from the File menu and you'll have a hardcopy of the online help file that's currently open. You can print them all in this manner if you like.

Peer Assistance

I'm a firm believer in peer assistance. America Online members are usually your best source of help because they can empathize; they understand your needs. Experts are often too far removed from your situation (and have too many other things to do) to help the way other members can. In other words: if you have a question, ask around.

You might start with the Internet Connection message boards. Use the keyword Internet, then double-click the Internet Connection Message Board listing in the main window. Though the contents of all boards change, this one will, no doubt, always offer a folder (see Figure 14-11), where you can post questions and receive replies from others who've experienced a similar situation.

An ambitious team of *CyberJockeys* patrols these boards as well, answering especially difficult questions. You can recognize CyberJockeys by the leading *CJ* in their screen names.

Figure 14-11: The Internet Connection message boards offer excellent help from fellow AOL members.

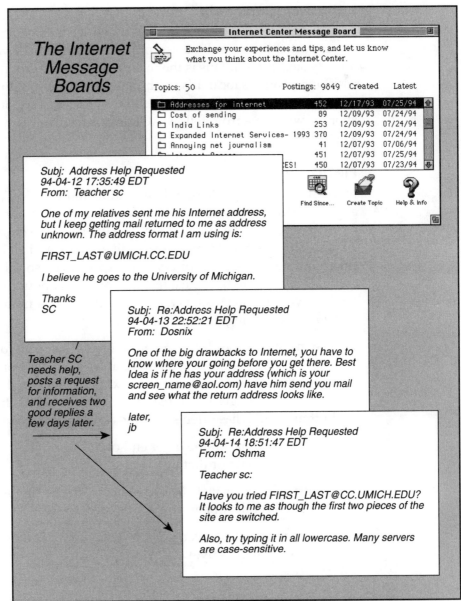

aol.newsgroups.help

Finally, be sure to subscribe to the aol.newsgroups.help newsgroup (it, too, is part of the default newsgroup subscription list—you're probably already subscribed). This is the most active location for newsgroup assistance, and it's local. It's not broadcast throughout the Internet—your questions are only seen by fellow AOL members, and your responses will come from fellow AOL members.

Netiquette

Nowhere is the etiquette of online conduct more critical (or more abused) than in newsgroups. Most faux pas are committed by newbies—people like you and me. The Internet is a community, after all: one with a particularly stalwart camaraderie and an intense adherence to an iconoclastic propriety. Most specialized social organizations are that way, and to become a member of one without first becoming familiar with its catechism is fishing for disgrace. A minicourse in Netiquette, then, might help:

- Having stung myself a number of times, I've taken to writing my missives and *not* posting them for at least a couple of hours. Rather, I save them and recall them the next time I sign on. For some reason, this obliges me to read them again before I click the post button—and it has often saved me considerable newsgroup face.

- There are people on the other end of the line: people with emotions and feelings. Honor them.

- Honor yourself as well. You are known on the Net by what you write. Project the image you want others to see.

- Brevity is admirable; verbosity is disfavored. If you say what you have to say succinctly, your words will carry greater authority and impact.

- Read before writing. Add something to the conversation; don't simply repeat what's already been said. Subscribe to the news.answers newsgroup and read the Frequently Asked Questions file (FAQ) for your newsgroup before posting. By reading before you write you'll have a better sense of the tenor and conventions of the newsgroup to which you are posting.

- Quote the messages to which you're responding. Edit the quoted material to oblige brevity (and indicate when you've done so), use the quoting fashion you see in other messages and always acknowledge the person you're quoting.

- Contribute something. Some people speak simply to be heard; these same people post simply to see their material online. Don't contribute to the tedium: look for a new perspective, ask a probing question, make an insightful comment. If none come to mind, wait for another opportunity. There are plenty of opportunities on the Net; we all have something worthy to contribute eventually.

- Use help. If the help files described in this chapter don't answer your question, post a message in aol.newsgroups.help. Lots of people are willing to help you if you ask.

Gopher & WAIS Databases

Growth on the Internet is a stupendous thing. Most everyone agrees that it exceeds 100 percent a year; some contend that it's as high as 20 percent *per month*. Regardless of the figure, navigating the Net has become about as convenient as navigating the Atlantic Ocean: relatively easy if you have the right tools, but impractical—some might say perilous—if you don't.

Gopher

One such tool is *Gopher*. Originating at the University of Minnesota (where the school mascot is the Golden Gopher), Gopher is a system that knows where things are on the Net and presents that knowledge as a series of nested menus. All you have to do is keep choosing menu items until you find what you're after, then Gopher "goes for" (it's kind of a double pun: mascot and "gofer") your material on the Net.

The Gopher system (keyword Gopher) is actually composed of a number of *Gopher servers*, located around the world. Each server is like a good librarian: it organizes content for your convenience. (Librarians organize libraries with card files; Gophers organize the Internet's content with menus.) When you find what you're looking for, it retrieves the information for you. Better yet, Gophers reference other Gophers: AOL's Gopher, for example, offers access to hundreds of other Gophers. It's as if you were given access to a librarian's convention, and the librarians, every one, brought their card files with them.

Though there are a number of Gopher servers, we're rarely made aware of them individually: AOL simply groups them all into one massive menu tree that we're free to peruse as we wish. In a way, that's too bad, because you're usually unaware of the vast distances you're traveling when you access the various Gopher servers on AOL's menus. You might be in Switzerland one moment and Germany the next. That's the nature of the Net: distance has no meaning in cyberspace.

The Comics Come to the Net

The original Gopher server at the University of Minnesota was established to bring convenience to the Net. Since copies of all of the Internet sites' directories were stored on the server, searching was local. No time was spent connecting to and disconnecting from the individual sites until data was located.

In time, more Gopher servers came along. There are scores of them now, and searching the *servers* has become a task.

Enter *Veronica*, a tool that searches databases. Veronica is simply a database of the Gophers' directories and menu item names.

Computer programmers are an iconoclastic lot, and many of them relax by reading comic books. The Archie comics are big in cyberspace, so the Veronica resource was named for the Veronica comic book character. (Searching for a name for your latest creation? Pick up the nearest literature.) Betty and Jughead can't be far behind.

To access Veronica, click the Search all Gophers button in the main Gopher and WAIS window.

Gopherspace is a crowded place during the academic year, especially during finals. Because of the crowding, don't be surprised if you receive connect errors. Crowded or not, Gopherspace is a wonderful place to browse. Browsing is what Gopher is all about. Plan to spend a lot of time here.

WAIS

Gopher isn't the only way of searching for data on the Net, *WAIS* (pronounced "wayz") is another. While Gopher is best suited for browsing, or poking around with no particular destination in mind, WAIS is best suited for searching, rather than browsing.

The Subtlety of Icons

Take a moment to look at Figure 14-12. Note the variety of icons pictured to the left of the menu topics.

Figure 14-12: The page, folder, and book icons on America Online's Gopher menus each have a specific meaning.

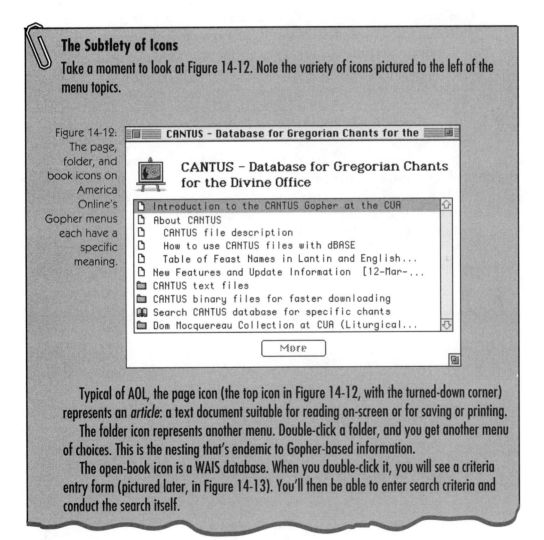

Typical of AOL, the page icon (the top icon in Figure 14-12, with the turned-down corner) represents an *article*: a text document suitable for reading on-screen or for saving or printing.

The folder icon represents another menu. Double-click a folder, and you get another menu of choices. This is the nesting that's endemic to Gopher-based information.

The open-book icon is a WAIS database. When you double-click it, you will see a criteria entry form (pictured later, in Figure 14-13). You'll then be able to enter search criteria and conduct the search itself.

WAIS servers contain custom indexes of data on the Internet, often limited to a single topic. Gopher indexes are more comprehensive, analogous to the card file in a public library. WAIS indexes are more like a private library; there are WAIS servers for computer science, molecular biology and literature, for example.

WAIS servers also offer a different "face" than Gophers do; while Gophers offer menus, WAIS servers offer a query form not unlike that of a database. You enter the criteria you're searching for and the WAIS server responds with data that match your query.

Conducting a WAIS Search

One of the Internet's finest jewels is its exhaustive collection of so-called "e-texts"—electronic texts of the world's literature. While there will always be a place for the smell of old books and the crackle of stiff pages, there are occasions where the immediacy of e-text retrieval makes the difference between reading the text or not.

There are so many e-texts now on the Internet that a number of searching mechanisms have emerged, including the ALEX retrieval system pictured in Figure 14-13.

Figure 14-13:
Searching the
ALEX retrieval
system for the
electronic text of
Lincoln's
Gettysburg
Address.

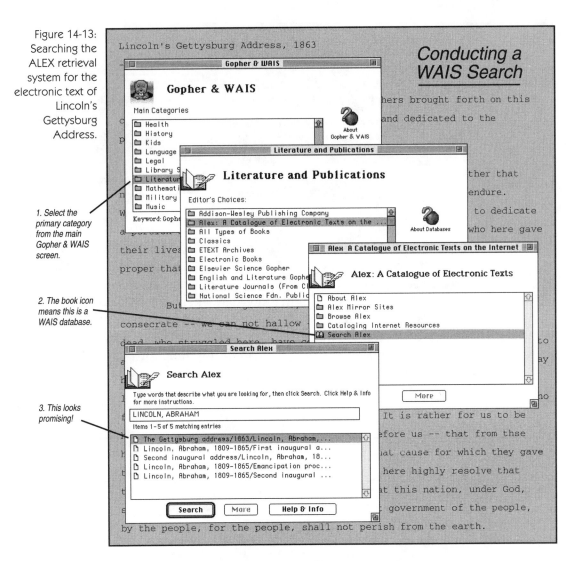

1. Select the
primary category
from the main
Gopher & WAIS
screen.

2. The book icon
means this is a
WAIS database.

3. This looks
promising!

Note that I had to know about ALEX, and I had to know that it's to be found in the Literature and Publishing section of AOL's Gopher. WAIS is for searching the Internet when you know what you're after and you know where to look for it. Developing an awareness of these things takes time. Don't expect to become a WAIS expert in a visit or two. Good things take time.

Editor's Choices

If you look carefully at the second window in Figure 14-13, you'll see the words "Editor's Choices." Each of the selections in the main Gopher and WAIS window leads to the Editor's Choices of resources available for that top menu item. These resources usually prove to be especially adroit: typically, they're comprehensive, intriguing and functional.

If you're browsing the Net, always try the Editor's Choices first. This is some of the best stuff the Internet has to offer.

FTP

Gopher, WAIS and the Web are nifty tools, but what if you want more direct access? What if you want to log on to another machine on the Net, see a directory of its files, and download a few? We're talking now about the engine room of the Internet, where you directly access other computers' holdings as if they were your own hard drive. FTP, or *File Transfer Protocol*, is that kind of access; it's how you download files from other machines, and files can be anything: programs, sounds, video and graphics.

Figure 14-14: Using FTP to download a Microsoft Word utility from Stanford University.

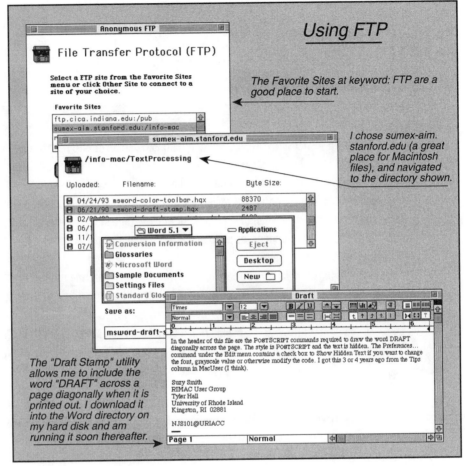

FTP is two things, actually. First, it's a protocol, allowing machines on the Net to exchange data (files) without concern for the type of machine that originated the file, the file's original format or even the operating systems of the machines involved. FTP is also a program—in which case it's called *ftp*, without the capitalization—that enables FTP. Just as the word *telephone* denotes both a device you hold in your hand and a system for international communications, ftp is both the message and the medium.

The term is also used as both a noun ("It's available via ftp") and a verb ("FTP to sri.com and look in the netinfo directory"). It's hard to misuse the term, in other words. Just don't try to pronounce it: this is one acronym that's always spelled out.

Anonymous FTP

Originally, most ftp sessions occurred between a site and a person at a remote location who had an account at that site. The person would log on by supplying an account name and a password, then conduct the appropriate file activities.

The need soon became apparent, however, for less restrictive access. What if a site wanted to post a file for *anyone* to download? A number of publicly funded agencies require such an arrangement. NASA's space images, as an example, are funded by public money, thus the public should have access to them.

The solution is *anonymous FTP*. During an anonymous FTP session, the user logs on to the remote site using the account name "anonymous" (AOL does this for you unless you supply a specific user name). The password for anonymous login, typically, is the user's Internet address—a common courtesy so the people at the remote site can determine who is using their system if they wish. Again, AOL does this for you unless you supply a specific password.

Operating FTP successfully and acquiring a library of fertile FTP locations (and when to access them) is a skill worthy of development, but it *does* require time to develop. Begin by reading the help files available at the keyword FTP (and pictured in Figure 14-10), and practice for a while using AOL's Favorite Sites, pictured in Figure 14-14. If you feel you need more help, post questions on the Internet Connection message boards. AOL's community is always ready to help you learn.

Moving On

Each of the Internet resources described on these pages is an existing AOL feature. Others will no doubt come along. That's part of the fun of telecommunications: this is just the beginning, and there's always more to come. Becoming a member of AOL (and exploring the Internet) is a little like planting a fruit tree: there's lots of diversity (blossoms, bees, fruit, firewood), and each year there's more than there was the year before.

It's positively organic. ;-)

Internet aside, our most precious resource as a society is our children, and AOL certainly hasn't forgotten them. In fact, there's an entire department dedicated to kids, and it's as palatial as the Internet itself. Shall we take a look? Turn the page....

Kids Only

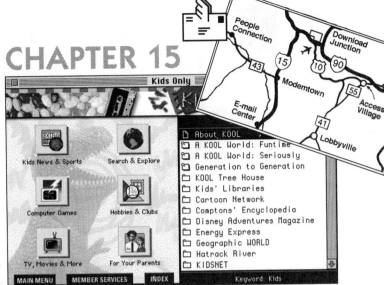

The introduction to Chapter 13 described the Clubs & Interests Department as "...as multiethnic as Ellis Island and as variegated as a harlequin's tights." It then went on to mention the African American, Asian, Hispanic, senior and gay boards and in so doing left out an entire segment of our society—kids.

Don't worry: kids get equal time in this book, and on AOL. In fact, they have an entire department. Kids Only Online (KOOL) was a mere forum a few months ago and now, deservedly, it's a department (see Figure 15-1).

This makes sense. Perhaps no other segment of our society adapts as well to computers as our kids do, and kids have no qualms about striking up a new online friendship, uploading original art or speaking their minds on a board topic.

Kids Only is AOL's Riviera for kids aged 6 to 13. Though adults occasionally drop by, this *is* the Kids Only Department, and kids are the ruling class. Click the Kids Only button on the Main Menu, or use the keyword: KOOL.

Figure 15-1: A montage of KOOL forums appears against a background by Chaz Pabst.

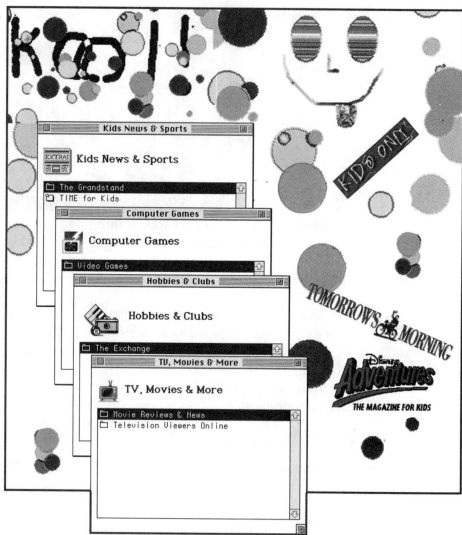

KOOL is hosted by Jack Powell—a kid person by choice and by profession. When he's not at home with his four daughters, he works as a pediatrician and pediatric cardiologist. Jack's wife Jean is a pediatric nurse, and cohost Genevieve Kazdin is a critic and reviewer of media for children. Gen has twin granddaughters to occupy her time when she's not online.

The Boards

Kids love to talk, so much so that KOOL offers not one, but three message boards for their comments. *Funtime* offers folders on annoying siblings, dinosaurs and the unexplained (among others); *Seriously* offers folders on AIDS, sexism and drugs; and *Generation to Generation* is the only board in the department where adult participation is encouraged. These boards are lively, unpredictable and often insightful. Even if you're not a kid, you'll enjoy reading the kids' comments.

Silly Putty

Sometimes you'll find the most interesting material in the least likely place. This most certainly was the case when I explored KOOL's Seriously board. Andy Baird, an AOL forum consultant in the graphics library, responded to a New Hampshire high school student's request for information about a now-famous synthetic rubber with the following piece:

"Silly Putty was indeed invented more or less by accident in the 1940s. A Scottish engineer named James Wright was working in the laboratories of General Electric in an attempt to create a superior synthetic rubber. (The battles in the Pacific had cut off the supplies of natural rubber from the Far East, so synthetic rubber was a hot priority during WWII.)

"Wright combined boric acid and silicone oil in a beaker, which resulted in a gooey mass. When he dropped a blob of the stuff, Wright was surprised to find that it bounced back and hit him in the face! Yet it could be stretched like putty, and if left to itself, would flow like a liquid. GE sent samples of the strange substance to engineers and researchers, hoping someone would find a use for it...but no one could.

"Six years later, an unemployed advertising executive named Peter Hodgson found out about the putty and tried selling it as a novelty gift item through a book catalog. To everyone's surprise, the putty outsold almost everything else in the catalog. Deeply in debt, Hodgson borrowed $147 and bought a big batch of the glop from GE; then he packaged it in plastic eggs, added the name Silly Putty and took some samples to the annual Toy Fair in New York. That led to an article in the *New Yorker* magazine, which in turn set off an avalanche of sales—250,000 orders came in in three days!

"The rest is history. Binney and Smith, the product's owners, say that over 200,000,000 eggs—that's 3,000 tons of Silly Putty!—have been sold over the years. (They're currently produced at the rate of 12,000 eggs a day at a putty plant in Pennsylvania.) Peter Hodgson died in 1975, leaving an estate of $140,000,000—and many happy Silly Putty owners!"

Andy Baird has his own folder in the Seriously board, called Ask Andy. If you have a science question that needs answering, Andy's the one to ask!

The Libraries

A colleague of mine—Craig Hickman from the University of Oregon's math department—loves to dabble with his computer. He also has kids of his own, and in his spare time he writes programs for his kids to use. He brought a little paint program he had written with him when he taught programming classes in my department at the University of Oregon in Portland. It was a great example of multimedia programming, but aside from his kids' use and the classroom example, he didn't have any plans for the program. He was just filling idle time when he wrote the program.

Until the software publisher Broderbund made him an offer he couldn't refuse. Almost overnight *KidPix* went from a plaything to one of the most successful painting programs for the Macintosh ever sold. It's cheap, it's colorful and makes lots of noise, and it has the kind of tools kids love to use.

Figure 15-2: A KidPix illustration by Scott Ostermiller, uploaded to KOOL s KidPix Trading Post.

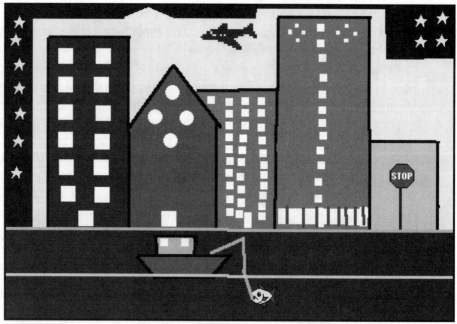

KidPix is such a hit that today it has its own KOOL library—the *KidPix Trading Post*. There are three others as well: *The KOOL Library* offers sounds, GIFs, smileys, morphs, HyperCard stacks, QuickTime movies, stories and icons; *Cartoon Images* are all GIF files, which display as they're downloaded (if you're using version 2.5 or later of the AOL software); *Apps for Kids* are all computer applications, including spelling checkers, typing tutors, word processors and trivia programs.

Hatrack River

Orson Scott Card has long been committed to online computer networks. His most famous novel, *Ender's Game*, not only showed many of the future possibilities of online services like AOL, but was quite possibly the first novel ever published online before it appeared in print.

Now on AOL, Orson Scott Card has opened his fictional town of Hatrack River. Hatrack River figures prominently in his series of American frontier fantasies called *The Tales of Alvin Maker*; it is also the name of a publishing company that Card and his wife, Kristine, own and operate.

Hatrack River is a particularly erudite and prophetic community—one of those niches marked by passion and intelligence that resonate with a number of onliners who can't find serendipity elsewhere. Hatrack River is founded on a healthy respect for the dignity and beliefs of others. We're all welcome at Hatrack, whether we choose to speak or simply to listen.

I mention Hatrack here because one of its libraries—the Dragon's Tale—is devoted to the writings of those who are under 18 (see Figure 15-3). If you're the parent of a youngster (or if you're under 18 yourself) with a literary penchant, take a moment to visit Hatrack River. The keyword Hatrack will get you there in a hurry.

Figure 15-3: Russell Miller s (age 15) Killing of the Veggies appears in the Dragon s Tale library at Hatrack River.

The Killing of the Veggies

by Russell Miller

The end is near, the cabbage cried,
the judgement is at hand
our time is done, the jig is up
now we're to be salads on demand.

The end is near, the cabbage cried,
the vegetarians' knives will swiftly fly
into our tender, ripening flesh
and I fear we all will die.

Hark unto sweet salvation,
cried the cabbage with loud and fierce voice
now we will die, but our souls all will live
if in religion we all do rejoice.

Bah said the carrot
Are you really so stupid you think we have souls?
That your god, he will hear us?
And save us from bowls?

Said the tomato: god's a veggie too
and protects us all from the knives
so that we never end up in salad bowls
and there forfeit our lives.

Wrong! said an olive, although god is up there
and god may just be a veggie too
but god, himself is a deist
and does not care one whit about you!

Or! said the carrot
what if you're half-right, and there is a god above,
but one who is human, however
and who looks on vegetables with no great love?

O swift was the blade and the cuts that it made
and like a vorpal sword it did go snicker-snack
and the vegetables were all brutally killed
their bodies split open and cracked.

Upon the large counter the bodies were strewn
no yard site; save bowls, for final bed.
Then they were tossed, and more insults ensued,
as then there was dressing for the dead.

An orange on the table had heard the whole talk
and had watched as they hawwed and they hemmed.
The talk on god had been quite impressive,
but in the end where had it got them?

What moral then was learned you ask
as the salad is interred,
eaten by hungry vegetarians,
with great gusto and nary a word.

As for the the orange, nothing at all.
He already knew that to be one must do.
And depending for help on a god who might be
is a path that is stupid and dangerous too.

As for the rest some had believed some had not
and really what more can be said?
Perhaps they'd been sinners, perhaps they'd been saints
but now they all were just dead.

And the souls? Well, not much is known
perhaps they were saved perhaps not.
But I don't think we'll ever truly know if they exist
and if so, where they go after veggie bodies rot.

The Tree House

The Tree House is KOOL's chat room (chat rooms are discussed in Chapter 12, "People Connection"), and it's one of the busiest—and most feature-packed—chats on AOL.

During the week that I'm writing this chapter, the Tree House discusses weather on Friday night, plays real-time games on Saturday and Sunday nights, offers a Star Trek simulation on Monday night, plays trivia on Tuesday, and offers video-game tips and tricks on Wednesday. Other times are set aside for specific age groups.

Double-click the Tree House listing in the main KOOL window and read the Tree House Calendar for the latest schedule.

TIME Online

Throwing its considerable weight behind the conviction that kids are our most precious resource, *Time* magazine launched TIME Online in late 1993. It has since become something of an *au fait* online community for kids—and kids only: participation by those over 14 years of age is discouraged. The topics are often substantial, the philosophies insightful, and the opinions articulate.

TIME Online's purpose is to see what young people think about *Time* magazine and the subjects of its stories in the context of kids' interests and kids' perceptions. Perhaps most significantly, it provides kids with an opportunity to talk directly to *Time*'s writers and editors. If you want to glimpse tomorrow's hopes and ambitions, read this board (see Figure 15-4).

Figure 15-4: Gun control isn t just an adult issue. The kids at TIME Online have resolute opinions too.

TIME Online

```
Subj:  Why?
Date:  94-04-10 16:44:55 EDT
From:  Julie B462

Last month there was a gun found at
school.

I live in Jonesboro, Ar ,a semi-sma
of 40,000 people. Im in seventh gra

A seventh grade boy had a .22 in hi
backpack. It was loaded with 6 bull
already cocked. If I or anyone else
bumped him too hard in the hall it
have gone off

I just wonder why this person didnt
the life of any students in the sch
```

```
Subj:  BAN ALL GUNS
Date:  94-04-16 21:38:24 EDT
From:  Julia89999

I think nobody should have a gun. And that
means nobody. The gov- ernment could tell
all factories that make guns to close
down.The hunters could make a sacrafice and
not hunt. Besides, the only thing that makes
hunting HUNTING is the guns. It doesn't
require much skill. With no guns, there
would be no one killed by guns. It's that
simple. People can't be stubborn and give
              to why they NEED guns. People would
           e murdered by knifes, but it wouldn't
           asy as a gun. With a gun you can
           omeone from thirty feet away. You
           be close to the person to stab them.
          ds gross. but it's true.
```

```
Subj:  Re:BAN ALL GUNS
Date:  94-04-19 16:45:58 EDT
From:  RickC0041

Dear Julia,
     Here's a scenario for you: you say
guns kill too many people,  if People we
being pushed out of windows, would you h
them to?

The constitution protects "the right to
arms"  and you want to take that Right a
But for your sake, if i ever want to kil
someone, i'll push Them out of a
window.(ha,ha)

P.S. Hunting does take skill,
RickC0041
```

```
Subj:  Re:BAN ALL GUNS
Date:  94-06-10 21:52:02 EDT
From:  NiteShaide

   It is against the constituition to ban all
guns also if they did how could they enforce
it besides searching your house which is
then an invasion of privacy.   I hope you
don't think banning guns will make things
better because i can prove it won't.

                                  JAMIE
```

A Word to Parents

Though it occurs throughout the service, harassment and exploitation are particularly obstructive at KOOL. To be effective, KOOL must be a place where kids are made to feel welcome: it's their online home, and a home—above all—must always be comfortable.

TOS

America Online's Terms of Service (keyword: TOS) clearly define the rules of acceptable online behavior. Parents should become familiar with them and share an understanding of them with their children before the kids first sign on.

When your child witnesses a TOS violation, he or she should be encouraged to use the keyword GuidePager and ask a Guide to enter the room where the violation is occurring. Not only will the offender encounter the significance of TOS enforcement (that's as politely as I can put it), your child will see what happens when these rules are broken. A witness to a "TOS event" rarely forgets the experience.

Instant Messages

Instant Messages often arrive unbidden, and when kids are involved they're occasionally unwelcome as well. Your child should know how to turn Instant Messages off (send an Instant Message to the screen name $im_off) and back on again (send an Instant Message to the screen name $im_on). Instant Messages are discussed in Chapter 12, "People Connection." Read about them if you haven't already.

Online Time

A friend of mine once recounted her horror when she discovered that her daughter had fallen asleep for two hours while making a call to a 900 number. While 900 numbers usually charge by the minute and AOL charges by the hour, AOL's charges can nonetheless add up quickly when a child—who can hardly be expected to understand the significance of a month of six-hour Saturdays in the KOOL Tree House—is left unattended online. The KOOL staff suggests you teach your children how to use FlashSessions for collecting and posting mail (FlashSessions are discussed in Chapter 19). Set limits on the amount of time they are allowed online much in the way television viewing is limited. KOOL should be a fun electronic clubhouse, but not a financial burden. America Online cannot be held responsible for charges you might deem excessive.

Parental Control

Finally, become familiar with AOL's Parental Control feature (keyword: ParentalControl). It's discussed in Chapter 12 (see the sidebar on pages 264–265) and it allows parents to determine where their children can go online and under what conditions they're allowed there.

Moving On

I don't want to become mired in negativity. Above all, KOOL is a place for kids. Shyness, introversion, even autism aren't uncommon in the ages between 6 and 13, and the anonymity offered by the online milieu is often therapeutic to these conditions. Shy kids nurture here; aggressive kids pacify; challenged kids thrive. Heck, even well-rounded kids like it. So do adults. Don't tell the kids.

If KOOL's the clubhouse in our online community, there must be a schoolhouse somewhere, and there is. It's called the Education Department and, delightfully, it's one of the most kaleidoscopic departments AOL offers. It's described in the next chapter. Don't miss it.

Education

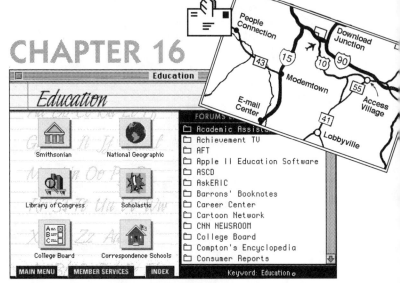

CHAPTER 16

I've read your letters. Many of you skip this department and this chapter. You're here to have fun, and education isn't your idea of a joyride on the infobahn. Too bad, because the rewards in the Education Department are as abundant as, well, June graduates in search of jobs.

Don't get me wrong: the emphasis here is on learning. Yes, the inquisitive browser will find scores of treasures here, but students, teachers and parents of students (or students-to-be) are especially well served by this department. If you fall into any of these categories, you should investigate the Education Department. Use the keyword Education, or click on the Department button on the Main Menu. Before you do, however, read this chapter. It's a big department, and this chapter will help you to refine your investigation and offer some tips as well.

This may be the most surprising department of them all. You expect to find students and teachers here, but mad Russians, giant lizards and supersonic spy planes? They're all in the Education Department (keyword: Education), along with much, much more.

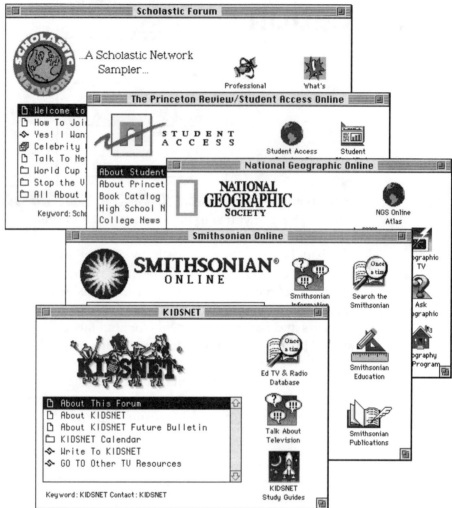

Figure 16-1: Just a few of the diverse offerings in the Education Department.

Education for Everyone

While teachers and students are exceptionally well served by this department, the rest of us are not overlooked. There's a Career Center; *National Geographic* and *Disney Adventures* magazines; the Smithsonian Institution; NPR, CNN and C-SPAN; and the Online Campus. Imagine having access to such resources without paying for magazine or cable subscriptions, or private tutoring fees!

National Geographic Online

Here you will find selections from *National Geographic* magazine and National Geographic's *Traveler* and *World* magazines, as well as a variety of news stories and press releases (keyword: Geographic). The television program is also featured in the Geographic TV Forum (see Figure 16-2).

Figure 16-2: *National Geographic, Traveler* and *World* magazines are all included in National Geographic Online.

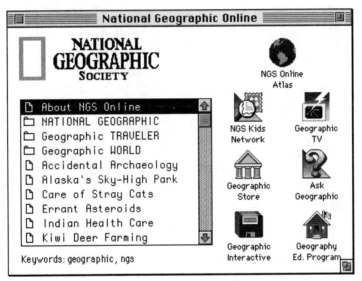

National Geographic's *Earth Almanac* tracks events on earth of particular interest to the Geographic reader. Written in the traditional Geographic style, the stories are always intriguing and often a little unusual. On the afternoon that I looked in, two stories struck me as particularly interesting—especially one recounting the adventures of ten-foot-long serpents intent on decimating the US territories in the South Pacific (see Figure 16-3).

Figure 16-3:
National
Geographic s *Earth
Almanac* regales
the reader with
reports on
rapacious reptiles
and recycled
rubber.

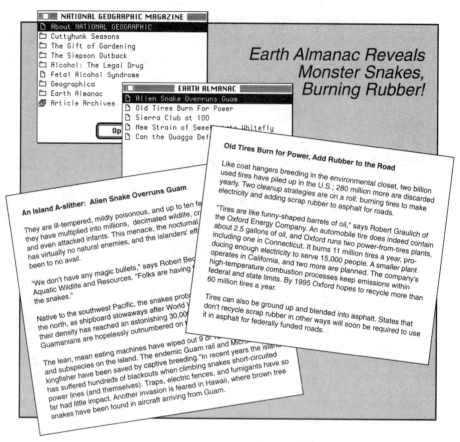

Earth Almanac Reveals
Monster Snakes,
Burning Rubber!

Old Tires Burn for Power, Add Rubber to the Road

Like coat hangers breeding in the environmental closet, two billion used tires have piled up in the U.S.; 280 million more are discarded yearly. Two cleanup strategies are on a roll: burning tires to make electricity and adding scrap rubber to asphalt for roads.

"Tires are like funny-shaped barrels of oil," says Robert Graulich of the Oxford Energy Company. An automobile tire does indeed contain about 2.5 gallons of oil, and Oxford runs two power-from-tires plants, including one in Connecticut. It burns 11 million tires a year, producing enough electricity to serve 15,000 people. A smaller plant operates in California, and two more are planned. The company's high-temperature combustion processes keep emissions within federal and state limits. By 1995 Oxford hopes to recycle more than 60 million tires a year.

Tires can also be ground up and blended into asphalt. States that don't recycle scrap rubber in other ways will soon be required to use it in asphalt for federally funded roads.

An Island A-slither: Alien Snake Overruns Guam

They are ill-tempered, mildly poisonous, and up to ten fe...
they have multiplied into millions, decimated wildlife, cr...
and even attacked infants. This menace, the nocturnal...
has virtually no natural enemies, and the islanders' eff...
been to no avail.

"We don't have any magic bullets," says Robert Be...
Aquatic Wildlife and Resources. "Folks are having...
the snakes."

Native to the southwest Pacific, the snakes prob...
the north, as shipboard stowaways after World...
their density has reached an astonishing 30,00...
Guamanians are hopelessly outnumbered on...

The lean, mean eating machines have wiped out 9 or...
and subspecies on the island. The endemic Guam rail and Micro...
kingfisher have been saved by captive breeding."In recent years the islan...
has suffered hundreds of blackouts when climbing snakes short-circuited
power lines (and themselves). Traps, electric fences, and fumigants have so
far had little impact. Another invasion is feared in Hawaii, where brown tree
snakes have been found in aircraft arriving from Guam.

 Constant Change

Perhaps you've noticed: this is not a conservative, tranquil industry. The waters of telecommunications are about as placid as an Atlantic storm. For this reason, America Online is in a state of constant change.

Case in point: as I write this, AOL has just announced an alliance with Simon & Schuster, the world's largest educational publisher. The service, called College Online, will create a new interactive experience for college professors and students—the first nationwide set of interactive services geared specifically to the higher education market.

Simon & Schuster will become a huge presence in the Education Department. Don't let changes like this annoy you. Seek them out and rejoice in their significance: AOL is always improving and we're the reason. To stay abreast of the changes, use the keyword New.

The Library of Congress Online

The *Secret Soviet Archives* are a temporary "exhibit" in the Education Department, not unlike the exhibit upon which they are based in the Library of Congress (keyword: Library). In the museum business, temporary (or traveling) exhibits don't stay in any one museum permanently; after an appropriate stay, they move on to other museums where others may see them. Indeed, the Library of Congress returned the Russian Archives exhibit to Moscow in July of 1992.

I include the Secret Soviet Archives as an example of the topical material endemic to this department and to impress you with the quality and opulence of its "traveling" exhibits. It also represents the world's first online version of a major national exhibit, and it appeared on America Online.

The Secret Soviet Archives (more properly, *Revelations from the Russian Archives*) is a collection of documents culled from several declassified secret files of the former Soviet Union. The full exhibit of some 300 Soviet documents, photographs and films—which were on display in the Library of Congress in the spring of 1992—is the first such exhibition in the West. It shed new light on some of the major events of the 20th century, from the Russian Revolution to recent times. Included in the exhibit are materials relating to such topics as Stalin's reign of terror, the Gulag system, censorship, the workings of the secret police, substandard construction practices at the Chernobyl nuclear plant and the 1962 Cuban Missile Crisis.

The online exhibit consists of excerpts from 25 of the 250 documents in the museum exhibit. Scans of the original documents are posted in GIF format (GIF is a graphics format that we'll discuss in Chapter 19, "FlashSessions & the Download Manager"). Each scanned original is accompanied by an English translation (which you can read online or save to your hard drive for further study) and a piece providing the appropriate historical background. Reading these documents is an experience never to be forgotten—a John Le Carre novel come to life, an event best illuminated by the Russian originals, downloaded and displayed on your screen, in heirloom color and Cyrillic mystery (see Figure 16-4).

The Russian Archives have been placed on exhibit on America Online "indefinitely." They make up a unique and most rewarding area on the service. Don't pass this one by!

Figure 16-4: The Chernobyl report exceeded 1,000 words and occupied nearly six pages. The page shown here, which documents early construction flaws, was written in early 1979. The plant exploded at 1:21 A.M. on April 26, 1986 a little over seven years later.

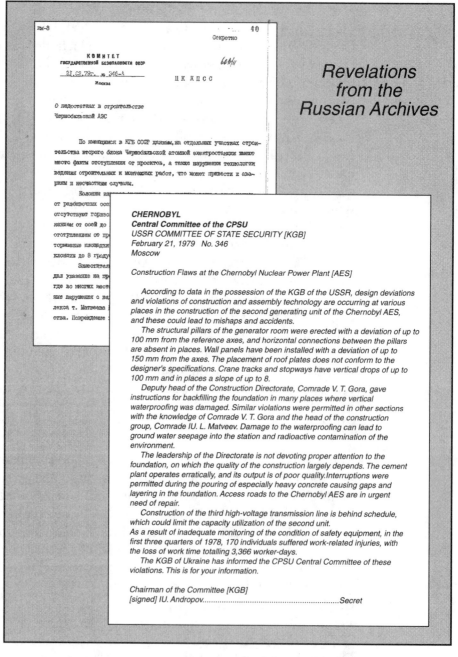

Revelations from the Russian Archives

CHERNOBYL
Central Committee of the CPSU
USSR COMMITTEE OF STATE SECURITY [KGB]
February 21, 1979   No. 346
Moscow

Construction Flaws at the Chernobyl Nuclear Power Plant [AES]

According to data in the possession of the KGB of the USSR, design deviations and violations of construction and assembly technology are occurring at various places in the construction of the second generating unit of the Chernobyl AES, and these could lead to mishaps and accidents.

The structural pillars of the generator room were erected with a deviation of up to 100 mm from the reference axes, and horizontal connections between the pillars are absent in places. Wall panels have been installed with a deviation of up to 150 mm from the axes. The placement of roof plates does not conform to the designer's specifications. Crane tracks and stopways have vertical drops of up to 100 mm and in places a slope of up to 8.

Deputy head of the Construction Directorate, Comrade V. T. Gora, gave instructions for backfilling the foundation in many places where vertical waterproofing was damaged. Similar violations were permitted in other sections with the knowledge of Comrade V. T. Gora and the head of the construction group, Comrade IU. L. Matveev. Damage to the waterproofing can lead to ground water seepage into the station and radioactive contamination of the environment.

The leadership of the Directorate is not devoting proper attention to the foundation, on which the quality of the construction largely depends. The cement plant operates erratically, and its output is of poor quality. Interruptions were permitted during the pouring of especially heavy concrete causing gaps and layering in the foundation. Access roads to the Chernobyl AES are in urgent need of repair.

Construction of the third high-voltage transmission line is behind schedule, which could limit the capacity utilization of the second unit.

As a result of inadequate monitoring of the condition of safety equipment, in the first three quarters of 1978, 170 individuals suffered work-related injuries, with the loss of work time totalling 3,366 worker-days.

The KGB of Ukraine has informed the CPSU Central Committee of these violations. This is for your information.

Chairman of the Committee [KGB]
[signed] IU. Andropov...Secret

As I write this, the Library of Congress features three additional online exhibits, including the Columbus Quincentenary, the Scrolls from the Dead Sea and Treasures of the Vatican. The Vatican exhibit includes such rare delights as love letters from Henry VIII to Anne Boleyn, Galileo's diaries and much more. The Library of Congress Online is not only fascinating and educational, it's a capital example of the benefits online access has to offer.

The Electronic University Network

The word "University" in academic circles implies accreditation and baccalaureate degrees recognized across the nation. The word also implies an accredited program of graduate studies leading to post-baccalaureate degrees. The Electronic University Network (keyword: EUN) offers both, each available without leaving your computer.

The University is based on the belief that quality education can be made available to people where they are—the home, the workplace, the barracks, the hotel room, the hospital; the belief that it's the quality of the dialog between the teacher and the student, not the distance between them, that determines the quality of education; the belief that reading, writing and thinking are at the heart of the educational process.

Figure 16-5: The Electronic University Network offers accredited learning, ranging from Associate s to Master s degrees.

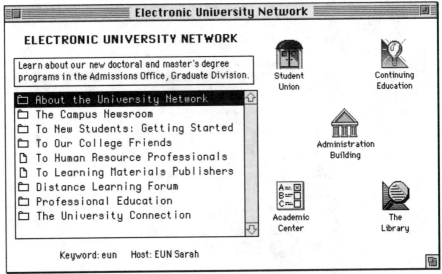

The University offers nearly 100 undergraduate courses that earn college credit and enable students to receive an Associate's or Bachelor's degree. You can also earn a Master of Business Administration (MBA) through the University. The MBA is offered in association with Saginaw Valley State University; the program is comprehensive (see sidebar) and nationally recognized.

Core Courses in the EUN MBA Program

SV 612 *Accounting for Management Decisions*
The uses of accounting information as it relates to decision making in business. Emphasizes current planning and control models, long-range decision making techniques, performance evaluation and accounting information for special decisions. The course may include current readings and case analysis.

SV 622 *Microeconomic Analysis*
Analysis of the behavior of consumers and business firms. Topics covered: the theory of demand, production, and supply, competitive and monopolistic markets, factor markets, general equilibrium and welfare economics, externality problems and public goods.

SV 604 *Financial Planning and Control*
Advanced application of selected finance topics to case studies. Specific topics include capital budgeting, dividend policy, leverage and working capital management. Current topics in finance, such as mergers and multinational corporations, will also be covered.

SV 620 *Quantitative Analysis for Decision Making*
The application of quantitative methods to managerial decision making with emphasis upon problem formulation, the analysis of the effects of changes in parameters and other aspects of model interpretation. The application of technique is emphasized.

SV 621 *Organizational Behavior*
Analysis of the effects of organizational roles in the behavior of people in organizations using an open system perspective. Through the analysis of research findings, the managerial implications of perception, communication, influence processes, technology and the motivational basis of behavior are examined.

SV 631 *Marketing Administration*
Analysis of marketing concepts and problems from the point of view of the business executive engaged in problem solving and decision making in formulating an effective marketing program. Emphasis on planning, organizing and controlling international as well as domestic marketing activities and their integration with objectives and policies of the firm.

SV 690 *Social Environment of Business*
An interdisciplinary course designed to develop students' ability to recognize, interpret and respond to major exogenous forces of concern in business. Topics include: ethical considerations, public policies, laws and regulations, economic environment, political and social influences, accounting practices, multinational corporations and other current concerns of national and international dimensions.

SV 695 *Executive Policies and Planning*
The study of the business enterprise from a top management point of view, emphasizing the formulation of strategies and policies for adapting to external influences and opportunities. The course requires the student to integrate knowledge of the functional areas in the development of comprehensive plans and policies. This course is taken after all other Core courses have been completed.

Speaking of home study, be sure to investigate International Correspondence Schools (keyword: ICS), the oldest and largest accredited home study school in the nation. Using ICS online, you can not only e-mail your instructors for overnight replies, you can talk to fellow students as well. AOL brings a new immediacy to correspondence schools, and ICS is a premier example of that potential.

Smithsonian Online

The Smithsonian Institution in Washington DC is probably America's most popular museum. Occupying a significant percentage of the District, the Institution is really a collection of 17 museums and galleries, including a zoo.

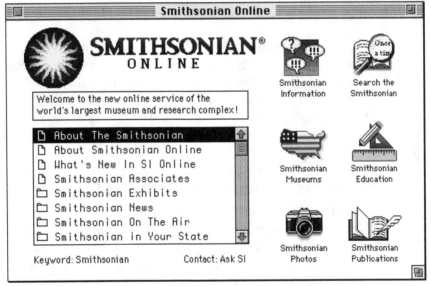

Figure 16-6: Smithsonian Online offers electronic, round-the-clock access to one of America's most comprehensive resources.

Smithsonian Online offers not only descriptions, articles and photos from many of these museums, it also offers a comprehensive planning guide for anyone planning to visit the Institution. Visiting the Smithsonian is not a casual event; planning is not only recommended, it's essential. And you can do all of your planning using America Online.

Figure 16-7: The SR-71 Blackbird spy plane touches down on the runway at Dulles International Airport near Washington, DC. The photo is available online and appears here courtesy of the Smithsonian Institution.

The thousands of Smithsonian Online images are scrupulously indexed; the Smithsonian Education Services area offers ideas, outlines, and publications for the teacher; and the Education Resource Guide catalogs educational materials available from the Smithsonian and several affiliated organizations. This is one of the richest environments available on the service, and it warrants your exploration.

Learning & Reference for the Student

As you can assume from its title, the emphasis in this department is education: learning more about it, getting more out of it and exploring new avenues. For the student, perhaps that last opportunity is the most valuable. Of all the online opportunities AOL provides for the student, three deserve specific mention here: Student Access, the Academic Assistance Center and College Board Online.

Princeton Review/Student Access

A number of resources are available to help students get more out of college, expand graduate school and career options, and network with other students nationwide. The Princeton Review, the nation's most effective test-prep company, has brought these resources together as an AOL service called The Princeton Review/Student Access Online (see Figure 16-8).

Figure 16-8: Student Access Online offers a number of educational, financial and career services.

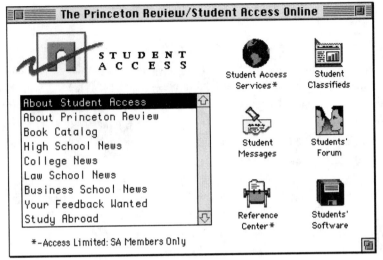

Membership in Student Access enables the student to take advantage of a variety of exclusive educational, financial and career services, including the following:

- Financial planning.

- Internship opportunities.

- Admissions counseling.

- Job-placement services.

- Group buying power offering hundreds of products and services at discounted rates.

- The service's greatest asset—the Student Access members themselves. Student Access forums and trips connect thousands of college students nationwide.

Student Access represents an almost unfair advantage to the student, yet membership is open to anyone. At this writing, the annual fee for this wealth of opportunity is $49.

Tom de Boor

Tom de Boor's office is devoid of ornamentation. The only break in the monotonous white sheetrock is a lone corkboard, suspended by a single nail at the upper left corner. The other nail—the one intended to hold the upper right corner—pulled out of the wall some time ago. The corkboard dangles at a 45 degree angle above Tom's IBM-PS1. Two other computers are present in the room: a terminal and a Macintosh SE. Neither is turned on; both are shrouded in opaque layers of dust. The terminal has been recently used: the dust has been wiped away from the area on the screen that Tom wanted to see.

Tom frequently brushes unruly hair from his eyes as he talks. And talking is something he's good at: animated, enthusiastic talk. In contrast to the disarray in Tom's office, his thinking is organized and methodical, and his conversation is compelling and ardent. As Manager/Senior Producer of Educational Services, Tom oversees AOL's most ambitious and scholarly effort, and he doesn't take this work lightly.

Tom's challenges are magnitude and access. An online service confronts two conflicting necessities: depth and convenience. The Education department is not unlike an immense public library: so diverse that it stimulates, but so large that it intimidates. Tom's solution is an environment that's more exploratory than linear. How often do you go to a video store in search of a specific movie and come home with something entirely different? People like to browse. Tom's objective is what he calls "Information Art": a browsing (rather than searching) environment—rich in graphics, sound and video—where education is as entertaining and diverse as a stroll down a midway or a visit to a mall: nonlinear and personal. It's about time education became fun.

Few can equal Tom's ambition, and that ambition is outwardly directed: Tom couldn't care less about the charm of his office or the pedigree of his coiffeur. He's singularly devoted to his department. Students, teachers, parents and administrators would have to search far and wide for a service that's as comprehensive, convenient and affordable as the Education Department, and Tom de Boor is the man to thank for it.

The Academic Assistance Center

The Academic Assistance Center (keyword: Homework) is designed for students who need additional reinforcement of the concepts they're learning, help with their homework or help with skills that have become rusty. In particular, this is the place to find teachers—teachers online and dedicated to the pursuit of academic goals.

Figure 16-9: The
Academic
Assistance Center
is where students
find teachers and
professionals to
help with
academic issues.

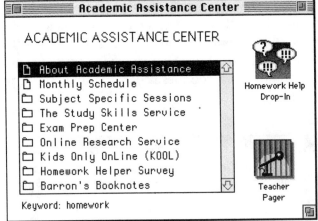

Academic Assistance Center

ACADEMIC ASSISTANCE CENTER

- About Academic Assistance
- Monthly Schedule
- Subject Specific Sessions
- The Study Skills Service
- Exam Prep Center
- Online Research Service
- Kids Only OnLine (KOOL)
- Homework Helper Survey
- Barron's Booknotes

Keyword: homework

Homework Help
Drop-In

Teacher
Pager

Figure 16-9: The Academic Assistance Center is where students find teachers and professionals to help with academic issues.

The Academic Assistance Center is dedicated to providing the student with academic assistance—online, without surcharge and guaranteed: all the message boards mentioned below are closely monitored—if a student posts a message on any of them and doesn't receive a response within 48 hours, AOL credits the student with an hour of free time.

- The Homework Help area is designed to help students who have a need for general help in several different areas.

- Live, real-time help with a specific subject area can be obtained in the Subject-Specific Instruction area, where students can post questions, attend one of many regularly scheduled sessions in a variety of subjects, or sign up for a special individual instruction session with one of AOL's instructors.

- During the evening, the Teacher Pager is ready to connect a student with a teacher online and live; all a student needs to do is use the keyword: TeacherPager. (The Teacher Pager is discussed in Chapter 17, "Reference Desk.")

- Help with research or term papers can be obtained through the Academic Research Service.

- Special help with end-of-term exams is available through the Exam Prep Center.

- Help in preparing for a standardized exam—like the GED and SAT exams—is available in the Study Skills Instruction area.

Homework is one area that's often foremost on the student's mind, and it's the subject that provokes most students to discover the Academic Assistance Center in the first place. Figure 16-10 identifies a few of the subject areas that were active when I visited—and I visited in the summer, when activity on these boards is slow in comparison to that of the school year.

Figure 16-10: At the height of the academic year, nearly 700 messages populate the Homework Q and A message board.

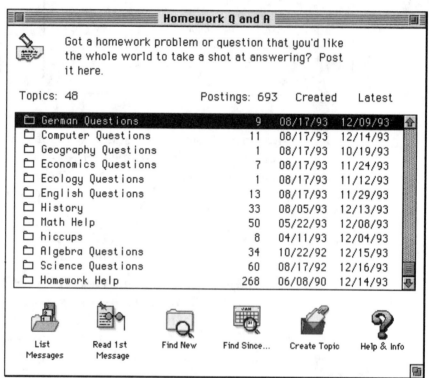

College Board Online

Founded in 1900, the College Board is a national, nonprofit association of more than 2,500 institutions and schools, systems, associations and agencies serving both higher and secondary education. The College Board assists students who are making the transition from high school to college through services that include guidance, admissions, placement, credit by examination and financial aid. In addition, the board is chartered to sponsor research, provide a forum to discuss common problems of secondary and higher education, and address questions of educational standards.

Which is a mouthful. This means that the College Board Online (keyword: CollegeBoard) is an invaluable service to the student faced with all the college-related questions: Where should I go? How much will it cost? What are the admission requirements? What are my chances of getting in?

Figure 16-11: The College Board Online is invaluable for the student contemplating a college education.

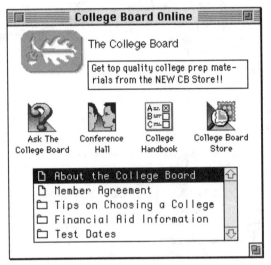

Perhaps the best way to introduce the College Board is to play the part of a prospective student and query the College Board Handbook. The handbook contains descriptions of over 3,100 colleges and universities. Information about each school includes majors offered, academic programs, freshman admissions, student life and athletics. The Handbook can be searched either by topic or college name.

Let's say I'm interested in journalism and black history, and I've decided to pursue the combination of the two as a career. For this, I need an education. Perhaps the College Board Handbook has the answer (see Figure 16-12).

Figure 16-12: A query of the College Handbook identifies the University of North Carolina at Chapel Hill as a possible candidate for my interests in journalism and black studies.

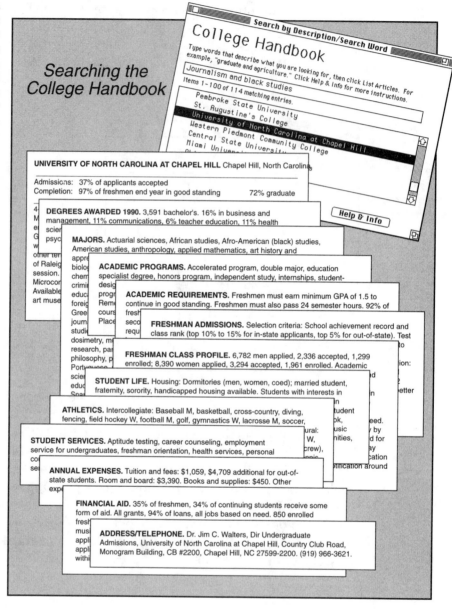

My search criteria for Figure 16-12 were "journalism" and "black studies." In response to these criteria, the College Handbook found 114 colleges that matched my criteria, one of which is the University of North Carolina at Chapel Hill. By selecting the UNC listing, I received all the text pictured in Figure 16-12. This is a profusion of information, and it's available for each of the other 113 candidates as well.

One thing I notice as I read the UNC admission requirements is that this is one tough school to get into. My credentials will have to be *sterling*. For this I need help, and for help I turn to the College Board Store (see Figure 16-13).

Figure 16-13: Shopping the College Board Store, I discover the perfect book and book/tape combination to help me hone my verbal communication skills so that I can submit a winning application.

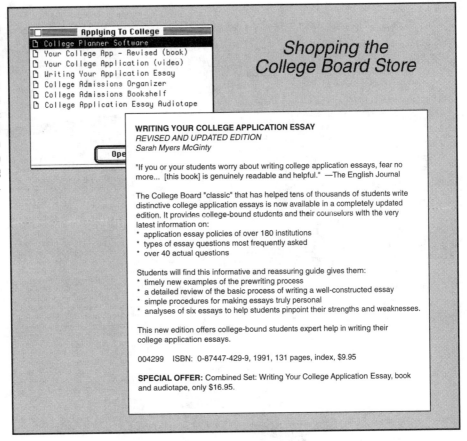

Learning & Reference for the Teacher

Education is not an isolated activity. Education involves the transfer of knowledge, and the transfer of knowledge typically begins with a teacher. The people at America Online know that; that's why the Learning & Reference Department features a number of areas specifically intended for teachers. Here we take a look at three of the service areas.

Teachers Information Network

The Teachers' Information Network (keyword: TIN) not only provides information pertaining to education; it also provides a gathering place where teachers can exchange information, ideas and experience (see Figure 16-14).

Figure 16-14: Clockwise from the upper left: a search of the TIN television and radio database for recommended music programs; the Electronic Schoolhouse; an exam from the Exam Exchange; FlashCard, a freeware application from the TIN libraries; and the Resource Pavilion. See the text for further description of these services.

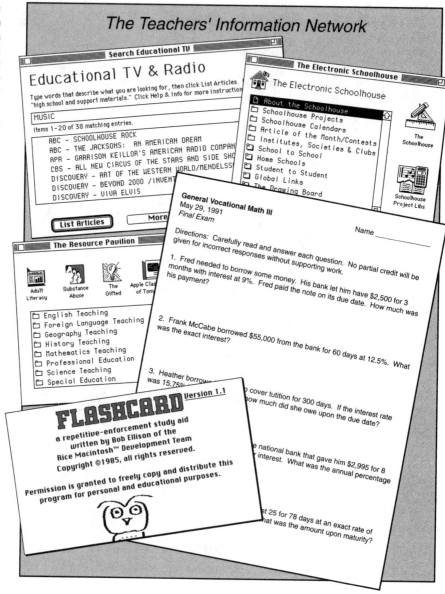

The Teachers' Information Network includes many more features than those pictured in Figure 16-14. Here are some of the sources:

- *KidsNet* is a nonprofit organization widely recognized as the most respected provider of information about and supplementary materials for educational television and radio programs. KidsNet offers the only computerized clearinghouse devoted exclusively to children's programming, primarily through the use of three searchable databases: cassette, on-air and home video. The databases are updated on a monthly basis. Use the keyword KidsNet. (KidsNet is also found in the Kids Only Department. See Chapter 15, "Kids Only.")

- *The Newsstand*, containing educational news items hot off the wires, regular feature articles from prestigious magazines such as Scholastic's *Electronic Learning* and the NSBA's *American School Board Journal*, articles of interest to educators from smaller presses, software reviews and a searchable database of information about more than 300 magazines.

- *The Resource Pavilion*, where experts and educational organizations with particular specialties wait to answer teachers' questions.

- *The Idea Exchange*, the TIN message board center, used for the creative exchange of information and ideas on a variety of topics.

- *The Multimedia Exchange*, for the development of joint multimedia projects and the exchange of software, building the education of tomorrow today.

- *The Electronic Schoolhouse*, dedicated to the creative use of telecommunications in education, where a variety of innovative telecommunications projects are posted or unfolding, and where teachers can arrange for joint connects with other schools or with home-schooling students.

- *Teachers' Libraries*, containing a rich array of public domain educational software programs, files, graphics, sounds, lesson plans and exams.

- *Teachers' University*, teachers teaching teachers in live seminar-style classes, an opportunity to learn new skills from old pros and to contribute to the education of the next generation of educators.

ⓐ *The Convention Center*, where teachers can learn about education conferences and events scheduled by various educational boards, associations and organizations across the country, and receive live reports from major conventions.

CNN NEWSROOM Online

In the past few months, CNN NEWSROOM Online has become one of America Online's most popular features (Figure 16-15). CNN (Cable News Network) is the largest news-gathering organization in the world, and CNN NEWSROOM Online brings the power of CNN to the classroom, complete with ready-to-use outlines and materials for the teacher.

Figure 16-15: CNN NEWSROOM Online not only offers the NEWSROOM, but access to CNN reporters, an idea exchange, and newsroom guides for the teacher.

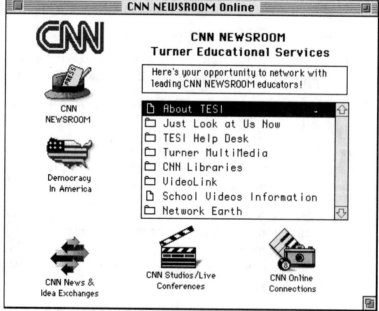

Much of CNN NEWSROOM Online is directed toward the teacher. Newsroom Guides offer classroom activities tied to *CNN NEWSROOM*, a daily 15-minute television news program that highlights the top stories of the day, presents student interest segments and features special newsroom "desks." The desks focus on science, international and business events. A Future Desk ponders events yet to happen, and

Friday's Editor's Desk offers opinion for students to analyze. Each day's program is accompanied by an online Classroom Guide, which provides teachers with key terms, suggested discussion topics, short- and long-term activities, and additional resources for easy follow-ups to viewing and discussion. The NEWSROOM is an extraordinary resource for the teacher. Who but CNN could offer a better look at current events? And who but AOL could bring it to the teacher in such a timely and convenient fashion.

NEA & ASCD Online

The National Education Association (keyword: NEA Public) is a teachers' union providing benefits, support, networking and—through related associations—accreditation for teachers and institutions. NEA Online is an ideal communications vehicle for the association: most teachers have access to a computer, and communication of this sort is best handled quickly, efficiently and bilaterally. AOL excels at this.

Figure 16-16: NEA Online offers a number of services for the teacher. Most of these services are available to anyone (including parents and students), not just NEA members.

ASCD's online area brings the resources of the association to members and the general public. Featured are articles from *Educational Leadership* (ASCD's flagship publication), catalogs of information about new ASCD products and services, an Ask ASCD research service, articles from *ASCD Update* and the *CTRC Quarterly*, and an opportunity to discuss curriculum issues on the area's "Talk About Curriculum" message board.

Figure 16-17: ASCD Online offers numerous resources for the educational administrator.

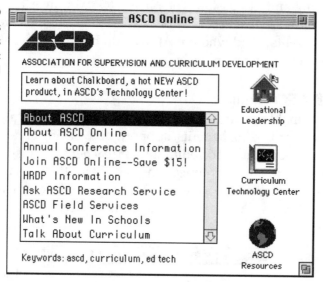

Learning & Reference for the Parent

The Parents' Information Network (keyword: PIN) is an integrated full-service set of online services for parents, offering interactive forums on issues of importance to parents, articles from educational periodicals, databases of useful information, real-time conferencing opportunities and parent-oriented guides to other parts of America Online.

Figure 16-18: The Parents Information Network gathers features from throughout the service and incorporates them into one easy-to-use resource.

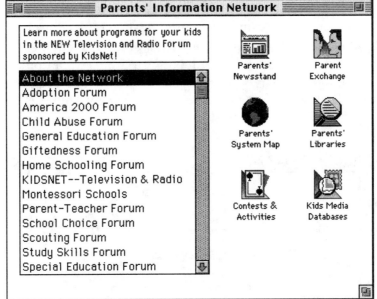

Of particular interest is the Parents' System Map—a guide to AOL from the parent's perspective. This is an innovative service, and a necessary one: AOL—as you have no doubt discovered—is huge. Learning the locations of forums, databases and libraries is a challenge, one that's well met by the Parents' System Map. If it is useful to a parent, it's no doubt on the map, including its title, brief description and location.

Look again at the forums in Figure 16-18: child abuse, giftedness, home schooling—here's where you can meet other parents who share the same interests as you and exchange concerns, techniques, successes and failures. When you need an empathetic friend, the Parents' Forum is the place to look.

The Broadcast Media

Though I've already mentioned CNN, there are two other broadcast services that should be of interest to you: National Public Radio Outreach and C-SPAN. An article I once read (found in *WIRED* magazine—see Chapter 14, "The Internet Connection") discussed the future of broadcast media and suggested that the era of passive, one-way broadcast communication was rapidly drawing to a close. I agree. We want more, and AOL's broadcast (and magazine) forums are burgeoning answers to that need.

National Public Radio Outreach Online

This is NPR's avenue of communication with educators and listeners alike. Educators will find a wealth of teacher's guides, newsletters and brochures which tie in with NPR programs—not unlike the strategy employed by CNN. The rest of us will find press releases, biographies (and photos) of on-air personalities, programming schedules and member station listings.

Figure 16-19: National Public Radio Outreach Online offers services for educators and listeners alike.

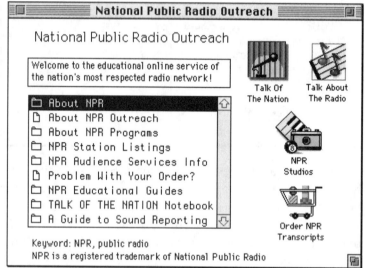

Two items are of particular interest: (1) Talk About the Radio provides direct access to NPR's listener-feedback loop. You're not only assured that your comment will be read, but you may receive a reply as well. (2) The Audience Services Information Area provides information on books, music and films reviewed on NPR's *All Things Considered*, *Morning Edition* and *Talk of the Nation*. Typically, contact information is included for individuals and organizations discussed in program features. The keyword? NPR, of course!

C-SPAN Online

Former House Speaker Jim Wright once called C-SPAN (Cable-Satellite Public Affairs Network) "America's Town Hall." Indeed, since 1977, C-SPAN has been providing live, unedited, balanced views of government forums unmatched in the broadcast industry. Now C-SPAN

Online brings C-SPAN's viewers even closer to cable television's public-affairs network.

Perhaps the most significant part of the online service is its program descriptions and long-range scheduling information: finally, we can tell what's coming up next!

Figure 16-20: C-SPAN Online offers schedules, feedback, educational services and a searchable database for its viewers.

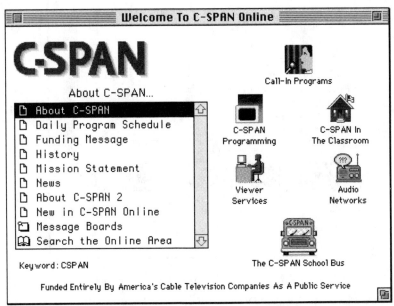

Educators who are interested in using C-SPAN as a teaching resource can join the network's free membership support service: C-SPAN In The Classroom. This service offers teaching guides, access to C-SPAN's archives, a toll-free educators' hotline and special issues of the *C-SPAN Digest*. Together with CNN and NPR, the C-SPAN Classroom offers a gold mine of current-affairs study material that's professionally produced, contemporary and—not to be forgotten— almost free. I wish my teachers had access to this material when I was in school.

Just Desserts

At the end of a heavy meal—your plate now emptied of consequences such as Chernobyl and post-graduate degrees—I like to serve a refreshing dessert. Something light, with a refreshing aftertaste. And what better than Disney Adventures Magazine (see Figure 16-21).

Figure 16-21:
Disney Adventures
Magazine offers a
searchable
database of
articles, a library of
pictures and
sounds, and a chat
room where kids
can gather every
Monday,
Wednesday and
Friday evenings.

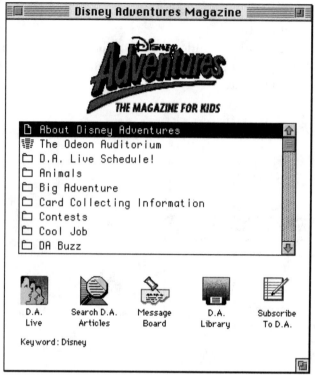

Disney Adventures is a magazine for kids, covering science, sports, entertainment, comics and puzzles. It's available at newsstands or grocery store checkout stands throughout the United States, or by subscription (you can subscribe online). More than 4 million kids read the magazine each month, and thousands of others visit the online forum every day.

Today I searched the Disney libraries and found the title song to Disney's film *Beauty and the Beast* in MIDI format. MIDI (Musical Instrument Digital Interface) is a hobby of mine, so naturally I downloaded the music and much to my delight, discovered not one but three versions of an arrangement of the Oscar-winning tune. The restrictions of the printed medium interfere here, or I'd play them for you. They're from Disney, after all, and they're exquisite.

(If you're interested in MIDI as I am, check out the Mac Music & Sound Forum, keyword MMS.)

Disney Adventures is AOL's lemon creme pie. It's rich and delicious, and the perfect end to a heavy online session. You don't have to be a kid to enjoy fresh pie, and the same's true for the Disney Adventures forum. Give it a try, and bring your appetite. Use the keyword Disney.

Moving On

The Education Department is a vast collection of resources: a joint venture by professionals, parents and students alike. Coupled with America Online's ease of use and graphical interface, it's not only one of the most comprehensive online resources available, it's really fun. Educators will tell you that learning is most effective when it's enjoyable—an experience that encourages the student's return. The Education Department is that kind of experience.

Anyone will tell you, however, that research is a significant portion of education. And research is rapidly becoming an electronic medium. There's good reason for that. Find out by turning the page...

Reference Desk

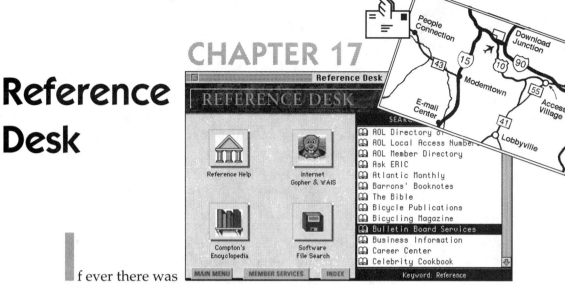

If ever there was a message in search of a medium, it's reference. The printed medium—home to reference works for centuries—is simply too inconvenient, too wasteful and too tardy to suit the information age. A printed encyclopedia, for example, might have made sense 60 years ago, but in order to describe every aspect of today's society—especially today's technological society—a comprehensive encyclopedia would have to fill a room, not a shelf. Even if you had the room, you would hesitate to use the thing: searching—especially cross-referencing—would be too tedious; it would probably be out of date by the time it was printed (it most certainly would by the time you paid for it); and its perpetual revisions would make indexing a nightmare.

Forget the printed encyclopedia. Forget the room to house it. Forget the payments and revisions. Turn on your computer, punch up AOL and click the Reference Desk button on the Main Menu, or use the keyword Reference. It's all here, it's all topical, it's all affordable and not a single tree fell to make it all possible.

Compton's Encyclopedia

Compton's Encyclopedia is published by Britannica Software, Inc., a division of Encyclopaedia Britannica, Inc. It features 8,784,000 words; 5,200 full-length articles; 26,023 capsule articles; and 63,503 index

---

The Reference Desk is America Online's access point to scores of online databases, reference works and information librarians. If you have a question, the Reference Desk probably has the answer. Click the Reference Desk button on the Main Menu, or use the keyword Reference.

entries. The multimedia version of this encyclopedia took top honors at the 1991 Software Publisher's Association awards ceremony, taking the annual prize awarded for the best stand-alone educational product, and a Critic's Choice award as Best Education Program. The online version (keyword: Encyclopedia) is continually updated and easy to search. Finding all the references—including cross references—to the word "mammal" takes only moments, and nothing is inadvertently omitted.

I love trains. I love the sound and smell—and the romance—of trains. I ride a light rail system to work—Metropolitan Area Express (MAX) in Portland, Oregon; voted America's Best in 1989—and Amtrak's most popular route—the Coast Starlight—passes within a few miles of my house. To test Compton's Encyclopedia as an effective resource, I searched for the word "train" and was more than gratified with the results.

Notable Passenger Trains

These are the trains I want to travel in someday. The text below is extracted from Compton's Encyclopedia, Online Edition, and downloaded from AOL.

 Blue Train, South Africa.
Said to be the most luxurious train in the world, the Blue Train makes a leisurely 1,000-mile, 26-hour trip once or twice a week between Pretoria and Cape Town.

Coast Starlight, United States.
Though I've already indicated that this is Amtrak's most popular train, it warrants a second mention here. The Coast Starlight crosses the Cascade Mountains and follows the coastline of California in a 1,400-mile, 33-hour trip between Seattle and Los Angeles. Save your pennies and get a sleeper.

More>

- Indian Pacific, Australia.
  Another luxury train, the Indian Pacific crosses the Australian continent, from Sydney to Perth, in less than three days.

- Orient Express, Europe.
  Europe's first transcontinental express, for years unmatched in luxury and comfort. From 1883 to 1977 (with interruptions during WWI and WWII), it ran from Paris, France, to Constantinople (now Istanbul), Turkey. Short runs are still made over portions of the original route.

- Rheingold, West Germany.
  One of Europe's finest trains, the Rheingold runs between Amsterdam, The Netherlands, and Basel, Switzerland, following the Rhine River and stopping at such cities as Cologne, Mainz and Munich.

- Rossiya, Trans-Siberian Railway.
  The Rossiya runs daily between Moscow and Vladivostok. The trip takes a week. Call your travel agent before you pack: things are changing over there.

- TGV, France.
  This is the fastest train in the world, cruising at 180 miles per hour and covering the 267 miles between Paris and Lyon in two hours.

Whoa! One hundred and eighty miles an hour! Few cars can reach that speed—in fact, few private aircraft can reach that speed. Let's hope no cows wander onto the tracks....

Reference Help

Forgive my rambling. I got sidetracked when the subject of trains came up. I was talking about online reference, and about some of the advantages it has over certain print reference materials. Online reference is convenient, it's inexpensive, and it's online 24 hours a day. Following are some of the other reference services available through America Online.

The Academic Research Service

America Online's Academic Research Service (ARS) provides research support for students at the high school, college or graduate level. It's populated by real people (Dr. Michael W. Popejoy is the administrator—he's also a professor, researcher and writer) who accept your e-mailed questions and respond with e-mailed replies (guaranteed within 24 to 72 hours). The service is especially effective at reducing research time for students who must conduct online research. Coupled with AOL's Internet gateway (the Internet is discussed in Chapter 14), a student's research potential is almost boundless.

AskERIC Online

This is the Academic Research Service for educators. The Educational Resources Information Center (ERIC) is a national information system designed to provide educators with ready access to an extensive body of education-related literature. It's funded by the US Department of Education.

AskERIC is ERIC's online information clearinghouse for teachers. It performs the same service as the ARS, but it's educator (rather than student) oriented and even more comprehensive. AskERIC is an Internet domain, and the staff is drawn from the faculties of institutions all over the world. As with the ARS, you submit your questions to the staff via e-mail and receive a reply 24 to 72 hours later.

Figure 17-1:
AskERIC Online is
America Online s
gateway to the
Internet-based
AskERIC
information
clearinghouse.

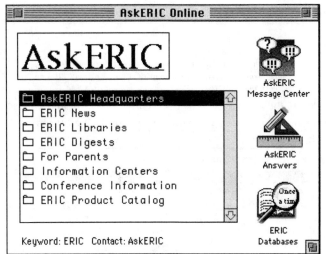

Though the AskERIC service is an Internet gateway (gateways are described in Chapter 10, "Personal Finance"), you won't even know you're on the Internet when you pose a question or receive a reply.

But there's more: AOL also offers a local (non-Internet) database of ERIC's digests, news and information centers. There's no waiting when you query this database; the answers are stored on the AOL host computer hard disks, so the response is immediate (see Figure 17-2).

Figure 17-2: It only seems appropriate to search AskERIC Online for information regarding online research, and it found 67 references to the topic! In fact, the paper shown here should be required reading for any educator who is contemplating the online research potential.

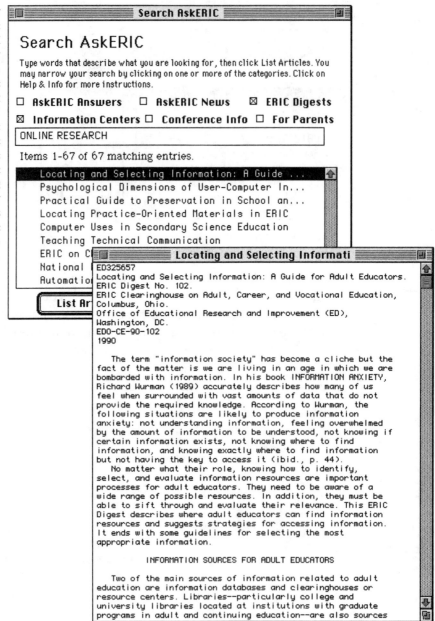

Like the Academic Research Service, AskERIC is free of extra charge on AOL. Just use the keyword AskERIC.

Teacher Pager

While ARS is intended for the use of secondary and college students, and ERIC is a service primarily intended for educators, the Teacher Pager is intended for the use of students of all ages, and it's even more personal. To access the Pager, use the keyword TeacherPager (see Figure 17-3).

Figure 17-3: The Teacher Pager puts students in direct, one-on-one contact with a teacher online.

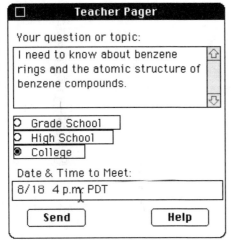

When the pager appears, type in your question or topic, select your grade level and a time you'd like to meet. When you click the Send button your message will automatically be sent to the Teacher Pager Coordinator, who will either get you help immediately (you should remain online for at least five minutes) or will e-mail you later. Over 500 teachers and professionals are on staff for this purpose.

There's More

The services mentioned here aren't the only reference services AOL offers. Be sure to investigate Ask Smithsonian, Ask Geographic and Ask NMAA (the Smithsonian's National Museum of American Art). There's a universe of professionals online, ready to help. All you have to do is ask.

File Search

You don't have to visit the Reference Desk in order to access AOL's file search. You can do this at any time, from any location, by using the keyword FileSearch.

File Search (you might hear it called "Quickfinder"—either term is accurate and the keyword Quickfinder works just as well) is AOL's mechanism for searching its list of online files. When you use either of these keywords, the Macintosh Software dialog box will appear (see Figure 17-4).

Figure 17-4: The File Search dialog box.

```
┌─────────────────────────────────────────────────────────────┐
│ ▣           Macintosh Software                             ▣ │
├─────────────────────────────────────────────────────────────┤
│ List files made available during: (Click one)              │
│     ◉ All dates        ○ Past month      ○ Past week        │
│ List files only in these categories: (Click on one or more) │
│                          ☐ All Categories                   │
│     ☐ Beginners      ☐ Business        ☐ Communications     │
│     ☐ DTP            ☐ Developer       ☐ Education          │
│     ☐ Games          ☐ Graphics        ☐ Hardware           │
│     ☐ Hypercard      ☐ Music & Sound   ☐ Utilities          │
│ List files with these words reflecting my interest: (Optional)│
│   ┌───────────────────────────────────────────────────────┐ │
│   │                                                       │ │
│   └───────────────────────────────────────────────────────┘ │
│  ┌─────────────┐  ┌──────────────────┐  ┌────────────────┐  │
│  │ Submit a File│  │ List Matching Files│ │ Get Help & Info│ │
│  └─────────────┘  └──────────────────┘  └────────────────┘  │
└─────────────────────────────────────────────────────────────┘
```

Most searches of AOL's online files are successful, but you might encounter situations where the search fails (no files are found) even though you know there are files online that meet your criteria, or where the search is too successful (wading through a hundred or more matches is just too much effort).

How Many Files Are Available?

One way of tracking AOL's growth is to make a periodic check of the total number of files available online. When I first joined the service (I'm a "charter member," having first signed on in early 1990), there were fewer than 10,000 files. When I checked today, there were over 60,000!

How did I determine the number of files available online? It's easy: just leave the file search dialog box empty (as it's pictured in Figure 17-4). Don't check any of the check boxes and don't put any criteria in the text box. Just leave the dialog as it appears when you first summon it, be sure the All dates button is selected, then click the List Matching Files button.

America Online will respond with a listing of all of the files available online, and a number indicating their total. With this many files, you won't want to even browse the list, but the total number might be informative. Do this occasionally and watch AOL grow.

Let's say that you received a file from a friend who is using a PC rather than a Mac. It's common to compress files before sending them, and your friend used PKZIP to do so. PKZIP is built into the Windows version of the AOL software, and most online files for PCs are "zipped," as they say, so this isn't uncommon.

Unfortunately, you've got a Mac, and Macs usually use the StuffIt compression software, not PKZIP. (StuffIt and PKZIP are discussed in Chapter 5, "Computing.") You need a Macintosh utility for unzipping PC compressed files. Amazingly, your Macintosh AOL software does this, but not for all versions of zipped files. Needing a utility that will decompress every imaginable zipped file, you sign on and use File Search to locate the utility.

Your first temptation is to simply type the category (or name) of the program you're looking for in the criteria text box, as shown at the top of Figure 17-5. You don't really want PKZIP itself: it only runs on PCs. You want something that will unzip zipped files on the Mac, so the generic term "zip" is about the best criterion for your purpose.

Figure 17-5:
Homing in on an
unzipping
program for the
Mac.

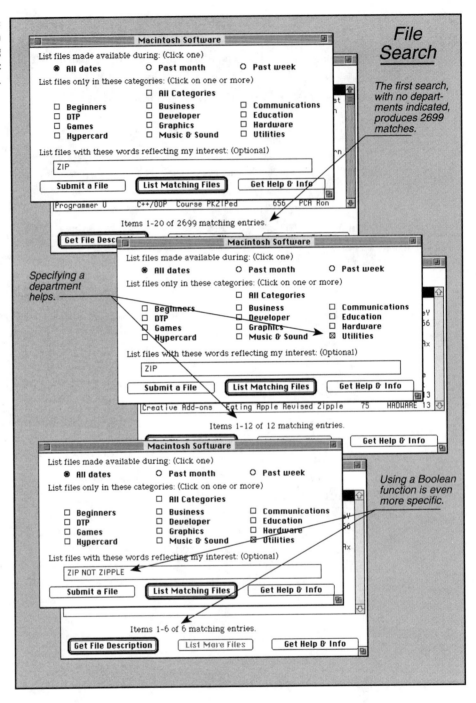

*File
Search*

*The first search,
with no depart-
ments indicated,
produces 2699
matches.*

*Specifying a
department
helps.*

*Using a Boolean
function is even
more specific.*

Referring to Figure 17-5, notice the results of the first search: 2699 files! Indeed, a few file searching tips seem in order:

🔺 Use check boxes to narrow your search. It's tempting to ignore the check boxes in the middle of the file search dialog box. If you do, All Categories is the default condition, even if it's not checked. By specifying a check box (I specified Utilities in the second example in Figure 17-5), my file search produced only 12 matches, a manageable number.

🔺 To further narrow a search, use Boolean functions (*and*s, *or*s and *not*s). I used a *not* function in the third example pictured in Figure 17-5 and eliminated all of the Zipples—whatever they are—that cluttered my results. (Be careful: mixing *and*s with *or*s or *not*s can sometimes produce misleading results. Read more about Boolean searches in Chapter 13, "Clubs & Interests.")

🔺 Don't specify version numbers. You might have heard that UnZIP 1.10 is the latest version. Searching with the criterion UnZIP 1.10 would produce UnZIP 1.10 all right, but not the latest version, UnZIP 2.0. Moreover, UnZIP 1.10 might have been removed from the libraries when UnZIP 2.0 was posted, thereby causing the search to fail altogether.

🔺 Criteria are not case-sensitive. Don't worry about uppercase and lowercase when you're typing criteria. America Online doesn't care. It also doesn't care if you make things plural or singular: "ZIPS" works no better or worse than "ZIP."

🔺 Use whole words. Abbreviations won't work, nor will wildcards. "UnZ" (for UnZip) or "UnZ*" (using a wildcard) won't find UnZIP.

🔺 Search specific libraries if File Search fails. Using File Search to find "MajorTom," for example, will fail. Since MajorTom is a graphic, and since it's stored in the Gallery (discussed in Chapter 12, "People Connection"), go to the Gallery and conduct your search there.

🔺 To find the latest files, leave everything blank and specify "Past week." This finds all of the files posted in just the past week.

Online Databases

With the fall 1994 release of the Reference Desk, AOL has effectively consolidated all of its online databases into one place. If you want information on water, for example, you can search over 70 databases, ranging from the Bible (317 references, including 80 for "holy water") to the White House (159 references, including 23 for "whitewater"). It's no longer necessary to roam all over the service, searching for databases and hoping you haven't missed one. They're all here; just use the keyword Reference.

Print the List

If you conduct much online research, it helps to have a printed listing of AOL's online databases, one that you can consult whether you're online or off. You can have one whenever the mail Reference Desk window is active: just choose Print List from the File menu.

We've explored many of AOL's databases in previous chapters, and others are highly specialized. But two warrant our attention here.

AOL Local Access Numbers

The listing of telephone numbers with which you can contact AOL is a prodigious database in itself. America Online serves all of North America, after all, and that's a lot of territory (and a lot of access numbers). If you plan to travel with your computer, search this database for a list of access numbers for the localities you'll be visiting. Print the list, pack it with your modem, and take it along. You can access the database from the Reference Desk, or by using the keyword Access.

If you are a frequent traveler, you'll want to read Appendix D, "On the Road." There are lots of tips there for the AOL road warrior.

BBS Search

America Online isn't the only electronic bulletin board system (BBS) available to you. Thousands of others dot the country. Few offer the breadth of service AOL does, but many offer the online community spirit, enhanced by their proximity to their members.

How do you find those that are near you? Search AOL's database of BBSes. It's available at the Reference Desk, or via the keyword BBS.

Moving On

With our explorations of the Education and Reference Departments, we've had a substantive experience. Though the online environment is an ideal platform for education and reference it's well suited to a number of others, including commerce.

You can buy (and sell) everything from art to videotapes online, from other members or from retail merchants. It all happens at the Marketplace, coming up next.

The Marketplace

If the X-genera-tion is to be believed, this is a material world. "Mall" is our mantra. But malls are a day's drive for some of us; others don't care for the crowds; still others would just as soon stay at home and do their shopping from there.

Forget the mall. Forget the shopping channel. Forget glossy catalogs. The Marketplace is as close as your computer.

Classifieds Online

This wouldn't be a fully operative communications medium without classified ads, and AOL has them—at no extra charge. Just select the Classifieds from the main Marketplace window, or use the keyword Classifieds (see Figure 18-1).

Classifieds Online offers, among other things, a library containing zip and area code directories; UPS, FedEx and US Mail rate charts; a UPS manifest printing program; and the complete American Computer Exchange used computer pricing guide.

The Marketplace is AOL's emporium—its flea market and bazaar, its supermarket and shopping mall. Leave the car in the driveway and the kids in the yard. We're ready to lend a little support to the private sector, and we don't even have to leave the comfort of home. Click the Marketplace button on the Main menu or use the keyword Marketplace and *shazam!*, we're ready to pursue Acquisition Mode.

Figure 18-1:
Classifieds Online,
where you can
buy and sell
computers and
components,
advertise your
professional
services, search
the job postings,
exchange
computer games
and software, and
take advantage
of business
opportunities—all
without extra
charges.

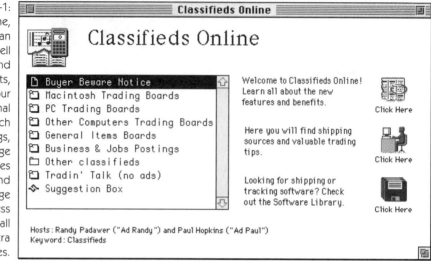

The Hard Sell

Browsing the Classifieds Online library the other day, I came across the following excerpt from *Direct-Marketing Firepower*, an intriguing book by Jonathan Mizel. He's describing his friend Joe, who placed an ad on a local bulletin board system—a similar situation (though much more parochial) to AOL's Classifieds Online:

"So he decided this local BBS would be just the place to advertise it (the hard disk) since they allowed free classifieds for computer items. Joe placed the ad for this item on a Monday. I think he said he was selling it for $120.00. Guess how many responses Joe got by Wednesday. Go on, guess.

"Within 48 hours, Joe had received 220 responses to his little classified ad on a system that was only used by San Francisco technical computer people. The total number of people who are on the system is probably less than 5,000. He was freaked out, even mad because people kept e-mailing him and calling him to get this damn piece of equipment (which, by the way, sold immediately)...

"Too bad old Joe didn't have 220 hard drives!"

Joe's experience occurred on a system with less than 5,000 members. America Online has over a million. When I last checked, over 11,000 classifieds were running, with more coming in every day. There's a portentous potential here.

And it's all free. All you pay is your regular AOL connect time.

Shoppers' Advantage

Speaking of numbers, approximately 3.1 million members (over one percent of the United States population!) shop through Shoppers' Advantage. This is a little like the shopping "clubs" that have sprouted up nationwide: you pay a small annual membership fee and you're rewarded with a warehouse full of products, attractively priced, in stock and ready for shipment. Shoppers' Advantage not only offers the convenience of online shopping, it guarantees the lowest prices anywhere, or it will refund the difference.

You can browse the store whether or not you're a member of Shoppers' Advantage—a significant advantage over local shopping clubs—and you can enroll online at any time.

Look at the benefits Shoppers' Advantage offers:

- Discounts of 10 to 50 percent on all manufacturers' list prices.

- Over 250,000 name-brand products, all in a searchable online database. If a product you're looking for is not on the database you can contact the Product Research team, and they will try and obtain the product for you.

- Automatic 2-year free warranty extension. Even if there is only a 3- or 6-month manufacturer's warranty, Shoppers' Advantage will extend the warranty on any product purchased through them to 2 years, at no cost.

- Merchandise from name-brand manufacturers, including Panasonic, GE, JVC, Nikon, Sony, Pioneer, AT&T, Nintendo, Whirlpool, Quasar, Jordache, Hoover, Pentax, Timex, Memorex, Rayban, Radio Shack, Pierre Cardin, Singer, Magnavox—an all-star roster of manufacturers.

- The Department Store, where browsing—rather than searching—is the order of the day, and the Best Buys section, where the staff posts their best bargains. If you want to compare prices and features for yourself, Shoppers' Advantage can compare up to 50 similar items at the same time and display the results for your consideration.

- Lowest price guarantee. If, within 30 days of buying something through Shoppers' Advantage, you find the same piece of merchandise being sold for a lower price by an authorized dealer, send Shoppers' Advantage a copy of the ad and they will send you the difference.

- A money-back guarantee. If you are not fully satisfied with Shoppers' Advantage, all you need do is call their toll-free number to cancel your membership. Your current membership fee will be refunded in full.

Mozart Mania

Searching the Shoppers' Advantage database the other day, I discovered the set of compact discs shown in Figure 18-2.

Figure 18-2: He only lived to see 37: Mozart was precocious, powdered and prolific. Now he is inexpensive as well.

```
Compact discs(STDK) Delta (DELT)
Model#: 358559 Title: 30 CD Mozart Collection
-----------------------------------------------------
Enjoy Mozart's timeless music over a lifetime with
this 30-CD commemorative collection. Features selec-
tions of Don Giovanni, Magic Flute, and Marriage of
Figaro; Violin Concerti 1, 2, and 3; early Symphonies
1, 2, and 3; Symphonies 21, 34, 35, 36, 38, 39, and
40; Piano Concerti 1, 2, and 3; Clarinet Concerto,
four horn concerti; the Flute Concerto, 21 songs,
piano sonatas, quintets and quartets, dances and
minuets, 11 marches and more.
-----------------------------------------------------
List Price:          open
Our Price:           $109.00
With Regular Delivery: $118.95 (delivery in 2-3 weeks)
```

Now there's a feast for Mozart mania!, at less than four bucks a disc, delivered to your door. There's probably a law against this, but I won't tell anyone if you don't.

Moving On

I've only scratched the surface of the Marketplace. You can order flowers online via the Flower Shop, or buy discounted books at the Online Bookstore. You not only can sell your old adding machine in the Classifieds, but you can buy a new one at the Penny Wise Office Products Store. Of course, you don't really need an adding machine because you have a computer, but isn't it time for a new one? Computer Express has not only computers, but components and software as well.

The pursuit of materialism, however, is no longer our concern. It's time to roll out the heavy armament. The next chapter explores AOL's Strategic Defense Initiative: FlashSessions and the Download Manager. America Online can sign on automatically, send and receive your mail, then sign back off—at any time of the day or night. It can queue files for later downloading and resume downloading files that have been interrupted.

Many of these features are unique to AOL. They're unprecedented, inconceivable and almost magical, but they're not indescribable. And describe them is what we're about to do. Read on. . .

FlashSessions & the Download Manager
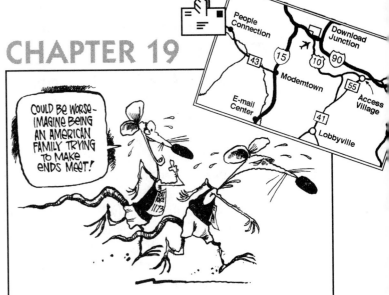

I've been getting a lot of e-mail lately. I've made a number of online friends and we correspond a lot, and I get tons of mail from readers. If I read all this mail online, they would have to deliver my AOL bill with a forklift.

There's an additional challenge to my finances: I'm a downloading zealot. I beta test a lot of software, all of which has to be downloaded. I collect utilities, fonts and graphics for my desktop-publishing ventures. I'm constantly downloading snippets from the Writers' Forum. I probably download three or four hours' worth of material a week. Starting a 58-minute download is one thing; remembering to return to the computer 58 minutes later is another. If I go outside to mow the lawn during a long download, there's a high probability I won't remember the computer when the download is finished. When I do remember it—usually about 20 minutes after the download is finished—I've just paid for 20 minutes of idle connect-time. This is not frugal.

Happily, AOL offers solutions to my problems: FlashSessions and the Download Manager.

Mike Keefe's editorial cartoons (keyword: Keefe) are a regular feature of America Online. His material is an ideal candidate for FlashSessions and the Download Manager, the two rat-race relieving features described in this chapter.

What Are FlashSessions?

Rather than try to explain FlashSessions, let me tell you about my typical morning. After fixing coffee, I sit down at my Mac and run AOL. I do not sign on; rather, I choose Read Incoming Mail from the Mail menu. All the mail I've received in the past 24 hours appears there. I read it all, forwarding, replying and composing new mail. Then I check the Online Downloads folder on my hard disk. A few downloaded files usually appear there, and I move them elsewhere on my hard drive, wherever I want them to be. All of this happens off-line, at my leisure: there are no clocks running. My Mac, you see, signed on at 4:00 A.M. It sent the mail I had prepared the previous day, retrieved and stored any mail AOL was holding for me, and downloaded the files I had requested. It did all this while I slept the sleep of innocence, while system activity was light and nobody wanted to use the phone.

On many days, that's all the computing I do. I'm sound asleep when the Mac is online, and my connect time is reduced to the absolute minimum: about a minute a day when I'm not downloading. This kind of absentee management is called a *FlashSession*. FlashSessions sign on, send and receive mail, download predesignated files, and sign off, all without human participation. You can schedule a FlashSession to occur at a predetermined (and unattended) time, you can invoke a Flash-Session manually (whether you're online or off), or you can conclude an online session with a FlashSession. They do their work quickly, efficiently and without complaint. This is what computing should be.

Futility Revisited

In Chapter 4, I had you send yourself a letter. Yes, it was an exercise in futility, but you saw e-mail in action. We're about to repeat the exercise, but this time we'll have the computer do it for us. We'll not only experience futility, we'll experience automated futility. This is not what computing is supposed to be, but it might prove to be enlightening.

🔺 Do not sign on. Rather, choose Compose Mail from the Mail menu. As you did in Chapter 4, prepare a short message to yourself. Your Compose Mail window should look something like that pictured in Figure 19-1. (Be sure to put *your* screen name in the To box, not mine. You have no idea how many people sent me FlashSession tests based on these instructions in the first edition of this book.)

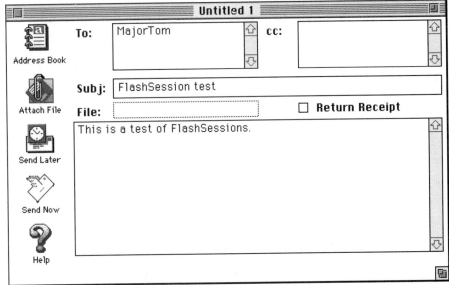

Figure 19-1:
Compose a
message to
yourself,
substituting your
screen name in the
To field.

▲ Note that the Send Now icon is dimmed. Since you're not online, this command is not available. Instead, click the Send Later icon. America Online will reply with the message pictured in Figure 19-2.

Figure 19-2:
America Online
confirms your
request to Send
Later.

▲ Note that two buttons are available. Click the one marked Set FlashSession.

▲ Your FlashSession window should look like the one in Figure 19-3, including all the check marks. If your window isn't displaying all three check marks, double-click any option that isn't checked.

Figure 19-3:
Configure
FlashSessions in
the FlashSession
window.

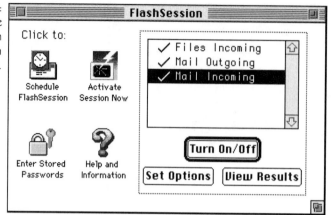

🔺 Now click the icon marked Enter Stored Passwords and complete the resulting form as pictured in Figure 19-4. Enter the password you use when you sign on to AOL. Your screen name will appear in place of mine, and the number of characters in your password will probably differ as well. (Notice that your password isn't displayed as you type: asterisks representing each letter in your password appear instead. That's as it should be. You never know who's looking over your shoulder.)

Figure 19-4:
Complete the
Stored Passwords
form.

Stored Passwords

Use Stored passwords for:

FlashSessions	Signon	Password:
☒	☐ MajorTom	********

[Cancel]   [Help]   [OK]

🔺 When you have completed the Stored Passwords form, click OK. America Online may respond with an online sermon regarding the advisability of using stored passwords. Read it carefully but don't worry: you've only stored a FlashSession password, and Flash-Session passwords are pretty benign.

🔺 Back at the FlashSession window, click the Activate Session Now icon. America Online will respond with the form in Figure 19-5.

Figure 19-5: The Activate FlashSession Now form makes more sense when you have more than one screen name.

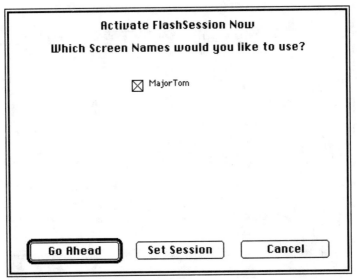

🔺 Understand that many people use more than one screen name. When multiple screen names are used, they all appear on this form. Nonetheless, you must turn on the check box for your screen name, even if you only have one (screen names are discussed in Chapter 2, "Making the Connection").

🔺 Click the button marked Go Ahead. America Online takes over (see Figure 19-6).

Figure 19-6: The FlashSession "flashes" your mail to AOL headquarters in Virginia and back in seconds.

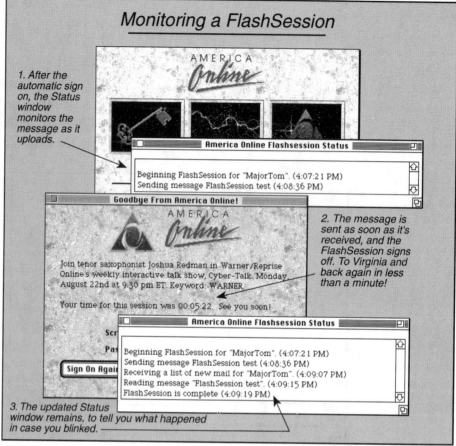

Monitoring a FlashSession

1. After the automatic sign on, the Status window monitors the message as it uploads.

AMERICA Online

America Online Flashsession Status

Beginning FlashSession for "MajorTom". (4:07:21 PM)
Sending message FlashSession test (4:08:36 PM)

Goodbye From America Online!

AMERICA Online

Join tenor saxophonist Joshua Redman in Warner/Reprise Online's weekly interactive talk show, Cyber-Talk, Monday, August 22nd at 9:30 pm ET. Keyword: WARNER

Your time for this session was 00:05:22. See you soon!

2. The message is sent as soon as it's received, and the FlashSession signs off. To Virginia and back again in less than a minute!

Scr

Pas

Sign On Again

America Online Flashsession Status

Beginning FlashSession for "MajorTom". (4:07:21 PM)
Sending message FlashSession test (4:08:36 PM)
Receiving a list of new mail for "MajorTom". (4:09:07 PM)
Reading message "FlashSession test". (4:09:15 PM)
FlashSession is complete (4:09:19 PM)

3. The updated Status window remains, to tell you what happened in case you blinked.

🔊 Because of AOL's rapid e-mail turnaround, this FlashSession has resulted in both an upload and a download. Not only did you send mail to yourself, you also received it. Did you hear your computer say, "You've got mail?" Whether you did or not, you've got mail and you need to read it. But you're not online. How do you read mail when you're off-line?

🔊 Pull down the Mail menu. The Read Incoming Mail command should be available (see the top portion of Figure 19-7). Choose it.

Figure 19-7: You can read mail off-line when it's convenient for you and the clock's not running.

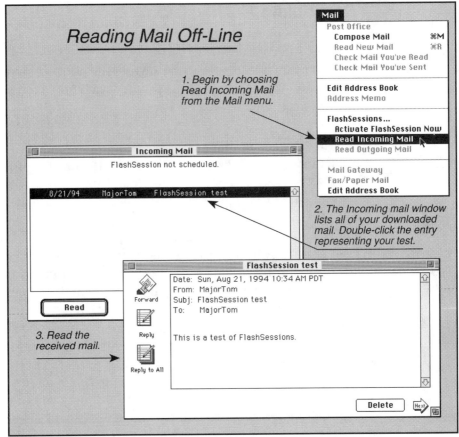

🔺 The Incoming Mail window will appear (see the middle portion of Figure 19-7). Double-click the entry representing your test.

🔺 A second window will open (Figure 19-7, bottom), containing the text of your test. After you've read it, delete it by clicking on the Delete button in the lower right corner.

I'm reminded of a big Mercedes sedan I read about the other day. In an irrational effort to remain the technological leader among motorcars, Mercedes equipped the car with motorized headrests! Now that's technology. Our exercise was a little like that. We threw technology at a task that was no doubt best left undone. At least we're in good company.

Scheduling FlashSessions

You can invoke a FlashSession at any time, whether you're online or off-line. Alternatively, you can schedule FlashSessions to occur at predetermined intervals: every day, every hour—whenever you please. Before any FlashSession can get under way, however, you have to tell AOL some things it needs to know.

FlashSession Setup

I can hear it now: It's 4 A.M. and AOL calls from the other room. "Tom," it says, "come out here and type in your password!" Bleary-eyed, I stumble to my Mac and type my password. I crawl back into bed and start to drift off when the voice calls again. "Tom," it says. (Is that a smirk in the voice?) "Come out here and tell me which screen name to use!" Again, I stumble to the Mac, tripping over the dog, who, rudely awakened, runs yelping into the hall table, spilling the Waterford crystal. I pick up the pieces, hiding those that don't seem to fit together any longer, and Band-Aid the laceration that has developed across the dog's nose. I do all this smiling, of course. Always smiling.

Do I make my point? The manual entry of passwords and screen names would defeat the whole purpose of unattended FlashSessions. These things have to be communicated to the Macintosh before the first FlashSession begins. Once communicated, they're stored on disk, eliminating the need for reentry.

Using Multiple Screen Names

I've talked about it before: many AOL members use more than one screen name. Perhaps more than one member of your family uses the service. Maybe you have an alter ego. Perhaps you're shy, or famous, or reclusive, and you don't want anyone to see your real name on-screen. Whatever the reason, if you use more than one screen name, you have to tell your Mac which of these screen names to use for its FlashSessions, and you'll have to enter a password for each name.

Entering Stored Passwords

Entering passwords is easy—perhaps a little too much so. Figure 19-8 shows you how to do it.

Figure 19-8: The
FlashSession
command under
the Mail menu
takes you to the
entry form for
stored passwords.

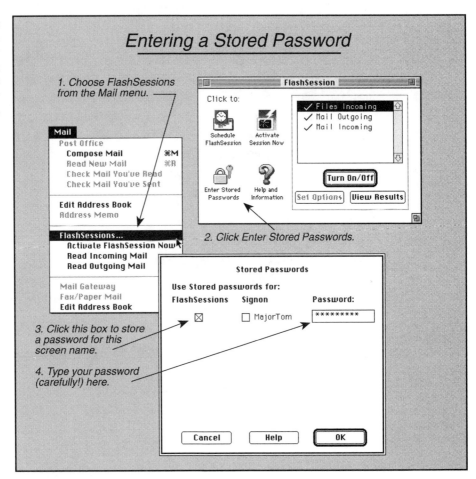

Figure 19-8: The FlashSession command under the Mail menu takes you to the entry form for stored passwords.

Though Figure 19-8 illustrates the entry of a single password for a single screen name, the Stored Passwords form can accommodate a number of each. Enter as many passwords as you wish for your various screen names—the same passwords you use when you sign on.

A Free Pass to Disneyland

Note that the form pictured in Figure 19-8 allows you to enter stored passwords not only for FlashSessions, but also for the attended sign-on sequence as well. Storing your sign-on password is a quick route to calamity. Once your sign-on password is stored, you can sign on to AOL without using your password. While this is convenient, it means that anyone with access to your computer can sign on using your account. This is like a free pass to Disneyland, with one significant exception: it's not free for you. At the end of the month, you're billed for the time, which can be a shocking experience if someone else has been discovering the wonders of AOL on your computer. While entering a stored password for FlashSessions isn't much of a risk (because it can only be used for a FlashSession), entering a sign-on password is. If access to your computer is absolutely secure, you might find this feature to be of convenience. If it isn't, or if you don't mind typing your password once in a while, leave the sign-on password box unchecked.

Declaring the Download Destination

One more setup task remains before you can start a FlashSession: you must declare a destination for downloaded files. Figure 19-9 illustrates the process and offers a brief glimpse of the Download Manager, a subject we will discuss later in this chapter.

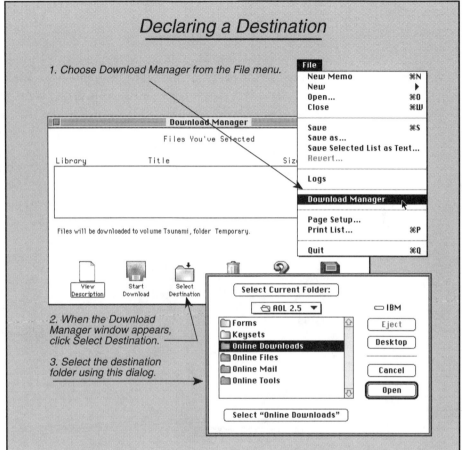

Attended FlashSessions

Now that you've stored your screen names, passwords and destinations, you're ready to run a FlashSession. The exercise that began this chapter describes an *attended FlashSession:* one that occurs when you issue a FlashSession command. Let's examine attended FlashSessions first.

Many FlashSessions occur when you're about to wrap up an online session. There's something organic about the flow of an online session: after a couple of months online, you'll glide from one task to another with all the fluidity of warm honey. About the last thing you'll want to do is interrupt your progress with a download or the transmission of a piece of mail. Instead, schedule a FlashSession to take care of these things when your session has concluded. More about this in a moment.

Another kind of attended FlashSession occurs when you're off-line and want your Mac to sign on, transfer files and sign off. As you saw during the earlier exercise, the advantage here is speed. FlashSessions know exactly what they're doing; they waste no time, they waste no money, and you don't have to stick around while they're under way.

Off-Line Attended FlashSessions

You begin an off-line FlashSession not by signing on, but by choosing Activate FlashSession Now from the Mail menu (shown at the top of Figure 19-10). When the Activate Session Now form appears (see the bottom of Figure 19-10), select the screen name you want to use, then click the Go Ahead button.

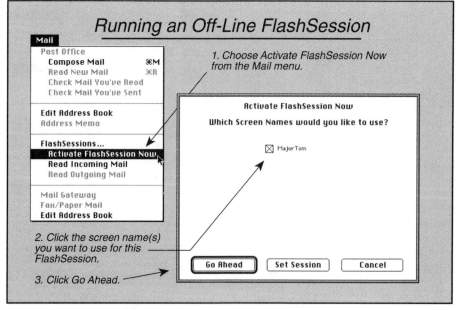

Figure 19-10: Once your screen name and password are stored, a menu selection and two mouse clicks are all it takes to run an off-line attended FlashSession.

Normally, this is all you need to do to run an off-line attended FlashSession. When you click the Go Ahead button, your Mac signs on, does everything it's been told to do, then signs off. It repeats the process for as many screen names as you've indicated. When the dust settles, a FlashSession Status window remains on your screen to inform you of what happened (Figure 19-11). This is more a necessity than a convenience. Without the FlashSession Status window, you might have to perform some major sleuthing to find out what happened during a FlashSession, especially one that occurred in your absence.

Figure 19-11: The FlashSession Status window lets you know what happened during a FlashSession, just in case you weren't watching.

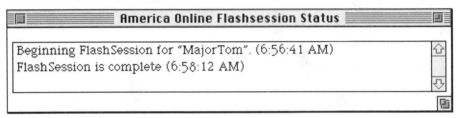

Look again at Figure 19-11. Note that only two entries appear there, representing the start and finish of my FlashSession. There's nothing in between. This session, in other words, had no activity. This isn't as meaningless as it might seem. Had this session occurred in the middle of the night, I would know the next morning that nothing happened during my 4 A.M. FlashSession, and I wouldn't waste my time looking for mail or files that were never there. Of additional benefit is notification of errors. If I misaddressed some mail or if the session was interrupted for some reason, I'd read about it here.

Online Attended FlashSessions

Another form of attended FlashSession is the one that occurs at sign-off. During a typical online event, you might visit a forum or two, mark some files for downloading, reply to some mail and perhaps compose some new mail. Downloads in particular can be disruptive to the flow of an online session. Sitting at your Mac watching a thermometer tally your tedium is not the best use of your time. That's why AOL provides sign-off FlashSessions.

When you've finished everything you want to do online, choose Activate FlashSession Now from the Mail menu rather than selecting Sign Off from the Go To menu (see the top of Figure 19-12), click Sign Off When Done, then click the Go Ahead button (see the bottom of Figure 19-12). This is one alternative to the Sign Off command; the other alternative is the Download Manager, which I'll discuss later in this chapter. Either one will work if activity remains that doesn't require your involvement.

Figure 19-12:
Rather than
choose Sign Off
from the Go To
menu, choose
Activate
FlashSession Now.
All of your queued
downloads and
mail routines will
become a part of
the sign-off
routine.

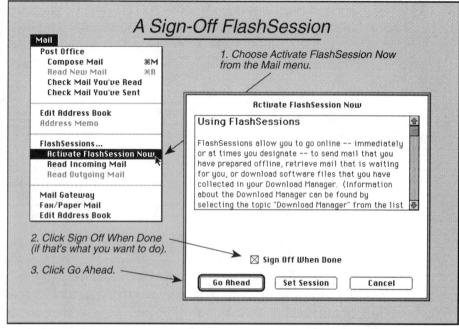

One more thing: If you accidentally choose Sign Off from the Go To menu while mail or files are queued for a FlashSession, AOL reminds you of your oversight (Figure 19-13). One way or another, you always have an opportunity to save queued material.

Figure 19-13:
America Online
politely reminds
you of your
oversight if you
choose Sign Off
with material
remaining in the
FlashSession queue.

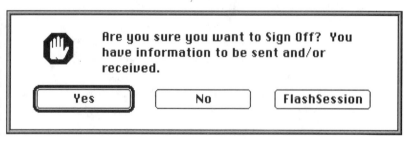

Delayed FlashSessions

A few months ago I went to the hardware store and purchased one of those timers that turns electrical appliances on and off automatically. I plugged my Mac into it and set it to come on at 4 A.M. I declared AOL as my startup application and instructed it to sign on and run my

FlashSession soon after the timer turns the Mac on. The key to all this automated profundity is the *delayed FlashSession*, which is our final FlashSession topic.

(I just displayed some old-Mac chauvinism. Old Macs turn on with a switch that stays turned on, not a button on top of the keyboard. Those less fortunate—those of you who have Macs with power-on buttons on top of the keyboard—must either discover alternative methods [see the sidebar] or forever suffer old-Mac envy.)

PowerKey

Users of Macintoshes with keyboard-activated power switches will revel in a tool called PowerKey from Sophisticated Circuits. It's a hardware device into which you plug your Mac. When you run the provided software, you can program PowerKey to turn on your Mac at a predetermined time and run your AOL software. At that point, a FlashSession can sign on, get your mail and sign off. PowerKey can turn the Mac off a few minutes after that.

PowerKey also enables the keyboard power switch for those Macs that don't normally use it (a raw nerve for some Mac owners: if it's there, why doesn't it work?). To learn more, send e-mail to the screen name "SophCir" and ask them to send product literature.

Setting the Startup Application

Buying a timer from the hardware store isn't enough. Normally, the Macintosh starts up with the Finder running, and the Finder can't sign on to AOL. Unless you are using the device mentioned in the sidebar, you must declare AOL as your startup application. That's easy enough, but it has to be done using the Finder, not the AOL software. If you're running System 6.0x, it's a relatively easy process:

🔺 If necessary, quit AOL. The Finder should be the only application running on your Macintosh.

🔺 Open all the necessary folders until you reach the one containing the AOL software.

🔺 Click the icon once to select it. Do not double-click.

🔺 Choose Set Startup from the Special menu.

That does it. The next time your Macintosh starts, it will start the AOL software automatically. You are still able to quit AOL and return to the Finder whenever you want to run other programs, and you can always follow the procedure described above to select the Finder as the startup application again. This will return your Mac to the condition in which you found it.

If you're running System 7.x, the process is just as easy:

🔺 First, make an alias of your AOL application by selecting the AOL icon (again, *don't* double-click it) and choosing Make Alias from the Finder's File menu.

🔺 Store the newly made alias in the Startup Items folder, located in your System Folder. This will instruct your Mac to launch AOL once your startup routine is complete. Everything else about how your Mac functions will remain exactly the same, except now, every time you start your Mac, AOL will automatically launch as soon as the Finder appears.

Note: If you don't want AOL to launch when you start your Mac, hold down the Shift key when you turn on your Mac and keep it held down until the Mac's boot-up operations conclude. This will disable (for that session only) any items stored in your Startup Items folder.

Scheduling the Date & Time

One more task remains before AOL will conduct its FlashSessions unattended: scheduling the time of day and the days of the week that you want AOL to conduct its FlashSessions. Figure 19-14 illustrates the procedure.

Figure 19-14: The
Schedule
FlashSession
window lets you
declare the days,
times and screen
names to be used
for unattended
FlashSessions. Be
sure to check the
box indicated in
step 2 or the
FlashSession
won't run.

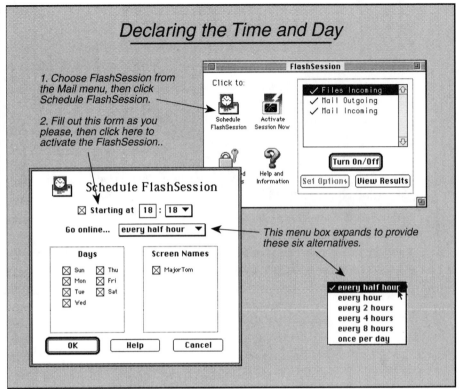

I've assumed here that you've checked all the activities you want
AOL to carry out during a FlashSession using the FlashSession window
(see the top of Figure 19-14). Usually you'll want to select all three
activities (Files Incoming, Mail Outgoing, Mail Incoming) shown in the
illustration.

Excepting Incoming Files

Just last week, I attempted to send some e-mail to a friend. Attached to the message was a 270k file. Unfortunately, I misspelled his name in the To box of the Compose Mail form. Even more unfortunately, the misspelling was a legitimate AOL member screen name, and the mail was sent to the wrong address. Though I re-sent the mail to the proper person later, the person who was on the receiving end of the misaddressed mail was no doubt quite displeased with me if he downloaded my file. My error might have cost him a half hour or more of connect time.

In other words, to protect yourself from encountering a mistake like the one I inadvertently inflicted on that unsuspecting AOL member, you might want to exercise an obscure command that's available from the FlashSession window. When you select Mail Incoming in that window, a button marked "Set Options" becomes active. When you click it, you're provided the opportunity to turn off the "Automatically download attached files" feature. The default is on; you might want to change that. After all, you can always sign back on to download files, but you can't undo the cost of a 40-minute download once it's done.

Look again at Figure 19-14. Note that my FlashSessions are scheduled for 18 minutes after the hour. In fact, I only have two choices: 18 or 48 minutes after the hour. America Online arbitrarily assigned these times when I joined. Yours will differ from mine, and so will everyone else's. America Online staggers FlashSession times to distribute the load on the AOL host computer. If given our druthers, most of us would probably choose to run our FlashSessions on the hour or the half-hour—that's human nature. But the host computer would bog down, answering thousands of simultaneous phone calls. Offering limited random times is AOL's way of avoiding FlashSession overload.

Reading Flashmail

It only makes sense that AOL lets you read incoming Flashmail. What's interesting is that you can read *outgoing* Flashmail as well. This is especially comforting for those of us who suffer from occasional bouts of incertitude. Until it's actually sent, mail is ours to edit, append, or wad up and throw away. (Now that I think about it, you can edit, append, or wad up and throw away mail even after it's sent—as long as no one has read it. Refer to Chapter 4, "Electronic Mail," if you're not familiar with this feature.)

Reading Incoming Mail

Incoming Flashmail is stored in a hidden file that AOL refers to as your "Flashbox." The Read Incoming Mail command is active whenever your Flashbox contains mail. Typically, this is the first command you'll choose after a FlashSession is finished. To read incoming mail, follow the steps illustrated in Figure 19-15.

Figure 19-15: Reading incoming mail is easy. Save it if you want, but don't forget to delete it (note the Delete button at the bottom of the illustration) after you read it!

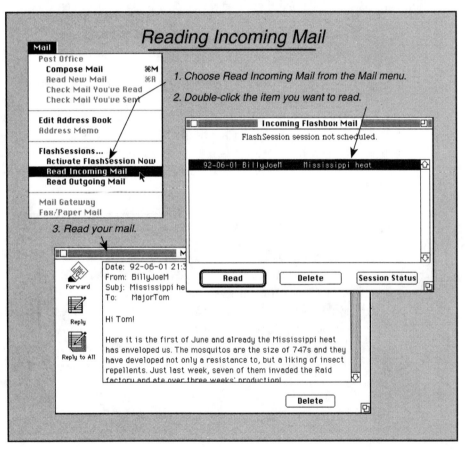

Watch Those Screen Names!

It's important to note that the only mail appearing in the Read Incoming Mail window is that which is addressed to the screen name currently appearing in the window that was onscreen when you signed on. If you've used a FlashSession to download mail for more than one screen name, you must change the screen name in the Welcome window (or the Goodbye window, if you've signed on and signed off earlier) to identify incoming mail for each of your screen names. Only then will you find all the mail that came in during the session.

Don't confuse this command with the Check Mail You've Read command, which also appears under the Mail menu. Check Mail You've Read is an online command that allows you to review mail you've already read. The Read Incoming Mail command discussed here is usually issued off-line, after a FlashSession has concluded. (Again, review Chapter 4 for a thorough explanation of e-mail commands.)

Avoid Clutter

Incoming Flashmail is stored in your Incoming Mail folder in a file with the same name as your screen name. All incoming mail messages are stored there until they're deleted, even after they have been read. In other words, if you don't delete incoming mail (by using the Delete button pictured at the bottom of Figure 19-15) after you've read it, the Read Incoming Mail command will remain active, and all incoming mail—past and present—will appear in the Incoming Flashmail window. This is confusing, to say the least. Save incoming Flashmail elsewhere on your hard drive if you wish, but always delete it from your Flashbox after you've read it.

Reading Outgoing Mail

The Read Outgoing Mail command allows you to read outgoing Flashmail before you send it. It can be invoked either online or off, as long as outgoing mail is in your Flashbox.

Figure 19-16: The
Read Outgoing
Mail command is
available only
when mail has
been scheduled
for delivery but
hasn't been sent.

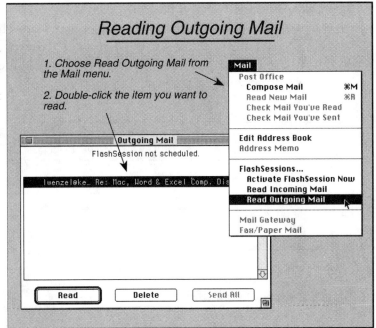

Again, don't confuse this command with the Check Mail You've Sent command. Check Mail You've Sent is an online command letting you review mail you've sent during the past week. The Read Outgoing Mail command pertains only to mail that you've scheduled for delivery and that hasn't been sent yet.

The Download Manager

Downloads probably offer more potential than any other AOL feature. Tens of thousands of files reside on the host computer's hard disks, and every one of them can be downloaded to your computer. Using the Download Manager, you can establish a queue of files while you're online, reading descriptions and estimating time. When your session is almost over, you then instruct the Download Manager to download the files and sign off. Once the process has begun, you can walk away.

Let's watch a typical Download Manager session to see what the screens look like. We'll schedule two files for downloading; then we'll instruct the Download Manager to handle the downloading process and sign off automatically.

Selecting Files for Downloading

Figure 19-17 illustrates the process of selecting a stock chart from the Decision Point Forum (discussed in Chapter 10, "Personal Finance") for downloading. Even if you don't invest in the market, these charts can be quite enlightening.

Figure 19-17: The last step in selecting a stock chart for delayed downloading is to click the Download Later button, which results in the dialog box at the bottom of the illustration.

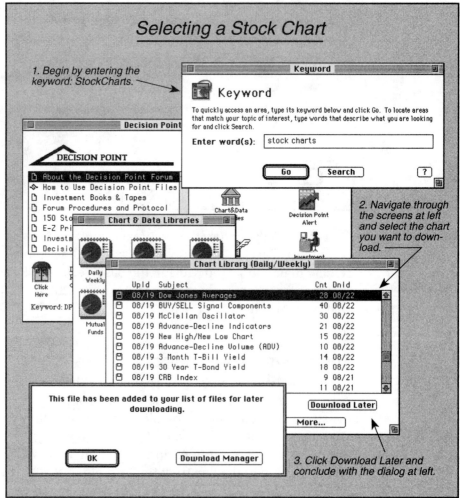

We might as well give the Download Manager more than one thing to do, so let's select another file to add to the download queue. A Mike Keefe political cartoon seems appropriate (Figure 19-18).

Figure 19-18:
Selecting a Mike
Keefe cartoon for
delayed
downloading.

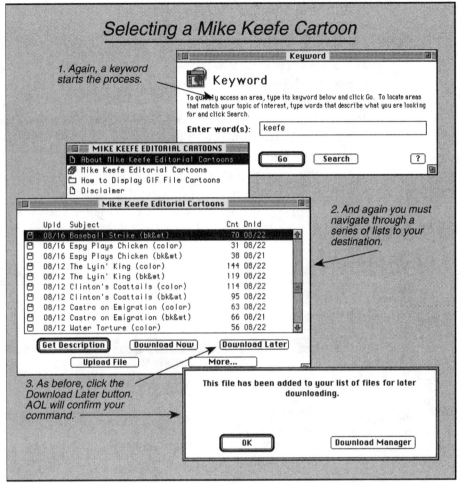

Selecting a Mike Keefe Cartoon

1. Again, a keyword
starts the process.

Keyword

To quickly access an area, type its keyword below and click Go. To locate areas that match your topic of interest, type words that describe what you are looking for and click Search.

Enter word(s): keefe

[Go]   [Search]   [?]

MIKE KEEFE EDITORIAL CARTOONS
- About Mike Keefe Editorial Cartoons
- Mike Keefe Editorial Cartoons
- How to Display GIF File Cartoons
- Disclaimer

Mike Keefe Editorial Cartoons

Upld	Subject	Cnt	Dnld
08/16	Baseball Strike (bk&wt)	70	08/22
08/16	Espy Plays Chicken (color)	31	08/22
08/16	Espy Plays Chicken (bk&wt)	38	08/21
08/12	The Lyin' King (color)	144	08/22
08/12	The Lyin' King (bk&wt)	119	08/22
08/12	Clinton's Coattails (color)	114	08/22
08/12	Clinton's Coattails (bk&wt)	95	08/22
08/12	Castro on Emigration (color)	63	08/22
08/12	Castro on Emigration (bk&wt)	66	08/21
08/12	Water Torture (color)	56	08/22

[Get Description]   [Download Now]   [Download Later]
[Upload File]   [More...]

2. And again you must
navigate through a
series of lists to your
destination.

3. As before, click the
Download Later button.
AOL will confirm your
command.

This file has been added to your list of files for later downloading.

[OK]   [Download Manager]

He's a Blues Musician Too

Mike Keefe has been drawing political cartoons for the *Denver Post* for 15 years. He won the 1991 Fischetti Editorial Cartoon Award, and has been recognized by Sigma Delta Chi and the National Headliners Club, winning their highest honors. His work also appears in *USA Today*, *New York Times*, *Washington Post*, *Time*, *Newsweek* and *U.S. News and World Report*. His online cartoons are available every Monday, Wednesday and Friday by 9 P.M. (Eastern time). You can reach him online via the screen name "dePIXion." You can find his cartoons by using the keyword Keefe. One graces the first page of this chapter.

Running the Download Manager

Meanwhile, back at the keyboard, we've decided to call it a day. Rather than sign off, we choose Download Manager from the File menu. This is a second alternative to the Sign Off command (the first being Activate FlashSession Now—under the Mail menu—described earlier in this chapter). The Activate FlashSession Now command accommodates both delayed mail and downloading activities, but it doesn't offer the control that the Download Manager does. The Download Manager—under the File menu—doesn't send queued mail, but it offers access to all of the options pictured in Figure 19-19. If you've mail to send and files to download when you sign off, choose Activate FlashSession Now (and configure the Download Manager ahead of time). If you've only files to download, choose the Download Manager.

Figure 19-19: The Download Manager window lists all files scheduled for download, including sizes, destinations and the estimated amount of time required to download the entire queue.

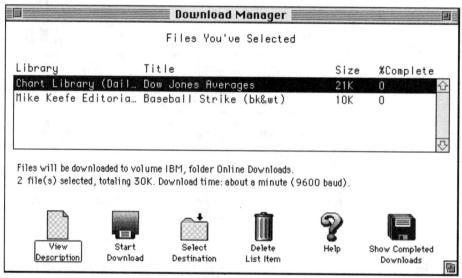

Note the icons across the bottom of Figure 19-19. This is an impressive array of commands. America Online wants you to have complete control over the downloading process, especially now that the download is about to begin.

View Description is the same as the View Description button when you're browsing a file library. It's handy to have this command here. Although you probably read a file's description half an hour ago, chances are you remember nothing about it now that you've reached the Download Manager window. Lots of things could have happened in the interim. This icon saves a long trip back to the file's original location to review its description.

 Start Download begins the download process. We'll use it in a moment.

 Select Destination allows you to declare a destination folder other than the Online Downloads folder, which is the default. *Note:* All the files in the queue must download to the same folder.

 Delete List Item allows you to remove a file (or two, or three) from the list. Sometimes, enthusiasm exceeds resources.

 The Help icon produces the Download Manager help screens.

 Show Completed Downloads lets you review your past 50 downloads. There's no value in downloading the same file twice. Though AOL will warn you if you try to download a file you've already downloaded, save yourself the trouble by checking this list first.

Pick Up Where You Left Off

Occasionally, the downloading process is interrupted. Lightning strikes. A power cord gets tripped over. The phone line develops a stutter. These kinds of things don't happen often; but when they do, they always occur when you're 80 percent of the way through a 47-minute download. *Poof!* There goes 35 minutes of connect time.

That's why the % Complete column appears (see Figure 19-19). If a file was interrupted during a download, this column declares the interruption and assures you that only the missing portion of the file will be downloaded—not all 47 minutes' worth—when you next activate the Download Manager.

The downloading process commences when the Start Download icon is clicked (Figure 19-20).

Figure 19-20: The FlashSession ends with a display of the information above.

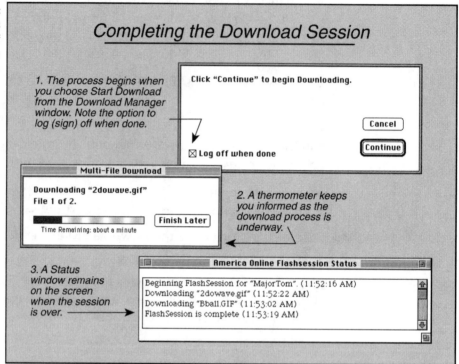

Completing the Download Session

1. The process begins when you choose Start Download from the Download Manager window. Note the option to log (sign) off when done.

Click "Continue" to begin Downloading.

☒ **Log off when done**

Cancel

Continue

Multi-File Download

Downloading "2dowave.gif"
File 1 of 2.

Finish Later

Time Remaining: about a minute

2. A thermometer keeps you informed as the download process is underway.

3. A Status window remains on the screen when the session is over.

America Online Flashsession Status

Beginning FlashSession for "MajorTom". (11:52:16 AM)
Downloading "2dowave.gif" (11:52:22 AM)
Downloading "Bball.GIF" (11:53:02 AM)
FlashSession is complete (11:53:19 AM)

Look again at Figure 19-20. When the Log Off When Done option is selected, you can walk away from the computer while all this is going on, secure in the knowledge that the Download Manager will sign off when everything has been downloaded satisfactorily.

When it's all over, we have two nice, big graphics to tack to the wall (Figure 19-21).

Figure 19-21: Tack the Dow Jones Averages and a political cartoon to your wall each day; people will think you're clever, erudite and urbane.

GIF Files

Macintoshes are fond of PICT and MacPaint graphics. Unfortunately, no other brand of computer is, and AOL serves a half-dozen different brands of computers.

Fortunately, a number of generic graphic formats have emerged, including TIFF, EPS and GIF. Perhaps you noticed that the stock charts and cartoons we just discussed were GIF files. Graphics Interchange Format (GIF) files were developed specifically for the telecommunications industry. The format accommodates color, grayscale, and black-and-white graphics with equal aplomb. It's also a very efficient format: more data is packed into each GIF byte than practically any other graphics format.

It makes little difference to you what format an online graphic is in, as the AOL software itself reads and displays most of them. It will convert them from one format to another as well, just choose Save from AOL's File menu whenever a graphic is displayed onscreen. You'll have a number of formats to choose from when you do.

Moving On

All this time spent talking about FlashSessions and the Download Manager might make you feel like a real yahoo if you don't use them. Don't worry about it: not all AOL members get enough mail or download enough files to make FlashSessions and the Download Manager worthwhile. In other words, you've got plenty of company: the yahoos are the majority.

There's a political statement there, I'm sure; but to explore it would hardly be the way to conclude a chapter. Instead, reward yourself for reading this far by turning the page. The "Ten Best" chapter follows. It's the pot of gold at the end of the rainbow.

Ten Best

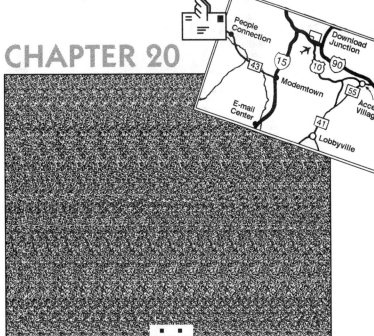

When I was a boy, I believed that if I remained quiet and cooperative all day and all night Christmas Eve, Santa would be especially generous to me. For one 24-hour period every year, I was a model child. I did everything that was asked of me, exactly as requested. I must have been right: nowadays I receive paperweights and paisley ties on Christmas mornings rather than the electric trains and red wagons I received back in the days of deference.

Have you been naughty or nice? You haven't turned to this chapter first, have you? This chapter is a reward for faithful readers only. This is my Ten Best chapter, and I award it only to those who have read all of the preceding 19 chapters. If that's you, read on…

Frontispiece graphic by Kai Krause, generated by his KPT 3D Stereo Noise filter for Photoshop. To find out more about Kai's filters, use the keyword PhotoShop and follow the path Software Libraries > KPT section. To find the graphic for download-ing, use the keyword FileSearch, then search the graphics files using the criterion 3D. To see the encoded image, stare at the two squares at the bottom of the graphic, allowing your eyes to go out of focus, until the two squares become three. Maintain-ing that focus (or lack of it), shift your gaze upward. You will see a familiar object in three dimensions. This is arguably one of the ten best graphics posted on AOL.

Ten Best Tips

Since we're discussing honor and privilege, let's begin with a list of the Ten Best Tips for using AOL. Most of these tips represent methods by which you can save time online (so you save money); all of them will make your online experience more efficient and effective; and not a one of them is dishonorable.

1. **Read this book.**
   If you're reading this paragraph in spite of the admonition on the previous page, at least plan to read the rest of the book eventually. It's full of insights and techniques—not only mine, but those of scores of other members as well. You don't have to be online to use this book. Take it on your next blue-water cruise: people will think you're very erudite, recondite and jocose.

2. **Use keywords and keyboard shortcuts.**
   This tip is so important that I've included two appendices—Appendix A and Appendix B—listing AOL's keywords and keyboard shortcuts, respectively. Keywords can save you tons of time. Don't worry about committing them all to memory, just memorize those you use often. (Your most frequently used keywords should be added to your Go To menu, which is explained in Chapter 13, "Clubs & Interests.") Keywords take you to locations that normally require the navigation of menus within menus within menus, and they do it in less than a second. To enter a keyword, type Command-K. To see an online list of keywords, type Command-K and click the Keyword Help button.
   America Online's keyboard shortcuts are so Mac-like that only a few require additional thought. A few are unique, and they're worth memorizing: Command-K to enter a keyword, Command-M to compose new mail, Command-F to find a member, Command-I to send an Instant Message—that's only four. It won't take long to learn them.

3. **Use Command-period and watch for the hollow arrow.**
   Speaking of Command-key combinations, don't forget Command-period. Command-period disconnects sluggish sign-ons, halts printing, and halts long articles, downloads and lists as they are received online. That's important: sometimes you'll double-click an article icon (articles are discussed in Chapter 13) only to find that

you got yourself into a four-minute feed that you don't want to read after all. No problem: type Command-period. The same goes for lists: Command-period stops my list of Mail You have Read, for instance, which contains hundreds of entries.

The hollow-arrow cursor is a little-known AOL feature, introduced with Version 2.0. Whenever you see the beachball cursor (the rotating black-and-white sphere that appears whenever your Mac is receiving data over the modem), try moving it around on the screen. Usually, the beachball will become a hollow arrow when you pass over scroll bars and menu bars. This is handy: when you're receiving a long list of items, you can start scrolling through that list using the hollow-arrow cursor without having to wait for the beachball to go away. All you have to do is explore a bit: move that beachball around and watch what happens.

4. **Use FlashSessions, and read and compose mail off-line.**
The Compose Mail command (Mail menu) works off-line as well as on. You can compose all your mail off-line while the clock's not running, perfecting every phrase. You can even attach files while you're composing mail off-line. When you have finished composing a piece of mail, click the Send Later icon at the left of the new mail (Untitled) window. America Online will store it (and any mail you compose) on your disk for transmission either later when you're online (choose Read Outgoing Mail from the Mail menu, then click the Send All button) or more likely via a FlashSession (discussed in Chapter 19).

Likewise, resist the urge to read new mail online. Rather, wait until you've finished all your other online activity, then choose Activate FlashSession Now from the Mail menu. America Online will download all of your incoming mail, then sign off. Once you're off-line, choose Read Incoming Mail from the Mail menu and read your mail at your own pace.

5. **Use help.**
Read the sidebar on pages 50–51 and follow the tips there, in the order in which they appear.

6. **Keep track of your time and money.**

   It's easy to lose track of time and money when you're online, but no one—neither you nor AOL—benefits from unexpected charges when the bill arrives. You can always check your current (and previous) month's bill by using the keyword Billing (which is free). The keyword Clock tells you how long you've been online during any particular session.

7. **Log your sessions and save to disk.**

   Don't spend time reading material online that can just as easily be saved and read later while off-line. Logging is a mechanism that allows you to capture all the text you encounter online without stopping to read it, whether it's text from the encyclopedia, messages on a board, or a discussion in a conference room. Any text that appears on your screen will be saved to a log if you open one before you start your online journey. (See Chapter 6, "Today's News," for a discussion of logging procedures.)

   Logging is particularly valuable for new members. Start a log, sign on and visit a few areas, then sign off. Once you're off-line, review the log (use the Open command under the File menu to open logs). You'll learn a lot about AOL when you can review an online session at your leisure.

   Of course, it's not easy to remember to open a log for each session, and sometimes you don't know you're going to run across something you want to save until you're there. Fortunately, all text received on AOL can be saved onto your hard drive for later review off-line. Simply go to the File menu and select Save. This causes all the text in the article or message in the front-most window on your screen to be transferred to any disk drive you specify, where it is saved as a plain text file that you can read using AOL or the word processor of your choice. Note that it isn't necessary for you to scroll through the entire article in order to save it. Even though you haven't seen the entire text of the article, your computer has, and everything is saved when you select Save.

8. **Multitask and download when system activity is minimal.**

   Your AOL software can download in the background while another application is running and you're working on a spreadsheet or using your word processor. If you start a long download—even if it's via a FlashSession—and you have something else to do with your Mac, use the procedures described in Chapter 13, "Clubs & Interests," to activate another application.

   Here's another downloading tip: The AOL system—the host computer and the long-distance carrier in your local area—gets very busy in the evenings and on weekends. Your time on the system is allocated in slices, and these time slices get smaller as the system becomes more active. Your computer spends more of its time waiting in line for data when these time slices get small, yet the clock keeps running regardless.

   Whenever you're planning a long download—say, anything over 10 minutes—plan it for the time of day when the system is least active. Typically, that's the morning: the earlier the better. Read about FlashSessions and the Download Manager in Chapter 19, and use both of them to tame your download time.

9. **Look for More buttons.**

   Lots of AOL windows include buttons or folders marked More. Don't neglect them. America Online doesn't tie up your system feeding you all 500 matching entries to a database search, for instance. Rather, it offers the first 20, then waits to see if you want more. You might want to cancel at that moment, or you might want to see more. When the conditions are appropriate, AOL always offers the More option, but it's only useful if you choose to exercise it. America Online users who neglect the More buttons online never know what they're missing.

10. **Manage your windows.**

    America Online's "modeless" strategy allows you to wander all over the service, leaving a litter of windows behind you. A mess like this quickly becomes unmanageable. You might spend needless time cleaning up after yourself or searching for a specific window onscreen while the online clock keeps running. Moreover, some of AOL's windows—the Main Menu and the Spotlight, in particular—are slow to redraw, and there's no need to pay for these windows' redrawing time while you're online. A number of techniques aid window management:

🔥 The Windows menu offers the Clean Up Windows and Close All Except Front commands. The Clean Up command arranges all of your windows in a cascade, filing them like folders in a file cabinet. Very tidy. Life could use a command like this.

🔥 The Close All Except Front command does what it's supposed to do, but there are alternatives: Command-W closes the front-most window, Option-Command-W closes them all. (This is something of a crisis-oriented command, but it's very satisfying to watch.) Alternatively, you can click the top window's close box to close it, or hold down the Option key while you click the top window's close box to close them all. This works while you're using the Finder too.

🔥 The bottom of the Windows menu lists the titles of all open windows. Use this menu to find the one you want quickly and easily, no matter how messy the screen becomes.

Ten Best Downloads

This list is hardly objective and is most certainly in no particular order. It is exclusive of fonts and graphics: you will have to explore those on your own. This is just a list of really great and useful stuff, all of which is available online for the cost of your connect time and perhaps a small shareware fee.

To find any of the downloads mentioned, use the keyword FileSearch, then specify the name of the file—excluding the version number (see the searching tips in Chapter 17, "Reference Desk")—as your search criteria. If you find more than one version of a particular program available, be sure to download the one with the highest version number, since it's the most recent release of that program.

1. **StuffIt**

   This software is offered both as a commercial product (StuffIt Deluxe), as shareware (previously StuffIt Classic, now StuffIt Lite) and as an integral feature of your AOL software. However, using AOL to stuff files that you don't intend to attach to email is a bit awkward. StuffIt's interface is as easy to learn as they come. StuffIt Lite should be on every Mac user's shelf, especially when you consider the minimal shareware fee. StuffIt is discussed in Chapter 4, "Electronic Mail," and again in Chapter 5, "Computing."

2. **Disinfectant**

   Disinfectant is virus detection freeware capable of eliminating many viruses as well as detecting them. Disinfectant is one of the best pieces of software—shareware or commercial—ever written, and it's free. It's updated faithfully, supported lovingly, and you can always count on it to beat everyone else to the punch in taking on new viruses. Disinfectant is discussed in Chapter 5, "Computing."

3. **GIFConverter**

   Most of the really spectacular graphics available on AOL are in a format that your AOL software can open and display. Occasionally, however, you might run into one that chokes AOL's software, or won't import into your word-processing or desktop-publishing program. For those occasions, you need a Swiss Army knife of a graphics program—one that opens anything and saves in formats that are useful to you. That program is GIFConverter, by Kevin Mitchell. Kevin is an AOL member and can answer your questions via the screen name "KevinM17."

4. **Sound Manager**

   If you're fond of chat room sounds, you must have this software. America Online offers hundreds of sounds for use in chat rooms, but they first have to be incorporated into your Mac's system. That's what Sound Manager does (among other things). Chat rooms, chat room sounds and Sound Manager are described in Chapter 12, "People Connection."

5. **KidPix**

   This is the shareware version of the KidPix program discussed in Chapter 15, "Kids Only." The shareware version offers no color, and you must send the shareware fee to the author to get the sound files (it's worth it), but it's a great way to try out KidPix before you buy the commercial version. Look in the Mac 500 Forum for this file (keyword: Mac500).

6. **Inigo Gets Out**

   This is the classic HyperCard stack that blossomed into a series of commercial releases. Its charm can't be equaled.

7. **Smileys**

   There are lots of lists of smileys posted online. Use the keyword FileSearch, then search with the criterion Smileys. With these lists at your side, you can smile with the best of 'em. ;-)

8. **FlashWrite**

   This is the best little notepad around, and it's a desk accessory that's available under your Apple menu no matter what you're doing with your Mac. In fact, if your word processing needs are basic (and 90 percent of most people's seem to be), this is all you may need. I find it especially valuable for searching my mail files for occurrences of words like "deadline."

9. **RoboWar**

   I forgive RoboWar for its combative title because it's such a kick. This shareware game allows you to program your own robots using a special scripting language, then send them into the field to battle with other robots—either others of your own making or any of the thousands posted on AOL. To get an idea of this game's popularity, use the keyword FileSearch and search with the criterion RoboWar. You'll find the program of course, but you'll also find all of the robots and tips other players have posted online.

10. **ZTerm**

    ZTerm is widely hailed by shareware fans as not just the best shareware telecommunications/modem program, but perhaps the best modem program of the bunch, regardless of the distribution method. ZTerm allows for a high degree of scripting and customization; something very important when using a telecommunications program for repeating the same boring steps over and over. You won't need it to work with AOL, but you will if you want to work with most other telecom packages.

11. **I Laughed So Hard I Cried**

    I know this is number 11 on a list of 10, but it's not really a download either. Rather, "I Laughed So Hard I Cried" is a series of humorous stories and anecdotes discovered online and compiled by Sandy Brockman (AFLSandyB). To find it, visit Sandy's Beginners Forum (keyword: Beginners—discussed in Chapter 5, "Computing"). This is spirit-lifting stuff, and we can all use a lift of spirits now and again.

Many thanks to Matt Triplett and Ruffin Prevost for their assistance with this list. Ruffin's book *The Mac Shareware 500* (published by Ventana Press) and its companion AOL library (keyword: Mac500) are invaluable resources for the download enthusiast.

Ten Most-Frequently Asked Questions of Customer Relations

As you might expect, the people in Customer Relations spend 90 percent of their time answering the same questions over and over again. Perhaps it will help if I answer them for you here. It might save you the trouble of contacting Customer Relations (and save them the trouble of replying).

1. **Where can I get help?**

   ▲ Read Chapter 3, "Online Help & the Members." Also, look up the topic in the index of this book to see if your question is answered here.

   ▲ Read the sidebar on pages 50–51 and follow the tips in the order in which they appear.

   ▲ Run the AOL software and choose Help from the Apple menu.

   ▲ Go online and choose the Member Services command from the Members menu (or use the keyword Help). The Member Services area provides information on how to access online and off-line help sources. Member Services is free. Spend as much time there as you like.

   ▲ Ask a Guide for help. Press Command-L and look for someone in the Lobby with the word "Guide" in his or her screen name.

   ▲ Ask the Technical Representatives in Tech Live who supply live, online support. Press Command-K and use the keyword TechLive.

   ▲ Get assistance from your fellow AOL members. Use the keyword MHM, which takes you to the Members Helping Members message boards.

- Send an e-mail message with your question to the AOL staff. Use the keyword Help, then click the EMail to the Staff button.

- If you have a fax machine or fax modem, call the AOL FaxLink service. This service provides information via fax concerning connectivity problems or error messages, and software and hardware incompatibilities. The phone number is toll free: 1-800-827-5551.

- Call AOL Market Support at 1-800-827-3338. This should be your last resort.

2. **Where can I ask questions?**

   - Ask the AOL staff for help. Use the keyword Help; click the EMail to the Staff button; then click the button that matches the topic of your question.

   - Ask Tech Live. Use the keyword TechLive. It's open from 9 A.M. to 2 A.M. (Eastern time) on weekdays, and from 12 P.M. to 1 A.M. on weekends.

   - Ask a Guide for help. Press Command-L and look for someone in the Lobby with the word "Guide" in their screen name.

   - Use the keyword MHM. This takes you to AOL's Members Helping Members message boards, where you can get help from your peers. Peer help is often the best of all.

3. **How do I find additional or closer access numbers?**
   America Online is always adding additional phone numbers. To stay in touch, use the keyword Access. If you're on the road and you need numbers for the area you're visiting, run the AOL software and choose the "Get Local #" locality setting in the Welcome window. Then click the Sign On button; you'll be connected to AOL's access-number database.

4. **Can I use the same AOL account from multiple computers?**
   No problem, even if they're different kinds of computers. All you need is AOL software for each (which is free). Use the keyword Upgrade to request additional copies of AOL software.

When you receive the additional copy of the software, do *not* use the registration number and password in the packet. Rather, enter the screen name and password you normally use when you're asked for the registration number and password. This will configure the new software to your existing account. But remember, only one screen name from an AOL account can be signed on at a time.

5. **Where do I begin?**

    - Try the Beginners Forum. Use the keyword Beginner. If you're using Version 2.5, begin at the Main Menu (if it's not displayed, select the Main Menu command from the Go To menu). From there, click any of the 14 Department buttons that closely match your interests. Also, click the Discover America Online button to find popular and new AOL areas.

    - The New Member Lounge in People Connection is also a good place to start. Choose Lobby from the Go To menu, then click the Rooms icon.

    - You might also visit the Clubs & Interests and Computing Departments. Find a forum there that interests you, read and reply to messages posted on the boards, and visit the forum's chat room when it's available.

    - Perhaps most important, though, is to do what you enjoy. There's no right or wrong place to begin your AOL travels. Feel free to explore uncharted territory. You can hardly get lost when you never leave home.

6. **How can I see how much time I have used and check my bill?**
    The keyword Clock displays the online clock; the keyword Billing displays your current charges, exclusive of the current session. You can get a complete explanation of charges here, and change your billing method if you want. The keyword Billing is a free area.

7. **How do I change my screen name?**
    Though you cannot change your original screen name, you can add up to four additional names and use them as you wish. Use the keyword Names. This is a free area as well.

8. **How do I change my profile?**
Use the keyword Help, then click the Billing Information icon. Alternatively, choose Edit Your Online Profile from the Members menu. The first method is free; the second is not.

9. **How do I disable Call Waiting?**
Call Waiting can disrupt online sessions, often resulting in a disconnect. To disable it, choose Setup from the Welcome window when you're not online. In most areas, you need only check the box labeled "Use this command to disable call waiting." (In Version 2.5, look for the "To disable call waiting, dial 1170" box.) In some places, you may need to change the command from "1170" to "*70." If you have trouble, ask Market Support (see item 1 of this list) or consult your local phone company.

10. **How do I turn off my modem's speaker when dialing?**
In Versions 2.1 and 2.5,

▲ While off-line, click the Setup button in the Sign On window.

▲ At the bottom of the Setup window, check to see what Modem Type is currently selected (write it down, if necessary).

▲ Click the Cancel button.

▲ Select the Open command from the File menu.

▲ In the dialog box that appears, double-click the Online Files folder.

▲ In the dialog box, scroll down until you see the file name of the modem type from the Setup window. Double-click this file to open it.

▲ Type "M0" (that's "M-zero") at the beginning of the Configuration box.

▲ Click the Save Changes button.

In Version 2.01,

▲ While off-line, click the Setup button in the Sign On window.

▲ Click the Edit Modem Strings button.

Type "M0" ("M-zero") at the end of the Configuration String box.

 Click the Save Changes button. Click the Save Changes button again to reach the Sign On window.

11. How can I turn off the Serial Port in Use message that pops up when I sign on?
In Version 2.5, you can turn this message off by selecting the Set Preferences command from the Members menu. When the Preferences window appears, double-click the Ask to Reset Serial Port option to uncheck it. In Version 2.1, you'll have to disable any other telecommunications software or extensions (such as FAX, Apple Remote Access, or Timbuktu) that might be using the modem port.

Thanks to Mary Daffron, Tracy McWilliams (whose enthusiasm exceeds his allotment, though I printed all eleven of his Ten Best nonetheless) and the AOL Technical Support Help Desk for help with this list.

Ten Best Ways to Make Friends Online

Perhaps above all, AOL is a community. If you're not a part of it, you're missing a wealth of opportunity. Like any community, you're ahead of the game if you know how to break into it. Here's how:

1. Visit the Lobby.
Read Chapter 12 ("People Connection"), then press Command-L for the Lobby. Say hello when you arrive. The Lobby is probably the greatest resource for online friends.

2. Find a favorite room and hang out there.
Chapter 12 describes the Event Rooms Guide (keyword: PC Studio). Look it over, find a room that interests you, and visit that room when it's available. You might also find a favorite room by visiting any of AOL's forums (forums are described in Chapter 13, "Clubs & Interests").

3. Visit the New Member Lounge.
If you're new to AOL, you'll find comfort in numbers in the New Member Lounge. Press Command-L, click the Rooms button, then select "New Members Lounge" from the Public Rooms list.

4. **Post your profile.**
   Don't neglect to post a profile for yourself. Use the keyword Help, then click the Billing Information icon. (You can also edit your profile by using the appropriate command under the Members menu, but the keyword method described above is free.) Talk about yourself. Make your personality irresistible. People in chat rooms often peek at other occupants' profiles, and if you haven't posted a profile, you're incognito.

5. **Use an effective screen name.**
   You can use the Help keyword technique described earlier to add a screen name to your account if the one you're using now isn't very effective in a social situation. People have a hard time relating to a screen name like "Tlich6734," but many find "MajorTom" worthy of comment. If nothing else, include your first name or your nickname in your screen name so people can address you like the friend you want to be.

6. **Search the membership for others with similar interests.**
   Use the keyword Directory to search the Member Directory for others with interests similar to yours. Read their profiles and send them e-mail. You'll be surprised at the number who reply.

7. **Read messages and reply.**
   Find a forum that interests you (see Chapter 13, "Clubs & Interests"), go to its message boards, and start reading messages. Eventually, you'll see some that provoke a response. Go ahead: post your comment. It gives you a great sense of purpose the next time you sign on: you'll scramble to that message board to see if anyone responded to your posting.

8. **Post a message soliciting replies.**
   Members Helping Members (keyword: MHM; see Chapter 3, "Online Help & the Members") is a great place for message posting, but any forum will do. Post a message asking for help or an opinion. People love to help, and everyone has an opinion.

9. **Read articles and reply.**
   This is similar to item 7. In forums like the Writers' Forum, people pour their hearts out in their articles, and they're always hoping for a little positive feedback.

10. Download a file posted by another member and reply.
This goes especially for fonts and graphics. Download a few files (downloading is discussed in Chapter 5, "Computing") and reply to the originator via e-mail. In selecting the graphics for this book, I sent e-mail to dozens of online artists, and every one of them replied within a day or two—most with two or three pages of enthusiastic banter.

Ten Best Smileys

I posted my own list of smileys in the first edition of this book, but I've since received mail from many readers with smileys of their own. Invariably, theirs are better. Perhaps the most charming was the list from Spencer Soloway, which appears below. For a complete list of smileys, use the keyword FileSearch, then use the criterion Smileys.

1. };^)' "lil devil"

2. B) "wearing shades"

3. :c) "pig headed"

4. [:-I] "robot"

5. $-) "lotto fever"

6. I-) "cyborg"

7. :-() "stubbed my toe"

8. @—>—>— "a rose"

9. O:) "Angel"

10. <:-) "I'm a dunce"

Everybody Out of the Bus!

Our tour has concluded. Typical of tours everywhere, ours has been an abridgment, a synopsis of things I find most interesting about AOL. You will find your own favorites, and in so doing discover things that I not only didn't mention, but didn't know myself. Moreover, AOL is a moving target: like most online services, AOL is almost a fluid— flowing from opportunity to opportunity, conforming to trends and advances, relentlessly expanding to fill new voids. I'll try to keep up, and no doubt there will be another edition of this book someday to describe an even bigger and better AOL than the one we know today.

Meanwhile, this edition has reached its end. While you're waiting for the next one, sign on to AOL and send me some e-mail. Tell me what you want included (or excluded) in the next edition. Tell me what you liked or disliked about this book. Send me logs, files, articles— anything you think might complement *The Official America Online Tour Guide*. I look forward to hearing from you.

—*MajorTom*

APPENDIX A
Keywords

Keywords are the fastest way to get from one place to another on America Online. To go to a specific forum or area, you just select Keyword from the Go To menu (or type Command-K), and enter the keyword.

Of course, you need to know the keyword before you can enter it. The most current list of keywords is always available by clicking the Keyword Help button in the Go To Keyword window. It's a long list, so long that it's divided into sub-lists by department. Because of its length, you might have trouble finding the keyword you're after by consulting the list online. (Printing it is an option.)

Allow me to suggest two alternatives: (1) Use the keyword Services (or choose Search Directory of Services from the Go To menu). The Directory of Services is a searchable database of services offered by America Online (and it's discussed in Chapter 3, "Online Help & the Members"). Because it's searchable, the Directory is a faster method of locating an online area than reading through the list of keywords, and the Directory always lists keywords when they're available. (2) Use the lists of keywords appearing below. They're alphabetical: one by keyword, the other by subject. They may save you the trouble of printing a list of your own.

Keyword Tips

The three little keyword tips below may be of help to you.

 Like screen names, keywords are neither case- nor space-sensitive. "directoryofservices" works just as well as "Directory of Services."

 Many of AOL's windows identify their associated keywords in the lower-left corner of the window. Look for these.

 Add frequently used keywords to your Go To menu. Editing the Go To menu is described in Chapter 13, "Clubs & Interests."

The keyword lists below were compiled by Jennifer Watson (screen name Jennifer) on 8/17/94. Please e-mail changes or additions to her, as she maintains the lists on a continuing basis. You can download the latest keyword lists by using the keyword FileSearch, then specifying the criterion: Keyword List. Thanks, Jennifer!

Entries with asterisks (*) are within free areas. Entries with daggers (†) are platform dependent. Some are for the Mac; some are for the PC. PC platform-dependent entries may not be available to Mac users.

Alphabetical by Keyword

@TIMES	@times/The New York Times Online
3DSIG	3D Special Interest Group
5.0	DOS Forum
5THGENERATION	Fifth Generation
25REASONS	Best of America Online showcase
9600	9600 Baud Access Center*
9600ACCESS	9600 Baud Access Center*
9600CENTER	9600 Baud Access Center*
A2APPLEWORKS	Apple Productivity Forum
A2ART	Apple Graphics and Sound Forum
A2DEVELOPMENT	Apple Development Forum
A2EDUCATION	Apple Education Forum
A2GAMES	Apple Games and Entertainment Forum
A2GRAPHICS	Apple Graphics and Sound Forum
A2HARDWARE	Apple Hardware Forum
A2MUSIC	Apple Graphics and Sound Forum
A2PERIPHERALS	Apple Hardware Forum
A2PRODUCT	Apple Hardware Forum
A2PRODUCTIVITY	Apple Productivity Forum
A2TELECOM	Apple Communications Forum
A2UTILITIES	Apple Utilities & Desk Accessories Forum
A2WORDPROCESSING	Apple Productivity Forum
AAII	AAII Online
AATRIX	Aatrix Software, Inc.
AAW	Apple Productivity Forum
ABBATEVIDEO	Abbate Video
ABF	Beginners' Forum
ABM	Adventures by Mail
ACADEMY	Starfleet Academy
ACCESS	Local access numbers*
ACCESSERIC	AskERIC
ACCESSNUMBERS	Local access numbers*
ACCESSSOFTWARE	Access Software
ACCOLADE	Accolade, Inc.
ACER	Acer America Corporation
ACHIEVEMENTTV	Achievement TV
ACM	Apple Communications Forum
ACOT	Apple Classrooms of Tomorrow
ACTIVISION	Activision
AD&D	AD&D Neverwinter Nights

ADD	AD&D Neverwinter Nights
ADOPTION	Adoption Forum
ADS	auto*des*sys, Inc.
ADSIG	Advertising Special Interest Group
ADV	Apple Development Forum
ADVANCED	Advanced Software, Inc.
ADVANCEDGRAVIS	Advanced Gravis
ADVENTURE	Games Forum †
ADVENTURESBYMAIL	Adventures by Mail
ADVERTISING	Advertising Special Interest Group
ADVERTISINGSIG	Advertising Special Interest Group
ADVICE	Advice & Tips
AECSIG	Architects, Engineers and Construction SIG
AED	Apple Education Forum
AFFINITY	Affinity Microsystems
AFRICANAMERICAN	The Exchange
AFT	American Federation of Teachers
AFTERWARDS	Afterwards Coffeehouse
AGM	Apple Games and Entertainment Forum
AGR	Apple Graphics and Sound Forum
AGS	Apple Graphics and Sound Forum
AHW	Apple Hardware Forum
ALADDIN	Aladdin Systems, Inc.
ALDUS	Aldus Corporation
ALPHATECH	Alpha Software Corporation
ALTSYS	Altsys Corporation
ALVIN	Hatrack River Town Meeting
ALYSIS	Alysis Software
AMATEURRADIO	Ham Radio Club
AMBROSIA	Ambrosia Software
AMERICANAIRLINES	EAASY SABRE
AMERICANDIALOGUE	American Dialogue
AMERICANINDIAN	The Exchange
AMS	Graphics and Sound Forum
ANALOG	Science Fiction Forum
ANIMATEDSOFTWARE	Animated Software
ANIMATION	Graphic Forum †
ANOTHERCO	Another Company
AOLBEGINNERS	Beginners' Forum
AOLPRODUCTS	AOL Products Center

APDA	Apple Professional Developer's Association
APOGEE	Apogee Software
APPLE	Apple II/Mac Computing & Software Department †
APPLE2	Apple II Computing & Software Department
APPLEII	Apple II Computing & Software Department
APPLEIIDEVELOPMENT	Apple Development Forum
APPLEIIEDUCATION	Apple Education Forum
APPLEIIGAMES	Apple Games and Entertainment Forum
APPLEIIGRAPHICS	Apple Graphics and Sound Forum
APPLEIIHARDWARE	Apple Hardware Forum
APPLEIIMUSIC	Apple Graphics and Sound Forum
APPLEIIPRODUCTIVITY	Apple Productivity Forum
APPLEIISOFTWARE	Apple II Software Center
APPLESCRIPT	AppleScript SIG
APPLEWORKS	Apple Productivity Forum
APPLICATIONS	Apple Applications Forum
APPLICATIONS	Apple Business Forum
APPMAKER	Bowers Development
APPS	Applications/Business Forum †
APR	Apple Productivity Forum
ARCADE	Games Forum †
ARES	Ares Microdevelopment, Inc.
ARGOSY	Argosy
ARIEL	Ariel Publishing
ARM	Real Estate Online
ART	Graphics Forum †
ARTICULATE	Articulate Systems
ARTIFICE	Artifice, Inc.
ARTS	Afterwards Coffeehouse
ASCD	Assoc. for Supervisor & Curriculum Development
ASCTECH	Alpha Software Corporation
ASCTS	Alpha Software Corporation
ASI	Articulate Systems
ASIAN	The Exchange
ASIMOV	Science Fiction Forum
ASKAMERICAONLINE	Member Services
ASKANDY	Advice & Tips
ASKANITA	Advice & Tips
ASKAOL	Member Services
ASKCS	Member Services
ASKERIC	AskERIC
ASKTHEDOCTOR	Advice & Tips
ASKTHEDR	Advice & Tips
ASKTHELAWYER	Advice & Tips
ASSEMBLY	Development Forum †\
ASTRONOMY	Astronomy Club
ASYMETRIX	Asymetrix Corporation
ATC	Apple Communications Forum
ATTIMES	@times/The New York Times Online
ATLANTIC	The Atlantic Monthly Online
ATLANTICMONTHLY	The Atlantic Monthly Online
ATLANTICONLINE	The Atlantic Monthly Online
ATTICUS	Atticus Software
AUDIO	Stereo Review Online magazine
AUDIO/VIDEO	Dolby Audio/Video Forum
AUDITORIUM	Center Stage auditorium
AUG	User Group Forum
AUT	Apple Utilities & Desk Accessories Forum
AUTO	AutoVantage
AUTOEXEC	Tune Up Your PC
AUTORACING	The Grandstand
AUTOS	Road & Track Magazine
AUTOVANTAGE	AutoVantage
AVIATION	Aviation Club
AVID	Avid DTV Group
AVIDDTV	Avid DTV Group
AVOCAT	Avocat Systems
AVT	Apple Utilities & Desk Accessories Forum
AW	Apple Productivity Forum
AWGS	Apple Productivity Forum
AWP	Apple Productivity Forum
AWS	Apple Productivity Forum
BABYBOOMERS	Baby Boomers area
BACKCOUNTRY	Backpacker Magazine
BACKPACKER	Backpacker Magazine
BARRONS	Barrons Booknotes
BASEBALL	The Grandstand
BASELINE	Baseline Publishing
BASEVIEW	Baseview Products, Inc.
BASIC	Development Forum †
BASKETBALL	The Grandstand
BBS	BBS Corner
BBSCORNER	BBS Corner
BCS	Boston Computer Society
BEER	Wine & Dine Online
BEGINNER	Beginners' Forum
BEGINNERS	Beginners' Forum
BERKELY	Berkeley Systems
BERKSYS	Berkeley Systems
BERKSYSWIN	Berkeley Systems
BESTOFAOL	Best of America Online showcase
BETHESDA	Bethesda Softworks
BETHESDA	Bethesda Softworks, Inc.
BEYOND	Beyond, Inc.
BFA	The Bicycle Network
BI	Gay & Lesbian Community Forum
BICMAG	Bicycling Magazine
BICYCLE	The Bicycle Network
BICYCLING	Bicycling Magazine
BICYCLINGMAGAZINE	Bicycling Magazine
BIKENET	The Bicycle Network
BILL	Billing Information and Changes
BILLING	Billing Information and Changes
BIOSCAN	OPTIMAS Corporation
BISEXUAL	Gay & Lesbian Community Forum
BITJUGGLERS	Bit Jugglers
BLIND	DisABILITIES Forum
BLOCDEVELOPMENT	TIGERDirect, Inc.
BMUG	Berkley Macintosh Users Group

BOARDWATCH	Boardwatch Magazine
BOATING	The Exchange
BOOKBESTSELLERS	Book Bestsellers area
BOOKNOTES	Barrons Booknotes
BOOKS	Book Bestsellers area
BOOKSTORE	Online Bookstore
BOWERS	Bowers Development
BOXING	The Grandstand
BRAINSTORM	Brainstorm Products
BREW	Wine & Dine Online
BREWING	Wine & Dine Online
BRODERBUND	Broderbund
BUDDHISM	Religion & Ethics Forum
BULLMOOSE	Bull Moose Tavern
BULLSANDBEARS	Bulls and Bears Game
BUNGIE	Bungie Software
BUSINESS	Business News area
BUSINESSFORUM	Applications/Business Forum †
BUSINESSKNOWHOW	Business Strategies
BUSINESSNEWS	Business News area
BUSINESSSENSE	Business Sense
BUSINESSSTRATEGIES	Business Strategies
BYTE	ByteWorks
BYTEBYBYTE	Byte By Byte Corporation
BYTEWORKS	ByteWorks
C	Development Forum †
C&S	Computing Department †
CAD	Graphics Forum †
CAERE	Caere Corporation
CAERECORPORATION	Caere Corporation
CALLISTO	Callisto Corporation
CAMERA	Kodak Photography Forum
CAMERAS	Popular Photography Online
CAMPING	Backpacker Magazine
CAMPUS	Interactive Education Services
CANCEL	Cancel Account*
CARANDDRIVER	Car and Driver Magazine
CARDINAL	Cardinal Technologies, Inc.
CAREER	Career Center
CAREERNEWS	USA Today Industry Watch section
CAREERS	Career Center
CARS	Road & Track Magazine
CARTOONNETWORK	Cartoon Network
CARTOONS	Cartoon collection
CARUSO	Inside Technology
CASABLANCA	Casa Blanca
CASADY	Casady & Greene
CASINO	RabbitJack's Casino
CB	College Board
CBD	Commerce Business Daily
CELEBRITYCOOKBOOK	Celebrity Cookbook
CENTERSTAGE	Center Stage auditorium
CENTRAL	Central Point Software
CENTRALPOINT	Central Point Software
CESOFTWARE	CE Software
CHANGEPASSWORD	Change your password*
CHANGES	Billing Information and Changes
CHANNELC	CNN Newsroom Online
CHAT	People Connection
CHECKFREE	CheckFree
CHESS	Play-By-Mail & Strategy Gaming Forum
CHICAGO	Chicago Online
CHICAGOONLINE	Chicago Online
CHICAGOTRIBUNE	Chicago Tribune
CHICO	California State University
CHRISTIAN	Religion & Ethics Forum
CHRISTIANS	Religion & Ethics Forum
CKFREE	CheckFree
CLARIS	Claris
CLASSES	Interactive Education Services
CLASSIFIED	Classifieds Online
CLASSIFIEDS	Classifieds Online
CLASSIFIEDSONLINE	Classifieds Online
CLINTON	White House Forum
CLOCK	Time of day and length of time online
CLUBPERFORMA	Apple Club Performa
CLUBS	Clubs & Interests Department
CMT	Coda Music Tech
CNN	CNN Newsroom Online
CNNNEWSROOM	CNN Newsroom Online
COBOL	Development Forum †
CODA	Coda Music Tech
CODAMUSIC	Coda Music Tech
COINS	The Exchange
COL	Chicago Online
COLCHAT	Chicago Online Chat
COLLIFESTYLES	Chicago Online Lifestyles
COLEDUCATION	Chicago Online Education
COLMARKETPLACE	Chicago Online Marketplace
COLNEWS	Chicago Online News, Business & Weather
COLPLANNER	Chicago Online Planner
COLSPORTS	Chicago Online Sports
COLLECTING	The Exchange
COLLEGE	College Board
COLLEGEBOARD	College Board
COLORIMAGING	Advanced Color Imaging Forum
COLORWEATHERMAPS	Color Weather Maps
COLUMNISTS	Columnists & Features Online
COLUMNS	Columnists & Features Online
COMMANDO	Kim Komando's Komputer Clinic
COMMUNICATIONS	Communications/Telecom/Networking Forum †
COMMUNITYCENTER	Clubs & Interests Department
COMPANIES	Industry Connection
COMPANY	Hoover's Handbook of Company Profiles
COMPANYPROFILES	Hoover's Handbook of Company Profiles
COMPAQ	Compaq
COMPOSER	Composer's Coffeehouse
COMPOSERS	Composer's Coffeehouse
COMPTONS	Encyclopedia
COMPUSTORE	Comp-u-Store Gateway
COMPUTE	Compute
COMPUTER	Computing Department †

COMPUTERAMERICA	Craig Crossman's Computer America
COMPUTEREXPRESS	Computer Express
COMPUTERLAW	CyberLaw, Cyberlex
COMPUTERPERIPHERALS	Computer Peripherals, Inc.
COMPUTERTERMS	Dictionary of Computer Terms
COMPUTING	Computing Department †
COMPUTOON	CompuToon area
COMPUTOON	CompuToon area
CONFERENCE	Weekly calendar of forum activity
CONFERENCECENTER	Weekly calendar of forum activity
CONFIG	Tune Up Your PC
CONNECTIX	Connectix
CONSERVATION	Backpacker Magazine
CONSUMER	Consumer Reports
CONSUMERREPORTS	Consumer Reports
CONSUMERS	Consumer Reports
CONTACTS	Employer Contacts
COOKBOOK	Celebrity Cookbook
COOKING	Cooking Club
COOPER	JLCooper Electronics
COSA	Company of Science and Art
COSN	Consortium for School Networking
COSTAR	CoStar
COURSES	Interactive Education Services
COURTROOMTELEVISION	Court TV
COURTTV	Court TV
COWLES	Cowles/SIMBA Media Information Network
COWLESSIMBA	Cowles/SIMBA Media Information Network
CPI	Computer Peripherals, Inc.
CPS	Central Point Software
CRAFTS	The Exchange
CRAIGCROSSMAN	Craig Crossman's Computer America
CREDIT	Credit for connect problems*
CREDITREQUEST	Credit for connect problems*
CRITICS	Critic's Choice
CRITICSCHOICE	Critic's Choice
CROSSMAN	Craig Crossman's Computer America
CRYSTALBALL	Advice & Tips
CSLIVE	Tech Help Live*
CSPAN	C-SPAN
CSPANCLASSROOM	C-SPAN Educational Services
CSPANONLINE	C-SPAN
CSUC	California State University
CURRICULUM	Assoc. for Supervisor & Curriculum Development
CUSTOMERSERVICE	Member Services
CYBERLAW	CyberLaw, Cyberlex
CYBERLEX	CyberLaw, Cyberlex
DACEASY	DacEasy, Inc.
DANCINGRABBIT	Dancing Rabbit Creations
DARTS	Darts [Apple II only]
DATABASE	Database Support SIG
DATABASES	Database Support SIG
DATAPAK	DataPak Software
DATAWATCH	Datawatch
DATING	Romance Connection message boards
DAVIDSON	Davidson & Associates
DAYNA	Dayna Communications
DAYSTAR	Daystar Digital
DCCOMICS	DC Comics Online Preview
DCOPREVIEW	DC Comics Online Preview
DEAD	Grateful Dead Forum
DEADSEA	Library of Congress Online
DEAF	DisABILITIES Forum
DEBATE	Express Yourself
DEBATEFORUM	Issues and Debate Forum
DECISION	Decision Point Forum
DECISIONPOINT	Decision Point Forum
DELL	Dell Computer Corporation
DELRINA	Delrina Corporation
DELTAPOINT	Delta Point
DELTATAO	Delta Tao
DEMOCRACY	CNN Newsroom Online
DENEBA	Deneba Software
DES	DeskMate
DESKMATE	DeskMate
DESKTOPPUBLISHING	Desktop Publishing area †
DEV	Development Forum †
DEVELOPER	Development Forum †
DEVELOPMENT	Development Forum †
DEVELOPMENTFORUM	Development Forum †
DFFOOD	Destination Florida: Restaurants and Nightlife
DFOUT	Destination Florida: Outdoors
DFPARKS	Destination Florida: Attractions
DFROOMS	Destination Florida: Places to Stay
DFSHOP	Destination Florida: Shopping
DFSPORTS	Destination Florida: Sports
DFX	Digital F/X
DIALOGUE	American Dialogue
DIAMOND	Diamond Computer Systems
DIGISOFT	DYA/Digisoft Innovations
DIGITAL	Digital Vision
DIGITALECLIPSE	Digital Eclipse
DIGITALF/X	Digital F/X
DIGITALRESEARCH	Novell Desktop Systems
DIGITALRESEARCHINC	Novell Desktop Systems
DIGITALTECH	Disney Technologies
DILBERT	Dilbert Cartoon area
DILBERTCOMICS	Dilbert Cartoon area
DINE	Wine & Dine Online
DIPLOMATS	Diplomats in the Classroom
DIRECT	Direct Software
DIRECTORY	Member Directory
DIRECTORYOFSERVICES	Directory of Services
DIROFSERVICES	Directory of Services
DIROFSVCS	Directory of Services
DIS	DisABILITIES Forum
DISABILITIES	DisABILITIES Forum
DISABILITY	DisABILITIES Forum
DISCOVER	Discover AOL area
DISNEY	Disney Adventures Magazine
DISNEYADVENTURES	Disney Adventures Magazine
DISNEYMAGAZINE	Disney Adventures Magazine

DISNEYSOFTWARE	Disney /Buene Vista Software
DOLBY	Dolby Audio/Video Forum
DOLBYAUDIO/VIDEO	Dolby Audio/Video Forum
DONTMISS	Directory of Services
DOS	DOS Forum
DOS5.0	DOS Forum
DOS6	MS-DOS 6.0 Resource Center
DOS60	MS-DOS 6.0 Resource Center
DOSFORUM	DOS Forum
DOSOMETHING	Do Something!
DOWNLOAD	Software Center †
DOWNLOADCREDIT	Credit for connect problems*
DOWNLOADGAMES	Free online game downloading*
DOWNLOADING	Software Center †
DP	Decision Point Forum
DPA	Decision Point Forum
DRDOS	DOS Forum
DREAMWORLD	Dreamworld
DRI	Novell Desktop Systems
DRIVING	Car and Driver Magazine
DTP	Desktop Publishing area †
DTSPORTS	DataTimes Sports Reports
DUBLCLICK	Dubl-Click Software
DYNAWARE	Dynaware USA
DYNAWAREUSA	Dynaware USA
DYNO	Portfolio Systems, Inc.
EAASY	EAASY SABRE
EARTH	Environmental Forum
EARTH	Network Earth
EASSYSABRE	EAASY SABRE
EASYSABRE	EAASY SABRE
EBBS	EBBS
ECON	Econ Technologies
ECOTOURISM	Backpacker Magazine
ECS	Electronic Courseware
EDFORUM	Education Forum
EDITPROFILE	Edit your member profile*
EDMARK	Edmark Technologies
EDTECH	Assoc. for Supervisor & Curriculum Development
EDTV	KIDSNET Forum
EDUCATION	Education Department
EFF	Electronic Frontier Foundation
EFORUM	Environmental Forum
ELECTRIC	Electric Image
ELECTRICIMAGE	Electric Image
ELECTRONICCOURSEWARE	Electronic Courseware
ELECTRONICS	Gadget Guru Electronics Forum
EMERGENCY	Emergency Response Club
EMERGENCYRESPONSE	Emergency Response Club
EMIGRE	Emigre Fonts
EN/X	Energy Express
ENCYCLOPEDIA	Encyclopedia
ENDER	Hatrack River Town Meeting
ENDNOTE	Niles and Associates
ENERGYEXPRESS	Energy Express
ENGLISH	Nat'l Council of Teachers of English
ENTERTAINMENT	Entertainment Department
ENVIRONMENT	Environmental Forum
ERC	Emergency Response Club
ERIC	AskERIC
ESH	Electronic Schoolhouse
ETHICS	Ethics and Religion Forum
EUN	Electronic University Network
EXAMPREP	Exam Prep Center
EXCHANGE	The Exchange
EXPERT	Expert Software, Inc
EXPERTSOFT	Expert Software, Inc
EXPRESSMUSIC	Bose Express Music
EXPRESSYOURSELF	Express Yourself
FANTASYFOOTBALL	The Grandstand
FANTASYLEAGUES	The Grandstand
FARALLON	Farallon
FAX	Fax/Paper Mail
FEATURES	Columnists & Features Online
FEEDBACK	Member Services
FELLOWSHIP	Fellowship of Online Gamers/RPGA Network
FFGF	Free-Form Gaming Forum
FIFTH	Fifth Generation
FILESEARCH	Search database of files
FINANCE	Personal Finance Department
FLIGHT	Flight Sim Resource Center
FLIGHTSIMS	Flight Sim Resource Center
FLIGHTSIMULATIONS	Flight Sim Resource Center
FLORIDA	Destination Florida
FLOWERSHOP	Flower Shop
FLY	Aviation Club
FLYING	Flying Magazine
FLYINGMAGAZINE	Flying Magazine
FOCUS	Focus Enhancements
FOCUSENHANCEMENTS	Focus Enhancements
FOG	Fellowship of Online Gamers/RPGA Network
FONTBANK	FontBank
FOOD	Cooking Club
FOOTBALL	The Grandstand
FORMZ	auto*des*sys, Inc.
FORUM	Computing Department †
FORUMAUD	Rotunda Forum Auditorium
FORUMAUDITORIUM	Rotunda Forum Auditorium
FORUMROT	Rotunda Forum Auditorium
FORUMS	Computing Department †
FRACTAL	Fractal Design
FRACTALDESIGN	Fractal Design
FRANKLIN	Franklin Quest
FREE	Member Services
FRIEND	Sign on a friend to AOL*
FSRC	Flight Sim Resource Center
FULLWRITE	FullWrite
FUND	Morningstar Mutual Funds
FUNDS	Morningstar Mutual Funds
FUTURELABS	Future Labs, Inc.
GADGETGURU	Gadget Guru Electronics Forum
GALLERY	Portrait Gallery
GAMEBASE	Game Base

GAMEDESIGN	Game Designers Forum
GAMEDESIGNER	Game Designers Forum
GAMEDESIGNERS	Game Designers Forum
GAMEROOMS	Games Parlor
GAMES	Entertainment Department
GAMES&ENTERTAINMENT	Entertainment Department
GAMESDOWNLOADING	Free online games downloading*
GAMESFORUM	Games Forum
GAMESFORUM	Games Forum †
GAMESPARLOR	Games Parlor
GAMING	Online Gaming Forums
GARDENING	The Exchange
GATEWAY	Gateway 2000, Inc
GATEWAY2000	Gateway 2000, Inc
GAY	Gay & Lesbian Community Forum
GCC	GCC Technologies
GCS	Gaming Company Support
GENEALOGY	Genealogy Club
GENEALOGYCLUB	Genealogy Club
GENERALMAGIC	General Magic
GEO	GeoWorks
GEOGRAPHIC	National Geographic Online
GEOWORKS	GeoWorks
GERALDO	The Geraldo Show
GERALDOSHOW	The Geraldo Show
GETTINGSTARTED	Beginners' Forum
GETTINGSTARTEDFORUM	Beginners' Forum
GFL	The Grandstand
GIFCONVERTER	GIF Converter
GIFTED	Giftedness Forum
GIX	Gaming Information Exchange
GLCF	Gay & Lesbian Community Forum
GLOBAL	Global Village Communication
GLOBALVILLAGE	Global Village Communication
GOLF	Sport News area
GOLFCOURSES	Golf Courses & Resort Information
GOLFRESORTS	Golf Courses & Resort Information
GOLFIS	Golf Courses & Resort Information
GOPHER	Internet Gopher & WAIS
GOSCUBA	Scuba Club
GOTAX	Tax Forum
GRANDSTAND	The Grandstand
GRAPHICARTS	Graphics Forum †
GRAPHICS	Graphics Forum †
GRAPHICSFORUM	Graphics Forum †
GRAPHICSIMULATIONS	Graphic Simulations
GRAPHISOFT	Graphisoft
GRATEFULDEAD	Grateful Dead Forum
GRAVIS	Advanced Gravis
GROUPWARE	GroupWare SIG
GRYPHON	Gryphon Software
GRYPHONSOFTWARE	Gryphon Software
GSMAG	GS+ Magazine
GSS	Global Software Suport
GTSF	Beginners' Forum
GUIDEPAGE	Page a Guide
GUIDEPAGER	Page a Guide
GUILD	Online Gaming Forums
HALLOFFAME	Downloading Hall of Fame
HAM	Ham Radio Club
HAMRADIO	Ham Radio Club
HANDLE	Add, change or delete screen names
HARDWARE	Hardware Forum †
HARDWARECOMPANIES	Industry Connection
HARDWAREFORUM	Hardware Forum †
HATRACK	Hatrack River Town Meeting
HATRACKRIVETTOWN	Hatrack River Town Meeting
HBSPUB	Harvard Business School Publishing
HCSSOFTWARE	HSC Software
HDC	hDC Corporation
HDCCORPORATION	hDC Corporation
HEADLINES	Top News area
HEALTH	Better Health & Medical Forum
HELIOS	Helios USA
HELIOSUSA	Helios USA
HELP	Member Services
HELPDESK	Beginners' Forum
HELPWANTED	Search Help Wanted USA
HERITAGEFOUNDATION	Heritage Foundation area
HIGHLIGHTS	AOL Highlights Tour
HIKER	Backpacker Magazine
HIKING	Backpacker Magazine
HISPANIC	The Exchange
HOBBIES	Clubs & Interests Department
HOCKEY	The Grandstand
HOLIDAY	AOL Holiday Central
HOLLYWOOD	Hollywood Online
HOLLYWOODONLINE	Hollywood Online
HOME	Homeowner's Forum
HOMEBREW	Wine & Dine Online
HOMEBREWING	Wine & Dine Online
HOMEEQUITYLOAN	Real Estate Online
HOMEOFFICE	Home Office Computing Magazine
HOMEOWNER	Homeowner's Forum
HOMEOWNERSFORUM	Homeowner's Forum
HOMEPC	HomePC Magazine
HOMEREFINANCING	Real Estate Online
HOMETHEATER	Stereo Review Online magazine
HOMEWORK	Academic Assistance Center
HOOVERS	Hoover's Handbook of Company Profiles
HOROSCOPE	Horoscopes
HOROSCOPES	Horoscopes
HORSERACING	The Grandstand
HOT	What's Hot This Month showcase
HOTLINE	Member Services
HROSSPEROT	Ross Perot/United We Stand area
HSC	HSC Software
HYPERCARD	HyperCard Forum
IBM	IBM Connection
IBMOS2	OS/2 Forum
IBVA	IBVA Technologies
IC	Industry Connection
ICF	International Corporate Forum
ICOM	Viacom New Media
ICOMSIMULATIONS	Viacom New Media

ICS	International Correspondence Schools	KIDSONLY	Kids Only Online
IES	Interactive Education Services	KITCHEN	Cooking Club
IIN	Redate/IIN Online	KIWI	Kiwi Software, Inc.
IMAGING	Advanced Color Imaging Forum	KNOWLEDGEBASE	Microsoft Knowledge Base
IMH	Issues in Mental Health	KOALA	Koala/MacVision
IMPACTII	IMPACT II: The Teachers Network	KODAK	Kodak Photography Forum
IMPROV	The Improv Forum	KOMANDO	Kim Komando's Komputer Clinic
IMPROVCLUB	The Improv Forum	KOMPUTERTUTOR	Kim Komando's Komputer Clinic
IMPROVCLUBS	The Improv Forum	KOOL	Kids Only Online
IMPROVFORUM	The Improv Forum	KPT	HSC Software
INCIDER	inCider	LABNET	TERC LabNet
INDUSTRY	Industry Connection	LAMBDA	Gay & Lesbian Community Forum
INDUSTRYCONNECTION	Industry Connection	LANGUAGESYS	SYS Language Systems
INFOCOM	Infocom	LAPIS	Lapis Technologies
INFORMATION	Member Services	LAPISTECHNOLOGIES	Lapis Technologies
INLINE	Inline Design	LAPUB	LaPub
INLINESOFTWARE	Inline Design	LAWRENCE	Lawrence Productions
INSIDEMEDIA	Cowles/SIMBA Media Information Network	LEADER	Leader Technologies
		LEADERTECH	Leader Technologies
INSIDETECH	Inside Technology	LEADERTECHNOLOGIES	Leader Technologies
INSIDETECHNOLOGY	Inside Technology	LEADINGEDGE	Leading Edge
INSIGNIA	Insignia Solutions	LEARN	Education Department
INTEL	Intel Corporation	LEARNING	Education Department
INTELLIMATION	Intellimation	LEARNINGCENTER	Education Department
INTERACTIVEDUCATION	Interactive Education Services	LEGAL	Legal SIG
INTERACTIVEED	Interactive Education Services	LEGALSIG	Legal SIG
INTERCON	InterCon Systems Corporation	LESBIAN	Gay & Lesbian Community Forum
INTEREST	Clubs & Interests Department	LETRASET	Letraset
INTERNATIONAL	International House	LETTER	A Letter From Steve Case*
INTERNET	Internet Center	LIBERTARIAN	Libertarian Party Forum
INTERNETCENTER	Internet Center	LIBRARIES	Software Center †
INTERPLAY	Interplay	LIBRARY	Library of Congress Online
INTHENEWS	Mercury Center In the News area	LIBS	Software Center †
INVESTING	Investors Network	LIFESTYLES	Clubs & Interests Department
INVESTMENTS	Investors Network	LIFESTYLES&HOBBIES	Clubs & Interests Department
INVESTORS	Investors Network	LIFESTYLES&INTEREST	Clubs & Interests Department
INVESTORSNETWORK	Investors Network	LIFESTYLES&INTERESTS	Clubs & Interests Department
IOMEGA	Iomega Corporation	LIFETIME	Lifetime Television
IPA	Advanced Color Imaging Forum	LIFETIMETELEVISION	Lifetime Television
ISIS	ISIS International	LIFETIMETV	Lifetime Television
ISISINTERNATIONAL	ISIS International	LINKS	Access Software
ISLAM	Religion & Ethics Forum	LINKSWARE	LinksWare, Inc.
ISLANDGRAPHICS	Island Graphics Corporation	LISTINGS	TMS TV Source
ISSUES	Issues and Debate Forum	LITERACY	Adult Literacy Forum
ISSUESANDDEBATE	Issues and Debate Forum	LITERATURE	Saturday Review Online
IYM	IYM Software Review	LOC	Library of Congress Online
IYMSOFTWAREREVIEW	IYM Software Review	LOCALNEWSPAPERS	Local Newspapers
JLCOOPER	JLCooper Electronics	LUCAS	LucasArts Games
JOBS	Job Listings Database	LUCASARTS	LucasArts Games
JPEGVIEW	JPEGView	MAC	Mac Computing & Software department
JUDAISM	Religion & Ethics Forum	MAC500	Mac Shareware 500
KAPLAN	Kaplan Online	MACART	Graphic Art & CAD Forum
KEEFE	Mike Keefe Cartoons	MACBIBLE	The Macintosh Bible/Peachpit Forum
KENSINGTON	Kensington Microware, Ltd.	MACBUSINESS	Business Forum
KENTMARSH	Kent*Marsh	MACCOMMUNICATION	Mac Communications Forum
KIDDESK	Edmark Technologies	MACCOMMUNICATIONS	Mac Communications Forum
KIDNET	KIDSNET Forum	MACCOMPUTING	Mac Computing & Software department
KIDSNET	KIDSNET	MACDESKTOP	Mac Desktop Publishing/WP Forum

MACDEVELOPMENT	Mac Development Forum
MACDTP	Mac Desktop Publishing/WP Forum
MACEDUCATION	Mac Education Forum
MACGAME	Mac Games Forum
MACGAMES	Mac Games Forum
MACGRAPHICS	Mac Graphic Art & CAD Forum
MACHARDWARE	Mac Hardware Forum
MACHOME	MacHome Journal
MACHOMEJOURNAL	MacHome Journal
MACHYPERCARD	Mac HyperCard Forum
MACINTOSH	Mac Computing & Software department
MACINTOSHBIBLE	The Macintosh Bible/Peachpit Forum
MACLIBRARIES	Mac Software Center
MACMULTIMEDIA	Mac Multimedia Forum
MACMUSIC	Mac Music & Sound Forum
MACO/S	Mac Operating Systems Forum
MACOPERATINGSYSTEMS	Mac Operating Systems Forum
MACOS	Mac Operating Systems Forum
MACPROGRAMMING	Mac Development Forum
MACROMEDIA	MacroMedia, Inc.
MACROMIND	MacroMedia, Inc.
MACSOFTWARE	Mac Software Center
MACSOUND	Mac Music & Sound Forum
MACSPEAKERZ	True Image Audio
MACTECH	MacTech Magazine
MACTECHMAG	MacTech Magazine
MACTECHMAGAZINE	MacTech Magazine
MACTELECOM	Mac Communications Forum
MACTELECOMM	Mac Communications Forum
MACTIVITY	Mactivity '94 Forum
MACUTILITIES	Mac Utilities Forum
MACVISION	Koala/MacVision
MACWORLD	MacWorld Magazine
MACWORLDEXPO	MacWorld Expo Center
MACWORLDPROCESSING	Mac Desktop Publishing/WP Forum
MADA	MacApp Developers Association
MAGAZINES	The Newsstand
MAILGATEWAY	Mail Gateway
MAIN	Reset Department menu to initial department [Apple II users only]*
MAINSTY	Mainstay
MALL	The Marketplace
MALLARD	Mallard Software
MANHATTANGRAPHICS	Manhattan Graphics (RSG)
MANUAL	Members' Online Support*
MARKET	Market Master
MARKETFIELD	Marketfield Software
MARKETMASTER	Market Master
MARKETNEWS	Market News area
MARKETS	Market News area
MARTINSEN	Martinsen's Software
MASS	Massachusetts Governor's Forum
MASSACHUSETTS	Massachusetts Governor's Forum
MASTERWORD	MasterWord
MAXIS	Maxis
MBS	Business Forum
MC	Military City Online
MCAFEE	McAfee Associates
MCBUSINESS	Mercury Center Business & Technology area
MCCLASSIFIEDS	Mercury Center Advertising
MCENTERTAINMENT	Mercury Center Entertainment area
MCLIBRARY	Mercury Center Newspaper Library
MCLIVING	Mercury Center Bay Area Living area
MCM	Communications Forum
MCMARKET	Mercury Center Advertising
MCNEW	Mercury Center In the News area
MCNEWS	Mercury Center In the News area
MCO	Military City Online
MCSPORTS	Mercury Center Sports area
MCTALK	Mercury Center Conference area
MDP	Mac Desktop Publishing/WP Forum
MDV	Mac Development Forum
MECC	MECC
MED	Mac Education Forum
MEDIAINFORMATION	Cowles/SIMBA Media Information Network
MEDICINE	Better Health & Medical Forum
MEMBERDIRECTORY	Member Directory
MEMBERPROFILE	Edit your member profile*
MEMBERS	Member Directory
MEMBERSGUIDE	Members' Online Support*
MEMBERSONLINEGUIDE	Members' Online Support*
MEN	The Exchange
MENSA	Giftedness Forum
MERCURY	Mercury Center
MERCURYCENTER	Mercury Center
MERIDIAN	Meridian Data
MESSAGEPAD	Personal Digital Assistants Forum
METROWERKS	Metrowerks
METZ	Metz
MGM	Mac Games Forum
MGR	Mac Graphic Art & CAD Forum
MGX	Micrografx, Inc.
MHC	Mac HyperCard Forum
MHM	Members Helping Members message board*
MHW	Mac Hardware Forum
MICHAELREAGAN	The Michael Reagan Show Online
MICHAELREAGANSHOW	The Michael Reagan Show Online
MICHIGAN	Michigan Governor's Forum
MICHIGANGOVERNOR	Michigan Governor's Forum
MICRODYNAMICS	Micro Dynamics, Ltd.
MICROFRONTIER	MicroFrontier, Ltd.
MICROGRAFX	Micrografx, Inc.
MICROJ	Micro J Systems, Inc
MICROMAT	MicroMat Computer Systems
MICRON	Xceed Technology
MICROPROSE	MicroProse
MICROSEEDS	Microseeds Publishing, Inc.
MICROSOFT	Microsoft Resource Center
MIDI	Graphics and Sound Forum
MIDI	Mac Music & Sound Forum
MIDI	PC Music and Sound Forum
MILITARY	Military and Vets Club
MILITARYCITYONLINE	Military City Online

MIRROR	Mirror Technologies	NATIONALGEOGRAPHIC	National Geographic Online
MLS	Real Estate Online	NBC	NBC Online
MMM	Mac Multimedia Forum	NBR	The Nightly Business Report
MMS	Mac Music & Sound Forum	NBRREPORT	The Nightly Business Report
MMW	Multimedia World Online [PC platform only]	NCTE	Nat'l Council of Teachers of English
		NEAONLINE	National Education Association
MMWORLD	Multimedia World Online [PC platform only]	NEAPUBLIC	National Education Association
		NEC	NEC Technologies
MOBILE	Mobile Office Online	NECTECH	NEC Technologies
MODEMHELP	Modem Help area* [PC platform only]	NEOLOGIC	NeoLogic
MOG	Members' Online Support*	NETWORKEARTH	Network Earth
MONEY	Business News area	NETWORKING	Communications/Telecom/Networking Forum †
MONSTERISLAND	Adventures by Mail		
MONTESSORI	Montessori Schools	NETWORKINGFORUM	Communications/Telecom/Networking Forum †
MOO	Gateway 2000, Inc		
MORAFFWARE	MoraffWare	NEVERWINTER	AD&D Neverwinter Nights
MORNINGSTAR	Morningstar Mutual Funds	NEW	New Features & Services showcase
MORPH	Gryphon Software	NEWAGE	Relgion & Ethics Forum
MORTAGE	Real Estate Online	NEWERA	Tactic Software
MORTAGERATES	Real Estate Online	NEWLINK	Beginners' Forum
MORTGAGES	Real Estate Online	NEWMAIL	New Mail Information area*
MOS	Mac Operating Systems Forum	NEWREPUBLIC	The New Republic Magazine
MOUNTAINBIKE	Bicycling Magazine	NEWS	Today's News
MOVIEREVIEWS	Movies menu	NEWS&FINANCE	Today's News
MOVIES	Movies menu	NEWS/SPORTS/MONEY	Today's News
MOVIES	Movies menu	NEWSANDFINANCE	Today's News
MS-DOS	DOS Forum	NEWSBYTES	Newsbytes
MS-DOSFORUM	DOS Forum	NEWSGROUPS	Internet Usenet Newsgroup area
MSA	Management Science Associates	NEWSLINK	Top News area
MSDOS6	MS-DOS 6.0 Resource Center	NEWSPAPER	Local Newspapers
MSDOS60	MS-DOS 6.0 Resource Center	NEWSPAPERS	Local Newspapers
MSFORUM	Microsoft Product Support	NEWSROOM	News Department
MSKB	Microsoft Knowledge Base	NEWSSEARCH	Search News Articles
MSSUPPORT	Microsoft Resource Center	NEWSSTAND	The Newsstand
MSTATION	Bentley Systems, Inc.	NEWSTEXT	Top News area
MTC	Communications Forum	NEWSWATCH	Search News Articles
MTV	MTV Online	NEWTON	Personal Digital Assistant's Forum
MUG	AOL Products Center	NEWWORLD	New World Computing
MULTIMEDIA	The Multimedia Exchange	NEWYORK	@times/The New York Times Online
MUSIC	Rocklink	NEWYORKCITY	@times/The New York Times Online
MUSIC&SOUND	Graphics and Sound Forum †	NEWYORKTIMES	@times/The New York Times Online
MUSICANDSOUNDFORUM	Graphics and Sound Forum †	NGLTF	Nation Gay & Lesbian Task Force
MUSICFORUM	Graphics and Sound Forum †	NGS	National Geographic Online
MUSTANG	Mustang Software	NIKON	Nikon Electronic Imaging
MUSTANGSOFTWARE	Mustang Software	NILES	Niles and Associates
MUT	Mac Utilities Forum	NINTENDO	Video Games area
MUTUALFUND	Morningstar Mutual Funds	NLF	Beginners' Forum
MUTUALFUNDS	Morningstar Mutual Funds	NMAA	National Museum of American Art
MVT	Mac Utilities Forum	NMSS	National Multiple Sclerosis Society
MW	MasterWord	NOHANDS	No Hands Software
MWORD	MasterWord	NOMADIC	Nomadic Computing Discussion SIG
NAESP	National Principals Center	NORTON	Symantec
NAME	Add, change or delete screen names	NOVELL	Novell Desktop Systems
NAMES	Add, change or delete screen names	NOW	Now Software
NAMI	National Alliance of Mentally Ill	NOWPLAYING	Directory of Services
NAPC	Employment Agency Database	NPR	National Public Radio Outreach
NAQP	National Association of Quick Printers area	NSDC	National Staff Development Council
		NSS	National Space Society

NUMBERS	Local access numbers*
NWN	AD&D Neverwinter Nights
NYC	@times/The New York Times Online
NYT	@times/The New York Times Online
NYTIMES	@times/The New York Times Online
OADD	AD&D Neverwinter Nights
OBJECTFACTORY	Object Factory
ODEON	Odeon Auditorium
OFFICE	Penny Wise Office Products Store
OFFICEPRODUCTS	Penny Wise Office Products Store
OGF	Online Gaming Forums
OLDUVAI	Olduvai Software, Inc.
OLT	OnLine Tonight
OMNI	OMNI Magazine Online
OMNIMAGAZINE	OMNI Magazine Online
ON	ON Technology
ONLINEBOOKSTORE	Online Bookstore
ONLINEGAMING	Online Gaming Forums
ONLINEGUIDE	Members' Online Support
ONLINETONIGHT	OnLine Tonight
ONYX	Onyx Technology
OPCODE	Opcode Systems, Inc.
OPCODESYSTEMS	Opcode Systems, Inc.
OPTIMAGE	OptImage Interactive Services
OPTIMAS	OPTIMAS Corporation
ORIGIN	Origin Systems
ORIGINSYSTEMS	Origin Systems
ORSONSCOTTCARD	Hatrack River Town Meeting
OS2	OS/2 Forum
OSTWO	OS/2 Forum
OTTER	Otter Solution
OTTERSOLUTION	Otter Solution
OURWORLD	Top News area
OUTDOORGEAR	Backpacker Magazine
OUTDOORS	The Exchange
PACEMARK	PaceMark Technologies, Inc.
PACKER	Packer Software
PAGAN	Religion & Ethics Forum
PALM	Palm Computing
PALMCOMPUTING	Palm Computing
PALMTOP	Personal Digital Assistants Forum
PAP	Applications Forum
PAPERMAIL	Fax/Paper Mail
PAPYRUS	Papyrus
PARENT	Parents' Information Network
PARENTALCONTROL	Parental Controls
PARLOR	Games Parlor
PASCAL	Development Forum †
PASSPORT	Passport Designs
PASSWORD	Change your password*
PBM	Play-By-Mail & Strategy Gaming Forum
PC	People Connection
PCANIMATION	PC Graphics Forum
PCAPPLICATIONS	PC Applications Forum
PCAPPLICATIONSFORUM	PC Applications Forum
PCAPS	PC Applications Forum
PCAUD	Center Stage auditorium
PCBEGINNERS	Beginners' Forum
PCBG	Beginners' Forum
PCCATALOG	PC Catalog
PCCATALOG	PC Catalog
PCCLASSIFIEDS	Browse the PC Catalog
PCCLASSIFIEDS	PC Catalog
PCDESKMATE	DeskMate
PCDEV	PC Development Forum
PCDEVELOPMENT	PC Development Forum
PCDEVELOPMENTFORUM	PC Development Forum
PCDM	DeskMate
PCEXPO	Redgate Online > PC Expo area
PCFORUMS	PC Computing & Software department
PCGAMES	PC Games Forum
PCGAMESFORUM	PC Games Forum
PCGRAPHICS	PC Graphics Forum
PCGRAPHICSFORUM	PC Graphics Forum
PCHARDWARE	PC Hardware Forum
PCHARDWAREFORUM	PC Hardware Forum
PCHELP	Beginners' Forum
PCHQ	Tandy Headquarters
PCLIBRARIES	PC Software Center
PCM	PC Telecom/Networking Forum
PCMU	PC Music and Sound Forum
PCMUSIC	PC Music and Sound Forum
PCMUSICANDSOUNDFORUM	PC Music and Sound Forum
PCMUSICFORUM	PC Music and Sound Forum
PCNOVICE	PC Novice & PC Today Online
PCPC	Personal Computer Peripherals
PCSECURITY	Computing Department †
PCSOFTWARE	PC Software Center
PCSOFTWARE	PC Software Center
PCSOUND	PC Music and Sound Forum
PCSOUNDFORUM	PC Music and Sound Forum
PCSTUDIO	PC Studio
PCSW	PC Software Center
PCTELECOM	PC Telecom/Networking Forum
PCTELECOMFORUM	PC Telecom/Networking Forum
PCTODAY	PC Novice & PC Today Online
PCUTILITIES	DOS Forum
PCWONLINE	PCWorld Online
PCWORLD	PCWorld Online
PCWORLDONLINE	PCWorld Online
PDA	Personal Digital Assistant's Forum
PDV	PC Development Forum
PEACHPIT	The Macintosh Bible/Peachpit Forum
PEACHTREE	Peachtree Software
PENNY	Penny Wise Office Products Store
PENNYWISE	Penny Wise Office Products Store
PENPAL	Edmark Technologies
PENTIUM	Intel Corporation
PEOPLE	People Connection
PEOPLECONNECTION	People Connection
PERFORMA	Apple Club Performa
PERFORMACENTER	Apple Club Performa
PERFORMARESOURCE	Apple Club Performa
PEROT	Ross Perot/United We Stand area
PERSONALFINANCE	Personal Finance Department
PET	Pet Care Club

PETCARE	Pet Care Club
PETERNORTON	Symantec
PETITIONS	Local access numbers*
PETS	Pet Care Club
PF	Personal Finance area
PGM	PC Games Forum
PGR	PC Graphics Forum
PHANTASYGUILD	Online Gaming Forums
PHOTO	Kodak Photography Forum
PHOTOS	Popular Photography Online
PHOTOGRAPHY	Photography Area
PHOTOSHOP	Photoshop SIG
PHOTOSHOPSIG	Photoshop SIG
PHW	PC Hardware Forum
PHYSICALLYDISABLED	DisABILITIES Forum
PICTURES	Pictures of the World
PIN	Parents' Information Network
PIXAR	Pixar
PIXEL	Pixel Resources
PIXELRESOURCES	Pixel Resources
PLAY-BY-MAIL	Play-By-Mail & Strategy Gaming Forum
PLAYMATION	Playmation
PMM	PC Multimedia Forum
PMU	PC Music and Sound Forum
POLITICS	Bull Moose Tavern
POPPHOTO	Popular Photography Online
POPULARPHOTOGRAPHY	Popular Photography Online
PORTABLE	Mobile Office Online
PORTABLECOMPUTING	Mobile Office Online
PORTFOLIO	Your Stock Portfolio
PORTFOLIOSOFTWARE	Portfolio Systems, Inc.
POWERBOOK	PowerBook Resource Center
POWERMAC	Power Mac Resource Center
POWERPC	Power Mac Resource Center
POWERUP	Power Up Software
PPI	Practical Peripherals, Inc.
PRACTICALPERIPHERALS	Practical Peripherals, Inc.
PRAIRIESOFT	PrairieSoft, Inc.
PRC	Apple Club Performa
PRESS	AOL Press Release Library
PRESSRELEASE	AOL Press Release Library
PREVENTION	Substance Abuse Forum
PRINCETONREVIEW	Student Access Online
PRINCIPALS	National Principals Center
PRODIGY	Prodigy Refugees' Forum
PRODIGYFORUM	Prodigy Refugees Forum
PRODIGYREFUGEES	Prodigy Refugees Forum
PRODUCTIVITY	Applications/Business/Productivity Forum †
PRODUCTIVITYFORUM	Applications/Business/Productivity Forum †
PROFILE	Edit your member profile*
PROGRAMMERU	Programmer University
PROGRAMMING	Development Forum †
PROGRAPH	Prograph International, Inc.
PROVUE	ProVUE Development
PS1	IBM Connection
PSION	Psion
PSL	IBM Connection
PSYCHICLABS	IBVA Technologies
PTC	PC Telecom/Networking Forum
PU	Programmer University
PUBLICRADIO	National Public Radio Outreach
PUBLISHERS	Industry Connection
PUNCHLINE	Comedy Club and Punchlines
QMMS	Mac Music & Sound Forum
QMODEM	Mustang Software
QUALITAS	Qualitas
QUARK	Quark, Inc.
QUE	The Quantum Que and Graffiti community message boards
QUEST	Adventures by Mail
QUICKFIND	Search database of files †
QUICKFINDER	Search database of files †
QUICKPRINTERS	National Association of Quick Printers area
QUOTE	Stock Market Timing & Charts area
QUOTES	Stock Market Timing & Charts area
RABBITJACKSCASINO	RabbitJack's Casino
RACING	Car and Driver Magazine
RADIO	Ham Radio Club
RADIUS	Radius, Inc.
RAILROADING	The Exchange
RASTEROPS	RasterOps
RAY	Ray Dream
RAYDREAM	Ray Dream
RDI	Free-Form Gaming Forum
REACTOR	Reactor
READ	Adult Literacy Forum
READING	Saturday Review Online
READUSA	Online Bookstore
REAGAN	The Michael Reagan Show Online
REALESTATE	Real Estate Online
RECCENTER	Entertainment Department
RECREATION	Entertainment Department
RECREATIONCENTER	Entertainment Department
REDGATE	Redgate/IIN Online
REFERENCE	Reference Desk
REFERENCEDESK	Reference Desk
REGISTER	IES Registration Center
REGISTRATION	IES Registration Center
RELIGION	Ethics and Religion Forum
RENDERMAN	Pixar
REPRISE	Warner/Reprise Records Online
RESEARCH	Academic Assistance Center
RESNOVA	ResNova Software (RESNOVASOFTWARE)
RESTAURANT	Wine & Dine Online
RESTAURANTS	Wine & Dine Online
RICKILAKE	The Ricki Lake Show
ROAD	Road & Track Magazine
ROADANDTRACK	Road & Track Magazine
ROCK	Rocklink
ROCKLAND	Rockland Software
ROCKLANDSOFTWARE	Rockland Software
ROCKLINK	Rocklink

ROGERWAGNER	Roger Wagner Publishing
ROLEPLAYING	Role-Playing Forum
ROMANCE	Romance Connection message boards
ROOTS	Genealogy Club
ROSSPEROT	Ross Perot/United We Stand area
ROTUNDA	Rotunda Forum Auditorium
RPG	Role-Playing Forum
RPGA	Fellowship of Online Gamers/RPGA Network
RPGANETWORK	Fellowship of Online Gamers/RPGA Network
SABRE	EAASY SABRE
SALIENT	Salient Software
SANJOSE	Mercury Center
SATELLITES	Ham Radio Club
SATREVIEW	Saturday Review Online
SATURDAYREVIEW	Saturday Review Online
SCHOLASTIC	Scholastic Network/Scholastic Forum
SCHOOLHOUSE	Electronic Schoolhouse
SCI-FI	Science Fiction Forum
SCIENCEFICTION	Science Fiction Forum
SCIFI	Science Fiction Forum
SCIFICHANNEL	The Sci-Fi Channel
SCOUTING	Scouting Forum
SCOUTS	Scouting Forum
SCREENNAME	Add, change or delete screen names
SCREENNAMES	Add, change or delete screen names
SCUBA	Scuba Club
SEGA	Video Games area
SENIOR	SeniorNet
SERIUS	Serius
SERVICE	Member Services
SERVICES	Directory of Services
SERVICESDIRECTORY	Directory of Services
SF	Science Fiction Forum
SHAREWARE500	Mac Shareware 500
SHAREWARESOLUTIONS	Shareware Solutions
SHIVA	Shiva Corporation
SHOPPING	The Marketplace
SHORTHAND	Online Shorthands
SHORTHANDS	Online Shorthands
SHOWS	Center Stage auditorium
SI	Smithsonian Online
SIERRA	Sierra On-Line
SIFS	Computing Department †
SIGNUP	IES Registration Center
SIGS	Computing Department †
SILICON	Hardware
SIMBA	Cowles/SIMBA Media Information Network
SIMULATOR	Games Forum †
SKI	Ski Reports
SKICONDITIONS	Ski Reports
SKIREPORTS	Ski Reports
SKIWEATHER	Ski Reports
SMITHSONIAN	Smithsonian Online
SOCEITY	Saturday Review Online
SOFT	Software Center †

SOFTARC	SoftArc
SOFTDISK	Softdisk Superstore [PC platform only]
SOFTSYNC	Expert Software, Inc
SOFTWARE	Software Center †
SOFTWARECENTER	Software Center †
SOFTWARECOMPANIES	Industry Connection
SOFTWARECREATIONS	Software Creations
SOFTWAREDIRECTORY	Software Center †
SOFTWAREHELP	Software Center †
SOFTWARELIBRARIES	Software Center †
SOFTWARELIBRARY	Software Center †
SOFTWAREPUBLISHERS	Industry Connection
SOFTWARETOOLWORKS	Software Toolworks
SOLIII	Sol III Play-by-Email Game
SOPHCIR	Sophisticated Circuits
SOS	Wall Street SOS Forum
SOVARC	Library of Congress Online
SOVIET	Library of Congress Online
SOVIETARCHIVES	Library of Congress Online
SPACE	National Space Society
SPECIALINTERESTS	Clubs & Interests Department
SPECTRUM	Spectrum HoloByte
SPECULAR	Specular International
SPORTS	Sport News area
SPORTSLINK	Sport News area
SPORTSNEWS	Sport News area
SRO	Saturday Review Online
SSI	Strategic Simulations
SSSI	SSSi
STAC	STAC Electronics
STAMPS	The Exchange
STARTER	Beginners' Forum
STARTREK	Star Trek Club
STEREO	Stereo Review Online magazine
STEREOREVIEW	Stereo Review Online magazine
STF	STF Technologies
STFTECHNOLOGIES	STF Technologies
STOCK	Stock Market Timing & Charts area
STOCKCHARTS	Decision Point Forum
STOCKLINK	Stock Market Timing & Charts area
STOCKPORTFOLIO	Your Stock Portfolio
STOCKQUOTES	Stock Market Timing & Charts area
STOCKS	Stock Market Timing & Charts area
STOCKTIMING	Decision Point Forum
STORE	The Marketplace
STORES	The Marketplace
STRATA	Strata, Inc.
STRATEGIC	Strategic Simulations
STRATEGY	Play-By-Mail & Strategy Gaming Forum
STUDENT	Student Access Online
STUDENTACCESS	Student Access Online
STUDY	Study Skills Service
STUDYSKILLS	Study Skills Service
STUFFIT	Aladdin Systems, Inc.
STUMP	Rotunda Forum Auditorium
SUBSTANCEABUSE	Substance Abuse Forum
SUGGESTION	Suggestion boxes*
SUGGESTIONS	Suggestion boxes*

SUPERCARD	Hardware
SUPERDISK	Alysis Software
SUPERMAC	SuperMac
SUPPORT	Member Services
SURVIVOR	Survivor Software
SURVIVORSOFTWARE	Survivor Software
SWC	Software Creations
SYMANTEC	Symantec
SYNEX	Synex
SYSOP	Member Services
SYSTEM7	Mac Operating Systems Forum
SYSTEM7.0	Mac Operating Systems Forum
SYSTEM7.1	Mac Operating Systems Forum
SYSTEM71	Mac Operating Systems Forum
TACTIC	Tactic Software
TALENT	Talent Bank
TALK	People Connection
TALKSHOW	Future Labs, Inc.
TANDY	Tandy Headquarters
TANDYHANDQUARTERS	Tandy Headquarters
TANDYHQ	Tandy Headquarters
TAROT	Advice & Tips
TAX	Tax Forum [seasonal]
TAXES	Tax Forum [seasonal]
TEACHER	Teachers' Information Network
TEACHERPAGER	Teacher Pager
TEACHERS	Teachers' Information Network
TEACHERU	Teachers' University
TECHHELPLIVE	Tech Help Live*
TECHNOLOGY	Computing Department †
TECHNOLOGYWORKS	Technology Works
TECHWORKS	Technology Works
TEEN	Teen Scene message boards
TEENS	Teen Scene message boards
TEENSCENE	Teen Scene message boards
TEKNOSYS	Teknosys Works
TELECOM	Communications/Telecom/Networking Forum †
TELECOMFORUM	Communications/Telecom/Networking Forum †
TELECOMMUNICATIONS	Communications/Telecom/Networking Forum †
TELEPORT	Global Village Communication
TELESCAN	Telescan Users Group Forum
TELEVISION	Soap Opera Summaries
TENNIS	The Grandstand
TERMS	Terms of Service*
TERMSOFSERVICE	Terms of Service*
TESTPREP	Kaplan Online
TEXASINSTRUMENTS	Texas Instrument
TGS	Prograph International, Inc.
THEATER	Saturday Review Online
THEATRE	Saturday Review Online
THEDEAD	Grateful Dead Forum
THEEXCHANGE	The Exchange
THEMALL	The Marketplace
THENEWREPUBLIC	The New Republic Magazine
THEWHITEHOUSE	White House Forum

THREESIXTY	Three-Sixty Software
THRUSTMASTER	Thrustmaster
THUNDERWARE	Thunderware
TI	Texas Instrument
TIA	True Image Audio
TICKET	Ticketmaster
TICKETMASTER	Chicago Online Ticketmaster
TIGER	TIGERDirect, Inc.
TIGERDIRECT	TIGERDirect, Inc.
TIME	Time Magazine Online
TIMES	@times/The New York Times Online
TIMESART	@times: Art & Photography
TIMESARTS	@times: The Arts
TIMESBOOKS	@times: Books of The Times
TIMESDINING	@times: Dining Out & Nightlife
TIMESLEISURE	@times: Leisure Guide
TIMESMOVIES	@times: Movies & Video
TIMESMUSIC	@times: Music & Dance
TIMESNEWS	@times/The New York Times Online
TIMESREGION	@times: In The Region
TIMESSPORTS	@times: Sports & Fitness
TIMESSTORIES	@times: Top Stories
TIMESTHEATER	@times: Theater
TIMESLIPS	Timeslips Corporation
TIMEWORKS	Timeworks
TIN	Teachers' Information Network
TIPS	Advice & Tips
TITF	Daily calender of forum activity
TMAKER	T/Maker
TMS	TMS TV Source
TNEWS	Teachers' Newsstand
TNPC	The National Parenting Center
TNR	The New Republic Magazine
TOMORROW	Tomorrow's Morning newspaper
TOMORROWSMORNING	Tomorrow's Morning newspaper
TOOLWORKS	Software Toolworks
TOPNEWS	Top News area
TOS	Terms of Service*
TOSADVISOR	Terms of Service*
TOTN	National Public Radio Outreach
TOUR	AOL Highlights Tour
TOURGUIDE	AOL Products Center
TRAILGUIDES	Backpacker Magazine
TRAILS	Backpacker Magazine
TRAINING	Career Development Training
TRAVEL	Travel Department
TRAVELER	Travel Forum
TRAVELERSCORNER	Traveler's Corner
TRAVELFORUM	Travel Forum
TRAVELHOLIDAY	Travel Holiday Magazine
TREK	Star Trek Club
TRIB	Chicago Tribune
TRIBADS	Chicago Online Classifieds
TRIBCLASSIFIED	Chicago Online Classifieds
TRIBUNE	Chicago Tribune
TRIVIA	Trivia Club
TRUEIMAGEAUDIO	True Image Audio
TSENG	Tseng

TSHIRT	AOL Products Center
TTALK	Teachers' Forum
TUNEUP	Tune Up Your PC
TUNEUPYOURPC	Tune Up Your PC
TUTORING	Academic Assistance Center
TV	Television
TVGOSSIP	TV Gossip
TVGUIDE	TMS TV Source
TVLISTINGS	TMS TV Source
TVSOURCE	TMS TV Source
UA	Unlimited Adventures
UCPA	United Cerebral Palsy Association, Inc.
UGC	User Group Forum
UGF	User Group Forum
UHA	Homeowner's Forum
UNIQUE	Best of America Online showcase
UNIVERSITIES	Electronic University Network
UNIVERSITY	Electronic University Network
UNLIMITEDADVENTURES	Unlimited Adventures
UPGRADE	Upgrade to the latest version of AOL*
USENET	Internet Usenet Newsgroup area
USERGROUP	User Group Forum
USERGROUPS	User Group Forum
USERLAND	Userland
USERNAME	Add, change or delete screen names
USF	University of San Francisco
USMAIL	Fax/Paper Mail
USNEWS	U.S. & World News area
UTAH	Utah Forum
UTAHFORUM	Utah Forum
VACATIONS	Backpacker Magazine
VATICAN	Library of Congress Online
VDISC	Videodiscovery
VENTANA	Mac Shareware 500
VENTANA500	Mac Shareware 500
VERTISOFT	Vertisoft
VETERANS	Military and Vets Club
VETS	Military and Vets Club
VETSCLUB	Military and Vets Club
VIACOM	Viacom New Media
VIDEODISC	Videodiscovery
VIDEODISCOVERY	Videodiscovery
VIDEOGAMES	Video Games area
VIDEOSIG	Video SIG
VIDEOTOOLKIT	Abbate Video
VIDI	VIDI
VIEWPOINT	Viewpoint DataLabs
VIREX	Datawatch
VIRTUALREALITY	Virtual Reality Resource Center
VIRTUS	Virtus Walkthrough
VIRUS	Virus Information Center SIG
VISIONARY	Visionary Software
VOYAGER	The Voyager Company
VOYETRA	Voyetra Technologies
VR	Virtual Reality Resource Center
VRLI	Virtual Reality Labs, Inc.
WAIS	Internet Gopher & WAIS
WALKTHROUGH	Virtus Walkthrough

WARNER	Warner/Reprise Records Online
WARNERMUSIC	Warner/Reprise Records Online
WEATHER	Weather
WEATHERMAPS	Color Weather Maps
WEIGAND	Weigand Report
WEISSMANN	Traveler's Corner
WESTWOOD	Westwood Studios
WESTWOODSTUDIOS	Westwood Studios
WHATSHOT	What's Hot This Month showcase
WHITEHOUSE	White House Forum
WILDCAT	Mustang Software
WILDCATBBS	Mustang Software
WILDERNESS	Backpacker Magazine
WIN	Windows Forum
WIN500	Windows Shareware 500
WINDOWS	Windows Forum
WINDOWS500	Windows Shareware 500
WINDOWSFORUM	Windows Forum
WINDOWSMAG	Windows Magazine
WINDOWSMAGAZINE	Windows Magazine
WINDOWWARE	Wilson Windowware
WINE	Wine & Dine Online
WINE&DINEONLINE	Wine & Dine Online
WINERIES	Wine & Dine Online
WINFORUM	Windows Forum
WINMAG	Windows Magazine
WINNEWS	Windows News area
WIRED	Wired Magazine
WOMEN	The Exchange
WOODSTOCK	Woodstock Online
WORDLIBRARY	MasterWord
WORDPERFECT	WordPerfect Support Center
WORKING	Working Software
WORLDNEWS	U.S. & World News area
WORTH	Worth Magazine Online
WORTHMAGAZINE	Worth Magazine Online
WORTHONLINE	Worth Magazine Online
WORTHPORTFOLIO	Worth Magazine Online Portfolio
WPMAG	WordPerfect Magazine
WRITER'S	Writer's Club
WRITERS	Writer's Club
WRITERSMARKET	Writers' Market Forum
WWIR	Washington Week in Review magazine
WWW	Wilson Windowware
XAOS	Xoas Tools
XAOSTOOLS	Xoas Tools
XCEED	Xceed Technology
YOURMONEY	Your Money area
YOURTOONS	Cartoon collection
ZEDCOR	Zedcor, Inc.

Alphabetical by Subject

@times/The New York Times Online	@TIMES	Advanced Color Imaging Forum	IPA
@times/The New York Times Online	ATTIMES	Advanced Gravis	ADVANCEDGRAVIS
@times/The New York Times Online	NEWYORK	Advanced Gravis	GRAVIS
@times/The New York Times Online	NEWYORKCITY	Advanced Software, Inc.	ADVANCED
@times/The New York Times Online	NEWYORKTIMES	Adventures by Mail	ABM
@times/The New York Times Online	NYC	Adventures by Mail	ADVENTURESBYMAIL
@times/The New York Times Online	NYT	Adventures by Mail	MONSTERISLAND
@times/The New York Times Online	NYTIMES	Adventures by Mail	QUEST
@times/The New York Times Online	TIMES	Advertising Special Interest Group	ADSIG
@times/The New York Times Online	TIMESNEWS	Advertising Special Interest Group	ADVERTISING
@times: Art & Photography	TIMESART	Advertising Special Interest Group	ADVERTISINGSIG
@times: Books of The Times	TIMESBOOKS	Advice & Tips	ADVICE
@times: Dining Out & Nightlife	TIMESDINING	Advice & Tips	ASKANDY
@times: In The Region	TIMESREGION	Advice & Tips	ASKANITA
@times: Leisure Guide	TIMESLEISURE	Advice & Tips	ASKTHEDOCTOR
@times: Movies & Video	TIMESMOVIES	Advice & Tips	ASKTHEDR
@times: Music & Dance	TIMESMUSIC	Advice & Tips	ASKTHELAWYER
@times: Sports & Fitness	TIMESSPORTS	Advice & Tips	CRYSTALBALL
@times: The Arts	TIMESARTS	Advice & Tips	TAROT
@times: Theater	TIMESTHEATER	Advice & Tips	TIPS
@times: Top Stories	TIMESSTORIES	Affinity Microsystems	AFFINITY
3D Special Interest Group	3DSIG	Afterwards Coffeehouse	AFTERWARDS
9600 Baud Access Center*	9600	Afterwards Coffeehouse	ARTS
9600 Baud Access Center*	9600ACCESS	Aladdin Systems, Inc.	ALADDIN
9600 Baud Access Center*	9600CENTER	Aladdin Systems, Inc.	STUFFIT
A Letter From Steve Case*	LETTER	Aldus Corporation	ALDUS
AAII Online	AAII	Alpha Software Corporation	ALPHATECH
Aatrix Software, Inc.	AATRIX	Alpha Software Corporation	ASCTECH
Abbate Video	ABBATEVIDEO	Alpha Software Corporation	ASCTS
Abbate Video	VIDEOTOOLKIT	Altsys Corporation	ALTSYS
Academic Assistance Center	HOMEWORK	Alysis Software	ALYSIS
Academic Assistance Center	RESEARCH	Alysis Software	SUPERDISK
Academic Assistance Center	TUTORING	Ambrosia Software	AMBROSIA
Access Software	ACCESSSOFTWARE	American Dialogue	AMERICANDIALOGUE
Access Software	LINKS	American Dialogue	DIALOGUE
Accolade, Inc.	ACCOLADE	American Federation of Teachers	AFT
Acer America Corporation	ACER	Animated Software	ANIMATEDSOFTWARE
Achievement TV	ACHIEVEMENTTV	Another Company	ANOTHERCO
Activision	ACTIVISION	AOL Highlights Tour	HIGHLIGHTS
AD&D Neverwinter Nights	AD&D	AOL Highlights Tour	TOUR
AD&D Neverwinter Nights	ADD	AOL Holiday Central	HOLIDAY
AD&D Neverwinter Nights	NEVERWINTER	AOL Press Release Library	PRESS
AD&D Neverwinter Nights	NWN	AOL Press Release Library	PRESSRELEASE
AD&D Neverwinter Nights	OADD	AOL Products Center	AOLPRODUCTS
Add, change or delete screen names	HANDLE	AOL Products Center	MUG
Add, change or delete screen names	NAME	AOL Products Center	TOURGUIDE
Add, change or delete screen names	NAMES	AOL Products Center	TSHIRT
Add, change or delete screen names	SCREENNAME	Apogee Software	APOGEE
Add, change or delete screen names	SCREENNAMES	Apple Applications Forum	APPLICATIONS
Add, change or delete screen names	USERNAME	Apple Business Forum	APPLICATIONS
Adoption Forum	ADOPTION	Apple Classrooms of Tomorrow	ACOT
Adult Literacy Forum	LITERACY	Apple Club Performa	CLUBPERFORMA
Adult Literacy Forum	READ	Apple Club Performa	PERFORMA
Advanced Color Imaging Forum	COLORIMAGING	Apple Club Performa	PERFORMACENTER
Advanced Color Imaging Forum	IMAGING	Apple Club Performa	PERFORMARESOURCE

Apple Club Performa	PRC	Articulate Systems	ASI
Apple Communications Forum	A2TELECOM	Artifice, Inc.	ARTIFICE
Apple Communications Forum	ACM	AskERIC	ACCESSERIC
Apple Communications Forum	ATC	AskERIC	ASKERIC
Apple Development Forum	A2DEVELOPMENT	AskERIC	ERIC
Apple Development Forum	ADV	Assoc. for Supervisor & Curriculum	
Apple Development Forum	APPLEIIDEVELOPMENT	Development	ASCD
Apple Education Forum	A2EDUCATION	Assoc. for Supervisor & Curriculum	
Apple Education Forum	AED	Development	CURRICULUM
Apple Education Forum	APPLEIIEDUCATION	Assoc. for Supervisor & Curriculum	
Apple Games and Entertainment Forum	A2GAMES	Development	EDTECH
Apple Games and Entertainment Forum	AGM	Astronomy Club	ASTRONOMY
Apple Games and Entertainment Forum	APPLEIIGAMES	Asymetrix Corporation	ASYMETRIX
Apple Graphics and Sound Forum	A2ART	Atticus Software	ATTICUS
Apple Graphics and Sound Forum	A2GRAPHICS	auto*des*sys, Inc.	FORMZ
Apple Graphics and Sound Forum	A2MUSIC	auto*des*sys, Inc.	ADS
Apple Graphics and Sound Forum	AGR	AutoVantage	AUTO
Apple Graphics and Sound Forum	AGS	AutoVantage	AUTOVANTAGE
Apple Graphics and Sound Forum	APPLEIIGRAPHICS	Aviation Club	AVIATION
Apple Graphics and Sound Forum	APPLEIIMUSIC	Aviation Club	FLY
Apple Hardware Forum	A2HARDWARE	Avid DTV Group	AVID
Apple Hardware Forum	A2PERIPHERALS	Avid DTV Group	AVIDDTV
Apple Hardware Forum	A2PRODUCT	Avocat Systems	AVOCAT
Apple Hardware Forum	AHW	Baby Boomers area	BABYBOOMERS
Apple Hardware Forum	APPLEIIHARDWARE	Backpacker Magazine	BACKCOUNTRY
Apple II Computing & Software Department	APPLE2	Backpacker Magazine	BACKPACKER
Apple II Computing & Software Department	APPLEII	Backpacker Magazine	CAMPING
Apple II Software Center	APPLEIISOFTWARE	Backpacker Magazine	CONSERVATION
Apple II/Mac Computing & Software		Backpacker Magazine	ECOTOURISM
Department †	APPLE	Backpacker Magazine	HIKER
Apple Productivity Forum	A2APPLEWORKS	Backpacker Magazine	HIKING
Apple Productivity Forum	A2PRODUCTIVITY	Backpacker Magazine	OUTDOORGEAR
Apple Productivity Forum	A2WORDPROCESSING	Backpacker Magazine	TRAILGUIDES
Apple Productivity Forum	AAW	Backpacker Magazine	TRAILS
Apple Productivity Forum	APPLEIIPRODUCTIVITY	Backpacker Magazine	VACATIONS
Apple Productivity Forum	APPLEWORKS	Backpacker Magazine	WILDERNESS
Apple Productivity Forum	APR	Barrons Booknotes	BARRONS
Apple Productivity Forum	AW	Barrons Booknotes	BOOKNOTES
Apple Productivity Forum	AWGS	Baseline Publishing	BASELINE
Apple Productivity Forum	AWP	Baseview Products, Inc.	BASEVIEW
Apple Productivity Forum	AWS	BBS Corner	BBS
Apple Professional Developer's Association	APDA	BBS Corner	BBSCORNER
Apple Utilities & Desk Accessories Forum	A2UTILITIES	Beginners' Forum	ABF
Apple Utilities & Desk Accessories Forum	AUT	Beginners' Forum	AOLBEGINNERS
Apple Utilities & Desk Accessories Forum	AVT	Beginners' Forum	BEGINNER
AppleScript SIG	APPLESCRIPT	Beginners' Forum	BEGINNERS
Applications Forum	PAP	Beginners' Forum	GETTINGSTARTED
Applications/Business Forum †	APPS	Beginners' Forum	GETTINGSTARTEDFORUM
Applications/Business Forum †	BUSINESSFORUM	Beginners' Forum	GTSF
Applications/Business/Productivity		Beginners' Forum	HELPDESK
Forum †	PRODUCTIVITY	Beginners' Forum	NEWLINK
Applications/Business/Productivity		Beginners' Forum	NLF
Forum †	PRODUCTIVITYFORUM	Beginners' Forum	PCBEGINNERS
Architects, Engineers and Construction SIG	AECSIG	Beginners' Forum	PCBG
Ares Microdevelopment, Inc.	ARES	Beginners' Forum	PCHELP
Argosy	ARGOSY	Beginners' Forum	STARTER
Ariel Publishing	ARIEL	Bentley Systems, Inc.	MSTATION
Articulate Systems	ARTICULATE	Berkeley Systems	BERKELY

Berkeley Systems	BERKSYS	Cardinal Technologies, Inc.	CARDINAL
Berkeley Systems	BERKSYSWIN	Career Center	CAREER
Berkley Macintosh Users Group	BMUG	Career Center	CAREERS
Best of America Online showcase	25REASONS	Career Development Training	TRAINING
Best of America Online showcase	BESTOFAOL	Cartoon collection	CARTOONS
Best of America Online showcase	UNIQUE	Cartoon collection	YOURTOONS
Bethesda Softworks	BETHESDA	Cartoon Network	CARTOONNETWORK
Bethesda Softworks, Inc.	BETHESDA	Casa Blanca	CASABLANCA
Better Health & Medical Forum	HEALTH	Casady & Greene	CASADY
Better Health & Medical Forum	MEDICINE	CE Software	CESOFTWARE
Beyond, Inc.	BEYOND	Celebrity Cookbook	CELEBRITYCOOKBOOK
Bicycling Magazine	BICMAG	Celebrity Cookbook	COOKBOOK
Bicycling Magazine	BICYCLING	Center Stage auditorium	AUDITORIUM
Bicycling Magazine	BICYCLINGMAGAZINE	Center Stage auditorium	CENTERSTAGE
Bicycling Magazine	MOUNTAINBIKE	Center Stage auditorium	PCAUD
Billing Information and Changes	BILL	Center Stage auditorium	SHOWS
Billing Information and Changes	BILLING	Central Point Software	CENTRAL
Billing Information and Changes	CHANGES	Central Point Software	CENTRALPOINT
Bit Jugglers	BITJUGGLERS	Central Point Software	CPS
Boardwatch Magazine	BOARDWATCH	Change your password*	CHANGEPASSWORD
Book Bestsellers area	BOOKBESTSELLERS	Change your password*	PASSWORD
Book Bestsellers area	BOOKS	CheckFree	CHECKFREE
Bose Express Music	EXPRESSMUSIC	CheckFree	CKFREE
Boston Computer Society	BCS	Chicago Online	CHICAGO
Bowers Development	APPMAKER	Chicago Online	CHICAGOONLINE
Bowers Development	BOWERS	Chicago Online	COL
Brainstorm Products	BRAINSTORM	Chicago Online Chat	COLCHAT
Broderbund	BRODERBUND	Chicago Online Classifieds	TRIBADS
Browse the PC Catalog	PCCLASSIFIEDS	Chicago Online Classifieds	TRIBCLASSIFIED
Bull Moose Tavern	BULLMOOSE	Chicago Online Education	COLEDUCATION
Bull Moose Tavern	POLITICS	Chicago Online Lifestyles	COLLIFESTYLES
Bulls and Bears Game	BULLSANDBEARS	Chicago Online Marketplace	COLMARKETPLACE
Bungie Software	BUNGIE	Chicago Online News, Business & Weather	COLNEWS
Business Forum	MACBUSINESS	Chicago Online Planner	COLPLANNER
Business Forum	MBS	Chicago Online Sports	COLSPORTS
Business News area	BUSINESS	Chicago Online Ticketmaster	TICKETMASTER
Business News area	BUSINESSNEWS	Chicago Tribune	TRIBUNE
Business News area	FINANCE	Chicago Tribune	CHICAGOTRIBUNE
Business News area	FINANCIALDISTRICT	Chicago Tribune	TRIB
Business News area	MONEY	Claris	CLARIS
Business Sense	BUSINESSSENSE	Classifieds Online	CLASSIFIED
Business Strategies	BUSINESSKNOWHOW	Classifieds Online	CLASSIFIEDS
Business Strategies	BUSINESSSTRATEGIES	Classifieds Online	CLASSIFIEDSONLINE
Byte By Byte Corporation	BYTEBYBYTE	Clubs & Interests Department	CLUBS
ByteWorks	BYTE	Clubs & Interests Department	COMMUNITYCENTER
ByteWorks	BYTEWORKS	Clubs & Interests Department	HOBBIES
C-SPAN	CSPAN	Clubs & Interests Department	INTEREST
C-SPAN	CSPANONLINE	Clubs & Interests Department	LIFESTYLES
C-SPAN Educational Services	CSPANCLASSROOM	Clubs & Interests Department	LIFESTYLES&HOBBIES
Caere Corporation	CAERE	Clubs & Interests Department	LIFESTYLES&INTEREST
Caere Corporation	CAERECORPORATION	Clubs & Interests Department	LIFESTYLES&INTERESTS
California State University	CHICO	Clubs & Interests Department	SPECIALINTERESTS
California State University	CSUC	CNN Newsroom Online	CHANNELC
Callisto Corporation	CALLISTO	CNN Newsroom Online	CNN
Cancel Account*	CANCEL	CNN Newsroom Online	CNNNEWSROOM
Car and Driver Magazine	CARANDDRIVER	CNN Newsroom Online	DEMOCRACY
Car and Driver Magazine	DRIVING	Coda Music Tech	CMT
Car and Driver Magazine	RACING	Coda Music Tech	CODA

Coda Music Tech	CODAMUSIC
College Board	CB
College Board	COLLEGE
College Board	COLLEGEBOARD
Color Weather Maps	COLORWEATHERMAPS
Color Weather Maps	WEATHERMAPS
Columnists & Features Online	COLUMNISTS
Columnists & Features Online	COLUMNS
Columnists & Features Online	FEATURES
Comedy Club and Punchlines	PUNCHLINE
Commerce Business Daily	CBD
Communications Forum	MCM
Communications Forum	MTC
Communications/Telecom/Networking Forum †	COMMUNICATIONS
Communications/Telecom/Networking Forum †	NETWORKING
Communications/Telecom/Networking Forum †	NETWORKINGFORUM
Communications/Telecom/Networking Forum †	TELECOM
Communications/Telecom/Networking Forum †	TELECOMFORUM
Communications/Telecom/Networking Forum †	TELECOMMUNICATIONS
Comp-u-Store Gateway	COMPUSTORE
Company of Science and Art	COSA
Compaq	COMPAQ
Composer's Coffeehouse	COMPOSER
Composer's Coffeehouse	COMPOSERS
Compute	COMPUTE
Computer Express	COMPUTEREXPRESS
Computer Peripherals, Inc.	COMPUTERPERIPHERALS
Computer Peripherals, Inc.	CPI
Computing Department †	C&S
Computing Department †	COMPUTING
Computing Department †	COMPUTER
Computing Department †	FORUM
Computing Department †	FORUMS
Computing Department †	PCSECURITY
Computing Department †	SIFS
Computing Department †	SIGS
Computing Department †	TECHNOLOGY
CompuToon area	COMPUTOON
CompuToon area	COMPUTOON
Connectix	CONNECTIX
Consortium for School Networking	COSN
Consumer Reports	CONSUMER
Consumer Reports	CONSUMERREPORTS
Consumer Reports	CONSUMERS
Cooking Club	COOKING
Cooking Club	FOOD
Cooking Club	KITCHEN
CoStar	COSTAR
Court TV	COURTROOMTELEVISION
Court TV	COURTTV
Cowles/SIMBA Media Information Network	COWLES
Cowles/SIMBA Media Information Network	COWLESSIMBA
Cowles/SIMBA Media Information Network	INSIDEMEDIA
Cowles/SIMBA Media Information Network	MEDIAINFORMATION
Cowles/SIMBA Media Information Network	SIMBA
Craig Crossman's Computer America	COMPUTERAMERICA
Craig Crossman's Computer America	CRAIGCROSSMAN
Craig Crossman's Computer America	CROSSMAN
Credit for connect problems*	CREDIT
Credit for connect problems*	CREDITREQUEST
Credit for connect problems*	DOWNLOADCREDIT
Critic's Choice	CRITICS
Critic's Choice	CRITICSCHOICE
CyberLaw, Cyberlex	COMPUTERLAW
CyberLaw, Cyberlex	CYBERLAW
CyberLaw, Cyberlex	CYBERLEX
DacEasy, Inc.	DACEASY
Daily calender of forum activity	TITF
Dancing Rabbit Creations	DANCINGRABBIT
Darts [Apple II only]	DARTS
Database Support SIG	DATABASE
Database Support SIG	DATABASES
DataPak Software	DATAPAK
DataTimes Sports Reports	DTSPORTS
Datawatch	DATAWATCH
Datawatch	VIREX
Davidson & Associates	DAVIDSON
Dayna Communications	DAYNA
Daystar Digital	DAYSTAR
DC Comics Online Preview	DCCOMICS
DC Comics Online Preview	DCOPREVIEW
Decision Point Forum	DECISION
Decision Point Forum	DECISIONPOINT
Decision Point Forum	DP
Decision Point Forum	DPA
Decision Point Forum	STOCKCHARTS
Decision Point Forum	STOCKTIMING
Dell Computer Corporation	DELL
Delrina Corporation	DELRINA
Delta Point	DELTAPOINT
Delta Tao	DELTATAO
Deneba Software	DENEBA
DeskMate	DES
DeskMate	DESKMATE
DeskMate	PCDESKMATE
DeskMate	PCDM
Desktop Publishing area †	DTP
Desktop Publishing area †	DESKTOPPUBLISHING
Destination Florida	FLORIDA
Destination Florida: Attractions	DFPARKS
Destination Florida: Outdoors	DFOUT
Destination Florida: Places to Stay	DFROOMS
Destination Florida: Restaurants and Nightlife	DFFOOD
Destination Florida: Shopping	DFSHOP
Destination Florida: Sports	DFSPORTS
Development Forum †	DEV
Development Forum †	DEVELOPER
Development Forum †	DEVELOPMENT
Development Forum †	DEVELOPMENTFORUM
Development Forum †	BASIC

Development Forum †	C	Econ Technologies	ECON
Development Forum †	COBOL	Edit your member profile*	EDITPROFILE
Development Forum †	PASCAL	Edit your member profile*	MEMBERPROFILE
Development Forum †	PROGRAMMING	Edit your member profile*	PROFILE
Development Forum †\	ASSEMBLY	Edmark Technologies	EDMARK
Diamond Computer Systems	DIAMOND	Edmark Technologies	KIDDESK
Dictionary of Computer Terms	COMPUTERTERMS	Edmark Technologies	PENPAL
Digital Eclipse	DIGITALECLIPSE	Education Department	EDUCATION
Digital F/X	DFX	Education Department	LEARN
Digital F/X	DIGITALF/X	Education Department	LEARNING
Digital Vision	DIGITAL	Education Department	LEARNINGCENTER
Dilbert Cartoon area	DILBERT	Education Forum	EDFORUM
Dilbert Cartoon area	DILBERTCOMICS	Electric Image	ELECTRIC
Diplomats in the Classroom	DIPLOMATS	Electric Image	ELECTRICIMAGE
Direct Software	DIRECT	Electronic Courseware	ECS
Directory of Services	DIRECTORYOFSERVICES	Electronic Courseware	ELECTRONICCOURSEWAre
Directory of Services	DIROFSERVICES	Electronic Frontier Foundation	EFF
Directory of Services	DIROFSVCS	Electronic Schoolhouse	ESH
Directory of Services	DONTMISS	Electronic Schoolhouse	SCHOOLHOUSE
Directory of Services	NOWPLAYING	Electronic University Network	EUN
Directory of Services	SERVICES	Electronic University Network	UNIVERSITIES
Directory of Services	SERVICESDIRECTORY	Electronic University Network	UNIVERSITY
DisABILITIES Forum	BLIND	Emergency Response Club	EMERGENCY
DisABILITIES Forum	DEAF	Emergency Response Club	EMERGENCYRESPONSE
DisABILITIES Forum	DIS	Emergency Response Club	ERC
DisABILITIES Forum	DISABILITIES	Emigre Fonts	EMIGRE
DisABILITIES Forum	DISABILITY	Employer Contacts	CONTACTS
DisABILITIES Forum	PHYSICALLYDISABLED	Employment Agency Database	NAPC
Discover AOL area	DISCOVER	Encyclopedia	COMPTONS
Disney /Buene Vista Software	DISNEYSOFTWARE	Encyclopedia	ENCYCLOPEDIA
Disney Adventures Magazine	DISNEY	Energy Express	EN/X
Disney Adventures Magazine	DISNEYADVENTURES	Energy Express	ENERGYEXPRESS
Disney Adventures Magazine	DISNEYMAGAZINE	Entertainment Department	ENTERTAINMENT
Disney Technologies	DIGITALTECH	Entertainment Department	GAMES
Do Something!	DOSOMETHING	Entertainment Department	RECCENTER
Dolby Audio/Video Forum	AUDIO/VIDEO	Entertainment Department	RECREATION
Dolby Audio/Video Forum	DOLBY	Entertainment Department	RECREATIONCENTER
Dolby Audio/Video Forum	DOLBYAUDIO/VIDEO	Environmental Forum	EARTH
DOS Forum	5.0	Environmental Forum	EFORUM
DOS Forum	DOS	Environmental Forum	ENVIRONMENT
DOS Forum	DOS5.0	Ethics and Religion Forum	ETHICS
DOS Forum	DOSFORUM	Ethics and Religion Forum	RELIGION
DOS Forum	DRDOS	Exam Prep Center	EXAMPREP
DOS Forum	MS-DOS	Expert Software, Inc	EXPERT
DOS Forum	MS-DOSFORUM	Expert Software, Inc	EXPERTSOFT
DOS Forum	PCUTILITIES	Expert Software, Inc	SOFTSYNC
Downloading Hall of Fame	HALLOFFAME	Express Yourself	DEBATE
Dreamworld	DREAMWORLD	Express Yourself	EXPRESSYOURSELF
Dubl-Click Software	DUBLCLICK	Farallon	FARALLON
DYA/Digisoft Innovations	DIGISOFT	Fax/Paper Mail	FAX
Dynaware USA	DYNAWARE	Fax/Paper Mail	PAPERMAIL
Dynaware USA	DYNAWAREUSA	Fax/Paper Mail	USMAIL
EAASY SABRE	AMERICANAIRLINES	Fellowship of Online Gamers/RPGA Network	
EAASY SABRE	EAASY		FELLOWSHIP
EAASY SABRE	EASSYSABRE	Fellowship of Online Gamers/RPGA Network	
EAASY SABRE	EASYSABRE		FOG
EAASY SABRE	SABRE	Fellowship of Online Gamers/RPGA Network	
EBBS	EBBS		RPGA

Fellowship of Online Gamers/RPGA Network	RPGANETWORK
Fifth Generation	5THGENERATION
Fifth Generation	FIFTH
Flight Sim Resource Center	FLIGHT
Flight Sim Resource Center	FLIGHTSIMS
Flight Sim Resource Center	FLIGHTSIMULATIONS
Flight Sim Resource Center	FSRC
Flower Shop	FLOWERSHOP
Flying Magazine	FLYING
Flying Magazine	FLYINGMAGAZINE
Focus Enhancements	FOCUS
Focus Enhancements	FOCUSENHANCEMENTS
FontBank	FONTBANK
Fractal Design	FRACTAL
Fractal Design	FRACTALDESIGN
Franklin Quest	FRANKLIN
Free online game downloading*	DOWNLOADGAMES
Free online games downloading*	GAMESDOWNLOADING
Free-Form Gaming Forum	FFGF
Free-Form Gaming Forum	RDI
FullWrite	FULLWRITE
Future Labs, Inc.	FUTURELABS
Future Labs, Inc.	TALKSHOW
Gadget Guru Electronics Forum	ELECTRONICS
Gadget Guru Electronics Forum	GADGETGURU
Game Base	GAMEBASE
Game Designers Forum	GAMEDESIGN
Game Designers Forum	GAMEDESIGNER
Game Designers Forum	GAMEDESIGNERS
Games Forum	GAMESFORUM
Games Forum †	ADVENTURE
Games Forum †	ARCADE
Games Forum †	GAMESFORUM
Games Forum †	SIMULATOR
Games Parlor	GAMEROOMS
Games Parlor	GAMESPARLOR
Games Parlor	PARLOR
Gaming Company Support	GCS
Gaming Information Exchange	GIX
Gateway 2000, Inc	GATEWAY
Gateway 2000, Inc	GATEWAY2000
Gateway 2000, Inc	MOO
Gay & Lesbian Community Forum	BI
Gay & Lesbian Community Forum	BISEXUAL
Gay & Lesbian Community Forum	GAY
Gay & Lesbian Community Forum	GLCF
Gay & Lesbian Community Forum	LAMBDA
Gay & Lesbian Community Forum	LESBIAN
GCC Technologies	GCC
Genealogy Club	GENEALOGY
Genealogy Club	GENEALOGYCLUB
Genealogy Club	ROOTS
General Magic	GENERALMAGIC
GeoWorks	GEO
GeoWorks	GEOWORKS
GIF Converter	GIFCONVERTER
Giftedness Forum	GIFTED
Giftedness Forum	MENSA
Global Software Suport	GSS
Global Village Communication	GLOBAL
Global Village Communication	GLOBALVILLAGE
Global Village Communication	TELEPORT
Golf Courses & Resort Information	GOLFCOURSES
Golf Courses & Resort Information	GOLFRESORTS
Golf Courses & Resort Information	GOLFIS
Graphic Art & CAD Forum	MACART
Graphic Forum †	ANIMATION
Graphic Simulations	GRAPHICSIMULATIONS
Graphics and Sound Forum	AMS
Graphics and Sound Forum	MIDI
Graphics and Sound Forum †	MUSIC&SOUND
Graphics and Sound Forum †	MUSICANDSOUNDFORUM
Graphics and Sound Forum †	MUSICFORUM
Graphics Forum †	ART
Graphics Forum †	CAD
Graphics Forum †	GRAPHICARTS
Graphics Forum †	GRAPHICS
Graphics Forum †	GRAPHICSFORUM
Graphisoft	GRAPHISOFT
Grateful Dead Forum	DEAD
Grateful Dead Forum	GRATEFULDEAD
Grateful Dead Forum	THEDEAD
GroupWare SIG	GROUPWARE
Gryphon Software	GRYPHON
Gryphon Software	GRYPHONSOFTWARE
Gryphon Software	MORPH
GS+ Magazine	GSMAG
Ham Radio Club	AMATEURRADIO
Ham Radio Club	HAM
Ham Radio Club	HAMRADIO
Ham Radio Club	RADIO
Ham Radio Club	SATELLITES
Hardware	SILICON
Hardware	SUPERCARD
Hardware Forum †	HARDWARE
Hardware Forum †	HARDWAREFORUM
Harvard Business School Publishing	HBSPUB
Hatrack River Town Meeting	ALVIN
Hatrack River Town Meeting	ENDER
Hatrack River Town Meeting	HATRACK
Hatrack River Town Meeting	HATRACKRIVETTOWN
Hatrack River Town Meeting	ORSONSCOTTCARD
hDC Corporation	HDC
hDC Corporation	HDCCORPORATION
Helios USA	HELIOS
Helios USA	HELIOSUSA
Heritage Foundation area	HERITAGEFOUNDATION
Hollywood Online	HOLLYWOOD
Hollywood Online	HOLLYWOODONLINE
Home Office Computing Magazine	HOMEOFFICE
Homeowner's Forum	HOME
Homeowner's Forum	HOMEOWNER
Homeowner's Forum	HOMEOWNERSFORUM
Homeowner's Forum	UHA
HomePC Magazine	HOMEPC

Hoover's Handbook of Company Profiles	COMPANY	Iomega Corporation	IOMEGA
Hoover's Handbook of Company Profiles	COMPANYPROFILES	ISIS International	ISIS
Hoover's Handbook of Company Profiles	HOOVERS	ISIS International	ISISINTERNATIONAL
Horoscopes	HOROSCOPE	Island Graphics Corporation	ISLANDGRAPHICS
Horoscopes	HOROSCOPES	Issues and Debate Forum	DEBATEFORUM
HSC Software	HCSSOFTWARE	Issues and Debate Forum	ISSUES
HSC Software	HSC	Issues and Debate Forum	ISSUESANDDEBATE
HSC Software	KPT	Issues in Mental Health	IMH
HyperCard Forum	HYPERCARD	IYM Software Review	IYM
IBM Connection	IBM	IYM Software Review	IYMSOFTWAREREVIEW
IBM Connection	PS1	JLCooper Electronics	COOPER
IBM Connection	PSL	JLCooper Electronics	JLCOOPER
IBVA Technologies	IBVA	Job Listings Database	JOBS
IBVA Technologies	PSYCHICLABS	JPEGView	JPEGVIEW
IES Registration Center	REGISTER	Kaplan Online	KAPLAN
IES Registration Center	REGISTRATION	Kaplan Online	TESTPREP
IES Registration Center	SIGNUP	Kensington Microware, Ltd.	KENSINGTON
IMPACT II: The Teachers Network	IMPACTII	Kent*Marsh	KENTMARSH
inCider	INCIDER	Kids Only Online	KIDSONLY
Industry Connection	COMPANIES	Kids Only Online	KOOL
Industry Connection	HARDWARECOMPANIES	KIDSNET	KIDSNET
Industry Connection	IC	KIDSNET Forum	EDTV
Industry Connection	INDUSTRY	KIDSNET Forum	KIDNET
Industry Connection	INDUSTRYCONNECTION	Kim Komando's Komputer Clinic	COMMANDO
Industry Connection	PUBLISHERS	Kim Komando's Komputer Clinic	KOMANDO
Industry Connection	SOFTWARECOMPANIES	Kim Komando's Komputer Clinic	KOMPUTERTUTOR
Industry Connection	SOFTWAREPUBLISHERS	Kiwi Software, Inc.	KIWI
Infocom	INFOCOM	Koala/MacVision	KOALA
Inline Design	INLINE	Koala/MacVision	MACVISION
Inline Design	INLINESOFTWARE	Kodak Photography Forum	CAMERA
Inside Technology	CARUSO	Kodak Photography Forum	KODAK
Inside Technology	INSIDETECH	Kodak Photography Forum	PHOTO
Inside Technology	INSIDETECHNOLOGY	Lapis Technologies	LAPIS
Insignia Solutions	INSIGNIA	Lapis Technologies	LAPISTECHNOLOGIES
Intel Corporation	INTEL	LaPub	LAPUB
Intel Corporation	PENTIUM	Lawrence Productions	LAWRENCE
Intellimation	INTELLIMATION	Leader Technologies	LEADER
Interactive Education Services	CAMPUS	Leader Technologies	LEADERTECH
Interactive Education Services	CLASSES	Leader Technologies	LEADERTECHNOLOGIES
Interactive Education Services	COURSES	Leading Edge	LEADINGEDGE
Interactive Education Services	IES	Legal SIG	LEGAL
Interactive Education Services	INTERACTIVEDUCATION	Legal SIG	LEGALSIG
Interactive Education Services	INTERACTIVEED	Letraset	LETRASET
InterCon Systems Corporation	INTERCON	Libertarian Party Forum	LIBERTARIAN
International Corporate Forum	ICF	Library of Congress Online	DEADSEA
International Correspondence Schools	ICS	Library of Congress Online	LIBRARY
International House	INTERNATIONAL	Library of Congress Online	LOC
Internet Center	INTERNET	Library of Congress Online	SOVARC
Internet Center	INTERNETCENTER	Library of Congress Online	SOVIET
Internet Gopher & WAIS	GOPHER	Library of Congress Online	SOVIETARCHIVES
Internet Gopher & WAIS	WAIS	Library of Congress Online	VATICAN
Internet Usenet Newsgroup area	NEWSGROUPS	Lifetime Television	LIFETIME
Internet Usenet Newsgroup area	USENET	Lifetime Television	LIFETIMETELEVISION
Interplay	INTERPLAY	Lifetime Television	LIFETIMETV
Investors Network	INVESTING	LinksWare, Inc.	LINKSWARE
Investors Network	INVESTMENTS	Local access numbers*	ACCESS
Investors Network	INVESTORS	Local access numbers*	ACCESSNUMBERS
Investors Network	INVESTORSNETWORK	Local access numbers*	NUMBERS

Local access numbers*	PETITIONS	MacroMedia, Inc.	MACROMEDIA
Local Newspapers	LOCALNEWSPAPERS	MacroMedia, Inc.	MACROMIND
Local Newspapers	NEWSPAPER	MacTech Magazine	MACTECH
Local Newspapers	NEWSPAPERS	MacTech Magazine	MACTECHMAG
LucasArts Games	LUCAS	MacTech Magazine	MACTECHMAGAZINE
LucasArts Games	LUCASARTS	Mactivity '94 Forum	MACTIVITY
Mac Communications Forum	MACCOMMUNICATION	MacWorld Expo Center	MACWORLDEXPO
Mac Communications Forum	MACCOMMUNICATIONS	MacWorld Magazine	MACWORLD
Mac Communications Forum	MACTELECOM	Mail Gateway	MAILGATEWAY
Mac Communications Forum	MACTELECOMM	Mainstay	MAINSTY
Mac Computing & Software department	MAC	Mallard Software	MALLARD
Mac Computing & Software department	MACCOMPUTING	Management Science Associates	MSA
Mac Computing & Software department	MACINTOSH	Manhattan Graphics (RSG)	MANHATTANGRAPHICS
Mac Desktop Publishing/WP Forum	MACDESKTOP	Market Master	MARKET
Mac Desktop Publishing/WP Forum	MACDTP	Market Master	MARKETMASTER
Mac Desktop Publishing/WP Forum	MACWORLDPROCESSING	Market News area	MARKETNEWS
Mac Desktop Publishing/WP Forum	MDP	Market News area	MARKETS
Mac Development Forum	MACDEVELOPMENT	Marketfield Software	MARKETFIELD
Mac Development Forum	MACPROGRAMMING	Martinsen's Software	MARTINSEN
Mac Development Forum	MDV	Massachusetts Governor's Forum	MASS
Mac Education Forum	MACEDUCATION	Massachusetts Governor's Forum	MASSACHUSETTS
Mac Education Forum	MED	MasterWord	MASTERWORD
Mac Games Forum	MACGAME	MasterWord	MW
Mac Games Forum	MACGAMES	MasterWord	MWORD
Mac Games Forum	MGM	MasterWord	WORDLIBRARY
Mac Graphic Art & CAD Forum	MACGRAPHICS	Maxis	MAXIS
Mac Graphic Art & CAD Forum	MGR	McAfee Associates	MCAFEE
Mac Hardware Forum	MACHARDWARE	MECC	MECC
Mac Hardware Forum	MHW	Member Directory	DIRECTORY
Mac HyperCard Forum	MACHYPERCARD	Member Directory	MEMBERDIRECTORY
Mac HyperCard Forum	MHC	Member Directory	MEMBERS
Mac Multimedia Forum	MACMULTIMEDIA	Members Helping Members message	
Mac Multimedia Forum	MMM	board*	MHM
Mac Music & Sound Forum	MACMUSIC	Member Services	ONLINEGUIDE
Mac Music & Sound Forum	MACSOUND	Member Services	ASKAMERICAONLINE
Mac Music & Sound Forum	MIDI	Member Services	ASKAOL
Mac Music & Sound Forum	MMS	Member Services	ASKCS
Mac Music & Sound Forum	QMMS	Member Services	CUSTOMERSERVICE
Mac Operating Systems Forum	MACO/S	Member Services	FEEDBACK
Mac Operating Systems Forum	MACOPERATINGSYSTEMS	Member Services	FREE
Mac Operating Systems Forum	MACOS	Member Services	HELP
Mac Operating Systems Forum	MOS	Member Services	HOTLINE
Mac Operating Systems Forum	SYSTEM7	Member Services	INFORMATION
Mac Operating Systems Forum	SYSTEM7.0	Member Services	MANUAL
Mac Operating Systems Forum	SYSTEM7.1	Member Services	MEMBERSGUIDE
Mac Operating Systems Forum	SYSTEM71	Member Services	MEMBERSONLINEGUIDE
Mac Shareware 500	MAC500	Member Services	MOG
Mac Shareware 500	SHAREWARE500	Member Services	SERVICE
Mac Shareware 500	VENTANA	Member Services	SUPPORT
Mac Shareware 500	VENTANA500	Member Services	SYSOP
Mac Software Center	MACLIBRARIES	Mercury Center	MERCURY
Mac Software Center	MACSOFTWARE	Mercury Center	MERCURYCENTER
Mac Utilities Forum	MACUTILITIES	Mercury Center	SANJOSE
Mac Utilities Forum	MUT	Mercury Center Advertising	MCCLASSIFIEDS
Mac Utilities Forum	MVT	Mercury Center Advertising	MCMARKET
MacApp Developers Association	MADA	Mercury Center Bay Area Living area	MCLIVING
MacHome Journal	MACHOME	Mercury Center Business & Technology area	MCBUSINESS
MacHome Journal	MACHOMEJOURNAL	Mercury Center Conference area	MCTALK

Mercury Center Entertainment area	MCENTERTAINMENT	Mustang Software	QMODEM
Mercury Center In the News area	INTHENEWS	Mustang Software	WILDCAT
Mercury Center In the News area	MCNEW	Mustang Software	WILDCATBBS
Mercury Center In the News area	MCNEWS	Nat'l Council of Teachers of English	ENGLISH
Mercury Center Newspaper Library	MCLIBRARY	Nat'l Council of Teachers of English	NCTE
Mercury Center Sports area	MCSPORTS	Nation Gay & Lesbian Task Force	NGLTF
Meridian Data	MERIDIAN	National Alliance of Mentally Ill	NAMI
Metrowerks	METROWERKS	National Association of Quick Printers area	NAQP
Metz	METZ	National Association of Quick Printers area	QUICKPRINTERS
Michigan Governor's Forum	MICHIGAN	National Education Association	NEAONLINE
Michigan Governor's Forum	MICHIGANGOVERNOR	National Education Association	NEAPUBLIC
Micro Dynamics, Ltd.	MICRODYNAMICS	National Geographic Online	GEOGRAPHIC
Micro J Systems, Inc	MICROJ	National Geographic Online	NATIONALGEOGRAPHIC
MicroFrontier, Ltd.	MICROFRONTIER	National Geographic Online	NGS
Micrografx, Inc.	MGX	National Multiple Sclerosis Society	NMSS
Micrografx, Inc.	MICROGRAFX	National Museum of American Art	NMAA
MicroMat Computer Systems	MICROMAT	National Principals Center	NAESP
MicroProse	MICROPROSE	National Principals Center	PRINCIPALS
Microseeds Publishing, Inc.	MICROSEEDS	National Public Radio Outreach	NPR
Microsoft Knowledge Base	KNOWLEDGEBASE	National Public Radio Outreach	PUBLICRADIO
Microsoft Knowledge Base	MSKB	National Public Radio Outreach	TOTN
Microsoft Product Support	MSFORUM	National Space Society	NSS
Microsoft Resource Center	MICROSOFT	National Space Society	SPACE
Microsoft Resource Center	MSSUPPORT	National Staff Development Council	NSDC
Mike Keefe Cartoons	KEEFE	NBC Online	NBC
Military and Vets Club	MILITARY	NEC Technologies	NEC
Military and Vets Club	VETERANS	NEC Technologies	NECTECH
Military and Vets Club	VETS	NeoLogic	NEOLOGIC
Military and Vets Club	VETSCLUB	Network Earth	EARTH
Military City Online	MC	Network Earth	NETWORKEARTH
Military City Online	MCO	New Features & Services showcase	NEW
Military City Online	MILITARYCITYONLINE	New Mail Information area*	NEWMAIL
Mirror Technologies	MIRROR	New World Computing	NEWWORLD
Mobile Office Online	MOBILE	Newsbytes	NEWSBYTES
Mobile Office Online	PORTABLE	Nikon Electronic Imaging	NIKON
Mobile Office Online	PORTABLECOMPUTING	Niles and Associates	ENDNOTE
Modem Help area* [PC platform only]	MODEMHELP	Niles and Associates	NILES
Montessori Schools	MONTESSORI	No Hands Software	NOHANDS
MoraffWare	MORAFFWARE	Nomadic Computing Discussion SIG	NOMADIC
Morningstar Mutual Funds	FUND	Novell Desktop Systems	DIGITALRESEARCH
Morningstar Mutual Funds	FUNDS	Novell Desktop Systems	DIGITALRESEARCHINC
Morningstar Mutual Funds	MORNINGSTAR	Novell Desktop Systems	DRI
Morningstar Mutual Funds	MUTUALFUND	Novell Desktop Systems	NOVELL
Morningstar Mutual Funds	MUTUALFUNDS	Now Software	NOW
Movies menu	MOVIEREVIEWS	Object Factory	OBJECTFACTORY
Movies menu	MOVIES	Odeon Auditorium	ODEON
Movies menu	MOVIES	Olduvai Software, Inc.	OLDUVAI
MS-DOS 6.0 Resource Center	DOS6	OMNI Magazine Online	OMNI
MS-DOS 6.0 Resource Center	DOS60	OMNI Magazine Online	OMNIMAGAZINE
MS-DOS 6.0 Resource Center	MSDOS6	ON Technology	ON
MS-DOS 6.0 Resource Center	MSDOS60	Online Bookstore	BOOKSTORE
MTV Online	MTV	Online Bookstore	ONLINEBOOKSTORE
Multimedia World Online		Online Bookstore	READUSA
[PC platform only]	MMW	Online Gaming Forums	GAMING
Multimedia World Online		Online Gaming Forums	GUILD
[PC platform only]	MMWORLD	Online Gaming Forums	OGF
Mustang Software	MUSTANG	Online Gaming Forums	ONLINEGAMING
Mustang Software	MUSTANGSOFTWARE	Online Gaming Forums	PHANTASYGUILD

Online Shorthands	SHORTHAND	PC Novice & PC Today Online	PCNOVICE
Online Shorthands	SHORTHANDS	PC Novice & PC Today Online	PCTODAY
OnLine Tonight	OLT	PC Software Center	PCLIBRARIES
OnLine Tonight	ONLINETONIGHT	PC Software Center	PCSOFTWARE
Onyx Technology	ONYX	PC Software Center	PCSOFTWARE
Opcode Systems, Inc.	OPCODE	PC Software Center	PCSW
Opcode Systems, Inc.	OPCODESYSTEMS	PC Studio	PCSTUDIO
OptImage Interactive Services	OPTIMAGE	PC Telecom/Networking Forum	PCM
OPTIMAS Corporation	BIOSCAN	PC Telecom/Networking Forum	PCTELECOM
OPTIMAS Corporation	OPTIMAS	PC Telecom/Networking Forum	PCTELECOMFORUM
Origin Systems	ORIGIN	PC Telecom/Networking Forum	PTC
Origin Systems	ORIGINSYSTEMS	PCWorld Online	PCWONLINE
OS/2 Forum	IBMOS2	PCWorld Online	PCWORLD
OS/2 Forum	OS2	PCWorld Online	PCWORLDONLINE
OS/2 Forum	OSTWO	Peachtree Software	PEACHTREE
Otter Solution	OTTER	Penny Wise Office Products Store	OFFICE
Otter Solution	OTTERSOLUTION	Penny Wise Office Products Store	OFFICEPRODUCTS
PaceMark Technologies, Inc.	PACEMARK	Penny Wise Office Products Store	PENNY
Packer Software	PACKER	Penny Wise Office Products Store	PENNYWISE
Page a Guide	GUIDEPAGE	People Connection	CHAT
Page a Guide	GUIDEPAGER	People Connection	PC
Palm Computing	PALM	People Connection	PEOPLE
Palm Computing	PALMCOMPUTING	People Connection	PEOPLECONNECTION
Papyrus	PAPYRUS	People Connection	TALK
Parental Controls	PARENTALCONTROL	Personal Computer Peripherals	PCPC
Parents' Information Network	PARENT	Personal Digital Assistant's Forum	NEWTON
Parents' Information Network	PIN	Personal Digital Assistant's Forum	PDA
Passport Designs	PASSPORT	Personal Digital Assistants Forum	MESSAGEPAD
PC Applications Forum	PCAPPLICATIONS	Personal Digital Assistants Forum	PALMTOP
PC Applications Forum	PCAPPLICATIONSFORUM	Personal Finance Department	PERSONALFINANCE
PC Applications Forum	PCAPS	Personal Finance Department	PF
PC Catalog	PCCATALOG	Pet Care Club	PET
PC Catalog	PCCATALOG	Pet Care Club	PETCARE
PC Catalog	PCCLASSIFIEDS	Pet Care Club	PETS
PC Computing & Software department	PCFORUMS	Photography Area	PHOTOGRAPHY
PC Development Forum	PCDEV	Photoshop SIG	PHOTOSHOP
PC Development Forum	PCDEVELOPMENT	Photoshop SIG	PHOTOSHOPSIG
PC Development Forum	PCDEVELOPMENTFORUM	Pictures of the World	PICTURES
PC Development Forum	PDV	Pixar	PIXAR
PC Games Forum	PCGAMES	Pixar	RENDERMAN
PC Games Forum	PCGAMESFORUM	Pixel Resources	PIXEL
PC Games Forum	PGM	Pixel Resources	PIXELRESOURCES
PC Graphics Forum	PCANIMATION	Play-By-Mail & Strategy Gaming Forum	CHESS
PC Graphics Forum	PCGRAPHICS	Play-By-Mail & Strategy Gaming Forum	PBM
PC Graphics Forum	PCGRAPHICSFORUM	Play-By-Mail & Strategy Gaming Forum	PLAY-BY-MAIL
PC Graphics Forum	PGR	Play-By-Mail & Strategy Gaming Forum	STRATEGY
PC Hardware Forum	PCHARDWARE	Playmation	PLAYMATION
PC Hardware Forum	PCHARDWAREFORUM	Popular Photography Online	CAMERAS
PC Hardware Forum	PHW	Popular Photography Online	PHOTOS
PC Multimedia Forum	PMM	Popular Photography Online	POPPHOTO
PC Music and Sound Forum	MIDI	Popular Photography Online	POPULARPHOTOGRAPHY
PC Music and Sound Forum	PCMU	Portfolio Systems, Inc.	DYNO
PC Music and Sound Forum	PCMUSIC	Portfolio Systems, Inc.	PORTFOLIOSOFTWARE
PC Music and Sound Forum	PCMUSICANDSOUNDFORUM	Portrait Gallery	GALLERY
PC Music and Sound Forum	PCMUSICFORUM	Power Mac Resource Center	POWERMAC
PC Music and Sound Forum	PCSOUND	Power Mac Resource Center	POWERPC
PC Music and Sound Forum	PCSOUNDFORUM	Power Up Software	POWERUP
PC Music and Sound Forum	PMU	PowerBook Resouce Center	POWERBOOK

Practical Peripherals, Inc.	PPI	Romance Connection message boards	ROMANCE
Practical Peripherals, Inc.	PRACTICALPERIPHERALS	Ross Perot/United We Stand area	HROSSPEROT
PrairieSoft, Inc.	PRAIRIESOFT	Ross Perot/United We Stand area	PEROT
Prodigy Refugees Forum	PRODIGYFORUM	Ross Perot/United We Stand area	ROSSPEROT
Prodigy Refugees Forum	PRODIGYREFUGEES	Rotunda Forum Auditorium	FORUMAUD
Prodigy Refugees' Forum	PRODIGY	Rotunda Forum Auditorium	FORUMAUDITORIUM
Programmer University	PROGRAMMERU	Rotunda Forum Auditorium	FORUMROT
Programmer University	PU	Rotunda Forum Auditorium	ROTUNDA
Prograph International, Inc.	PROGRAPH	Rotunda Forum Auditorium	STUMP
Prograph International, Inc.	TGS	Salient Software	SALIENT
ProVUE Development	PROVUE	Saturday Review Online	LITERATURE
Psion	PSION	Saturday Review Online	READING
Qualitas	QUALITAS	Saturday Review Online	SATREVIEW
Quark, Inc.	QUARK	Saturday Review Online	SATURDAYREVIEW
RabbitJack's Casino	CASINO	Saturday Review Online	SOCEITY
RabbitJack's Casino	RABBITJACKSCASINO	Saturday Review Online	SRO
Radius, Inc.	RADIUS	Saturday Review Online	THEATER
RasterOps	RASTEROPS	Saturday Review Online	THEATRE
Ray Dream	RAY	Scholastic Network/Scholastic Forum	SCHOLASTIC
Ray Dream	RAYDREAM	Science Fiction Forum	ANALOG
Reactor	REACTOR	Science Fiction Forum	ASIMOV
Real Estate Online	ARM	Science Fiction Forum	SCI-FI
Real Estate Online	HOMEEQUITYLOAN	Science Fiction Forum	SCIENCEFICTION
Real Estate Online	HOMEREFINANCING	Science Fiction Forum	SCIFI
Real Estate Online	MLS	Science Fiction Forum	SF
Real Estate Online	MORTAGE	Scouting Forum	SCOUTING
Real Estate Online	MORTAGERATES	Scouting Forum	SCOUTS
Real Estate Online	MORTGAGES	Scuba Club	GOSCUBA
Real Estate Online	REALESTATE	Scuba Club	SCUBA
Redate/IIN Online	IIN	Search database of files	FILESEARCH
Redgate Online > PC Expo area	PCEXPO	Search database of files †	QUICKFIND
Redgate/IIN Online	REDGATE	Search database of files †	QUICKFINDER
Reference Desk	REFERENCE	Search Help Wanted	HELPWANTED
Reference Desk	REFERENCEDESK	Search News Articles	NEWSSEARCH
Relgion & Ethics Forum	NEWAGE	Search News Articles	NEWSWATCH
Religion & Ethics Forum	BUDDHISM	SeniorNet	SENIOR
Religion & Ethics Forum	CHRISTIAN	Serius	SERIUS
Religion & Ethics Forum	CHRISTIANS	Shareware Solutions	SHAREWARESOLUTIONS
Religion & Ethics Forum	ISLAM	Shiva Corporation	SHIVA
Religion & Ethics Forum	JUDAISM	Sierra On-Line	SIERRA
Religion & Ethics Forum	PAGAN	Sign on a friend to AOL*	FRIEND
Reset Department menu to initial		Ski Reports	SKI
department [Apple II users only]*	MAIN	Ski Reports	SKICONDITIONS
ResNova Software		Ski Reports	SKIREPORTS
(RESNOVASOFTWARE)	RESNOVA	Ski Reports	SKIWEATHER
Road & Track Magazine	AUTOS	Smithsonian Online	SI
Road & Track Magazine	CARS	Smithsonian Online	SMITHSONIAN
Road & Track Magazine	ROAD	Soap Opera Summaries	TELEVISION
Road & Track Magazine	ROADANDTRACK	SoftArc	SOFTARC
Rockland Software	ROCKLAND	Softdisk Superstore [PC platform only]	SOFTDISK
Rockland Software	ROCKLANDSOFTWARE	Software Center †	DOWNLOAD
Rocklink	MUSIC	Software Center †	DOWNLOADING
Rocklink	ROCK	Software Center †	LIBRARIES
Rocklink	ROCKLINK	Software Center †	LIBS
Roger Wagner Publishing	ROGERWAGNER	Software Center †	SOFT
Role-Playing Forum	ROLEPLAYING	Software Center †	SOFTWARE
Role-Playing Forum	RPG	Software Center †	SOFTWARECENTER
Romance Connection message boards	DATING	Software Center †	SOFTWAREDIRECTORY

Software Center †	SOFTWAREHELP	Tandy Headquarters	TANDYHANDQUARTERS
Software Center †	SOFTWARELIBRARIES	Tandy Headquarters	TANDYHQ
Software Center †	SOFTWARELIBRARY	Tax Forum	GOTAX
Software Creations	SOFTWARECREATIONS	Tax Forum [seasonal]	TAX
Software Creations	SWC	Tax Forum [seasonal]	TAXES
Software Toolworks	SOFTWARETOOLWORKS	Teacher Pager	TEACHERPAGER
Software Toolworks	TOOLWORKS	Teachers' Forum	TTALK
Sol III Play-by-Email Game	SOLIII	Teachers' Information Network	TEACHER
Sophisticated Circuits	SOPHCIR	Teachers' Information Network	TEACHERS
Spectrum HoloByte	SPECTRUM	Teachers' Information Network	TIN
Specular International	SPECULAR	Teachers' Newsstand	TNEWS
Sport News area	GOLF	Teachers' University	TEACHERU
Sport News area	SPORTS	Tech Help Live*	CSLIVE
Sport News area	SPORTSLINK	Tech Help Live*	TECHHELPLIVE
Sport News area	SPORTSNEWS	Technology Works	TECHNOLOGYWORKS
SSSi	SSSI	Technology Works	TECHWORKS
STAC Electronics	STAC	Teen Scene message boards	TEEN
Star Trek Club	STARTREK	Teen Scene message boards	TEENS
Star Trek Club	TREK	Teen Scene message boards	TEENSCENE
Starfleet Academy	ACADEMY	Teknosys Works	TEKNOSYS
Stereo Review Online magazine	AUDIO	Telescan Users Group Forum	TELESCAN
Stereo Review Online magazine	HOMETHEATER	Television	TV
Stereo Review Online magazine	STEREO	TERC LabNet	LABNET
Stereo Review Online magazine	STEREOREVIEW	Terms of Service*	TERMS
STF Technologies	STF	Terms of Service*	TERMSOFSERVICE
STF Technologies	STFTECHNOLOGIES	Terms of Service*	TOS
Stock Market Timing & Charts area	QUOTE	Terms of Service*	TOSADVISOR
Stock Market Timing & Charts area	QUOTES	Texas Instrument	TEXASINSTRUMENTS
Stock Market Timing & Charts area	STOCK	Texas Instrument	TI
Stock Market Timing & Charts area	STOCKLINK	The Atlantic Monthly Online	ATLANTIC
Stock Market Timing & Charts area	STOCKQUOTES	The Atlantic Monthly Online	ATLANTICMONTHLY
Stock Market Timing & Charts area	STOCKS	The Atlantic Monthly Online	ATLANTICONLINE
Strata, Inc.	STRATA	The Bicycle Network	BFA
Strategic Simulations	SSI	The Bicycle Network	BICYCLE
Strategic Simulations	STRATEGIC	The Bicycle Network	BIKENET
Student Access Online	PRINCETONREVIEW	The Exchange	AFRICANAMERICAN
Student Access Online	STUDENT	The Exchange	AMERICANINDIAN
Student Access Online	STUDENTACCESS	The Exchange	ASIAN
Study Skills Service	STUDY	The Exchange	BOATING
Study Skills Service	STUDYSKILLS	The Exchange	COINS
Substance Abuse Forum	PREVENTION	The Exchange	COLLECTING
Substance Abuse Forum	SUBSTANCEABUSE	The Exchange	CRAFTS
Suggestion boxes*	SUGGESTION	The Exchange	EXCHANGE
Suggestion boxes*	SUGGESTIONS	The Exchange	GARDENING
SuperMac	SUPERMAC	The Exchange	HISPANIC
Survivor Software	SURVIVOR	The Exchange	MEN
Survivor Software	SURVIVORSOFTWARE	The Exchange	OUTDOORS
Symantec	NORTON	The Exchange	RAILROADING
Symantec	PETERNORTON	The Exchange	STAMPS
Symantec	SYMANTEC	The Exchange	THEEXCHANGE
Synex	SYNEX	The Exchange	WOMEN
SYS Language Systems	LANGUAGESYS	The Geraldo Show	GERALDO
T/Maker	TMAKER	The Geraldo Show	GERALDOSHOW
Tactic Software	NEWERA	The Grandstand	AUTORACING
Tactic Software	TACTIC	The Grandstand	BASEBALL
Talent Bank	TALENT	The Grandstand	BASKETBALL
Tandy Headquarters	PCHQ	The Grandstand	BOXING
Tandy Headquarters	TANDY	The Grandstand	FANTASYFOOTBALL

The Grandstand	FANTASYLEAGUES	Tomorrow's Morning newspaper	TOMORROWSMORNING
The Grandstand	FOOTBALL	Top News area	HEADLINES
The Grandstand	GFL	Top News area	NEWSLINK
The Grandstand	GRANDSTAND	Top News area	NEWSTEXT
The Grandstand	HOCKEY	Top News area	OURWORLD
The Grandstand	HORSERACING	Top News area	TOPNEWS
The Grandstand	TENNIS	Travel Department	TRAVEL
The Improv Forum	IMPROV	Travel Forum	TRAVELER
The Improv Forum	IMPROVCLUB	Travel Forum	TRAVELFORUM
The Improv Forum	IMPROVCLUBS	Travel Holiday Magazine	TRAVELHOLIDAY
The Improv Forum	IMPROVFORUM	Traveler's Corner	TRAVELERSCORNER
The Macintosh Bible/Peachpit Forum	MACBIBLE	Traveler's Corner	WEISSMANN
The Macintosh Bible/Peachpit Forum	MACINTOSHBIBLE	Trivia Club	TRIVIA
The Macintosh Bible/Peachpit Forum	PEACHPIT	True Image Audio	MACSPEAKERZ
The Marketplace	MALL	True Image Audio	TIA
The Marketplace	SHOPPING	True Image Audio	TRUEIMAGEAUDIO
The Marketplace	STORE	Tseng	TSENG
The Marketplace	STORES	Tune Up Your PC	AUTOEXEC
The Marketplace	THEMALL	Tune Up Your PC	CONFIG
The Michael Reagan Show Online	MICHAELREAGAN	Tune Up Your PC	TUNEUP
The Michael Reagan Show Online	MICHAELREAGANSHOW	Tune Up Your PC	TUNEUPYOURPC
The Michael Reagan Show Online	REAGAN	TV Gossip	TVGOSSIP
The Multimedia Exchange	MULTIMEDIA	U.S. & World News area	USNEWS
The National Parenting Center	TNPC	U.S. & World News area	WORLDNEWS
The New Republic Magazine	NEWREPUBLIC	United Cerebral Palsy Association, Inc.	UCPA
The New Republic Magazine	THENEWREPUBLIC	University of San Francisco	USF
The New Republic Magazine	TNR	Unlimited Adventures	UA
The Newsstand	MAGAZINES	Unlimited Adventures	UNLIMITEDADVENTURES
The Newsstand	NEWSSTAND	Upgrade to the latest version of AOL*	UPGRADE
The Nightly Business Report	NBR	USA Today Industry Watch section	CAREERNEWS
The Nightly Business Report	NBRREPORT	User Group Forum	AUG
The Quantum Que and Graffiti		User Group Forum	UGC
community message boards	QUE	User Group Forum	UGF
The Ricki Lake Show	RICKILAKE	User Group Forum	USERGROUP
The Sci-Fi Channel	SCIFICHANNEL	User Group Forum	USERGROUPS
The Voyager Company	VOYAGER	Userland	USERLAND
Three-Sixty Software	THREESIXTY	Utah Forum	UTAH
Thrustmaster	THRUSTMASTER	Utah Forum	UTAHFORUM
Thunderware	THUNDERWARE	Vertisoft	VERTISOFT
Ticketmaster	TICKET	Viacom New Media	ICOM
TIGERDirect, Inc.	BLOCDEVELOPMENT	Viacom New Media	ICOMSIMULATIONS
TIGERDirect, Inc.	TIGER	Viacom New Media	VIACOM
TIGERDirect, Inc.	TIGERDIRECT	Video Games area	NINTENDO
Time Magazine Online	TIME	Video Games area	SEGA
Time of day and length of time online	CLOCK	Video Games area	VIDEOGAMES
Timeslips Corporation	TIMESLIPS	Video SIG	VIDEOSIG
Timeworks	TIMEWORKS	Videodiscovery	VDISC
TMS TV Source	LISTINGS	Videodiscovery	VIDEODISC
TMS TV Source	TMS	Videodiscovery	VIDEODISCOVERY
TMS TV Source	TVGUIDE	VIDI	VIDI
TMS TV Source	TVLISTINGS	Viewpoint DataLabs	VIEWPOINT
TMS TV Source	TVSOURCE	Virtual Reality Labs, Inc.	VRLI
Today's News	NEWS	Virtual Reality Resource Center	VIRTUALREALITY
Today's News	NEWS&FINANCE	Virtual Reality Resource Center	VR
Today's News	NEWS/SPORTS/MONEY	Virtus Walkthrough	VIRTUS
Today's News	NEWSANDFINANCE	Virtus Walkthrough	WALKTHROUGH
Today's News	NEWSROOM	Virus Information Center SIG	VIRUS
Tomorrow's Morning newspaper	TOMORROW	Visionary Software	VISIONARY

Voyetra Technologies	VOYETRA
Wall Street SOS Forum	SOS
Warner/Reprise Records Online	REPRISE
Warner/Reprise Records Online	WARNER
Warner/Reprise Records Online	WARNERMUSIC
Washington Week in Review magazine	WWIR
Weather	WEATHER
Weekly calendar of forum activity	CONFERENCE
Weekly calendar of forum activity	CONFERENCECENTER
Weigand Report	WEIGAND
Westwood Studios	WESTWOOD
Westwood Studios	WESTWOODSTUDIOS
What's Hot This Month showcase	HOT
What's Hot This Month showcase	WHATSHOT
White House Forum	CLINTON
White House Forum	THEWHITEHOUSE
White House Forum	WHITEHOUSE
Wilson Windowware	WINDOWWARE
Wilson Windowware	WWW
Windows Forum	WIN
Windows Forum	WINDOWS
Windows Forum	WINDOWSFORUM
Windows Forum	WINFORUM
Windows Magazine	WINDOWSMAG
Windows Magazine	WINDOWSMAGAZINE
Windows Magazine	WINMAG
Windows News area	WINNEWS
Windows Shareware 500	WIN500
Windows Shareware 500	WINDOWS500
Wine & Dine Online	BEER
Wine & Dine Online	BREW
Wine & Dine Online	BREWING
Wine & Dine Online	DINE
Wine & Dine Online	HOMEBREW
Wine & Dine Online	HOMEBREWING
Wine & Dine Online	RESTAURANT
Wine & Dine Online	RESTAURANTS
Wine & Dine Online	WINE
Wine & Dine Online	WINE&DINEONLINE
Wine & Dine Online	WINERIES
Wired Magazine	WIRED
Woodstock Online	WOODSTOCK
WordPerfect Magazine	WPMAG
WordPerfect Support Center	WORDPERFECT
Working Software	WORKING
Worth Magazine Online	WORTH
Worth Magazine Online	WORTHMAGAZINE
Worth Magazine Online	WORTHONLINE
Worth Magazine Online Portfolio	WORTHPORTFOLIO
Writer's Club	WRITER'S
Writer's Club	WRITERS
Writers' Market Forum	WRITERSMARKET
Xceed Technology	XCEED
Xceed Technology	MICRON
Xoas Tools	XAOS
Xoas Tools	XAOSTOOLS
Your Money area	YOURMONEY
Your Stock Portfolio	PORTFOLIO
Your Stock Portfolio	STOCKPORTFOLIO
Zedcor, Inc.	ZEDCOR

APPENDIX B
Command Keys

Many of America Online's most frequently used commands have Command-key combinations that you can use instead of using the standard pull-down menus. Many people prefer command keys because they are faster than using pull-down menus, and they can be executed without using the mouse, a big plus if you do a lot of typing.

You can press a Command-key combination from anywhere within the America Online application to perform a command without using the mouse.

Remember, you can press Command-period at any time to cancel a long listing, a print job or most other time-consuming activities that you may not want to wait through while you're online.

The Command key is the located next to the Spacebar and is designated by either the familiar Apple logo or the cloverleaf symbol, or perhaps both, depending on which model of Mac and keyboard you own. To execute any of the commands listed below, you should press and hold the Command key, and then (without releasing the Command key) press the appropriate letter key. You don't need to press the Shift key, even though the letters are shown here in uppercase.

Sorted by Menu Command

Help	⌘ - /
File New Memo	⌘ - N
File Open	⌘ - O
File Close	⌘ - W
File Save	⌘ - S
File Print	⌘ - P
File Quit	⌘ - Q
Edit Undo	⌘ - Z
Edit Cut	⌘ - X
Edit Copy	⌘ - C
Edit Paste	⌘ - V
Edit Select All	⌘ - A
Go To Keyword	⌘ - K

Go To Lobby	⌘ - L
Go To Favorite Places	⌘ - 1 through ⌘ - 9
Mail Compose Mail	⌘ - M
Mail Read New Mail	⌘ - R
Members Send Instant Message	⌘ - I
Members Get a Member's Profile	⌘ - G
Members Locate a Member Online	⌘ - F

Sorted by Command-Key Combination

⌘ - /	Help
⌘ - 1 through ⌘ - 9	Go To Favorite Places
⌘ - A	Edit Select All
⌘ - C	Edit Copy
⌘ - D	Edit Duplicate
⌘ - F	Members Locate a Member Online
⌘ - G	Members Get a Member's Profile
⌘ - I	Members Send Instant Message
⌘ - K	Go To Keyword
⌘ - L	Go To Lobby
⌘ - M	Mail Compose Mail
⌘ - N	File New Memo
⌘ - O	File Open
⌘ - P	File Print
⌘ - Q	File Quit
⌘ - R	Mail Read New Mail
⌘ - S	File Save
⌘ - V	Edit Paste
⌘ - W	File Close
⌘ - X	Edit Cut
⌘ - Z	Edit Undo

APPENDIX C
Modems, Localities & CCL Files

America Online's custom software is not only user-friendly, it's also modem-friendly. The first time you sign on to America Online, the software asks you several questions as part of the initial installation process. Your answers determine such things as modem speed and type, local access telephone numbers to use and so on. This information automatically configures your America Online software to connect effortlessly. However, you may need to modify this information: for example, if you change your location, upgrade your modem, or discover that your non-standard modem needs special configuration. This appendix will show you how to create and save multiple setups and how to modify your configuration. Modem files and CCL scripts as they relate to successful America Online connection are also covered.

Localities

Your America Online software allows you to create and store multiple sets of modem setup and connection information. These sets of information are called "Localities," and while they are handy for folks who move from location to location, they are also very useful for those who like to stay put. You can store configurations for different connection speeds as well as access numbers for various locations.

Think of localities as coats. If you live in a temperate region of the country, you may only own one light windbreaker. On the other hand, if you call a more diverse climate your home, you may collect an entire wardrobe of coats for any weather condition. Localities are no different: they allow you to successfully step out into the world of America Online, regardless of where you are or what modem you are using. Best of all, creating and choosing your locality before signing on is easier than purchasing and deciding which coat to wear.

New localities are simple to create. Launch the America Online software and instead of signing on as you normally would, choose New from the File menu and select Locality from the submenu to the right. In the new, untitled Connection Settings window that appears, enter your setup information (described below in "Changing Your Setup"). When you're finished, save your new locality by clicking the Save button in the lower right-hand corner of the window. When you're prompted to name the locality, choose a title that reflects the function of the new information, such as "Ann Arbor" (for a different location) or "9600 Access" (for a different connection speed). To use the locality you've just created, click the Locality pop-up menu in your Sign On window and select it. The next time you sign on, your software will use the setup information in the chosen locality.

Changing Your Setup

To create or modify localities, you need to change your setup options. Creation is simple, as described earlier in this appendix. To modify a locality, click the Setup button in the Welcome window, then choose the locality you wish to alter from the Network and Modem Setup list. Finally, click the Setup button at the bottom of the Sign On window (see Figure C-1). In either creation or modification, your software displays a window titled "Connection Settings" with a number of options. Be sure to make a note of your current settings in case you need to return to them. You can use this screen to change any of a number of options, all described below.

Figure C-1: Working off-line, click the Setup button in the Sign On window to access your setup information.

Home – 9600

Connection Settings

First Try	**Second Try**
Connection File: SprintNet ▼	Connection File: SprintNet ▼
Connection Speed: 9600 bps ▼	Connection Speed: 2400 bps ▼
Phone Number: 295-0337	Phone Number: 241-0496
☐ To reach outside line, dial 9,	☐ To reach outside line, dial 9,
☐ To disable call waiting, dial 1170,	☐ To disable call waiting, dial 1170,
☒ TouchTone	☒ TouchTone
☐ Hardware Handshaking	☐ Hardware Handshaking
Connection Port: Modem Port ▼	Connection Port: Modem Port ▼
Modem Type: Intel 14.4 EX ▼	Modem Type: Intel 14.4 EX ▼

[Help]   [Cancel]   [Save]

Connection File

This pop-up menu is used to select which phone carrier handles your calls from the local access node to America Online's host computer. SprintNet is the most widely used carrier for America Online in the US; Datapac is used in Canada. You can use the Connection File pop-up menu to select the appropriate network as specified for your access number. (The keyword Access—available only when you're online—lists all of AOL's access numbers.)

Connection Speed

You'll most likely need to change only this if you get a new modem with a speed different than your usual modem, or if you're currently using a local access node that doesn't take full advantage of your modem's speed capabilities. For instance, you may use a local access number that can only handle 2400 baud. But if you later switch to a different number that can serve 9600 baud modems and you have a 9600 baud modem, you need to change the baud rate setting that your America Online software uses. Use the Connection Speed pop-up menu to set the baud rate to the highest speed your modem and node can handle.

Phone Numbers

The First Try and Second Try fields contain the phone numbers your America Online software uses to connect with the host computer. The Second Try number is used only if the First Try number is busy or does not respond properly. You will need to change these numbers if you're moving to a new area, if you're traveling or if you want to try a different local access number.

You can find local access numbers for America Online by using the keyword: Access. If there is only one number for an area, use that as both your First and Second Try numbers to allow for automatic redialing should the number be busy the first try. If you don't want to dial a second number, leave the Second Try number blank.

Tip: If you use a 9600-baud number for your First Try, list a slower (probably 2400 baud) number for your Second Try. High-speed access is occasionally capricious; 2400-baud access is not.

Another tip: In some areas you may need to dial an area code, even for a local call. If you normally need to do this when you place voice calls, you will need to do it for America Online access as well.

Note: Remember, any long-distance charges you incur reaching the America Online access number are your responsibility. They're not included as a part of your monthly America Online fee. If you have to dial the number 1 before you can reach AOL's nearest access number, you're no doubt incurring long-distance charges.

Outside Line Prefix

Some telephone systems, particularly those in hotels, offices and schools, require that you dial a "9" or other prefix to get an outside line. To enable the outside line prefix, click the check box. Enter the number you want America Online to dial; then enter a comma. The comma tells the modem to wait two seconds before dialing the next number. If it takes longer than two seconds for your phone system to access an outside line and generate a dial tone, you might want to add a second comma just to be sure.

Disable Call Waiting

When you're connected to America Online and someone tries to call you, he or she would normally get a busy signal. If you have Call Waiting, however, the caller hears a normal ring and your modem hears the beep that normally lets you know you've got a call waiting. As you can imagine, this tends to confuse your Mac (not to mention the AOL host computer). That which is a convenience for voice communications is an interference for telecommunications and will cause your modem to disconnect from America Online. To configure your software to turn off Call Waiting whenever you dial America Online (but not any other time), all you have to do is click this check box. If you use Call Waiting, you can (and should) temporarily disable it on most phone systems by entering a code such as "1170," or "*70," before dialing America Online. Be sure to include the comma after the string of numbers: it tells the modem to wait two seconds before dialing the next number. Note that the America Online software has already entered "1170," for you in the Disable Call Waiting field. If you aren't sure what numbers you should enter to disable Call Waiting, check with your local telephone company or look in the front section of your local phone book, under Call Waiting.

TouchTone

Touch-tone phones are standard equipment today in homes and hotels. However, there are still a few local phone exchanges (or homes) that do not support tone-dialing. If your America Online software seems to be having trouble when first dialing the local access number, disable the TouchTone option by clicking this box to remove the check.

Hardware Handshaking

This check box is used to turn the hardware handshaking features of your modem on or off. Hardware handshaking requires the use of a special cable. Very few modems come with a hardware handshaking cable. Hardware handshaking is necessary to fully utilize modem speeds over 9600 baud. Consult your modem manual to see if your modem supports hardware handshaking. Note that if you wish to use this option, you must check this box for both the First and Second Try numbers. Some older Macintosh modem cables cannot support hardware handshaking; if you are experiencing problems with this option enabled, turn it off.

Connection Port

This tells the software where to look for the modem's physical connection to your computer, with the default being the modem port. If you want to use a modem connected to your Mac's printer port rather than the modem port, use the Connection Port pop-up menu to make your selection. If you have and use a Geoport, the option "Geoport" should appear.

Modem Type

This pop-up menu allows you to designate the type of modem you are using, enabling proper setup for connection to America Online. If your modem is not listed, you can use a generic modem (such as Hayes Basic for 2400 baud and below or Hayes Extended for faster speeds) or use a custom modem file (described below in "Modem Files").

Once you've customized your locality setup, be sure to save your changes. To save, choose Save from the File menu. However, if this locality setup includes a different modem, configuration or location than what you generally use, you may want to use Save As to give it a unique name and keep the original settings intact. (Make sure you save the file to the Online Files folder.) Once saved, you can use your new locality setup by selecting it from your Locality pop-up menu on your Sign On window before initiating your connection.

Tip: If you use both 2400 and 9600 baud access to connect to AOL, set up a locality for each along with the appropriate numbers and even modem files, if necessary. This will allow you to choose between 2400 and 9600 baud connection before signing on at the click of the mouse.

Modem Files

For the majority of members, America Online has made it unnecessary to worry about such things as data bits, stop bits or parity. All your connection information is collected when you initially run America Online. Should you need to change your modem setup for any reason, follow the steps below:

⚫ Click the Setup button at the bottom of the Welcome window.

⚫ America Online's user-friendliness doesn't stop there, though. They've gone the extra step of allowing you to customize your modem setup should you need it. If you use a modem that's not included in America Online's preconfigured modem settings, you may need to create a custom modem file. A modem file is simply information that allows your modem and the America Online software to work together smoothly. It tells the modem how to set itself up for dialing out, how to place a call and how to behave once it is connected. Fortunately, you hardly ever need to alter your modem file, but the option is available on those rare occasions when it is necessary. In these cases, a number of simple solutions are available.

⚫ If you are able to sign on, drop by the free Tech Live area online (keyword: TechLive), available both weekdays and weekends. An America Online representative will guide you through the process of configuring the software for your modem.

⚫ If it is after hours for Tech Live (and you're able to sign on), you may be able to find a preconfigured file for your modem already available. Go to keyword HELP, enter Members' Online Support, click the Technical Help icon and then the Modem Help icon. The well-stocked Modem Drivers library is very likely to contain what you need. If you find a file for your modem, download it to your Online Files folder. After you've downloaded the file, sign off and click Setup in the Welcome window (actually, it'll be the Goodbye window if you've just signed off) and your modem type will appear in the pop-up menu for selecting.

🔺 If you are unable to sign on, call America Online Technical Support at 1-800-827-3338. Like the Tech Live area, this service is available seven days a week and the representatives can offer considerable guidance.

🔺 If you are an advanced user, you can create a custom modem file suited to your own needs. Please note that even as an expert telecommunicator, you are advised to consult your modem's manual or technical support line for the features you can enable or disable before making changes. If you'd like to give this option a go, read on!

Customizing Your Modem File

To customize your modem file, choose Open from the File menu To customize your modem file, follow the steps below:

🔺 Working off-line, choose Open from the File menu.

🔺 Find the Online Files folder that's in your America Online folder.

🔺 Select a pre-configured modem file from those that appear in the Online Files folder. Use the one that's closest to describing your modem make and model.

🔺 Make a copy of this file by choosing Save As from the File menu and giving your file a distinctive name.

🔺 You can also create a new modem file by choosing New from the File menu and selecting Modem file. Whether it's a new file or one you're about to modify, a modem-file modification form appears (see Figure C-2).

Figure C-2:
America Online
offers a built-in
editor to create or
modify a custom
modem file.

Untitled

Modem Configuration

PLEASE NOTE : This area is designed for advanced modem users only! Please consult your modem manual BEFORE making any changes. You may customize your modem configuration by editing the appropriate commands below.

Attention :

Enable Hardware Handshaking :

Initialization :

Disable Hardware Handshaking :

Configuration :

Future Use String #1 :

Reset :

Future Use String #2 :

| Help | Cancel | **Save Changes** |

Attention

This command precedes all others that are sent to your modem. Normally, this string of characters is "AT" for Hayes-compatible modems. These attention characters communicate to your modem the speed, format and parity used by your computer.

Initialization

This is only needed if you must initialize your modem into the Hayes Command Mode. This box is usually left empty.

Configuration

This command is used to optimize your modem settings for connection to America Online. This string varies, depending on which modem type you're using for your connection. New modem users can add "X4" to allow the modem to detect a busy signal quicker.

Reset

This restores your modem to the settings it was using before signing on to America Online. The character "Z" is the default for this string.

Enable Hardware Handshaking

This is used to configure the hardware handshaking features of your modem. Consult your modem's manual to see if your modem supports hardware handshaking, and which codes are to be used if it does.

Disable Hardware Handshaking

Again, consult your modem's manual to see if your modem supports hardware handshaking, and which codes are to be used if it does.

Future Use String #1 & #2

These two strings are reserved for future enhancements to the America Online software and should be left empty.

Tip: Be sure to save an unmodified copy of your modem file or make a note of the modem strings as they are before you change them. This will allow you to restore your modem file to its previous settings if need be.

Solving Common Modem Problems

Here are some common modem problems and solutions:

Modem Won't Dial

America Online's software requires echo off, verbose mode, and responses on. To verify that these are enabled, open the modem file you've designated in Setup with the Open option under the File menu. Add "Q0V1E0" to the Configuration string. If something similar is in your Configuration string, your modem file is already set correctly.

Modem Dials but Won't Connect

If your connection fails at some point between the high-pitched carrier tone and the Welcome window, or if it fails after the first thing you try to do online, flow control (XON/XOFF) is probably the culprit. Make sure that it's disabled: adding "&K0" to your Initialization string should do the trick.

Modem Disconnects on Call Waiting

Sudden disconnections can also be caused by Call Waiting. The click that indicates a call is waiting on the line sounds like a "break" (disconnect immediately) signal to the modem, which obligingly hangs up. If this is a problem, you should disable Call Waiting when you connect to America Online. You can disable it off-line by selecting the Setup button in the Sign On window and clicking in the check box marked "To disable call waiting, dial..." The input field to the right of this line contains the pulse code to disable Call Waiting, which also works for touch-tone users in most areas. In some areas, you may need to change the default of "*70," to "1170," for touch-tone use. Include a comma after the code: it tells the modem to wait two seconds before dialing the next number. If you aren't sure what numbers you should enter to disable Call Waiting, check with your local telephone company or look in the front section of your local phone book under Call Waiting.

Modem Disconnects Frequently

If you have problems with line noise (static on your phone line while signed on to America Online), the result may be file-transfer errors, strange characters on the screen or occasional disconnections from America Online. One step you can take to cut down on line noise is to temporarily set your baud rate to a lower speed. Try the speed one step down from your current setting. You can also try another local access number (if available).

Another common cause of frequent disconnects is a phone cord with a bad connector (or jack) on one or both ends, or a faulty wall jack. If you hear lots of static when you're talking on the phone, odds are that the same amount of static (line noise) is present when you use America Online. Check with your telephone company or an electrician to find out what can be done to improve your line quality.

Modem Speaker Stays On

To disable your modem speaker, open your modem file and add "M0" (the letter M and a zero) to the Configuration string. If there are already characters present, add "M0" at the end. Alternatively, "M1" will enable the speaker until a connection is made, and "M2" will keep the speaker turned on after a connection has been established.

CCL Files

The dysfunctionally curious will note AOL's ability to save a file created with the New command as a "CCL File." A CCL file (Communication Control Language) is a modem "script" that allows your modem to talk to certain communication systems. Your America Online software comes with CCLs for networks like SprintNet, Tymnet and Datapac, enabling them to work with America Online. CCL scripts are written in a programming language and can be modified with a simple text editor. The CCLs come preconfigured and already in place; you needn't do anything to take advantage of these other than verify that the appropriate CCL for your access number is selected in the Connection File pop-up menu on the Setup screen. Additionally, it is unlikely that you will need to alter a CCL script, as modem files can handle virtually all of your needs.

APPENDIX D
On the Road

Your access to America Online need not end where your wanderlust begins. Whether you travel across the country or use your PowerBook at work and at home, AOL is only a phone call away. This appendix gives you tips for calling AOL while traveling, finding local access numbers, and signing on with a computer other than your own.

Using America Online on the Road

Using AOL when you are traveling is easy with these few preparations and helpful hints:

- Inexpensive kits are available that help in setting up your modem when traveling. It's also a good idea to travel with an extra length of standard phone line with modular (RJ-11) jacks on each end, and also a phone splitter. These items are available at many phone or electronics store.

- If you're going to be staying in a hotel, ask for a "computer-ready" room: one with an extra phone jack for your modem. If the hotel doesn't have phones set up for computer users, you can usually remove the phone cable from its phone jack and connect your modem cable.

- If you need to dial a long-distance access number and want to avoid the hotel's long-distance charges or charges on a friend's phone bill, you can use your calling card. Edit your locality setup (detailed in Appendix C) by inserting the following in the Phone Number field:

  <Long distance carrier number, if needed> + 0 + <area code> + <access number> + ,,,,, + <calling card number> + PIN (personal identification number, which may be optional)

  For example: 10333-0-313-665-2900,,,,,12312312341234#

  Those five commas cause AOL to wait ten seconds while your long-distance carrier comes on the line and asks for your calling-card number.

🔺 Note that your long-distance carrier number might be needed to override the default carrier for the phone you are calling from: AT&T is 10288 and Sprint is 10333. Call Waiting might cause problems with this procedure, so disable Call Waiting if you are having difficulties.

🔺 Use AOL to back up your work while traveling. Send mail to yourself and attach the file you want to save. If you need to restore the file, you can read the mail and download the saved file. If you lose your work while you're on the road, or even after you return, you'll have a backup waiting online when you get home.

🔺 In your travels, you might find yourself using AOL in places where loud sounds could be disruptive to others around you, such as a friend's guest room or a waiting room. In these situations, you can disable your AOL sounds (check your System Preferences under the Members menu) or turn your modem speaker off (refer to Chapter 20, "Ten Best," or check your modem manual).

🔺 Look up the local access numbers (by using the keyword Access) for the area you'll be visiting. Do this before you leave: it's much easier. Create individual localities (discussed in Appendix C) for your most frequent destinations and name them appropriately. When you need to sign on you can simply select your location, say, Work, Branch Office, Home or Cottage, from the Locality pop-up menu of the Sign On window, and you're ready!

Tips for travelers and general help signing on are all available in the AOL software by selecting Help under the File menu.

Finding Local Access Numbers Off-Line

If you discover that you need a new access number while you're on the road, but you are unable to get online to search the number directory, you aren't alone. Many others have traveled down this path and a variety of options have opened up:

▲ Sign on with the Get Local # option in the Locality pop-up menu of the Welcome (sign-on) window. With this option enabled, AOL will automatically call a toll-free number and present you with a list of access numbers to choose from.

 Note: If you are calling from a hotel and need to dial an outside line prefix, like an "8" or a "9," select that from Setup before selecting the Get Local # option. The Setup button is grayed out once the Get Local # option is selected.

▲ Call AOL's Customer Service Hotline at 1-800-827-6364 (in the US) or 1-703-893-6288 (from Canada or overseas), open Monday through Friday from 9 A.M. to 2 A.M. and weekends from 12 P.M. to 1 A.M. (Eastern time).

▲ Phone the carrier network: Tymnet can be reached at 1-800-336-0149; SprintNet at 1-800-877-5045 ext. 5, and SprintNet's automatic access number listings at 1-800-473-7983.

▲ If you have a fax modem or access to a fax machine, call AOL's FAXLink service at 1-800-827-5551 and request that a list of access numbers be faxed to you. An automated voice menu will guide you through the choices.

▲ If you're within the United States, you can connect to SprintNet's Local Access Numbers Directory with a standard telecommunications program. To access, simply dial any SprintNet node directly, and once connected type "@D" and press the Return key twice. At the @ prompt, type "c mail" and press Return, then type "PHONES" for the user name and "PHONES" again for the password. You can look up any local SprintNet number available.

Signing On as a Guest

In your travels you are likely to visit others who have AOL on their computers. While your screen names won't appear in their software, you can still use their machine to sign on with your account. Just select the "Guest" screen name from the pop-up menu of the Welcome (sign-on) window and then click the Sign On button. (The "Guest" name always appears in the list of screen names, no matter whose machine you're using or what kind of computer it is.) The software will dial the local access number and connect to AOL.

After you've made the connection, you'll see a dialog box that asks for your screen name and password. America Online will connect using your account. Charges (other than long-distance charges, if any) you accrue during the session will be billed to your account rather than your friend's.

Note: Data such as your Address Book and FlashSession information is stored locally in your AOL software rather than on the AOL host computer. As a result, you will not be able to see this information when signed on as a Guest on another computer. You are also unable to edit your screen names while signed on as a Guest.

To sign off from a Guest session, simply choose Sign Off from the Go To menu as you normally would.

APPENDIX E
Preferences

By selecting the Preferences feature, you can customize several AOL functions. The AOL software was shipped with preferences preselected for you ("defaults"). You will probably like them the way they are. But Mac users are independent thinkers and like to make these decisions for themselves, thus the Preferences command. Don't worry about experimenting—you can always change things back.

When you choose Set Preferences from the Members menu, the preference categories are listed on the left side of your screen (see Figure E-1). To select a preference category, click it once. Then you can double-click any item from the preference list on the right side of the screen to turn it on or off. A preference that's turned on is indicated by a check mark next to it.

Figure E-1: The Preferences dialog box.

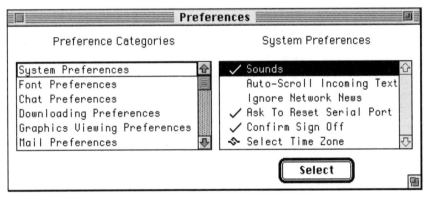

System Preferences
These are preferences that apply to your AOL software.

Sounds
The AOL software is shipped with Sounds activated. These sounds include "Welcome," "Good-bye" and "File's done." Other sounds are controlled from within their own preference category, including chat sounds and the mail's "You've got mail" notification.

When the chat room sounds are turned on, you can receive audible "sound bites" from other members when you're in a People Connection chat room or in a Conference Room elsewhere online. (To learn more about sending, receiving and installing chat sounds, refer to Chapter 12, "People Connection.")

Auto-Scroll Incoming Text

If you select this option, incoming text (for example, a news article or email) automatically scrolls on your screen as it is sent from the AOL host computer. If you leave the option as is (the default) you can manually scroll text using the scroll bar on the right of your incoming text window, even before the text has completely arrived.

Ignore Network News

From time to time (it isn't often, but it does occur) AOL sends informational bulletins called "Network News" to members. These bulletins summarize special events happening on the service, or events of particular significance.

You don't need to do anything to get these messages—they automatically appear at the top of your screen, and they don't interrupt what you're doing. If you would prefer not to receive these messages while you're online, leave the "Ignore Network News" feature turned off (which is the default).

Ask to Reset Serial Port

Occasionally, software will leave your serial port (the socket in the back of your Mac that's connected to your modem) active, even though the software is finished with it. The AOL software itself does this occasionally if you're disconnected from the service abruptly.

The Ask to Reset Serial Port option (which defaults to on) simply asks you, whenever AOL determines that the serial port is on, if the port is in use. You can turn it off if your modem is the only device connected to that port.

Confirm Sign Off

Some people are annoyed by the "Are you sure you want to sign off?" dialog box that appears when you select Sign Off from the Go To menu.

It's a good idea to leave this one turned on, however, in case you accidentally hit Command-Q (for Quit), which signs you off before it quits. Left on (which is the default), this command interrupts that potential accident.

Select Time Zone

This is nice: if you don't live in the Eastern time zone, this preference allows you to change the time locality of AOL's "date stamps." This means that your incoming mail, for instance, can be stamped with the time that the sender sent it, using your time zone. For most members, this is best left on.

Font Preferences

Have fun with this one! America Online allows you to change your preference for the font and size of the type you see in online text, articles, in chat and conference rooms, and in your mail. For example, if you have difficulty reading text online, you might be more comfortable with a larger size, or even a different font. You can select any font and size that you have installed on your Macintosh system. The font you select as your mail font will be seen when you compose and receive mail, *but the formatting of other Mac users who send you mail will be seen when you receive it.*

Note that you can turn colored text off for received mail. You will want to do this if you have a monochrome screen. (Formatting mail is discussed in Chapter 4, "Electronic Mail.")

Tip
A few areas of AOL use a "tabular" arrangement for information (that is, text and numbers in columns and rows). If you receive or send a lot of mail in this format, or if you frequently access information formatted in this way, you might prefer to use a monospaced font, such as Monaco or Courier.

Chat Preferences

Here you can opt to have incoming text in chat rooms (such as People Connection, or other conference rooms located throughout AOL) appear on your screen double-spaced. Also, you can turn off sounds that other members might send you in chat areas. (Chat sounds are discussed in Chapter 12, "People Connection.")

Downloading Preferences

Your AOL software is shipped with a decompression utility called StuffIt (discussed in Chapter 5, "Computing"). You will find that many downloadable AOL files are "stuffed"—that is, they've been compressed so that they take up less space. The advantage to this is that they take less time to download, which saves you time and money. Your software also contains the routines necessary to expand self-extracting archives (SEA files). Before you can use these files, however, they must be expanded using the decompression utilities that come free with your AOL software.

Auto-Expand Files

America Online automatically expands any compressed files you've downloaded when you sign off. If you prefer that these files not be expanded, you can turn off this preference. You'll want to do this if you download to floppies, which might not be capable of holding both the downloaded archive and the files it creates when it's expanded.

Delete Compressed Files

If you turn on this preference (which is defaulted to off), AOL will automatically delete the compressed version of any file that was expanded when you signed off. This will save space on your hard drive. On the other hand, the compressed file is a form of insurance, and you might want to save it on a floppy for archival purposes. You be the judge. The default is off.

Confirm "Download Later"

When you tell your AOL software that you want to download a file later, it will normally respond with a message confirming your request. This preference turns the message off if you wish.

Graphics Preferences

These preferences pertain to the onscreen viewing of graphics as they're received.

Auto-View Graphics

This is the preference that allows you to view most graphics as they're received. Viewing them allows you to abort the download if you don't like (or need) what you see. It's best to leave this preference on unless your Mac is very low on memory, or very slow.

Use Mac System Colors

Some graphics arrive with their own color "palette." While this usually makes them look better, these palettes are actually tables that your Mac has to consult for every pixel that comprises the graphic. Using the Mac's system colors eliminates the need for this consultation and speeds things up a bit. Leave this on if you want speed; turn it off if you want the most faithful colors in your graphics.

Mail Preferences

Electronic mail is discussed in Chapter 4. Here are the preferences that apply.

Mail Voice Announcement

If you have mail when you first sign on, or if you receive a piece of mail in your empty mailbox while you're online, a voice announces, "You've Got Mail." If you prefer not to be interrupted by the announcement, turn off the Mail Voice Announcement.

Mail Waiting Notice

When you have mail, a little mailbox icon flashes on your menu bar. If you don't like this notice, you can turn it off.

Close Mail After Sending

America Online is automatically set to close a mail document after you've sent it to the recipient. If you would like to keep a document you've already sent open on your screen, turn this preference off.

Close Mail on Next/Previous

When you use the "Next/Previous" arrows (located at the bottom right side of the mail window) to scroll through your mail messages, AOL automatically closes old mail windows after you've finished reading them. (This prevents leaving a "bread crumb" trail of open windows across your screen.) If you want these windows to stay open, turn this preference off.

Save FlashMail as Text

FlashMail (FlashSessions are discussed in Chapter 19) is normally saved using a proprietary format on your disk and isn't available for use by other software, such as word processors. If you want to review your FlashMail with other software, you'll have to turn this option on. If you do, however, you'll not have access to automated replies and forwards—a major convenience.

Confirm "Send Later"

When you compose mail off-line and click the Send Later button, AOL normally displays a message that confirms your intention. If you would rather not encounter that message, turn this option off.

Members Preferences

These preferences have to do with Instant Messages, which are discussed in Chapter 12, "People Connection."

Instant Message Notice

If you receive an Instant Message (IM) while you're online, an "IM" icon will flash on your menu bar. If you don't want the notice to appear, you can turn it off.

Tip

If you see the IM notice flashing, but you don't see the Instant Message window at the top of your screen, select the Windows menu on your menu bar. You might find that your Instant Message is hiding under your active window. (This happens if you receive your Instant Message while you're typing text.)

Incoming IMs to Front

Normally, an incoming Instant Message pops onto the top of your screen, demanding attention. This can be a problem for people who receive a lot of IMs, because an IM can interrupt your typing. If you don't want IMs on top, turn this preference off.

Play IM Sounds

This preference turns off the "tinkerbell" sound that you hear when Instant Messages are received.

Glossary

This glossary was prepared by Jennifer Watson (screen name: Jennifer) and George Louie (screen name: NumbersMan) of the America Online staff (to whom I express my heartfelt thanks for a job very well done). It's updated regularly and posted online. To find it, use the keyword FileSearch, then search with the criterion VirtualLingo.

access number — A phone number (usually local) your modem uses to access America Online. To find an access number online, go to keyword: ACCESS. If you aren't signed on to AOL, there are a number of ways to get access numbers:

- ▲ Sign on with the "New Local#" (WAOL) or "Get Local#" (Mac AOL 2.1 or higher) option in the "Set Up & Sign On" window.

- ▲ Delete all your numbers in Setup; AOL will automatically call the 800 number and let you choose from the list of access numbers.

- ▲ Phone the network: Call SprintNet at 1-800-877-5045 ext. 5 or SprintNet's automatic access number listings at 1-800-473-7983; call Tymnet at 1-800-336-0149.

- ▲ Dial up SprintNet's Local Access Numbers Directory: Using a general telecommunications program, you can call in to a SprintNet node directly. Once connected, type "@D" and hit the Enter key twice. At the @ prompt given, type "c mail" and hit Enter, then type "PHONES" for the username and "PHONES" again for the password. You can look up any local SprintNet number available.

- ▲ Call America Online's Customer Service Hotline at 1-800-827-6364 (within U.S.) or 1-703-893-6288 (from Canada or overseas), open from 9 a.m. to 2 a.m. ET, Monday through Friday and 12 noon to 1 a.m. ET on weekends.

- ▲ Call AOL's FAXLink service at 1-800-827-5551 and request that a list of access numbers be faxed to you. An automated voice menu will guide you through the choices.

- ▲ Dial up AOL's Customer Service BBS with a standard telecommunications program at 1-800-827-5808 (settings: 8 data bits, no parity, 1 stop bit, up to 14.4K).

If you don't have a local access number, read the information in the Access Number area (keyword: HELP) on how to obtain one. See also Datapac, SprintNet, Tymnet and node.

Address Book — An AOL software feature that allows you to store screen names for easy access. Your Address Book may be created, edited or used through the Address Book icon available when composing mail. You can also create or edit them with the Edit Address Book option under your Mail menu. See also e-mail and screen names.

afk — Common shorthand for "away from keyboard." It's most often used in chat and IMs when it's necessary to leave the keyboard for an extended length of time. See also shorthands, abbreviations and chat.

America Online, Incorporated (AOL) — The Vienna, Virginia-based parent company of the three online services—America Online, PC-Link and Q-Link. PC-Link and Q-Link are going offline fall 1994, however. Formerly known as Quantum Computer Services and founded in 1985, AOL has grown rapidly in both size and scope. AOL has over 1 million members and dozens of alliances with major companies. America Online's stock exchange symbol is AMER. To contact AOL headquarters, call 1-800-827-6364. See also AOL.

analog — Information composed of continuous and varying levels of intensity, such as sound and light.

AOL — Abbreviation for America Online, Inc. Occasionally abbreviated as AO. See also America Online, Incorporated.

AOLiversary — A date celebrated yearly on which a member first became an active on America Online. Considered an accurate yardstick by some to determine their state of addiction. See AOLoholic.

AOLoholic — A member of AOL who begins to display any of the following behaviors: spending most of their free time online; thinking about AOL even when off-line (evidenced by the addition of shorthands to non-AOL writings); attempting to bring all their friends and family online; and/or thinking AOL is the best invention since the wheel. A 12-step plan is in development. Many, but not all AOLoholics, go on to become remote staff. See also member and remote staff.

archive (ARC) — (1) A file that has been compressed smaller with file compression software. See also file, file compression, PKZIP, and StuffIt. (2) A file that contains message board postings that may be of value, but have been removed from a message board due to their age, inactivity of topic, or lack of message board space. These messages are usually bundled into one document, and placed in a file library for retrieval later. See also file and library.

article — A text document intended to be read online, but may be printed or saved for later examination offline. On MacAOL, the limit is 25k; if longer it will scroll off the top of the window (the "More" feature is not

ASCII — Acronym for American Standard for Computer Information Interchange (or American Standard Code for Information Interchange). ASCII is the numeric code used to represent computer characters on computers around the world.

Ask the Staff button — See Comment to Staff button.

asynchronous — Data communication via modem of the start-stop variety where characters do not need to be transmitted constantly. Each character is transmitted as a discrete unit with its own start bit and one or more stop bits. AOL is asynchronous. See also synchronous.

attached file — A file that hitches a ride with e-mail. Be the file text, sound or pictures of your hamster "Bruno," it is said to be attached if it has been included with the e-mail for separate downloading by the recipient (whether addressed directly, carbon copied, forwarded or blind carbon copied.) See also archive, download, e-mail and file.

auditorium — Auditoriums are specially equipped online "rooms" that allow large groups of AOL members (up to 300–500) to meet in a structured setting. Currently, there are four auditoriums: The Coliseum, a.k.a. Center Stage (for special and general events), Rotunda (for computing-related topics or computing company representatives), the Odeon (for Information Providers) and Tech Live (for questions and help on AOL — this is in the free area). The auditoriums are divided into two parts: the stage, where the emcee and the guest speaker(s) are located, and the chat rows, where the audience is located. More information on auditoriums can be found at keyword: SHOWS or ROTUNDA. See also emcee, OnlineHost, Coliseum, Odeon, Rotunda and Tech Live.

bandwidth — A measure of the amount of information that can flow through a given point at any given time. To use a popular analogy, a low bandwidth is a two-lane road while a high bandwidth is a six-lane super-highway.

baud rate — A unit for measuring the speed of data transmission. Technically baud rates refer to the number of times the communications line changes states each second. Strictly speaking, baud and bits per second (bps) are not identical measurements, but most non-technical people use the terms interchangeably. See also bps.

BBS (Bulletin Board Service) — A system offering information that can be accessed via computer, modem and phone lines. For more information online, go to keyword: BBS.

blind carbon copy (bcc) — A feature of the AOL e-mail system that allows you to send e-mail to a member or members without anyone other than you being aware of it. See also e-mail.

board — An abbreviated reference to a message board or bulletin board service (BBS). See also message board and BBS.

bps (bits per second) — A method of measuring data transmission speed. Currently, 1200, 2400 and 9600 bps are supported on AOL. 14,400 may be available in larger cities, but unreliably as it is still in testing. See also baud.

brb — Common shorthand for "be right back." It is used by AOL members when participating in chat/conference rooms or talking in IMs (Instant Messages). See also shorthands, abbreviations and chat.

browse — To casually explore rather than examine in detail. Typically used in reference to message boards and file libraries.

btw — Common shorthand for "by the way." It is used in IMs, chat/conference rooms, e-mail and message postings. See also shorthands, abbreviations and chat.

bulletin board — See message board and BBS.

carbon copy (cc) — A feature of the AOL e-mail system that allows you to address e-mail to a member for whom the e-mail is not directly intended or is of secondary interest. See also e-mail.

CCL (Communication Control Language) — A script that allows you to control your modem. CCL scripts are most useful when the connection process is more complicated than can be handled by a modem file. See also modem files.

Center Stage — See Coliseum.

chat — To engage in real-time communications with other members. See also Instant Message, chat room, conference room and auditorium.

chat rooms — Online areas where members may meet to communicate and interact with others. There are two kinds of chat areas — public and private. Public chat areas can be found in the People Connection area (keyword: PEOPLE) or in the many forums around AOL. Public rooms may either be officially-sanctioned rooms or member-created rooms (which are listed separately). All public rooms are governed by AOL's Terms of Service (TOS) and are open to anyone interested. See also private room, chat, host, Guide, TOS and People Connection.

chat sounds — Sounds may be played and broadcast to others in chat areas by selecting "Chat Sounds..." under the "Chat" menu. You can also play them by typing: {S <sound>} and sending it to the chat area. Be sure to type it exactly as shown and insert the exact name of the sound you wish to play where <sound> appears in the example. See also chat room and library.

CIS — Short for CompuServe Information Service. May also be abbreviated as CI$. See also Compuserve.

client — A computer that requests information from another.

close box — The small box in the upper-left corner of your window. Clicking on this box closes the window. Not to be confused with a shoe box, boom box or even clothes box. See also window.

club — See forum.

Coliseum — Previously known as Center Stage, The Coliseum is an auditorium located in People Connection or via the keyword: SHOWS. See also auditorium and emcee.

Command key — Usually located near the Spacebar, you'll find printed on it either an open Apple symbol or a clover-leaf symbol (or both). Holding down the Command key while another key is pressed will often activate a special function. See also Option key and Open-Apple key.

Comment to Staff button — A button available in file libraries that will allow you to send a note to the managers of the library. See also download and library.

CompuServe (CIS) — A large, established commercial online service similar to America Online. While CompuServe Information Service (CIS) has more databases available, their service is priced higher and is less user-friendly than AOL. CIS is owned by H&R Block. May be referred to as "CIS" or "CI$" in shorthand during chat.

conference room — A specific kind of chat area found in forums all around AOL where members can meet, hold conferences and interact in real-time. Conference rooms can hold up to 23 or 48 members at any one time (depending on location), and are located outside of the People Connection. See also host, moderator and protocol.

corporate staff — Members who are usually company or IP (information provider) employees and work at the corporate offices of the company. In-house AOL, Inc. staff is often referred to in this manner as well. See also in-house and IP.

CS Live — See Tech Live.

Customer Relations — America Online's Customer Relations Hotline is open from 9 a.m. to 2 a.m. Eastern time Monday through Friday, and noon to 1 a.m. on weekends. Call 1-800-827-6364 during these hours. See also Tech Live.

cyberpunk — First used to designate a body of speculative fiction literature focusing on marginalized people in technologically-enhanced cultural "systems." Within the last few years, the mass media has used this term to catergorize the denizens of cyberspace. Cyberpunks are known to cruise the information landscapes with alacrity, or lacking that, eagerness.

cyberspace — An infinite world created by our computer networks. Cyberspace is no less real than the real world—people are born, grow, learn, fall in love and die in cyberspace. These effects may or may not be carried over into the physical world. America Online is an example of cyberspace created through interaction between the energies of the members, staff and computers. See also online community.

daemon — An automatic program that performs a maintenance function on AOL. For example, a board daemon may run at 3 A.M. and clean up old posts on a message board.

database — A collection of information, stored and organized for easy searching. A database can refer to something as simple as a well-sorted filing cabinet, but today most databases reside on computers because they offer better access. See also Directory of Services, Member Directory and searchable.

Datapac — A packet-switching network operated by Bell Canada that provides local access numbers for Canadian members at an extra fee. See also packet-switching network and access number.

Delete — An AOL e-mail system feature that allows you to permanently remove a piece of mail from any and all of your mailboxes. See also e-mail and Status.

demoware (demonstration software) — These are often full-featured versions of commercial software, with the exception being that the Save or Print features are often disabled. Some demos are only functional for certain periods of time. Like shareware, demonstration software is a great way to try before you buy.

department — This is the broadest category of information into which America Online divides its material. There are 14 departments, corresponding with the departmental organization of this book.

digital — Information that is represented by two discrete states (either 1 or 0) and also referred to as binary information. Most information in the real world is not digital, but must be converted into this form to be used by computers.

Directory of Services — A searchable database that allows AOL members to quickly locate AOL's available services. This is available at keyword: SERVICES. See also database and searchable.

document — An information file, usually relating specific details on a topic. See also article and file.

DOD — Abbreviation for Data On Demand, a method of receiving artwork updates. AOL is unique in that as it grows and new areas are added, the custom artwork associated with new services and areas can be added on the fly. At the time of this writing, DODs are only available on the Mac AOL and WAOL platforms; PC/GEOS users receive artwork updates via UDOs.

download — The transfer of information stored on a remote computer to a storage device on your personal computer. This information can come from AOL via its file libraries, or from other AOL members via attached files in e-mail. See also archive, attached file, file, library, download count and download manager.

download count — The download count (often abbreviated "Cnt" in a library window) refers to the number of times that file has been downloaded. This is often used as a gauge of the file's popularity. See also file, library and download.

download manager — An AOL software feature that allows you to keep a queue of files to download at a later time. You can even set up your software to automatically sign off when your download session is complete. You can schedule your software to sign on and grab files listed in the queue at times you specify. See also download and file.

e-mail — Short for electronic mail. One of the most popular features of online services, e-mail allows you to send private communications electronically from one person to another. See also attached file, carbon copy, blind carbon copy, return receipt, Keep As New, Delete, Status, e-mail address and gateway.

e-mail address — A cyberspace mailbox. On AOL, your e-mail address is simply your screen name; for folks outside of AOL, you address is yourscreenname@aol.com. For mail outgoing from AOL, check out the Internet Center (keyword: INTERNET) for more information. See also e-mail and screen name.

echo — A rare AOL system bug that rapidly repeats a person's chat over and over in a chat or conference room. Also known as a system scroll. If this occurs, you should leave the room immediately and page a Guide using keyword: GUIDEPAGER.

emcee — A member who has been trained to moderate and host events held in auditoriums. See also auditorium.

emoticons — Symbols consisting of characters found on any keyboard which are used to give and gain insight on emotional states. For example, the symbol :) is a smile — just tilt your head to the left and you'll see the : (eyes) and the) (smile). A brief list of emoticons is available at keyword: SHORTHANDS. See also shorthands and chat.

eWorld — Apple Computer's newest online service. Based on AOL's client system, eWorld is expected to be a popular service with its stylized graphics and Apple support. eWorld opened to the public on June 20, 1994.

FAQ — Short for "Frequently Asked Questions." FAQs may take the form of an informational file containing questions and answers to common concerns/issues. See also message board and library.

fax (facsimile) — A technique for sending graphical images (such as text or pictures) over phone lines. While faxes are usually sent and received with a stand-alone fax machine, faxes may also be sent to or from computers using fax software and a modem. You can also send a fax through AOL at keyword: FAX.

file — Any amount of information that is grouped together as one unit. On AOL, a file can be anything from text to sounds and can be transferred to and from your computer via AOL. See also download, library and software file.

file compression — A programming technique by which many files can be reduced in size. Files are usually compressed so that they take up less storage space, can be transferred quicker and/or can be bundled with others. See also file and download.

file name extensions — These are usually three-character codes found suffixing a file name, and are primarily used for PC files.

flame — Made popular on the Internet, this means to chat, post messages, or send e-mail about something that is considered inflammatory by other members, and may cause fires among those who read and respond to it. Harassment and vulgarity are not allowed on America Online, and if you see this occurring, you may report the occurrence at keyword: TOS. See also chat, message board, e-mail and TOS.

flashmail — On the Mac, this is a feature of the AOL software that allows you to save your outgoing e-mail to disk to send at a later time, or save your incoming e-mail so you can look at it later, online or off-line. These e-mails are stored in your flashbox, and the outgoing files are sent with FlashSessions. See also e-mail.

folder — Groupings of messages by topic within message boards are termed "folders" on America Online. See also message and message boards.

form — A window for an area online—usually comprised of a text field, a list box (scrollable), and one or more icons. See also icon and window.

forum — A place online where members with similar interests may find valuable information, exchange ideas, share files and get help on a particular area of interest. Forums (also known simply as areas or clubs) are found everywhere online, represent almost every interest under the sun, and usually offer message boards, articles, chat rooms and libraries, all organized and accessible by a keyword. Forums are moderated by forum hosts or forum leaders. See also form and keyword.

freeware — A file that is completely free and often made available in libraries of online services like AOL for downloading. Unlike public domain files, you are not able to modify it and the author retains the copyright. Since the author or programmer usually posts freeware and the user downloads it, distribution is direct and nearly without cost. See also file, shareware and public domain.

gateway — A link to another service, such as the Internet, EAASY SABRE or StockLink. Gateways allow members to access these independent services through AOL. See also Internet.

GIF (Graphic Interchange Format) — A type of graphic file that can be read by most platforms; the electronic version of photographs. GIFs can be viewed with a GIF viewer utility, which are located at keyword: GALLERY.

Gopher — A feature of the Internet that allows you to browse huge amounts of information. The terms implies that it will "go-pher" you to retrieve information. It also refers to the way in which you "tunnel" through the various menus, much like a gopher would. See also WAIS and Internet.

GUI — Graphical User Interface. Some examples of GUIs include the Mac Operating System, OS/2 and Windows. See also operating system, system, OS/2 and Windows.

Guide — Experienced AOL members who have been specially chosen and trained to help other members enjoy their time online. All on-duty Guides wear their "uniforms"—the letters "Guide" followed by a space and a two- or three-letter suffix in all caps. See also Guide Pager, Lobby and uniform.

Guide Pager — A feature of AOL that allows you to page a Guide when there is a problem in a chat or conference room. Simply go to keyword: GUIDEPAGER, and you will be presented with a simple form to complete regarding the problem. See also Guide and TOS.

hacker — Not to be confused with hamsters, hackers are self-taught computer gurus who take an unholy delight in discovering the well-hidden secrets of computer systems. Blighted by a bad reputation of late, hackers do not necessarily denote those who intend harm or damage. There are those, however, who feed upon the pain inflicted by viruses. See also virus.

hamster — Unbeknownst to most users, AOL's host computers are actually powered by these small, efficient creatures with large cheek pouches. They are notorious for being temperamental workers. When things slow down or troubles mount online, it is a sure sign that an AOL employee forgot to feed the hamsters.

help room — Online "rooms" where members can go to get live help with the AOL software/system as well as assistance in finding things online. See also Guide, Help, MHM and Tech Live.

host — (1) The AOL computer system. (2) An AOL member who facilitates discussion in chat rooms. You can find hosts all over the system, and they will often be wearing "uniforms" —letters in front of their names (usually in all caps) to designate the forum they host for. See also Guide, chat room, conference room and uniform.

hot chat — A safe, euphemistic term which means to chat about (read "flirt") and engage in the popular online dance of human attraction and consummation. Virtually, of course. And usually in private rooms or IMs.

icon — A graphic image of a recognizable thing or action that leads to somewhere or initiates a process. See also keyboard shortcuts.

Ignore — (1) Chat blinders; a way of blocking a member's chat from your view in a chat/conference room window. Ignore is most useful when the chat of another member becomes disruptive in the chat room. (2) An AOL e-mail system feature that allows you to ignore mail in your New Mail box, causing it to be moved to your Old Mail box without having to read it first. See also e-mail and Status.

in-house — Used to describe those employees that actually work at AOL in Vienna, Virginia. May also be referred to as corporate staff. This is contrasted with remote staff, many of whom are actually volunteers and work from their homes. See also corporate staff and remote staff.

IP (Information Provider) — A person or party supplying material for use on AOL's services, and/or responsible for the content of an area on America Online's services. See also corporate staff and remote staff.

interactive — Having the ability to act on each another. AOL is interactive in the sense that you can send information and, based upon that, have information sent back (and vice versa). The chat rooms are an excellent example.

insertion point — The blinking vertical line in a document marking the place where text is being edited. The insertion point may be navigated through a document with either the mouse or the arrow keys.

IM (Instant Message) — AOL's equivalent of passing notes to another person during a meeting, as opposed to speaking up in the room (chat) or writing out a letter or memo (e-mail). Instant Messages (IMs) may be exchanged between two AOL members signed on at the same time and are useful for conducting conversations when a chat room isn't appropriate, available or practical.

Internet — The mother of all networks is not an online service itself, but rather serves to interconnect computer systems and networks all over the world. The Internet is managed by the National Science Foundation (NSF). AOL features an Internet Center which includes access to e-mail service to and from Internet addresses, USENET Newsgroups, and Gopher & WAIS Databases, among other features. FTP and Telnet access will be offered within 1994. AOL has even provided "Net Guides" who rove among the areas helping members out. To receive mail through the Internet gateway, you need to give others your Internet mailing address which consists of your AOL screen name (without any blank spaces) followed by the "@" symbol and "aol.com" (i.e., jennilynn@aol.com). To obtain more information about the Internet, use the keyword: INTERNET to go to the Internet Center. For information about TCP/IP access to America Online, see TCP/IP. See also gateway, gopher, newsgroups and WAIS.

Keep As New — An AOL e-mail system feature that allows you to keep mail in your New Mail box, even after you've read or ignored it. See also e-mail.

keyboard shortcuts — The AOL software provides us with keyboard command equivalents for menu selections. For example, rather than selecting "Send Instant Message" from the menu, you could type Command-I on the Mac or Open-Apple-I on the Apple II. For a complete list of these keyboard shortcuts, see the Keyboard Shortcuts Chart included as a supplement to the VirtuaLingo Glossary.

keyword — (1) A fast way to move around within America Online. To use a keyword, type Command-K on the Mac and then the keyword, followed by the Enter key. Keywords are communicated to others in a standard format: Keyword: NAME. An updated list of all public keywords is available in the AOL file libraries by searching for "keyword surf" (don't include the quotes) at keyword: FILESEARCH. (2) A single word you feel is likely to be included in any database on a particular subject. A keyword is usually a word that comes as close as possible to describing the topic or piece of information you are looking for. Many of AOL's software libraries can be searched for keywords.

library — An area online in which files may be uploaded to and downloaded from. The files may be of any type: text, graphics, software, sounds, etc. To search libraries available for your platform, go to keyword: FILESEARCH. See also file, download, upload, search and browse.

line noise — Extraneous noise on telephone lines that is often heard as clicks or static. While line noise is usually only a nuisance to voice communications, it means trouble for data being transmitted through modems. If you are having problems remaining connected, it may be the result of line noise. Signing off, redialing and getting a new connection will often help this problem.

Lobby — Often seeming more like the Grand Central Station of AOL rather than a sedate hotel foyer, the Lobby is the default chat room of the People Connection. See also chat, chat room and Guide.

LOL — Shorthand for "Laughing Out Loud," often used in chat areas and Instant Messages. Another variation is ROFL, for "Rolling On Floor Laughing." See also shorthands, abbreviations and chat.

lurk — To sit in a chat room or read a message board, yet contribute little or nothing at all. Hamsters are known lurkers. See also chat and conference room.

Mac AOL — The Apple Macintosh version of the AOL client software. The current version is 2.5. May also be referred to as MAOL.

macro — A "recording" of keystrokes or mouse movements/clicks on a computer that allows you to automate a task. Macros are usually created with shareware and commercial software and can be initiated with a single key.

megabyte — 1,048,576 bytes of data.

member — An AOL subscriber. The term "member" is embraced because AOLers are members of the online community. See also Online Community.

Member Directory — The database of AOL member screen names that have profiles. To be included in this database, the member only needs to have created a Member Profile. The Member Directory is located at keyword: MEMBERS. See also member, Member Profile, database and searchable.

Member Profile — A voluntary online information document that describes oneself. Name, address information, birthday, sex, marital status, hobbies, computers used, occupation and a personal quote may be provided. This is located at keyword: MEMBERS or PROFILE. See also member and Member Directory.

message — A note posted on a message board for others members to read. A message may also be referred to as a post. See also message board.

message board — An area where members can post messages to exchange information, ask a question or reply to another message. All AOL members are welcome and encouraged to post messages in message boards (or boards). Message boards are occasionally called bulletin boards. See also message, folder, thread and Message Center.

message board pointer — An automatic place-marker for message boards. AOL keeps track of the areas you have visited by date, allowing you to pick up where you left off upon your return. Once you've visited a message board, clicking on the "Find New" button will show you only the new messages that have been posted since your last visit. The pointers are updated each time you return. These pointers stay in effect for 60 days after your last visit.

Message Center — A collection of message boards in one convenient area. See also message board.

MHM (Members Helping Members) — A message board in the free area where America Online members can assist and get assistance from other members. Located at keyword: MHM.

modem — An acronym for modulator/demodulator. This is the device that translates the signals coming from your computer into a form that can be transmitted over standard telephone lines. A modem also translates incoming signals into a form that your computer can understand.

modem file — An information file which stores your modem settings for connecting to AOL. As modems differ, you often need to use a modem file configured specifically for your modem. See also CCL.

moderator — Typically a host who facilitates a discussion during a conference. The moderator usually manages protocol, if used. See also host, conference room and protocol.

MorF — Acronym for Male or Female. To ask another member their sex. This happens frequently in Lobbies and chat rooms in the People Connection, but it is considered ill-mannered by most seasoned onliners. BorG (Boy or Girl?) is another manifestation of this virus that seems to infect some members. See also Lobby, chat room and People Connection.

netiquette — 'Net manners. Cyberspace is a subculture with norms and rules of conduct all its own—understanding of these will often make your online life more enjoyable and allow you to move through more smoothly. Online etiquette includes such things as proper capitalization (don't use all caps unless you mean to shout). Basically, the most important rule to keep in mind is one we learned offline and in kindergarten of all places: Do unto others as you'd have them do unto you (a.k.a. The Golden Rule). See keyword: SHORTHANDS for a primer in AOL etiquette.

Network News — AOL maintenance broadcasts and feedback that are displayed in a small window. Network News can be enabled or disabled with the AOL software (select Preferences under the Members menu).

newbie — Affectionate term for a new member (under six months). The New Member Lounge in the People Connection is a popular haunt for the newly initiated.

newsgroups — Internet's version of a public message board. Available on AOL at keyword: NEWSGROUPS. See also Internet.

node — A single computer or device accessible via a phone number and used by one or more persons to connect to a telecommunications network, such as AOL. See also packet-switching network, access number, Datapac, SprintNet and Tymnet.

Odeon — An auditorium which focuses on conferences for media providers online, such as OMNI Magazine Online or NBC Online. The Odeon is accessible through individual forums or through keyword: ODEON. See also Auditorium.

online — The condition of a computer when it is connected to another machine via modem.

online community — A group of people bound together by their shared interest or characteristic of interacting with other computer users through online services, BBSes or networks. Because of the pioneer aspects of an online community, established onliners will welcome newcomers and educate them freely, in most cases. See also cyberspace.

OnlineHost — The screen name of AOL's host computer used to send information and usually seen in chat rooms, conference rooms and auditoriums. See also chat room, conference room and auditorium.

Open-Apple key — A special function key on the Apple II series keyboard. Usually located near the Spacebar, with an outline of the Apple Computer Logo on the key. Holding down the Open-Apple key while another key is pressed will often activate a special function. See also Command key, Option key and keyboard shortcuts.

OS (operating system) — The software that is used to control the basic functions of a computer. Operating systems are generally responsible for allocation and control of a computer's resources. Some common operating systems are: System 7, MS-DOS, UNIX, and OS/2. See also System, UNIX and Windows.

Option key — A special function key commonly found on Mac keyboards. Usually located on the bottom row of keys and labeled "Option." Holding down the Option key while another key is pressed will often activate a special function.

OS/2 — IBM's 32-bit operating system which offers a Macintosh-like interface for IBM PC and compatible machines. The current release of OS/2, version 2.1, runs Windows 3.1, Dos and OS/2 specific applications. See also operating system and Windows.

P* — shorthand for Prodigy Service. See also Prodigy Service.

packet-switching network (PSN) — The electronic networks that enable you to access a remote online service by dialing a local phone number. See also access number, node, Datapac, SprintNet and Tymnet.

palmtop — See PDA.

parental chat controls — Parental Control enables the master account holder to restrict access to certain areas and features on AOL (such as blocking IMs and rooms). It can be set for one or all screen names on the account; once Parental Control is set for a particular screen name, it is active each time that screen name signs on. Changes can be made by the master account holder at any time. To access controls, go to keyword: PARENTALCONTROL.

PDA — Short for Personal Digital Assistant. A hand-held computer that performs a variety of tasks, including personal information management.

People Connection (PC) — The AOL department dedicated to real-time chat. Many different rooms can be found here: Lobbies, officially-sanctioned rooms, member-created rooms, private rooms, the Center Stage auditorium and PC Studio. You can access this area with keyword: PEOPLE. Feel free to surf PC, but please obey hamster crossing signs. See also department, chat room.

PKZIP — A compression utility for PCs to compress one file, or multiple files, into a smaller file (called an archive), which will make for shorter up/downloading. The latest version is 2.04g. See also archive, download, file, file compression, archive and StuffIt.

post — (1) The act of putting something online, usually into a message board. (2) A message in a message board. See also message board and message.

private — The state of being in a private room. It is considered taboo by some members to be "seen" in a private room because this is often the communication channel of choice for "hot chatters." In reality, however, private rooms are a convenient way to meet with someone when IMs would get in the way. See also private room and hot chat.

private room — A chat room which is created by a member via an option in People Connection where the name is not public knowledge.

Prodigy — An information service founded as a joint venture between IBM and Sears. It is currently one of the larger competitors that AOL faces. Prodigy is marred by continuous online advertising, screening of messages before they're allowed to be posted, and other quirks. For all it's drawbacks, Prodigy still has a enormous subscriber base. For those members who defected from Prodigy to AOL, there is a Prodigy Refugees Forum online (keyword: PRODIGY). See also P*.

profile — AOL allows each screen name to have a "profile" attached to it. A profile tells a bit about who you are, where you live, what your interests are — anything you want others to know about you. A profile can be created or updated at keyword: PROFILE. See also member, Member Directory and screen name.

protocol — A system used in conference rooms to keep order and facilitate a discussion. When you have a question, you type "?," when you have a comment, you type "!" and when you are finished, you type "/ga" A queue of those waiting with questions and answers is displayed at regular points throughout the conference, and members will be invited to speak by the moderator or host. It is considered impolite and a breach of protocol to speak out of turn. See also conference room, host and moderator.

public domain — A file that's completely free, uncopyrighted, and typically posted on services like AOL for distribution (via downloading) directly to the user. Since the producer (or programmer) usually posts this and the user downloads it, distribution is direct and nearly without cost.

punt — The act of being disconnected from AOL often as a result of difficulties at AOL or interference on your node (such as line noise). See also node and line noise.

punt pillows — Virtual "pillows" given, via chat or IMs, to cushion the posterior of a member who was punted. Often depicted as () () () () or [] [] [] [] (the harder, concrete variety). See also chat, IMs and punt.

'puter — An affectionate abbreviation for one's computer; often employed by enthusiasts and AOLoholics.

Q-Link — AOL's service for Commodore 64 and 128 users.

Q-Pons — Points Q-Link members may win through participation in special events. These may be accrued and "traded in" for free time or collectibles (5000 Q-Pons are the equivalent of one free hour of online access on Q-Link). There is no equivalent on America Online or PC-Link. See also Q-Link.

quoting — To include parts of an original message in a reply. One or two greater-than characters > is the standard method for setting off a quote from the rest of the message. They are usually placed to the left of the sentence, followed by a space, but may also be placed on the right as well.

release — To make something available to the general public, such as a file in a file library. See also file and library.

remote staff — AOL members who staff the various forums and areas. They usually work from their homes, not AOL headquarters, hence "remote." Often these are Guides, Hosts, Forum leaders/assistants/consultants, etc. See also IP, corporate staff, in-house, Guide and host.

return receipt — A feature available with the Mac AOL software that returns a piece of e-mail acknowledging that mail you sent to another AOL member (or members) has been received. To enable this function, you must check the "Return Receipt" box on the e-mail window before it is sent. See also e-mail, carbon copy, blind carbon copy and status.

revolving door — A chat or conference room has a "revolving door" when members are quickly moving in and out of the room. Lobbies and many popular chat rooms in the People Connection will often have "revolving doors." See also chat room, conference room and Lobby.

Rotunda — An auditorium that features conferences with companies or areas in the Computing & Software department. Accessible via keyword: ROTUNDA. See also auditorium.

screen name — The names—pseudonyms, more often than not—that identify AOL members online. Screen names may contain no fewer than three and no more than ten characters, must be unique, and cannot contain vulgarity or vulgar references. Also, some combinations of letters are reserved for online staff (such as "Guide" or "OMNI"). Screen names may not start with a number. See also member and e-mail address.

scroll — (1) Refers to the movement of incoming text and other information on your computer screen. See scroll bar. (2) The act of repeatedly typing similar words on screen, or spacing out the letters of a word. See keyword: TOS for more information.

scroll bar — The bar on the right hand side of a window which allows you to move the contents up and down, or on the bottom of a window for moving things to the left or right. The area on the scroll bar between the up and down arrows is shaded if there is more information than fits in the window, or white if the entire content of the window is already visible. See also scroll (1).

search — Typically used in association with libraries and other searchable databases, the term search refers to a specific exploration of files or entries themselves, rather than a causal examination done line by line. See also searchable, database, file and library.

searchable — A collection of logically related records or database files which serve as a single central reference; a searchable database accepts input and yields all matching entries containing that character string. The Members Directory is an example of a searchable database. See also search, database, Directory of Services and Members Directory.

self-extracting archive — A compressed file that contains instructions to automatically decompress itself when opened; the software that decompressed it originally is not needed. On the Mac, these files can be decompressed simply by double-clicking on the icon. Self-extracting archive files are usually identifiable by the ".sea" extension. See also file compression and StuffIt.

shareware — A fully-functional file that is distributed with the promise of "try before you buy." Made available with the downloader's good conscience in mind, the authors of shareware ask that if you continue to use their product, you pay the fee requested in their documentation. See also file.

ShrinkIt — A compression utility for Apple IIs to compress one or more files into a smaller file, called an archive. See also archive, file, file compression, archive, PKZIP and StuffIt.

shorthands — The collective term for the many emoticons and abbreviations used during chat. These devices were developed by members over time to give information on the writer's emotional state when ASCII text only is available. A brief list of these is available at keyword: SHORTHANDS. See also emoticons, abbreviations and chat.

sign-on kit — The free software, registration codes and directions for creating a new AOL account. There are a number of ways to obtain sign-on kits. Online, go to keyword: FRIEND and follow the directions there to have kit sent via snail mail. Off-line, you can always find a "free offer" card in a magazine, particularly those magazines which have online forums like

OMNI Magazine. You may also find the sign-on kits themselves bundled in one or more newsstand magazines, such as *MacWorld,* or with commercial software, modems and computers. Sign-on kits can also be ordered via phone (1-800-827-6364, ext. 7776). Of course, you can always purchase *The Official America Online Membership Kit & Tour Guide* from your local bookstore; a sign-on kit is included in the back of the book. If you simply need new AOL software but not a entirely new account, you can download the latest software for your platform at keyword: UPGRADE or use the AOL Support BBS (see the access number entry for information regarding the AOL Support BBS).

simulchat — A chat held simultaneously with a radio call-in broadcast. Online chat participants listen to the broadcast and discuss the same topics being discussed on the air. The radio broadcast takes questions and comments from the online chat as well as from callers. See also chat.

smileys — See shorthands and emoticons.

snail mail — Mail that is sent via the U.S. Postal Service. Not meant as derogatory, but to point out the difference between nearly instantaneous e-mail versus the delivery of tangible packages. See also e-mail.

snert — Acronym for Sexually Nerdishly Expressive Recidivistic Trolls. A member who is disruptive or annoying.

software file — A file available in an AOL software library. Often, a software file online is actually multiple files (a program, its documentation, etc.) which are compressed together for shorter uploading or downloading. Every file posted online for download must meet AOL's Terms of Service standards and be checked for functionality and viruses. See also archive, file, file compression, library, TOS, virus, ARC, PKZIP, ShrinkIt and StuffIt.

sounds — See chat sounds.

Spam — A luncheon meat produced by the Hormel Foods Corporation. Spam is frequently the butt of many online jokes originally due to Monty Python's use of Spam as the topic of some of their skits. Lately, Spam jokes have taken on a life of their own online and you may see references to it in chat rooms or message boards. Fortunately, hamsters consider Spam a delicacy. See chat, chat rooms and message boards.

SprintNet — Formerly known as Telenet, SprintNet is a packet-switching network that provides members with 1200, 2400 and 9600 bps local access numbers to America Online. SprintNet networks are owned and operated by US Sprint. See also packet-switching and access number.

StuffIt — A popular compression program for the Apple Macintosh currently published by Aladdin Software and written by Raymond Lau. Stuffit is the standard method of compressing Mac files for uploading to AOL's file libraries. See also archive, file compression, self-extracting archive, download and shareware.

Status (of e-mail) — An AOL feature that allows you to check if e-mail has been read yet and, if read, when. The status for an e-mail message will be either "(not yet read)," "(ignored)," or will show the precise date and time when the mail was read. See also e-mail, carbon copy, blind carbon copy and return receipt.

surf — To cruise in search of information not readily evident in the hope of discovering something new. Usually paired with another word to describe the type of information being sought.

synchronous — Data communication technique in which bits are transmitted and received at a fixed rate. Used to transmit large blocks of data over special communications lines. Much more complex than asynchronous communication, this technique has little application for most personal computer users. See also asynchronous.

sysop — Abbreviation for system operator. The individual who operates and maintains a computer service — usually including a message board, a library or collection of libraries, and a chat room. Pronounced "sis-op." See also forum.

system — Short for operating system, this refers to the software that controls the basic operations of a computer. System can also refer to the collection of components that have a functional existence when combined. Some examples of this include your computer system, the telephone system, or the AOL system. See also operating system, OS/2 and Windows.

TCP/IP — Acronym for Transmission Control Protocol/Internet Protocol. The protocol language that Internet machines use to communicate. AOL announced that they are testing a version of the AOL client software that allows users to use TCP/IP to sign on to AOL. To get this beta software, apply at keyword: TCP on AOL, or get it from ftp.aol.com. Note that beta software is not supported by AOL's Technical Support Staff. See also Internet.

Tech Live — Also known as CS Live, this is a free area where you can ask questions of AOL staff live. The Tech Live Auditorium is open from 9 a.m. to 2 a.m. Eastern time, Monday through Friday, and 12 noon to 1 a.m. Saturday and Sunday. Here you can get live help from experienced Customer Relations staff working in-house at AOL headquarters. This service is available in the Free Area through keyword: CSLIVE. You can get to Tech Live without entering the Free Area if you are on a Mac or PC; simply go to keyword: PEOPLE, click on Rooms, go to the Members Rooms list and create a room called "Tech Live" — you'll be taken to the Tech Live auditorium. See also Customer Relations.

thread — In general terms, a discussion that travels along the same subject line. More specifically, a thread refers a group of posts in a message board under the same subject and (hopefully) topic. See also message board.

thwapp — To hit someone upside their screen name; a virtual slap. For example you may be ::thwapped:: for requesting an age/sex check in a chat room.

timeout — (1) What happens when you've got two computers connected online and one gets tired of waiting for the other (i.e., when the hourglass [PC] or beachball [Mac] cursor comes up and the "host fails to respond"). (2) The result of remaining idle for a certain amount of time while signed on to AOL. This timeout time is usually thirty minutes, but may vary with different modems. In this case, AOL's computers are tired of waiting for you. It's also protection against staying signed on all night when an AOLoholic falls asleep at the keyboard.

title bar — The portion of a window where the name of the window is displayed. On the Mac the title bar also may include the close box and the zoom box. See also close box, window and zoom box.

TOS — Short for America Online's Terms of Service—the terms of agreement everyone agrees to when registering for and becoming a member of America Online. These terms apply to all accounts on the service(s). The areas covered include General Information, Payment Information, Third Party Sales and Service, Termination Information, Disclaimer and Liability Notices, Online Conduct, America Online Software License, Copyright Notices, Information Supplied By Members, Electronic Mail, Other Provisions. You can read these terms at keyword: TOS. Also included are avenues of reporting TOS violations to AOL. See TOSAdvisor and TOS warning.

TOSAdvisor — In days of olde, this was the screen name to which all TOS violations observed by members are sent to. These days, if you feel something violates TOS, you should go to keyword: TOS to report it (with the exception of Apple and PC-Link members — they still e-mail TOSAdvisor). The Terms of Service Staff area can also be reached at keyword: PCSTUDIO > Terms of Service/Parental Controls > Write to Terms of Service Staff. See TOS, TOS warning and OSW.

TOSsable — The state of being likely to receive a TOS warning. For example, a TOSsable word is one which a TOS warning could be given to if typed online. See TOS and TOS warning.

TOS warning — An on screen warning given by a trained Guide or Host for violating AOL's Terms of Service. These warnings are reported to AOL who takes action (or not, depending on the severity of the breach). See TOS.

Tour Guide — Short for *The Official America Online Membership Kit & Tour Guide*—this book.

troll — An online wanderer that often leaves a wake of disgruntled members before crawling back under their rock. It is unclear why trolls find AOL a popular watering hole, but it could be because they consider hamsters a delicacy. See also snert.

Tymnet — A packet-switching network that provides members with 1200 and 2400 bps local access numbers to America Online. Tymnet networks are owned and operated by BT Tymnet. To find Tymnet local access numbers, go to keyword: ACCESS or call 1-800-336-0149. See also packet-switching network and access number.

typo — (1) A typographical error. (2) A dialect that many onliners have mastered with the advent of keyboards and late nights.

UDO — A method of receiving updates to the AOL software. Upon signing-on to AOL, the UDO sends all the necessary updates to your computer before you can do anything else.

uniform — The screen name that's often "worn" by a staff member, either in-house or remote, when working online. The screen name usually consists of a identifiable prefix and a personal name or initials. See also Guide and Host. Some current uniforms include:

AFL	Apple/Mac Forum Leader
AFA	Apple/Mac Forum Assistant
AFC	Apple/Mac Forum Consultant
CNR	CNN News Room staff
CSS	Company Support Staff
GLCF	Gay and Lesbian Community Forum staff
Guide	General system guide
GWRep	GeoWorks Representative
IC	Industry Connection

NPR	National Public Radio Outreach staff
OMNI	OMNI Magazine Online staff
PC	PC Forum Leader
PCA	PC Forum Assistant
PCC	PC Forum Consultant
PCW	PC World Online
PS1	PS1 Connection staff
Teacher	IES Teacher
TECHLive	Tech Live representative
VGS	Video Game Systems staff
WCC	Chicago Online/Windy City Chat staff

UNIX — An easy-to-use operating system developed by Ken Thompson, Dennis Ritchie and coworkers at Bell Laboratories. Since it also has superior capabilities as a program development system, UNIX should become even more widely used in the future. AOL does not currently have software for the UNIX platform. See also operating system.

Unsend — An AOL e-mail system feature that allows you to retrieve mail that has been sent but not yet read. See also e-mail.

upload — (1) The transfer of information from a storage device on your computer to a remote computer, such as AOL's host computer. This information may be uploaded to one of AOL's file libraries or it may be up-loaded with a piece of e-mail as an attached file. See also file, file compression and library. (2) The file or information which is sent or uploaded.

virus — Computer software that has the ability to attach itself to other software or files, does so without the permission or knowledge of the user, and is generally designed with one intent—to propagate themselves. They *may* also be intentionally destructive, however not all virus damage is intentional. Some benign viruses suffer from having been poorly written and have been known to cause damage as well. Virus prevention software and information may be found at keyword: VIRUS (on the Mac platform) or keyword: MCAFEE (on the PC platform).

WAIS — (Wide Area Information Server) A database that allows you to search through huge amounts of information on the Internet, similar in some respects to a Gopher. WAIS databases are now widespread through the Internet. See also Gopher and Internet.

WAOL — The PC platform's Windows version of the AOL client software. The current version is 1.1 — rev. 38.

weeding — (Yes, that's "weeding" as in a garden of bliss.) An online wedding. Often held in the People Connection chat rooms like Romance Connection or in the LaPub. Nuptial announcements and well-wishes can be found in The Que message board at keyword: QUE.

window — A portion of the computer screen in which related information is contained, usually with a graphical border to distinguish it from the rest of the screen.

Windows — A graphical extension to the DOS operating system used on IBM PCs and compatibles. Developed by Microsoft, the Windows environment offers drop-down menus, multitasking and mouse-oriented operation. See also system and UNIX.

ZIP — see PKZIP.

zoom box — The zoom box is the small box in the upper-right corner of the window. Clicking on the zoom box will cause a reduced window to zoom up to fill the entire screen; clicking on the zoom box of a maximized window will cause it to zoom down to its reduced size.

Bibliography

Aboba, Bernard. *The BMUG Guide to Bulletin Boards and Beyond*. Berkeley, CA: BMUG, 1992.
Though BMUG is an acronym for the Berkeley Macintosh Users' Group, this book is not particularly Macintosh-specific. Aside from the 100 or so pages devoted to use of the BMUG Bulletin Board System (BBS), this book is a thorough presentation of telecommunications subjects, including a quick-start chapter; using USENET UUCP and FidoNew netmail; a BBS Network Guide; sending mail around the world; jargon; buying a modem; how to save money on your phone bill; file transfer between Macs, PCs and Unix; and file compression. Excellent basic reference for any telecomunicator, especially the Internet user.

Dvorak, John C. *Dvorak's Guide to PC Connectivity*. New York: Bantam, 1991. 3 disks.
As its title suggests, this book is more about connectivity, not telecommunications (Dvorak's telecommunications book appears below). It is divided into four parts: cables, hardware (modems, fax, scanners, storage, printers), connectivity software and networks.

Dvorak, John C. and Nick Anis. *Dvorak's Guide to PC Telecommunications*. Berkeley, CA: Osborne-McGraw Hill, 1990. 2 disks.
A comprehensive examination of telecommunications divided into four parts: layman's view, technical view, user guides (to the programs on the enclosed disks) and appendices.

Glossbrenner, Alfred. *The Complete Handbook of Personal Computer Communications: Everything You Need to Know to Go Online With the World* (3rd ed.). New York: St. Martin's Press, 1989.
This is the book to get if you're after a listing of all the commercial online services available and what they have to offer. Includes CompuServe, Delphi, Dow Jones, Huttonline, Investor's Express, NewsMet, MCI Mail and, of course, America Online.

Pournelle, Jerry and Michael Banks. *Pournelle's PC Communications Bible*. Redmond, WA: Microsoft Press, 1992.
More of a practical view of telecommunications than a technical one, this book features chapters on online research, doing business by modem and international communications (with emphasis on Japan and Europe).

Prevost, Ruffin and Rob Terrell. *The Mac Shareware 500: The Last Word on the Best Virus-free Macintosh Shareware*. Chapel Hill, NC: Ventana Press, 1992. 4 disks (including AOL software).
The heart of this book is its Macintosh shareware reviews: games, fonts, graphics, utilities, sound and music, education and more. The book includes five hours of connect time on AOL for new or existing members, which nearly offsets the purchase price. If you download data for your Macintosh, you must have this book.

Rittner Don. *EcoLinking: Everyone's Guide to Online Environmental Information*. Berkeley, CA: Peachpit Press, 1992.
The first guide to the growing phenomenon of activists and researchers using computers to link up with each other. Excellent guide to online research—including the Internet—in the layperson's lexicon.

Robinson, Phillip. *Delivering Electronic Mail*. San Mateo, CA: M&T Books, 1992.
A thorough treatise on electronic mail, including chapters on terminology, security, choosing an e-mail system, using an e-mail system, managing an e-mail system, LAN e-mail programs, public e-mail systems and the Internet. Excellent resource for the person in charge of a local e-mail system.

Stoll, Cliff. *The Cuckoo's Egg*. New York: Pocket Books (Simon & Schuster), 1990.
Reads like a spy novel, but it's a true story of computer espionage via the Internet. This is great reading, regardless of whether you're interested in telecommunications. It's required reading if you want to know more about the Internet. Cliff nailed the spy (after three years of tracking—when the CIA, FBI and NSA could not) and made the front page of the *New York Times*.

Index

S

Colophon

This book was produced on several different Macintosh Quadras using PageMaker 5.0. It was output directly to film using a Linotronic 330 imagesetter.

The body text is set in Palatino. Subheads, running heads and folios are set in varying weights of DTC Kabel. The sidebars are set in Adobe Futura Condensed. Some of the illustrations were produced in Aldus Freehand 3.1.

Design & Conquer

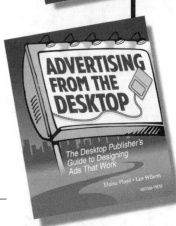

Looking Good in Color

$29.95

272 pages, illustrated

Like effective design, using color properly is an essential part of a desktop publishing investment. This richly illustrated four-color book addresses basic issues from color theory—through computer technologies, printing processes and budget issues—to final design. Even the graphically challenged can make immediate use of the practical advice in *Looking Good in Color*.

Looking Good in Print, Third Edition

$24.95

462 pages, illustrated

For use with any software or hardware, this desktop design bible has become the standard among novice and experienced desktop publishers alike. With more than 300,000 copies in print, *Looking Good in Print, Third Edition,* is even better—with new sections on photography and scanning. Learn the fundamentals of professional-quality design along with tips on resources and reference materials.

Newsletters From the Desktop, Second Edition

$24.95

392 pages, illustrated

Now the millions of desktop publishers who produce newsletters can learn how to improve the designs of their publications. Filled with helpful tips and illustrations, as well as hands-on tips for building a great-looking publication. Includes an all-new color gallery of professionally designed newsletters, offering desktop publishers at all levels a wealth of ideas and inspiration.

Maximize Your Mac

Voodoo Mac, Second Edition

$24.95
472 pages, illustrated

Whether you're a power user looking for new shortcuts or a beginner trying to make sense of it all, *Voodoo Mac* has something for everyone! Computer veteran Kay Nelson has compiled hundreds of invaluable tips, tricks, hints and shortcuts that simplify your Macintosh tasks and save time, including disk and drive magic, font and printing tips, alias alchemy and more!

The System 7.5 Book, Third Edition

$24.95
736 pages, illustrated

The all-time best-selling *System 7 Book*, now revised, updated and retitled! *The System 7.5 Book* is the industry's recognized standard and the last word on the Macintosh and PowerMac operating systems. A complete overview of AppleHelp, AOCE, e-mail, fax, PC Exchange, MacTCP, QuickTime and more!

Mac, Word & Excel Desktop Companion, Second Edition
$24.95
362 pages, illustrated

Why clutter your desk with three guides? This money saver gets you up and running with Apple's System 7.1 software and the latest versions of Microsoft Word and Excel for the Mac. A complete overview; examples of each program's commands, tools and features; and step-by-step tutorials guide you easily along the learning curve for maximum Macintosh productivity!

HTML Publishing on the Internet for Macintosh

$49.95
500 pages, illustrated

Create your own Web page! *HTML Publishing on the Internet* covers everything from using a service provider to constructing information centers and virtual storefronts. Offers step-by-step instructions for creating a site that meets the needs of developers and viewers alike. Packed with tools for publishing documents on the Internet, the included CD-ROM contains HotMetal PRO™, Internet Assistant™, Netscape Navigator™ plus additional graphics viewers, templates, conversion software and more!

The Official America Online Membership Kit & Tour Guide, Second Edition

$27.95
575 pages, illustrated

This book takes Mac users on a lively romp through the friendly AOL cyberscape. Bestselling author Tom Lichty, a.k.a. MajorTom, shows you how to make friends; find your way around; and save time and money online. Complete with software to get you started. BONUS: 20 free hours of online time for new members. Also available for Windows.

America Online's Internet for Macintosh, Second Edition

$19.95
315 pages, illustrated

Forget about expensive, inscrutable Internet connections! AOL members can slide onto the Infobahn with a mere mouse-click. Same easy, graphical interface, no extra charges. This new edition adds tips on using AOL's new Web browser along with FTP, newsgroups and more.

A Great Gift Idea!

Give your friends or relatives everything they need to join the digital revolution and juice up their online literacy. With *The Official America Online Membership Kit & Tour Guide, Second Edition*, they can explore the nation's fastest-growing commercial online service **at no risk**.

The Tour Guide shows readers how to

- **Get news** from dozens of online wire services, newspapers and magazines.
- **Exchange e-mail** with friends on the other side of the world.
- **Explore the Internet** through America Online's new Internet services.
- **Download** tens of thousands of software files for a Macintosh or PC.
- **Get expert computing advice** from top hardware and software companies.
- **Access stock quotes**, buy and sell stocks online and track investments with an online portfolio management system.
- **Discuss politics** and current affairs in AOL's chat rooms.
- **And much more!**

Get the most from your time online! This readable, richly illustrated "traveling companion" includes the America Online starter disk and **20 FREE hours of online time** for new members!

Find your place in the emerging digital global village. While you're at it, find a place for a friend, too—a great gift for novice and experienced online users alike!

Kits available for Windows and Macintosh.

To order, use the form on the order page, or contact your local book or computer store.

To order any Ventana Press title, complete this order form and mail or fax it to us, with payment, for quick shipment.

TITLE	ISBN	Quantity		Price		Total
Advertising From the Desktop	1-56604-064-7	_____	x	$24.95	=	$ _____
America Online's Internet for Mac, 2nd Edition	1-56604-305-0	_____	x	$19.95	=	$ _____
HTML Publishing on the Internet for Mac	1-56604-228-3	_____	x	$49.95	=	$ _____
Looking Good in Color	1-56604-219-4	_____	x	$29.95	=	$ _____
Looking Good in Print, 3rd Edition	1-56604-047-7	_____	x	$24.95	=	$ _____
Looking Good With QuarkXPress	1-56604-148-1	_____	x	$34.95	=	$ _____
Mac, Word & Excel Desktop Companion, 2nd Edition	1-56604-130-9	_____	x	$24.95	=	$ _____
Newsletters From the Desktop, 2nd Edition	1-56604-133-3	_____	x	$24.95	=	$ _____
The Official America Online for Macintosh Membership Kit & Tour Guide, 2nd Edition	1-56604-127-9	_____	x	$27.95	=	$ _____
The Official America Online for Windows Membership Kit & Tour Guide, 2nd Edition	1-56604-128-7	_____	x	$27.95	=	$ _____
Photoshop f/x	1-56604-179-1	_____	x	$39.95	=	$ _____
The System 7.5 Book, 3rd Edition	1-56604-129-5	_____	x	$24.95	=	$ _____
Voodoo Mac, 2nd Edition	1-56604-177-5	_____	x	$24.95	=	$ _____

Subtotal = $ _____

Shipping = $ _____

TOTAL = $ _____

SHIPPING:

For all standard orders, please ADD $4.50/first book, $1.35/each additional.
For "two-day air," ADD $8.25/first book, $2.25/each additional.
For orders to Canada, ADD $6.50/book.
For orders sent C.O.D., ADD $4.50 to your shipping rate.
North Carolina residents must ADD 6% sales tax.
International orders require additional shipping charges.

Name _____ Daytime telephone _____

Company _____

Address (No PO Box) _____

City _____ State_____ Zip _____

Payment enclosed ____VISA ____MC ____ Acc't # _____ Exp. date_____

Exact name on card _____ Signature _____

Mail to: Ventana • PO Box 13964 • Research Triangle Park, NC 27709-3964 ☎ 800/743-5369 • Fax 919/544-9472

Check your local bookstore or software retailer for these and other bestselling titles, or call toll free: 800/743-5369